"This study can be called Catholic in the broad sense of the word. Theologians from Roman-Catholic and Protestant origin get to speak about themes, related to God's election. Professor Echeverria listens attentively to his theological discussion partners and weighs their vision from a systematic theological and ecumenical perspective. The books requires an attentive reading, but those who are prepared to do so definitely receive a reward for their efforts."

—**Gerard de Korte**, Bishop of the Diocese of 's-Hertogenbosch, The Netherlands

"Imagine that a Jesuit, a Dominican, a Barthian, and an Evangelical were locked in the Vatican Library and fed sparingly until they came to a consensus on predestination. What conclusion might they reach? Clear, clean, and cogent in argumentation, Echeverria's superb study juxtaposes and synthesizes diverse perspectives, offering a viewpoint that is Catholic in the preeminent sense, congruent with the church's magisterial teaching, yet open to insights from such Protestant thinkers as John Calvin, Karl Barth, Herman Bavinck, G. C. Berkouwer, William Lane Craig, and Oliver Crisp. One concludes the book with a sense that the long-controverted doctrine of predestination is not an impossible riddle or logical muddle, but a core Catholic teaching that reconciles the priority of God's grace with the reality of a human response in faith and obedience. This work will appeal to Catholic, Orthodox, Protestant, and Pentecostal scholars, and to others intrigued by this notoriously challenging doctrine."

—**Michael J. McClymond**, Professor of Modern Christianity, Saint Louis University

Divine Election

Divine Election

*A Catholic Orientation in Dogmatic
and Ecumenical Perspective*

Eduardo J. Echeverria

PICKWICK *Publications* · Eugene, Oregon

DIVINE ELECTION
A Catholic Orientation in Dogmatic and Ecumenical Perspective

Copyright © 2016 Eduardo J. Echeverria. All rights reserved. Except for brief quotations in critical publications or reviews, no part of this book may be reproduced in any manner without prior written permission from the publisher. Write: Permissions, Wipf and Stock Publishers, 199 W. 8th Ave., Suite 3, Eugene, OR 97401.

Pickwick Publications
An Imprint of Wipf and Stock Publishers
199 W. 8th Ave., Suite 3
Eugene, OR 97401

www.wipfandstock.com

PAPERBACK ISBN: 978-1-62564-992-8
HARDCOVER ISBN: 978-1-4982-8566-7
EBOOK ISBN: 978-1-5326-0602-1

Cataloguing-in-Publication data:

Names: Echeverria, Eduardo J.

Title: Divine election : a catholic orientation in dogmatic and ecumenical perspective / Eduardo J. Echeverria.

Description: Eugene, OR: Pickwick Publications, 2016 | Includes bibliographical references and index.

Identifiers: ISBN 978-1-62564-992-8 (paperback) | ISBN 978-1-4982-8566-7 (hardcover) | ISBN 978-1-5326-0602-1 (ebook)

Subjects: LSCH: Election (Theology) | Theology, Doctrinal | Calvin, Jean, 1509–1564 | Scheeben, Matthias Joseph, 1835–1888 | Barth, Karl, 1887–1968 | Bavinck, J. H. (Johann Hermann), 1895–1964 | Berkouwer, G. C. (Gerrit Cornelis), 1903–1996 | Balthasar, Hans Urs von, 1905–1988

Classification: BT810.3 E24 2016 (print) | BT810.3 (ebook)

Manufactured in the U.S.A.   09/07/16

To my grandchildren

Penelope Grace Deely

&

Samuel Benjamin Warburton

Further let me ask of my reader, wherever, alike with myself, he is certain, there to go on with me; wherever, alike with myself, he hesitates, there to join with me in inquiring; wherever he recognizes himself to be in error, there to return to me; wherever he recognizes me to be so, there to call me back: so that we may enter together upon the path of charity, and advance towards Him of whom it is said, "Seek His face evermore" [Ps 105:4].

—*ST. AUGUSTINE, DE TRINITATE, I, 3, 5*

Let it be presupposed that every good Christian is to be more ready to save his neighbor's proposition than to condemn it. If he cannot save it, let him inquire how he means it; and if he means it badly, let him correct him with charity. If that is not enough, let him seek all the suitable means to bring him to mean it well, and save himself.

—*ST. IGNATIUS OF LOYOLA, SPIRITUAL EXERCISES, PRESUPPOSITION*

Contents

Acknowledgments | ix

Chapter 1. Revelation, Faith, Doctrine, and Theological Authority | 1

Chapter 2. Calvin on the Will | 35

Chapter 3. Scheeben on God's Universal Salvific Will, Predestination, Grace, and Freedom | 77

Chapter 4. Barth on Predestination and Its Implications | 126

Chapter 5. Bavinck and Berkouwer on Double Predestination | 171

Chapter 6. Balthasar's Hopeful Universalism? | 217

Chapter 7. A Catholic Synthesis | 274

Bibliography | 289

Index | 299

Acknowledgments

I AM IMMENSELY GRATEFUL for the ongoing support of the administrators and staff of Sacred Heart Major Seminary, Detroit, Michigan, and for my many friends and colleagues, especially for their deep commitment to the Catholic faith and the teachings of the Church. To them all who provide me with a sanctuary, indeed, a home for teaching and writing, I owe a debt of gratitude. I am thankful to Hans Boersma and Anthony Lane for their comments on earlier versions of the chapter on John Calvin, to Aidan Nichols, O.P., for his encouraging words on the chapters dealing with Balthasar and Scheeben, and to Fr. Thomas Guarino for his comments regarding the chapter on a Catholic Synthesis. An earlier version of the chapter on Bavinck and Berkouwer was first given as a lecture at Hillsdale College, Michigan, Dominican House of Studies, Cambridge, England, and Oak Hill Theological College, London. The chapter on Balthasar was given as a lecture at the Catholic Studies Center, University of Durham, England. I am grateful to the colleagues and students of all these institution for their probing questions. Many thanks to René van Woudenberg for the main title of the book. Last, but certainly not least, I am grateful beyond words to my wife, Donna Rose, for her wonderful and enduring support in all things, making it possible for me to do my work. Indeed, she is *sine qua non.*

> May God grant that I speak with judgment and have thoughts worthy of what I have received, for he is the guide even of wisdom and the corrector of the wise. For both we and our words are in his hand, with all our understanding, too (Wis 7:15–16).

CHAPTER 1

Revelation, Faith, Doctrine, and Theological Authority

If we take seriously the conviction that election lies at the *cor ecclesiae*, at the heart of the church, we find ourselves at the center of the church's faith when we focus on the question of election.[1]

Predestination is the cause of our salvation, and therefore is of the utmost importance in theology; it is also the object of lively controversy.[2]

Salvation and damnation are equally grounded in the ineluctable decision of God.... They do not, however, stand alongside each other having the same rank, for God's universal saving will has been revealed in the gospel of Jesus Christ, whereas God's no is a mystery withdrawn from human knowledge.[3]

Theology, *auditus fidei* and *intellectus fidei*

THE PRACTICE OF CHRISTIAN theology presupposes the principle that faith seeks a disciplined understanding (*intellectus fidei*) of the content of revelation. The role of the Christian theologian "is to pursue in a particular way an ever deeper understanding of the Word of God found in the inspired

---

1. Berkouwer, *Een Halve Eeuw Theologie, Motieven en Stromingen van 1920 to Heden*, 102; in English, *A Half Century of Theology: Movements and Motives*, 79. Both sources will be cited throughout this work, first the original followed by the pagination of the English translation in square brackets [ ]. Quotations are from the English translation unless otherwise indicated.

2. Scheeben, *The Mysteries of Christianity*, 701–2.

3. Schnelle, *Theology of the New Testament*, 214.

Scriptures and handed on by the living Tradition of the Church. He does this in communion with the Magisterium which has been charged with the responsibility of preserving the deposit of faith."[4] This book takes up the topic of the mystery of God in himself and his relationship with human persons, in short, divine election and human freedom. In other words, how do we reconcile God's sovereignty of grace with human freedom, not just in general, but particularly with respect to the Church's full understanding of God's plan of salvation as a work of grace? Equally crucial to this study is the question of how do we reconcile God's universal salvific will with the mystery of predestination, election and reprobation.

Divine election is a revealed truth, that is, salvation is a work of God. In this book, I shall reflect, in the light of reason, on this revealed truth and the received tradition and doctrines of the Christian faith. This principle of *intellectus fidei* is expressive of the dynamism of faith seeking understanding that is found in a correlation of faith and revelation. Inherent, then, within the very nature of Christian revelation is this principle because "rational persons are the beneficiaries of this revelation" who are "impelled by the Spirit of truth, to deepen their understanding of what they believe" (*fides quae creditur*).[5] In short, says Ratzinger, "theological science responds to the invitation of truth as it seeks to understand the faith."[6] The corollary of this theological quest for insight is the *auditus fidei*—"Faith comes by hearing, and hearing by the Word of God" (Rom 10:17). "Hearing the Word in faith" is followed up by the first theological act of attentive listening to the Word of God. The faith with which one believes (*fides qua creditur*) is an act of faith that is embedded in and flows from the theological virtue of faith. That virtue—which is a gift of God's grace—is the permanent disposition in which the theological habit of mind is rooted. "Faith is the theological virtue by which we believe in God and believe all that he has said and revealed to us, and that Holy Church proposes for our belief, because he is truth itself."[7] This theological habit of mind properly orders the mind to the "knowledge that God has revealed in his Word to the church concerning himself and all creatures as they stand in relation to him."[8] The disciplined exploration of the content of revelation involves human reason illuminated by faith, attaining a certain understanding of the mysteries of faith.

---

4. Congregation for the Doctrine of the Faith, *Donum Veritatis*, §6.

5. Weinandy, *Does God Suffer?*, 28.

6. Congregation for the Doctrine of the Faith, *Donum Veritatis*, §6.

7. *CCC*, §1861.

8. Bavinck, *GD* I, 13 [38].

Furthermore, the discipline of theology involves philosophy, indeed, a Christian way of philosophizing that is conceived and practiced in dynamic union with faith.[9] God's revelation discloses truth that exceeds human reason's capacity, but it is not opposed to human reason. "Revelation in fact penetrates human reason, elevates it, and calls it to give an account of itself (cf. 1 Pet 3:15)."[10] As John Paul II rightly notes: "Indeed without the help of philosophy theological issues cannot be clarified, as, for example, language concerning God, the personal relations within the Trinity, God's creative activity in the world, the relationship between God and man, and the identity of Christ as true God and true man. The same applies in various assertions of moral theology, in which certain concepts recur, like the moral law, conscience, freedom, personal responsibility, guilt, and so forth, all of which are defined with reference to philosophical ethics."[11] In addition, the role of reason in doing theology therefore involves not only defending by reasoned argument the truths of revelation, but also demonstrating "the interrelationship between the various truths of faith. This too clarifies and expands the understanding of the truths related."[12] Here, too, John Paul is insightful: ""We ought above all to remember that the divine Truth 'which is proposed to us in Holy Scripture understood in accordance with the teaching of the Church' [Aquinas, *Summa theologiae*, IIa IIae, Q. 5, Art. 3 ad 2] enjoys its own natural intelligibility, which is so logically coherent, that it stands as an authentic wisdom." The pope continues to explain the intellectual structure of Christian doctrine:

> The *understanding of faith* opens up this truth more clearly, both by perceiving the logical and intellectual structures of the propositions which make up Christian doctrine, and above all by making quite clear the salvific meaning contained by these propositions for the good of individuals and of humanity. From the sum of these propositions taken together the faithful undoubtedly come to knowledge of the history of salvation, the summit of which is found in Christ and in his Pascal Mystery. By their assent of faith they then share in this mystery.[13]

9. John Paul II, *Fides et Ratio*, §76.

10. Congregation for the Doctrine of the Faith, *Donum Veritatis*, §1.

11. John Paul II, *Fides et Ratio*, §66.

12. Weinandy, *Does God Suffer?*, 29.

13. John Paul II, *Fides et Ratio*, §66. For an excellent study by Paul Helm on the "intellectual structure of Christian systematic theology" from the perspective of classical Reformed theology that has many points of convergence with the Catholic tradition, see his *Faith, Form, and Fashion*, 11–38.

Yet, as the concluding sentence insists, the assent of faith isn't just a matter
of the internal coherence of the intellectual structure of Christian doctrine,
but rather this assent is about participating in the mysteries of faith. In what
sense, then, is faith a way of knowing divine reality, sharing in Christ's Pas-
cal Mystery, and how, as Romanus Cessario asks, "can propositions serve
as true objects of faith, even though the act of faith finds its ultimate term
in the divine reality?"[14] Cessario adds, "For Catholic theology, the act of
faith reaches beyond the formal content of doctrines and attains the very
referent—'*res ipsa*'—of theological faith."[15] Aquinas understood this matter
well. Yes, he does say, "Actus autem credentis non terminator ad enuntiabile
sed ad rem" [The believer's act (of faith) does not terminate in the propositions, but the realities [which they express].[16] While it is true to say that the
ultimate term of faith is not a set of theological formulas that we confess, but
rather God himself, it is also the case that for Aquinas articles of faith are
necessary for knowing God. Aquinas explains: "We do not form statements
except so that we may have apprehension of things through them. As it is
in knowledge, so also in faith."[17] In other words, one knows primarily God
himself but as mediated in and through determinate propositions. Propositions are an authentic mediation of God's self-revelation because faith involves belief, and to have a belief means that one is intellectually committed,
or has mentally assented, to the truth of some proposition or other. Faith
involves belief, continues Aquinas, and "belief is called assent, and it can
only be about a proposition, in which truth or falsity is found."[18]

As Charles Cardinal Journet puts Aquinas' point, "The object of faith
is both the statement so far as this touches reality, and reality so far as this is
shown in the statement. It is both the statement to which faith assents, and
reality which becomes open to it by its assent, towards which it tends, and
in which it terminates."[19] In reply to those who pit the statement or proposition over against reality by claiming that the reality remains essentially
unknowable because inexpressible, Journet adds, "Some people have supposed that faith is not concerned with the statement but with reality, *non est
de enumtiabili sed de re. . . .* This is false, for faith involves assent, and hence
involves a judgment based on the true and the false, *non potest esse nisi de*

---

14. Cessario, *Christian Faith*, 71.

15. Ibid.

16. Aquinas, *Summa Theologiae*, II-II, q. 1, a. 2, ad. 2.

17. Ibid.

18. Aquinas, *Disputed Questions on Truth*, q. 14, art. 8, ad. 12.

19. Journet, *What is Dogma?*, 11–12.

compositione, in qua verum et falsum invenitur."[20] In short, propositions of faith are true because they correspond to reality; they are as true judgments an "adaequatio intellectus et rei," corresponding to what is, and hence "a claim to the possession in knowledge of what is."[21]

Moreover, the dynamic—faith seeking understanding—of this two-fold methodological principle of the *auditus fidei* and the *intellectus fidei*,[22] which is expressive of a true and fruitful relationship between faith and reason, is "marked by a kind of circular progress." Since one is not always standing in the same place because a certain growth in the understanding of revelation, "of the realities and the words [about those realities] which have been handed down," according to *Dei Verbum*,[23] is cultivated by theological inquiry, it is probably best to think of this progress as a hermeneutical spiral. John Paul explains:

> Theology's source and starting point must always be the Word of God revealed in history, while its final goal is necessarily the understanding of that Word, which increases with each passing generation. Yet, since God's Word is Truth (cf. Jn 17:17), the human search for truth—philosophy, pursued in keeping with its own rules—can only help to understand God's Word better. We are not dealing here with the simple adoption of this or that concept or element of a philosophical system in theological discourse ; what is important above all is that the reason of the believer should employ his own capacity for reflection in the discovery of truth, in the course of the movement which, beginning by taking up the Word of God, tries to gain a fuller comprehension of it. It is very evident that, moving between these two poles—that is between the Word of God and its deeper comprehension—reason is offered guidance and is warned against paths which would lead it to stray from revealed Truth and to stray in the end from the truth pure and simple. Instead, reason is in this way spurred on to exploring new paths

20. Ibid., 12. *Catechism of the Catholic Church*, no. 170: "We do not believe in formulas, but in those realities they express, which faith allows us to touch. 'The believer's act [of faith] does not terminate in the propositions, but in the realities [which they express]' [St. Thomas Aquinas, *STh* II-II, 1, 2, ad. 2]. *All the same*, we do approach these realities with the help of formulations of the faith which permit us to express the faith and to hand it on, to celebrate it in community, to assimilate and live on it more and more" (emphasis added). See also, Guarino, *Vattimo and Theology*, 103–18, for a defense of propositional revelation and faith's knowledge of God as mediated through determinate propositions.

21. Mansini, "Dogma," 242.

22. John Paul II, *Fides et Ratio*, §65.

23. Vatican II, *Dei Verbum*, §8.

which, left to itself, it could hardly imagine that it could find. From this circular movement philosophy emerges the richer from its contact with the Word of God in its attainment of new and unexpected ends.[24]

In addition, theological exploration of the content of revelation is done within a historical context and within some normative tradition[25] of reflection and argument in light of ecclesial warrants, namely, the authoritative sources of the faith, such as, firstly, the Sacred Scripture, and secondly, tradition that consists of ecumenical councils, creeds and confessions, theological masters, the *sensus fidelium,* and the teaching office of the Church. Without these ecclesial warrants, the study of theology would be epistemologically defective.[26]

Problems and Mysteries

Herman Bavinck, the great Dutch master of Reformed dogmatics of the late nineteenth and early twentieth century, opens volume 2 of his *Gereformeerde Dogmatiek* (1897) with the assertion that "Mystery is the lifeblood of dogmatics."[27] Similarly, some fifteen years earlier, Vatican Council I teaches that human reason, illuminated by faith, can gain, by God's grace, a certain rational understanding of the revealed mysteries, truths such as the Trinity, but it can never grasp them in the way it can those truths which are proper to the domain of natural reason—either by being evident to the human mind such that we grasp their intrinsic truth or by being inferred from other things that we know to be true. Indeed, "The Catholic Church professes that this faith, which is the beginning of man's salvation is a super-

24. John Paul II, *Fides et Ratio,* §73.

25. Although I am a committed Catholic theologian doing theology within the normative tradition of confessional Catholicism, and thus in the light of Catholic teaching, this study is an ecumenical work, indeed, a work in receptive ecumenism, and hence I am listening attentively to the writings of fellow Christian theologians from other traditions of reflection and argument. Receptive Ecumenism means : "Dialogue is not simply an exchange of ideas. In some way it is always an 'exchange of gifts'. . . . Dialogue does not extend exclusively to matters of doctrine but engages the whole person; it is also a dialogue of love" (John Paul II, *Ut Unum Sint,* 1995 Encyclical, §§28, 47, respectively. For a further analysis of receptive ecumenism, see Eduardo Echeverria, *Pope Francis,* 145–81.

26. Nichols, *Shape of Catholic Theology,* 15.

27. Bavinck, *Gereformeerde Dogmatiek* II, 1 (hereafter *GD*); in English, *Reformed Dogmatics*: Vol. 2, *God and Creation,* 29. Both sources will be cited throughout this work, first the original followed by the pagination of the English translation in square brackets [ ]. Quotations are from the English translation unless otherwise indicated.

natural virtue whereby, inspired and assisted by the grace of God, we believe that what he has revealed is true . . . because of the authority of God himself who reveals them."[28] Therefore, "For divine mysteries by their very nature so exceed the created intellect that, even when they have been communicated in revelation and received by faith, they remain covered by the veil of faith itself and shrouded, as it were, in darkness as long as in this mortal life 'we are away from the Lord; for we walk by faith, not by sight" [2 Cor 5:6]."[29] Still, inadequacy of expression does not mean inexpressibility of truth.

Now, although Bavinck, in volume 1 of *Gereformeerde Dogmatiek* (1895) agrees with Vatican I's teaching that faith's knowledge of God is a gift of God's grace, believing that what God has revealed in these mysteries of faith is true, he alleges that Rome characterizes these truths as incomprehensible, meaning thereby that "they belong to another, higher, supernatural order, which surpasses the human intellect as such." Bavinck adds, "It [Rome] therefore has to put a heavy accent on the incomprehensibility of the mysteries, as well as protect and maintain it [incomprehensibility]. The dimension of incomprehensibility seems by itself to be a proof of validity and truth."[30] In fact, Bavincks adds, "an urgent appeal was now made to reason to blindly accept revelation's content in faith."[31] He then cites—inexplicably!—an infamous saying of Tertullian: "It is believable because it is absurd . . . . Certain, because it is impossible."[32] Whether this is a correct understanding of Tertullian is not our concern here. What is of concern is that Bavinck seems oblivious to the claim of Vatican I that "the assent of faith is by no means a blind impulse of the mind." Furthermore, the council adds, "though faith is above reason, there can never be a real discrepancy between faith and reason."[33] Moreover, as a consequence of this emphasis on incomprehensibility, argues Bavinck, faith's assent is then reduced to the blind acceptance of these mysteries—a blind faith, a blind trust, a mute submission—rather than seeing in these mysteries, even if through a glass darkly, "the wisdom and grace of God." By contrast, then, Bavinck wants to put the emphasis on the fact that faith's knowledge of these mysteries "turns

28. Denzinger §3009.

29. Denzinger §3016.

30. Bavinck, *Gereformeerde Dogmatiek* I, 590; English translation, *Reformed Dogmatics*, 1:620. Both sources will be cited throughout this work, first the original followed by the pagination of the English translation in square brackets [ ]. Quotations are from the English translation unless otherwise indicated.

31. Ibid., 476 [510].

32. Ibid., 590 [620].

33. Denzinger, §§3010, 3017.

into wonder; knowledge terminates in adoration. And their confession becomes a song of praise and thanksgiving."[34]

Pace Bavinck,[35] Vatican Council I did *not* put an emphasis on the incomprehensibility of the mysteries, as if to say that God has revealed something that is incomprehensible and that is that. What the council actually says is this, "The Catholic Church professes that this faith, which is the beginning of man's salvation is a supernatural virtue whereby, inspired and assisted by the grace of God, we believe that what he has revealed is true, not because the intrinsic truth of things is recognized by the natural light of reason, but because of the authority of God himself who reveals them, who can neither err nor deceive." Of course Bavinck agrees that the mysteries of faith are not evident to mind. Still, he adds, "believers do know these mysteries." The Catholic tradition agrees with Bavinck that the mysteries of faith are knowable, and that faith is a way of knowing. Indeed, Catholic theologians, such as Josef Pieper, for one, have developed an epistemology of testimony in order to give an account of how we come to know these mysteries in faith.[36] I have developed this epistemology elsewhere.[37] For now, let me make the point that the Catholic sense of mystery is about truth, an excess, a superabundance, of wisdom and intelligibility. "Mystery means never being able to say the last word about something which is rich in meaning; there is always more to say; there is not too little but too much to be known."[38] In sum, let us not confuse mystery with contradiction, paradox, antinomy; otherwise, we may fall prey to the identification of mystery and irrationality.[39]

It is precisely in this connection that the distinction between problems and mystery is relevant. This distinction originates with the French Catholic philosopher Gabriel Marcel[40] and it is later developed by another French

---

34. Bavinck, *GD* I, 591 [621].

35. Berkouwer echoes a similar criticism of Roman Catholicism. I respond to it, briefly, in Echeverria, "Revelation and Authority," 18–28; more extensively, Echeverria, *Berkouwer and Catholicism*, 242–65.

36. Pieper, *Belief and Faith*.

37. Echeverria, *Berkouwer and Catholicism*, 242–65.

38. Saward, "Christ The Light of the Nations, Part II." Paul Helm agrees: "We may be able to clarify the mystery further, but a Christian theologian is certainly not in the business of eliminating divine mysteries as a matter of principle" (*Faith, Form, and Fashion*, 32).

39. Sproul, *Chosen by God*, 43–47, has a brief but helpful discussion of the differences between mystery, on the one hand, and contradiction, paradox, and antinomy, on the other. See also, Olson, "A Crucial but Much Ignored (or Misunderstood) Distinction for Theology: "Mystery" versus "Contradiction.""

40. Gabriel Marcel, *The Mystery of Being*, I, *Reflection and Mystery*, 204–19.

Catholic, the neo-Thomist philosopher Jacques Maritain.[41] The distinction highlights two different approaches that one can take in a field of inquiry, for instance, to issues of faith and theology. Maritain says, "It is a mystery and at the same time a problem, a mystery in regard to the thing, the object as it exists outside the mind, a problem in regard to our formulae."[42] For instance, that our salvation is a work of God's divine election in his dealings with human persons is a mystery; the way in which this mystery has been grasped and formulated is a problem. It is the former in the sense—keeping with our understanding of mystery above—that "no matter how much one said and no matter how true it may be, there is always more to be understood and articulated."[43] The latter in the sense that some formulations of the mystery of divine election have marred this mystery because they leave us concluding that divine election is inconsistent with human freedom, because the statement that God ordains whatsoever comes to pass is interpreted as a version of determinism (soft or hard) and the latter is incompatible with libertarian freedom, that God is unjust, that divine election makes God the author of sin, that election and reprobation are symmetrically related to the will of God, and that it results in spiritual inertia and evangelistic apathy.[44]

These are all problems that originate in our theological formulations of the mystery of divine election and human freedom. The theological enterprise, engaged in faith seeking understanding, is situated between mystery and problem. Weinandy correctly says, "The true goal of theological inquiry is not the resolution of theological *problems*, but the discernment of what the *mystery* of faith is. Because God, who can never be fully comprehended, lies at the heart of all theological inquiry, theology by its nature is not a problem solving enterprise, but rather a mystery discerning enterprise. . . . True Christian theology has to do with clarifying, and so developing, the understanding of the mysteries of faith and not the dissolving of the mysteries into complete comprehension."[45]

Consider, then, the theological formulations of the mystery of divine election and human freedom that has resulted in the apparent loss of man's authentic freedom; the reconciliation of God's foreknowledge, decrees, and efficacious grace with our freedom of will. Alternatively, there are those formulations that in explaining human freedom present us with the problem of showing how God's sovereignty in knowledge is such that he has

41. Jacques Maritain, *A Preface to Metaphysics*, 3–11.
42. Ibid., 4.
43. Weinandy, *Does God Suffer?*, 31.
44. Three problems identified by Henry, *God, Revelation and Authority*, 84–87.
45. Weinandy, *Does God Suffer?*, 32, 35.

infallible knowledge of man's free future acts. Or formulations about the reconciliation of the mystery of predestination (possibly restricted pre-destining grace) with God's universal will to save; or how infinite justice, mercy, goodness, and sovereign freedom are intimately reconciled in the incomprehensible union of the Godhead itself. All the theologians that I will consider in this book have tried to clarify the mystery in light of these formulations and others, ever mindful that it is not fully comprehensible, and so the mystery of God in himself and his relationships with human person in time and history always remains open to further clarification and development. As John Paul II has stated: "In short, the knowledge proper to faith does not destroy the mystery; it only reveals it the more, showing how necessary it is for people's lives."[46] Before turning to define the terms of the problem of divine election and human freedom, I shall now take a look at G.C. Berkouwer's clarification of the "boundaries of reflection" regarding the mystery of divine election.[47]

The Boundaries of Reflection

Berkouwer rightly notes: "Man's resistance to the doctrine of election can-not be explained by merely pointing to his reluctance to accept and bow be-fore the *skandalon* of sovereign grace."[48] John Calvin responds to his critics that those who reject the doctrine of election are guilty of "impious pride" because they "measure the justice of God by their own comprehension."[49] In some cases, however, resistance is motivated by one-sided formula-tions of the doctrine. For instance, "whenever the 'fatherly countenance of God,'" is obscured by being "hidden behind the concept of the 'absolute power of God' or behind the frightening idol of a mechanistic-deterministic causality."[50] Consider in this connection, first, Calvin's discussion of election

---

46. John Paul II, *Fides et Ratio*, §13.

47. Berkouwer, *De Verkiezing Gods*, 5–27; in English, *Divine Election*, 7–27. Both sources will be cited throughout this work, first the original followed by the pagina-tion of the English translation in square brackets [ ]. Quotations are from the English translation unless otherwise indicated.

48. Ibid., 7 [8].

49. Calvin, *Concerning the Eternal Predestination of God*, 87–88. Reid asks criti-cally of Calvin's rejoinder to his critics: "Is it possible that Calvin in fact is applying a metaphysical solution to what is really a moral problem? Does he here slip from the moral sphere where the problem [of God's justice] has arisen over to the metaphysical sphere?" (Reid, "Introduction," 31).

50. Berkouwer, *De Verkiezing Gods*, 9 [10]

and reprobation in light of the absolute power of God, and his claim that "God's will is the rule of righteousness." He says:

> Foolish men contend with God in many ways, as though they held him liable to their accusations. They first ask, therefore, by what right the Lord becomes angry at his creatures who have not provoked him by any previous offense; for to devote to destruction whomever he pleases is more like the caprice of a tyrant than the lawful sentence of a judge. It therefore seems to them that men have reason to expostulate with God if they are predestined to eternal death solely by his decision, apart from their own merit. If thoughts of this kind ever occur to pious men, they will be sufficiently armed to break their force by the one consideration that it is very wicked merely to investigate *the causes of God's will.* For his will is, and rightly ought to be, the cause of all things that are. For if it has any cause, something must precede it, to which it is, and rightly ought to be, the cause of all things that are. . . . For God's will is so much the highest rule of righteousness that whatever he wills, by the very fact that he wills it, must be considered righteous. When, therefore, one asks why God has so done, we must reply: because he has willed it. But if you proceed further to ask why he so willed, you are seeking something greater and higher than God's will, which cannot be found. Let men's rashness, then, restrain itself, and not seek *what does not exist.*[51]

Calvin leaves us here with a sense that God is arbitrary, namely, that there are no reasons for what God does, and hence with the notion of a *decretum absolutum* that is behind the bifurcation of election and reprobation. As Helm puts it, "God acts because he wills so: end of story."[52] This conclusion raises the question whether God then operates voluntaristically? Does he retreat to a sheer, impenetrable voluntarism? Helm helpfully explains voluntarism. "That God is able to choose between A and B does not give us a 'voluntaristic' God. Voluntarism has to do with the absence of grounds or reasons for any such choice, leaving the choosing to an arbitrary (ungrounded or reasonless) volition. If for God there are no reasons for acting or commanding as he does, what he does is an act of will alone, and this is voluntarism."[53] Put differently, voluntarism deprives God's sovereignty—*potentia Dei absoluta*—of all internal intelligibility because he is thought to act

---

51. Calvin, *Institutes of the Christian Religion*, 3.23.2.

52. Helm, "The Will of Calvin's God?"

53. Ibid.

independently of his wisdom and goodness.[54] Still, Calvin is quick to tell us, however, "We do not advocate the fiction of 'absolute might': because this is profane, it ought rightly to be hateful to us. We fancy no lawless God who is a law unto himself . . . But we deny that he is liable to render an account; we also deny that we are competent judges to pronounce judgment in this cause according to our own understanding." So, Calvin, on the one hand, resists the claim that God is arbitrary, but, on the other hand, he insists that we are not competent judges of God's will. God has reasons for doing what he does, but we don't have access to those reasons. He adds again this:

> God does nothing without the best of reasons. But since the most certain rule of righteousness is his will, it ought, as I may say, to be the principal reason of all our reasonings. For the humility of faith, as it is born out of a living reverence for the divine righteousness, is no figment of ignorance. For who that does not have the persuasion fixed deeply in his mind that God is righteous and all His works are right, can acquiesce simply in His good pleasure? Hence, I detest the doctrine of the Sorbonne, for which the papal theologians applaud themselves, that invents for God an absolute power. For it is easier to dissever the light of the sun from its heat, or for that matter its heat from fire, than to separate God's power from His righteousness. Let these monstrous speculations be put far away from pious minds, that God should be able to do more than is proper to Him or to act without rule or reason. Nor indeed do I accept the suggestion that, because God in doing anything is free from all law, He therefore is without censure. For to make God beyond law is to rob Him of the greatest part of His glory, for it destroys His rectitude and His righteousness. Not that God is subject to law, except in so far as He Himself is law. For such is the consent and agreement between His power and His righteousness, that nothing proceeds from Him that is not considered, legitimate and regular. And certainly the faithful both preach His omnipotence and necessarily acknowledge at the same time that He is judge of the world, so that they understand His power, in their meaning of the term, to be tempered with righteousness and equity.[55]

For now, I will make two remarks on this passage. One, Calvin affirms God's will as the last and highest rule of righteousness, and so even though he rejects the fiction of the "absolute power" of God, he does not want to

54. International Theological Commission, "In Search of a Universal Ethic: A New Look at the Natural Law," §30.

55. Calvin, *Concerning the Eternal Predestination of God*, 178–79.

diminish God's sovereignty. Regarding the former, Calvin warns against isolating the will of God from the fullness of God's Holy nature and then conceiving his sovereign power as the absolute might of a tyrant. So, God's will is bound to his nature and hence he necessarily acts in accordance with it.[56] Two, God's will is not subject to a standard, a law, standing above God. Rather, God is a law unto himself, but that doesn't mean that we can detach God's power and sovereignty from his justice. As Berkouwer says, "Whenever Calvin spoke of these things he repeatedly spoke of the impossibility of separating God's power from His justice and holiness. . . . For that reason he employed the expression that God is a law unto Himself, an expression in which he rejected the *potentia absoluta* as well as a law above God. It is the will of the God who is a law unto Himself that Calvin called 'pure' and perfect. In other words, in his rejection of the *potentia absoluta* he pointed to the perfection of all God's virtues. This, in all modesty and reverence, is the ultimate of what can be said."[57]

And yet since Calvin denies that God must give an account of himself, the specter of God's inscrutable arbitrariness looms its dreaded face such that man has no choice but to bend. This is particularly the case because the decree of reprobation includes the preterition, or an act of God's sovereign will to pass over by divine grace some men. Louis Berkhof is right that "those who are passed by are condemned on account of their sin."[58] But they are not passed over by divine grace *because* of their sin, and hence this raises the question regarding their moral responsibility for their preterition. This decree of rejection is about God passing some by ("preterition") for good reasons known only to God himself. It is sometimes called negative reprobation, for example, by Thomists.[59] Be that as it may, Calvin says, "God chooses some, and passes over others according to his own decision. . . . God has always been free to bestow his grace on whom he wills."[60] So, the question remains to be asked whether divine election places us "before an arbitrary God who decides, acts, and wills, not in reaction to human deeds, and not on the level of good order and morality, but according to the absolute *liberum arbitrium* in which He elects and rejects?"[61]

Similar objections to this view were raised by the nineteenth-century philosopher, John Stuart Mill. He rejected the defense of God's absolute

---

56. Helm, "The Will of Calvin's God?"

57. Berkouwer, *De Verkiezing Gods*, 59 [61].

58. Berkhof, *Systematic Theology*, 116–17.

59. Ott, *Fundamentals of Catholic Dogma*, 245.

60. Calvin, *Institutes of the Christian Religion*, 3.22.1.

61. Berkouwer, *De Verkiezing Gods*, 64 [68].

power as the putative basis of a theory of religious morality, a defense that insists on the limits of human knowledge in the face of the *deus absconditus*. Mill says, "If in ascribing goodness to God I do not mean what I mean by goodness; if I do not mean the goodness of which I have some knowledge, but an incomprehensible attribute of an incomprehensible substance, which for aught I know may be a totally different quality from that which I love and venerate—and even must, if Mr Mansel is to be believed, be in some important particulars opposed to this—what do I mean by calling it goodness? and what reason have I for venerating it?" [62] Mill vehemently reject the concept of God in Mansel's theory of religious morality in which right actions are right just because God approves of them and wrong actions are wrong just because God disapproves of them. This concept of God remains incomprehensible to Mill. When we apply the concept of goodness to man and God this concept has a completely different meaning in each instance of application which brings with it a threat to our moral certainty, indeed, moral knowledge because of the hiddenness of God's moral nature—*deus absconditus*—in regard to man's understanding of right and wrong. Paul Helm, a Calvinist philosophical theologian, rightly rejects this view: "If God is worshipful as good (because of his goodness), then . . . [t]he goodness of God must bear some positive relation to the sorts of human actions we regard as good. Otherwise, why ascribe *goodness* to God?"[63]

Something similar has taken place in respect of understanding divine election as a powerless submission to God's sovereignty. Here the consolation of election "cannot be distinguished from [a powerless] submission to destiny and fate, and in which the Savior of the world can no longer be detected."[64] Berkouwer explains,

> In theology and preaching the doctrine of election has often been interpreted from a deterministic point of view. This has had serious results in the life of the Church and has often ended in disdain of and vexation about the doctrine of election itself. In the background of election—and of the preaching of it—a dark concept of God then becomes visible, which originates from the mutilation of Biblical testimony, no matter how often one appeals to all sorts of Biblical references. The counsel of God is then discussed in a deterministic or even fatalistic manner so that the faithful have no choice but to draw their conclusions of

62. Mill, *An Examination*, 128–29. According to Max Weber, a similar cry was heard from John Milton, "I may go to hell, but such a God (as that of the Calvinistic teaching) will never command my respect" (in Barth, *Church Dogmatics* (*CD*), II.2, 13).

63. Helm, *Providence of God*, 167.

64. Berkouwer, *De Verkiezing Gods*, 11 [13].

passivity, quietism, and tormenting uncertainty. And that uncertainty is then not ascribed to the result of littleness of faith or
of unbelief—this is the crisis of certainty—but to the unavoidable correlation of the fact of an election which is and remains
hidden in complete mystery. No connection can then be made
between election and consolation, but only between election
and fear and uncertainty.[65]

In reaction to the deterministic scheme, as described in the above passage
by Berkouwer, in which the doctrine of predestination is interpreted, some
retreat to indeterminism, meaning thereby libertarian freedom.[66] In this
connection, there is the question of determinism versus freedom when
God's sovereignty, namely, that "God eternally ordains whatsoever comes
to pass," is understood to mean, as Oliver Crisp describes this view, that "I
am not free at any moment to choose to act contrary to what God ordains
I do at that moment." Crisp adds, "But free will requires the ability to do
otherwise at the moment of choice, in which case the Reformed view must
deny that I have free will." He continues:

Freedom, in the full-blooded sense of the term relevant to questions of free will, requires alternate possibilities. If a particular
choice is really free, in this sense, then it must be one that was
not determined in advance, whether by God or by any other
cause. It must be up to me how the choice goes, and it must be
the case that at the moment of choice I was able to do something
other than what I actually chose to do. If the Reformed deny
this, then they deny human freedom in the sense relevant to the
free-will debate.[67]

Human freedom in this sense is libertarian freedom, and indeed, hard determinism is incompatible with human free will in this sense. Calvin, as I
understand him, rejects libertarian freedom as a consequence of the fall,
but he distinguishes "freedom from compulsion" from "freedom of choice."
Calvin says, "For Lombard finally declares that we have free will, not in that
we are equally capable of doing so or thinking good and evil, but merely
that we are freed from compulsion. According to Lombard, this freedom is
not hindered, even if we be wicked and slaves of sin, and can do nothing but
sin."[68] Elsewhere he explains, "If freedom is opposed to coercion, I both acknowledge and consistently maintain that choice is free, and I hold anyone

65. Ibid., 9 [10].
66. Barth, CD II.2, 45.
67. Crisp, Deviant Calvinism, 75–76. I have learned much from Crisp's book.
68. Institutes, 2.2.6.

who thinks otherwise to be a heretic. If, I say, it were called free in the sense of not being coerced nor forcibly moved by an external impulse, but moving of its own accord, I have no objection."[69] Still, voluntarily choosing is not the same as libertarian freedom, the freedom to do otherwise, adds Calvin. "We deny that choice is free, because through man's innate wickedness it is of necessity driven to what is evil and cannot seek anything but evil. . . . [A] ecause his will is corrupt he is held captive under the yoke of sin and therefore of necessity wills in an evil way. For where there is bondage [of the will], there is necessity."[70] It seems that Calvin is a soft determinist, a theological compatibilist, regarding free will, in the sense of voluntarily choosing, and determinism. And it is as a theological compatibilist that he seems to address the question of grace and freedom. A series of questions emerge at this point regarding the compatibility of free will and determinism.

Two questions in particular shall engage my attention in the second chapter where I treat Calvin. First, given the effect of the fall upon human free will, man is incapable of freely choosing, in the sense of cooperating freely, to be reconciled to God. Berkouwer refers to the criticism of this view by, for one, Erich Przywara (1889–1972), that it teaches "a monergism of grace, an exclusive activity on God's part against all human endeavor becomes mere nothingness, a divine superiority in which humans decisions are no longer of any consequence."[71] Second, fallen human beings can only choose to do evil and hence the will is bereft not only of an inclination to goodness but also of the power to choose between good and evil. This position raises the question of the relationship between nature and grace. Do aspects of man's natural will persist in the regime of the fallen human condition able to produce some moral good? If yes, this does not mean that the will contributes to salvation, but only whether it is active, in some sense whatsoever, in the process of salvation. If not, the question arises whether grace builds upon human nature in any sense whatsoever, or is human nature a corrupt vessel such that it must be replaced altogether by something altogether new?

Enough has been said by way of introduction to see how "the 'fatherly countenance of God,'" is obscured by being "hidden behind the concept of the 'absolute power of God' or behind the frightening idol of a mechanistic-deterministic causality."[72] But how then can we rightly understand the doctrine of election as *cor ecclesiae*? "Can we really speak of the consolation

69. Calvin, *Bondage and Liberation of the Will*, 2.279.

70. Ibid., 2.280.

71. Berkouwer, *De Verkiezing Gods*, 46 [44].

72. Ibid., 9 [10].

of election, or must we conclude that this doctrine undermines the basic foundation of our lives, devastating all certainty and stability? Is that perhaps the last and unavoidable consequence, when the apriori character of the eternal counsel of God, of predestination, is so much emphasized, and when not only theology but Scripture itself keeps us spellbound with the words 'before the foundation of the world'?"[73] Berkouwer is alluding here to Ephesians 1: 4, "Just as He chose us in Him before the foundation of the world" (cf. Rom 8:29–30). This verse refers to God's eternal decision, his pretemporal, superhistorical eternal election, which flows from the divine counsel of his absolute freedom. "How can we discuss election without marring this mystery?"[74]

For instance, critics of the Canons of Dort (1618–1619) have argued that this Reformed confession teaches a "double predestination." This teaching means that "God, by a mere arbitrary act of his will, without the least respect or view to any sin, has predestinated the greatest part of the world to eternal damnation, and has created them for this very purpose; that in the same manner in which election is the fountain and cause of faith and good works, reprobation is the cause of unbelief and impiety."[75] The Canons unequivocally reject this charge. "The Reformed churches not only do not acknowledge [this teaching], but even detest [it] with their whole soul."

And yet, the Council of Trent makes it: "If anyone shall say that the grace of justification is attained by those only who are predestined unto life, but that all others, who are called, are called indeed, but do not receive grace, as if they are by divine power predestine to evil; let him be anathema."[76] We shall return to discuss this charge in chapter 5. For now, let it suffice to say that addressing the topic of the mystery of God's divine counsel, especially his relationship with human freedom, is not that those who emphasize the God's eternal decision, his pretemporal, superhistorical eternal election, which flows from the divine counsel of his absolute freedom are more consistent with biblical revelation than others who want to safeguard human freedom. Says Berkouwer, "After all, the point at issue [is] not a more or less logical and consistent mode of thinking so that the one draws every possible conclusion while the other refuses to go beyond a certain point and for no apparent reason suddenly stops drawing conclusions." Berkouwer explains:

> It has often happened, for instance, that from the doctrine of
> divine sovereignty the conclusion was drawn that man could

---

73. Ibid., 10 [12].

74. Ibid., 5 [7].

75. Canons of Dort (1618–1619), in Dennison, *Reformed Confessions*, 120–53.

76. Denzinger, §1567.

not be held fully responsible for his deeds, while from the acceptance of man's responsibility as Scripture presents it the
conclusion was drawn that there could be no mention of an absolute sovereignty and of a truly apriori and sovereign election.
It was believed that only logical consequences had been drawn,
while actually the correct insight had been abandoned from the
very beginning because divine sovereignty and human freedom
had been seen as factors that limited one another on one and
the same level, and this meant a deviation from the message of
Scripture.[77]

In short, adds Berkouwer, "the polemics about election cannot be interpreted as only a difference in the extent of consistency." Rather, he concludes,
"the question is whether one speaks in the light of the full context of the
gospel message." Berkouwer is alluding here to the "unity of scripture" in
the sense that Sacred Scripture possesses a unity and self-consistency. The
content and unity of the whole of Scripture is the first hermeneutical norm
proposed by *Dei Verbum* §12. "There are profound interrelations in the truth
of God but we are not to think that they are to be seen and understood by
drawing some logical consequences from a number of presupposed truths
about election as they are revealed to us in Scripture."[78] But how do we get
at those "profound interrelations in the truth of God?"

Berkouwer notes that theological exegesis must confront the question
about "what can be deduced from the testimony of Scripture, and what consequences does it imply." He adds, "This question, important in all doctrinal
reflection, is of particular importance regarding the doctrine of election.
The Westminster Confession [of Faith] has specifically connected [this
question] with the counsel of God, 'The whole counsel of God concerning
all things necessary for his glory, man's salvation, faith, and life, is either
expressly set down in Scripture or by good and necessary consequence may
be deduced from Scripture.'"[79]

Still, there are limits here to using deductive reasoning as an in-
strument of theological exegesis given, says Berkouwer, that all sorts of
conclusions have been drawn, not the least of which "culminated in the
well-known [hard] phrase '*destinare ad peccatum*'."[80] This phrase belongs to
the view that takes predestination to be double. This is, in the strict sense,
when both election and reprobation are symmetrical with respect to the

77. Berkouwer, *De Verkiezing Gods*, 20 [21].

78. Ibid., 22 [28].

79. Ibid., 16 [17].

80. Ibid., 17 [18].

mode of divine causality. On this view, the logical implication of divine sovereignty is pressed to the point where a strict parallelism of divine operation is affirmed and the asymmetry between salvation and reprobation is denied. Berkouwer responds to the "good and necessary consequence" hermeneutical norm. He says, "The heart of the matter was not simply a formal epistemological debate about the range of man's logic and about his right to draw conclusions concerning election, but the structure of the whole doctrine of election."[81]

Unfortunately, Berkouwer has no hermeneutical approach that will free his theological exegesis from the limitations he identifies. And that is because he takes Scripture to be a self-sufficient source of revelation. I think *Dei Verbum* 9 is right: "It is not from sacred Scripture alone that the Church draws her certainty about everything which has been revealed." Berkouwer rightly notes elsewhere that this is not a return to the "two-source" theory of revelation. He argues that the meaning of "not from Sacred Scripture alone" ("non per solam Scripturam") need not be taken to question the material completeness of Scripture and opting for the two-source theory in which Scripture must be completed by tradition.[82] He makes the point that the formulation in this passage concerns the *certainty* of the Church regarding the teachings of the Scripture rather than the question of its material sufficiency or insufficiency. In other words, the role of tradition in this passage pertains to the matter of how the Church arrives at the epistemic certainty of the truth. Quoting E. Stakemeier, a German Catholic commentator of *Dei Verbum*, Berkouwer defends this reading on *"non per solam Scripturam."*

> Roman Catholic commentators appropriately lay heavy emphasis on this: "One takes note of the word *certitudinem*. This formulation sheds light on the irreplacable importance of tradition without either exaggerating or minimizing its function." This explains the way in which *knowing*, the process of knowing within the church, is considered and for which the traditions are indispensable, but not the way in which the material *insufficientia* of Scripture is expressed. These commentators do not want to fix the traditions as being either complementary or as being merely interpretative. . . .The council . . . limited the significance of tradition to indicating *certitude*,the church's *knowledge of the faith*. This is the point at which the *non per solam Scripturam* functions in the life of the church, for here the

81. Ibid., 17 [18].

82. Not everyone would agree with Berkouwer's interpretation that the two-source theory is not being reasserted here. For a contrary view, see George, "An Evangelical Reflection," 34.

believer is confronted with Scripture in its connection with tradition and church. But this does not yet imply that traditions are
an independent source of revelation alongside Holy Scripture.[83]

Dei Verbum 12 frees us from limitations of the "good and necessary
consequences" hermeneutical approach by proposing a second hermeneutical criterion for theological exegesis of the meaning of the biblical text:
"The living tradition of the Church must be taken into account." In addition,
there is a third criterion that will assist us in getting at the "profound interrelations of truth" and this is called in Latin "*analogia fidei.*" In Romans 12:6,
St. Paul says that each one was to exercise his gifts, for instance, of teaching,
"according to the proportion of our faith." The Greek word for *proportion*
here is *analogia*, from whence comes the phrase *analogy of faith.* The Catholic tradition understands the "analogy of faith" in a way that Berkouwer
seems to be suggesting.[84] Yves Congar has explained the "analogy of faith":

> This expression, borrowed from St. Paul (Rom 12:6), signifies,
> in theology, the relationship and proportions existing between
> the different statements or articles that have been revealed: re-
> lationship and proportions such that new statements, not made
> explicitly in the documents of Revelation, appear possible and
> even necessary.[85]

83. Berkouwer, *Nabetrachting op het Concilie*, 115–16. This, too, is the view of Ratzinger in his commentary on the meaning of "non per solam Scripturam": "The function
of tradition is seen here as a making certain of the truth, i.e., it belongs in the formal
and gnoseological sphere—and, in fact, this is the sphere in which the significance of
tradition is to be sought" (Ratzinger in his commentary on *Dei Verbum*, the Dogmatic
Constitution on Divine Revelation, 195). It is also the view of Yves Congar, but now
with respect to the disputed passage of Trent upon which *Dei Verbum* 9, is based. He
rejects the interpretation that Trent had a two-source theory of revelation. "That kind of
affirmation does not lie within the *text* of the decree. It does not say that such truths do
not lay *embedded* in the writings, but only that they *cannot be discerned* through Scripture *alone*: for this we need the traditions. But this means no more than what people
assert when they maintain the thesis of the formal insufficiency of Scripture" ("De
    Omstreden Kwestie," 92).

84. Vatican II, *Dei Verbum*, §12, "Sed, cum Sacra Scriptura eodem Spiritu quo
scripta est etiam legenda et interpretanda sit (25), ad recte sacrorum textuum sensum
eruendum, non minus diligenter respiciendum est ad contentum et unitatem totius
Scripturae, ratione habita vivae totius Ecclesiae Traditionis et *analogiae fidei*" (italics
added). According to Avery Cardinal Dulles, "The Abbott edition translates this term
rather felicitously as 'the harmony that exists between elements of the faith'. We know
a priori that God could not inspire a meaning that was contrary to the truth embodied
in the dogmas of the Church. The dogmas serve as negative norms for excluding mis-
interpretations. More than this, they throw positive light on what the Holy Spirit was
intimating in various biblical texts" (Dulles, "Vatican II.").

85. Congar, *Meaning of Tradition*, 120.

I turn now to say something specifically about the boundaries of reflection in respect of the doctrine of election. This will require a brief discussion of the notion of "theological notes" in the Catholic tradition.

Theological Notes

It is important to describe briefly the theological notes—"what doctrines are binding, on what grounds, and in what measure"[86]—by explaining them briefly and the corresponding authority of doctrinal statements. Given the limitations of this chapter, I can best begin here by citing Karl Rahner's statement regarding the Second Vatican Council's assumptions about levels of authoritative teaching. These assumptions, I contend, are necessary for a clear and fruitful discussion of the boundaries of reflection in respect of the doctrine of election in a Catholic perspective. The Council assumes:

> [1] the distinctions to be made between the wielders of the teaching authority in the Church (individual bishops, the collective episcopate, the pope, a general council); [2] the distinctions to be made between the doctrine taught (revealed truths, truths not revealed but necessarily linked with revelation as its presupposition or its consequence etc.); [3] the distinctions to be made between the types of authority claimed by the teacher and his intention of binding his hearers; [4] the distinctions to be made between the "theological qualifications" of the truths proposed (dogma, common teaching, irreformable truths, reformable truths which still demand a conditional assent, etc.); [5] the distinctions to be made in the assent of the hearer (from the absolute assent of faith to a genuine but not necessarily irreformable inner assent and on to mere "obedient silence").[87]

Pared down for my purpose here, I shall summarize the different levels of magisterial authority to be attributed to dogmas and doctrines as follows:

1. *De fide*: dogmas of the faith. These are divinely revealed truths *contained in the Word of God, written or handed down,* either (a) formally defined by a pope or Council; or (b) taught by the ordinary and universal magisterium. They constitute basic beliefs that must be held by Catholics, and they are called the primary objects of infallibility.

2. *Fides ecclesiastica*: doctrines that are infallibly taught as inseparably connected with revelation, called secondary objects of infallibility.

---

86. Dulles, *Magisterium*, 84.

87. Rahner, "Dogmatic Constitution," 208–16, and 209.

These truths are necessarily connected with revelation by virtue of either an *historical relationship, or* a *logical connection,* expressing a stage in the development of the understanding of revelation. These truths are (a) formally defined by a pope or Council; or (b) taught infallibly by the ordinary and universal magisterium of the Church as a *"sententia definitive tenenda."* This is why these are called the "faith of the Church."

3. *Sententia fidei proxima*: doctrine authoritatively but non-infallibly taught by the magisterium. This is for a doctrine that is not formally promulgated, but is regarded as teaching a truth of revelation. It is proximate to the faith.

4. *Sententia ad fidem pertinens,* or *theologice certa*: theological conclusions logically deduced from a proposition of faith and taught by the magisterium, which have a high degree of certainty.

5. *Sententia probabilis*: denotes probable opinion, although in theological discussion there are many other levels operating: well founded, pious, and tolerated opinions (with the least authority).[88]

Regarding level 1, namely, dogmas, which are a primary object of infallibility, and which should be held as a matter of divine faith, we have the teaching of the Council of Trent in the Decree on Justification.[89] For example, man cannot make himself right, that is, justify himself, with God; salvation is a work of God; God brings about justification through the atoning work of Christ that has the power to forgive all the sins of men; the scope of Christ's atoning work is universal, and yet "even though 'Christ died for all' [2 Cor 5:15], still not all receive the benefit of his death, but only those to whom the merit of his Passion is imparted."[90] As I argue below, this theological claim regarding the universal scope of Christ's atonement, and its application only to some, presupposes the sufficiency-efficacy distinction. Furthermore, there are also the dogmas regarding grace and freedom and the rejection of the "error and heresy of the Pelagians and the semi-Pelagians, as well as that of Calvin."[91] The former heresy in the theology of grace "rejects the doctrine of original sin, overlooks the pressure of concupiscence and the nature of

88. D'Costa, *Vatican II*, 14–15, with some adaptations I have made. Similarly, Ott, *Fundamentals of Dogma*, 9–10; and Dulles, *Magisterium*, 83–84. Helpful here is Ratzinger, "Doctrinal Commentary." See also Ernst, "The Theological Notes," 813–25.

89. Denzinger §1997a, "Address to the Legate of King Philip III of Spain, July 26, 1611."

90. Ibid., §1523.

91. Ibid., §1997a.

suffering and death as consequence of sin." Furthermore, "it conceives of human freedom as (created but) complete autonomy which by itself can and must observe the law of God, thus denying the necessity of grace for natural and salutary observance of the moral law." Semi-pelagianism "divides salvation between God and man in a primitive synergism: man begins his salvation by his own unaided powers; then God responds to this independent 'good will' by granting the grace to complete the work of salvation."[92] In response, the church affirms the teaching of the second council of Orange (529) that divine grace is the beginning of faith—the *initium fidei*. Trent, in particular, states that "the beginning of justification must be attributed to God's prevenient grace through Jesus Christ, that is, to his call to them without any previous merits of theirs."[93] Furthermore,

> When the apostle [Paul] says that man is justified 'through faith' and 'gratuitously' [Rom 3:22, 24], those words are to be understood in the sense in which the Catholic Church has held and declared them with uninterrupted unanimity, namely, that we are said to be justified through faith because 'faith is the beginning of man's salvation', the foundation and root of all justification, 'without which it is impossible to please God' [Heb 11:6] and to come into the fellowship of his sons. And we are said to be justified gratuitously because nothing that precedes justification, neither faith nor works, merits the grace of justification; for 'if it is by grace, it is no longer on the basis of works; otherwise (as the same apostle says) grace would no longer be grace' [Rom 11:6].[94]

In respect of Calvin, it isn't clear at all what teaching of his Trent has in mind that it is rejecting. I think we can surmise, however, that the teaching in question is about Calvin's denial that man retains in the fallen state any freedom of choice between good and evil, indeed, any power to do any good whatsoever.[95] Consider Calvin's attack on Lombard for a "hint that man by his very own nature somehow seeks the good," so that "we cooperate with the assisting grace of God."[96] As Dewy Hoitenga rightly says, "Calvin rejects the notions that our natural but corrupted will can 'prepare' us for conversion ([*Institutes*] 2.3.7). He believes that both ideas—cooperation and preparation—undermine the complete dependence of the will upon saving

---

92. Rahner and Vorgrimler, *Theological Dictionary*, 343, 431, respectively.
93. Denzinger, §1525.
94. Ibid., §1532.
95. Calvin, *Institutes of the Christian Religion*, 2.1.8, 2.3.1, 2.3.6, and 2.3.8.
96. Ibid., 2.2.6.

grace for conversion."[97] In this light, then, we can easily understand Trent's point. This is a second level teaching, an infallible doctrine about cooperating with the assisting grace of God, and the denial that grace is irresistible:

> Thus, those who through their sins were turned away from God, awakened and assisted by his grace, are disposed to turn to their own justification by freely assenting to and cooperating with that grace [cann. 4 and 5]. In this way, God touches the heart of man with the illumination of the Holy Spirit, but man himself is not entirely inactive while receiving that inspiration, since he can reject it; and yet, without God's grace, he cannot by his own free will move toward justice in God's sight [can. 3]. Hence, when it is said in Sacred Scripture: "Return to me and I will return to you" [Zech 1:3], we are reminded of our freedom, but when we reply: "Return us to yourself, O Lord, that we may be restored" [Lam 5:21], we acknowledge that God's grace precedes us.[98]

Or as the Address to the Legate of King Philip III of Spain states, according to Catholic doctrine "It is necessary that the free will be moved, stirred up, and assisted by the grace of God and that it can freely assent and dissent."[99]

We come now to level 5 teaching regarding the "question of the way grace works."[100] Trent does not address this question raised by the theological dispute between the Thomists and the Molinists. "Both parties agree in substance with Catholic truth, namely, that God cause us to act with the

97. Hoitenga, *John Calvin*, 115.

98. Denzinger, §1525.

99. Ibid., §1997a.

100. Formula for Ending the Controversies on the Aids of Grace sent to the General Superiors of the Order of Preachers and the Society of Jesus, September 5, 1607, §1997: "What is called the 'controversy on grace' constitutes the most important internal Catholic discussion concerning grace in the sixteenth and seventeenth centuries. The theologians of the Order of Preachers understood grace not only as a condition but also as the cause of the human assent in the sense of a 'physical predetermination' (praedeterminatio physica). The theologians of the Society of Jesus in general taught that grace is always given to man in equal measure, with God, in so doing, knowing by means of *scientia media* [middle knowledge] the free decisions of man. An important role was played in this regard by the work of Luis de Molina, S.J., *Liberi arbitrii cum gratiae donis, divina praescientia, provenditia, praedestinatione et reprobation concordia*. . . . It was first published in Lisbon in 1588 and then in Amsterdam in 1595. Molina's opponents attacked it harshly. In November 1597, Clement VIII established a commission to examine it, and the *Concordia* came close to being censure, but was not. Paul V maintained contact with the Molinists (e.g., Francis de Sales). After more than 120 congregations and sessions held between 1598 and 1607, he finally ended the dispute. He imposed silence regarding the achieved results. He ordered the general superiors of the Order of Preachers and the Society of Jesus to make known within their order the formula given below [§1997a, and quoted in the body of this chapter]."

efficacy of his grace; that he makes those to will who are unwilling, and he bends and changes the wills of men, from which the question arises; but they only disagree as to the manner; because the Dominicans [Thomists] say he predetermines our will physically, that is, really and efficiently, while the Jesuits [Molinists] maintain that he does so congruently and morally: opinions which can both be defended."[101] More than two centuries later in Pope Benedict XIV's Letter, "Dum praeterito," to the Grand Inquisitor of Spain, July 31, 1748, he states the boundaries of reflection on the question regarding the way grace works: "You know that there are numerous opinions in the schools on the very famous questions concerning predestination and grace and the manner of reconciling human liberty with the omnipotence of God." He elaborates:

> The Thomists are defamed as destroyers of human liberty and followers of not only Jansen but also of Calvin; but since they answer the objections in a most satisfactory manner, and their view has never been condemned by the Apostolic See, the Thomists remain unscathed in this, and in the present state of things, it is not permitted for any ecclesiastical superior to deprive them of their opinion. The Augustinians are defamed as followers of Baius and Jansen. They reply that they are advocates of human liberty, and they resists such objections with all their strength; and since, up till now, the Holy See has not condemned their view, there is no one who does not see that it cannot be demanded by anyone that they swerve from their opinion. The followers of Molina and Suarez are denounced by their adversaries as being Semipelagians; the Roman Pontiffs up till now have not pronounced a judgment on this Molinist system, and for this reason, they continue and can continue to defend it.[102]

Against this background, I now want to say something about the boundaries of reflection regarding divine election. Catholics generally give the impression that predestination is a product of the Protestant Reformation and the exclusive concern of the Reformed (in particular, Calvinist) tradition. But, as Margaret H. McCarthy correctly states, "predestination is no stranger to the Catholic theological tradition." "Indeed," she adds, "it was Augustine, the Father of Western theology, not John Calvin, who first turned his attention directly to the question of predestination found in the

---

101. Denzinger, §1997a.
102. Ibid., §§2564–2565.

Pauline writings and who first articulated a bonafide doctrine."[103] Furthermore, turning to the biblical warrant for predestation, we can sample a
few New Testament texts:[104] Jesus said, "You did not choose me, but I chose
you and appointed you to go and bear fruit—fruit that will last" (John
15:16); "When the Gentiles heard [that God had made the Jews a light for
the Gentiles], they were glad and honored the word of the Lord; and all
who were appointed for eternal life believed" (Acts 13:48); "For he chose
us in him before the foundation of the world to be holy and blameless in
his sight. In love he predestined us to be adopted as his sons through Jesus
Christ, in accordance with his pleasure and will—the praise of his glorious
grace, which he has freely given us in the One he loves" (Eph 1:4–6; see also,
1:11); "But we ought always to thank God for you, brothers loved by the
Lord, because from the beginning God chose you to be saved through the
sanctifying work of the Spirit and through belief in the truth" (2 Thess 2:13);
"Who has saved us and called us to a holy life—not because of anything we
have done but because of his own purpose and grace. This grace was given
us in Christ Jesus before the beginning of time" (2 Tim 1:9); "No one can
come to me unless the Father who sent me draws him, and I will raise him
on the last day" (John 6:44); "This is love: not that we loved God, but that he
loved us and sent his Son as an atoning sacrifice for our sins" (1 John 4:10).
In short, election is God's choice, not the sinner's choice.

In articulating a Catholic doctrine of election, predestination and reprobation, we must be mindful of the specific boundaries that protect the
mystery of grace and election and prevent the distortion of the gospel, as in
the heresy of predestinarianism, otherwise known as "double predestination." As I understand Barth, he sides with Trent's rejection of this heresy.
"At any rate, in Holy Scripture there is no parallelism of this kind in the
treatment and proclamation of the divine election and rejection."[105] Predestination is parallel, and hence double in the strict sense, when both election
and reprobation are symmetrical with respect to the mode of divine causality. On this view, the logical implication of divine sovereignty is pressed
to the point where a strict parallelism of divine operation is affirmed and
the asymmetry between salvation and reprobation is denied. This results in
the heresy of *predestinarianism*,[106] which is the false teaching that God does
foreordain to damnation and to the means that lead to it, namely, sins, *in*

103. McCarthy, "Recent Developments," 1.

104. For a detailed account of both Old and New Testaments texts, see Bavinck,
Gereformeerde Dogmatiek, II, 302–8 [343–47].

105. Barth, *CD* II.2, 17.

106. For a brief review of the Church's condemnation of "Heretical Predestinarianism," see Pohle, *Grace, Actual and Habitual*, 201–2, 205–6, 212–21.

the same sense in which he foreordains to salvation and to the means that lead to it, namely faith. "That is to say, from all eternity God decreed some to election and by divine initiative works faith in their hearts and brings them actively to salvation. By the same token, from all eternity God decrees some to sin and damnation (*destinare ad peccatum*) and actively intervenes to work sin in their lives, bringing them to damnation by divine initiative."[107]

The heresy of *predestinarianism* was rejected by the decisions of the councils of Quiersy (853), Valence (855), Langres, Toul, and Thuzey.[108] The sum and substance of these decisions were, one, "that God wills in a certain sense to save all men," and two, "that there is no such thing as predestination to evil."[109] The former refers to the universal scope of the atoning work of Christ. Innocent X (May 31, 1653) condemned as false and heretical the following proposition of Cornelius Jansen: "It is Semipelagian to say that Christ died or shed His blood for all men without exception."[110] This means not only that the merit of his atonement is intrinsically sufficient, in principle, to forgive all human sin (1 Pet 1:18–19; Heb 8:18), but also that God wills to save all fallen men from sin and hence it is extrinsically sufficient for their sins.[111] Now, that God wills to save all men from sin by virtue of the universal scope of Christ's atoning work does not mean that his work is universally efficacious for the salvation of all, and hence the doctrine of universal atonement is not the same as universalism, namely, that God will necessarily save all men. Furthermore, that there is such a thing as "predestination to evil" rests on the heresy—double predestination—that was also rejected by the Council of Trent, Canon XVII: "If anyone shall say that the grace of justification is attained by those only who are predestined unto life, but that all others, who are called, are called indeed, but do not receive grace, as if they are by divine power predestines to evil; let him be anathema."[112] The upshot is that God does not predestine the unregenerate or reprobate to damnation—this claim is essential to maintaining the "essential *asymmetry*"[113] between salvation and reprobation.

107. Sproul, "Double Predestination."

108. Denzinger, Council of Quiersy, §621–624; Council of Valence III, §625–633.

109. Garrigou-Lagrange, *Predestination*, 18.

110. Denzinger, §2005.

111. In am indebted to Oliver Crisp for helping me to understand the conceptual difference between Christ's death being intrinsically and extrinsically sufficient (*Deviant Calvinism*, 215–23).

112. Denzinger, §1567.

113. Berkouwer remarks that "this term comes from [Gérard]. Philips, [the Belgian Catholic ecclesiologist, and key drafter of Vatican II's *Lumen Gentium*] who sees in it a mark of Roman Catholic theology" (*De Verkiezing Gods*, 213n34 [182n16]). Berkouwer

Mindful, then, that a Catholic view of predestination must reject that heresy, in order to maintain the basic asymmetry between salvation and reprobation, one of the main difficulties of the doctrine of predestination that I shall treat in this book is how to reconcile particular predestination with God's will to save all mankind (1 Tim 2:4–6; John 3:16). Reconciling predestination with God's universal salvific will presents us with the deep problem of showing how God does not work in the same manner (*in eodem modo*) with respect to the elect and to the reprobate once every form of logical symmetry or parallelism between election and reprobation is rejected. A related question to this main issue is whether God eternally predestines some to life with or without consideration of their foreseen merits. The former approach favors absolute (unconditional) predestination *ante praevisa merita*, whereas the latter favors hypothetical (conditioned) predestination *post praevisa merita*. In other words, either God elects independently of any knowledge he might have concerning foreseen faith or his election depends on foreseen faith. In light of the essential asymmetry between election and reprobation, there are five truths that act as boundaries in our reflection on predestination. [114]

First, in his infinite, all-embracing love, God truly and sincerely desires the salvation of all men in Christ. As I stated above, Innocent X (May 31, 1653) condemned as false and heretical the following proposition of Cornelius Jansen: "It is Semipelagian to say that Christ died or shed His blood for all men without exception."[115] The universal scope of the atoning work of Christ and also that God wills to save all men from sin is foundational to the received tradition and doctrines of the Church, particularly the magisterial teaching of Vatican II, John Paul II, and the *Catechism of the Catholic Church* (*CCC*). In the words of the *CCC*, "Jesus, the Son of God, freely suffered death for us in complete and free submission to the will of God, his Father. By his death he has conquered death, and so opened the possibility of salvation to all men."[116] Even more explicitly, the *CCC* states:

> The Scriptures had foretold this divine plan of salvation through
> the putting to death of "the righteous, my Servant" as a mystery
> of universal redemption, that is, as the ransom that would free
> men from the slavery of sin" [Isa 53:11; cf. 53:12; Jn 8:34–36;

---

holds that this "essential asymmetry" is one of Reformed theology's "most important characteristics" (213 [182]).

114. Helpful to me in formulating these boundaries is Kimel, "Predestination," as well as Ott, *Fundamentals of Catholic Dogma*, 238–45.

115. Denzinger, §2005.

116. *CCC*, §1019.

Acts 3:14]. . . . Having thus established him in solidarity with us sinners, God "did not spare his own Son but gave him up for us all," so that we might be "reconciled to God by the death of his Son" [Rom 8:32, 5:10]. . . . At the end of the parable of the lost sheep Jesus recalled that God's love excludes no one: "So it is not the will of your Father who is in heaven that one of these little ones should perish" [Mt 18:14]. He affirms that he came "to give his life as a ransom for many" [Mt 20:28; cf. 26:28; Mark 14:24]; this last term is not restrictive, but contrasts the whole of humanity with the unique person of the redeemer who hands himself over to save us [Mt 20:28; cf. Rom 5:18–19]. The Church, following the apostles, teaches that Christ died for all men without exception: "There is not, never has been, and never will be a single human being, for whom Christ did not suffer" [Council of Quiercy].[117]

Actually, the *Catechism* overlooks here a significant distinction between the universal sufficiency of Christ's atoning work and its efficacy. Trent doesn't.[118]

This raises a second truth that is a boundary to our reflection on divine election. In its Decree on Justification Trent states: "even though 'Christ died for all' [2 Cor 5:15], still not all do receive the benefit of His death, but those only to whom the merit of His passion is imparted."[119] As I said above, the merit of Christ's atonement is intrinsically sufficient, in principle, to forgive all human sin (1 Pet 1:18–19; Heb 8:18), but also that God wills to save all fallen men from sin and hence it is extrinsically sufficient for their sins.[120] Now, that God wills to save all men from sin by virtue of the universal scope of Christ's atoning work does not mean that his work is efficacious for the salvation of all. So, in respect of its efficacy, Christ's atoning work

117. Ibid., §§601, 603, 605.

118. According to Aquinas, Christ is "the propitiation for our sins, efficaciously for some, but sufficiently for all, because the price of his blood is sufficient for the salvation of all; but it has its effect only in the elect" (*Commentary on Titus* 1:2:6. See also, *Summa theologiae* III. 48.2.

119. Denzinger, §1523.

120. Six Questions on the Translation of the *Pro Multis*: Question 3: "Does this mean that Christ did not die for everyone? No. It is a dogmatic teaching of the Church that Christ died on the Cross for all men and women (cf. John 11:52; 2 Corinthians 5:14–15; Titus 2:11; 1 John 2:2). The expression for many, while remaining open to the inclusion of each human person, is reflective also of the fact that this salvation is not brought about in some mechanistic way, without ones own willing or participation; rather, the believer is invited to accept in faith the gift that is being offered and to receive the supernatural life that is given to those who participate in this mystery, living it out in their lives as well so as to be numbered among the many to whom the text refers."

is restricted to the many. Second, in his infinite, all-embracive love, God provides sufficient grace to all men so that they might turn to him and be saved. In other words, the scope of Christ's atoning work is universal having died for all humanity, but it is efficacious only for the many. A corollary of this second boundary regarding God's sufficient grace is the rejection of the Jansenists[121] assertion that all grace is necessarily efficacious if that means that it is irresistible. As Alvin Kimel puts it,

> In 1713 Pope Clement XI condemned the proposition that "Grace is the working of the omnipotent hand of God which nothing can hinder or retard" (*Unigenitus Dei Filius*)[[122]]. There is an authentic grace that is truly sufficient for salvation, which provides to the sinner the Spirit-enabled freedom to turn to God but does not necessarily and irresistibly realize its salvific end, a grace that [although sufficient] man may mysteriously and inexplicably reject. Even those who have been born again by water and Holy Spirit may fail to persevere in faith and good works. Or as the Synod of Quiersy taught: "The Omnipotent God wishes *all men* without exception *to be saved*, although not all will be saved."[123]

Third, the Catholic Church definitively rejects Pelagianism and semi-Pelagianism: the claims that we cause our own salvation, or that we initiate our own salvation. Salvation is the work of God's grace, from beginning to end; Christ is the full and sufficient cause of our salvation. Semi-pelagianism, in particular, affirms that the *initium fidei*, the beginning of faith, is in the human will, and not in God's grace, and consequently isolates the will from the *gratia praeveniens* (prevenient grace).[124] But we are not Calvinists: man

121. Innocent X condemned as false and heretical the following proposition of Cornelius Jansen: "In the state of fallen nature interior grace is never resisted" (Denzinger, §2002).

122. Clement XI, Errors of Paschasius Quesnel, Condemned in the dogmatic Constitution, *Unigenitus*, September 8, 1713: proposition no. 10 (Denzinger, §2410).

123. Kimel, "Predestination." The Council of Quiersy, 853 A.D., was against Gottschalk of Orbais (800–868) and the Predestinarian controversy.

124. Pelagianism was condemned at the Council of Ephesus (431 A.D.) and the Second Council of Orange (529 A.D.) The latter Council explicitly rejects this tenet of semi-Pelagianism: "If anyone says that the increase as well as the beginning of faith and the very desire of faith—by which we believe in him who justifies the sinner and by which we come to the regeneration of holy baptism—proceeds from our own nature and not from a gift of grace . . . such a one reveals [him]self in contradiction with the apostolic doctrine" [Phil. 1:6; Eph. 2:8] (Denzinger, §375). The third Council of Valencia (855 A.D.), in its third canon, spoke of the predestination of the wicked to death in the following terms: "We unhesitatingly admit the predestination of the elect to life and of the wicked to death." Then it immediately adds: "But God foreknew the malice

is not purely passive, since prevenient grace enables man freely to love and obey God and to cooperate with him and hence to participate in God's justifying and sanctifying grace of salvation. But this synergism is neither pelagian nor semi-pelagian, which are its heretical forms.[125] "When Catholics say that persons 'cooperate' in preparing for and accepting justification by consenting to God's justifying action, they see such personal consent *as itself an effect of grace*, not as an action arising from innate human abilities."[126] But this cooperation does not mean that God does part of the work of salvation and man does the rest.

Nevertheless, the question remains exactly how is grace bestowed upon us and how does it effect our salvation, and, as Crisp states, "how much the will of a fallen individual awakened or invigorated by the secret working of the Holy Spirit may be said to be active in the process of salvation [?]" Crisp rightly adds, "This is not the same thing as claiming that the will of a fallen individual contributes in any substantive way to salvation. It is not even clear what it would mean for 'the will' to contribute to salvation, other than as a euphemism for the agent contributing to her or his salvation. And no evangelical theologian, Arminian or Reformed, would countenance that."[127] And I would add—neither would a Catholic theologian that remains within the boundaries of confessional Catholicism.

Fourth, God does not predestine anyone to sin or Hell, and he does not reprobate independently of an individual's demerits and sins. Denying this proposition makes "it difficult to believe that God is merciful, and this difficult to believe in God."[128] Earlier I quoted the Council of Trent, Canon XVII, on this very point, but the Church made the same point much earlier at the Synod of Orange: "We not only do not believe that any are foreordained to evil by the power of God, but even state with utter abhorrence that

---

of the wicked, and because it was their own and he was not the cause of it, He did not predestine it. The punishment, of course, following their demerit, this He foreknew and predestined" (Denzinger, §628, as cited in Garrigou-Lagrange, *Predestination*, 183–84). See also, Council of Trent, Sixth Session, On Justification, Canon III, "If anyone saith, that without the prevenient inspiration of the Holy Ghost, and without his help, man can believe, hope, love, or be penitent as he ought, so that the grace of Justification may be bestowed upon him: let him be anathema" (Denzinger, §1553). This Augustinian teaching is found in the *CCC*, no. 2001: "The *preparation of man* for the reception of grace is already a work of grace. This latter is needed to arouse and sustain our collaboration in justification through faith, and in sanctification through charity."

125. Olson, *Arminian Theology*, 17–18.

126. Joint Declaration on the Doctrine of Justification, 4.1.20; emphasis added.

127. Crisp, *Deviant Calvinism*, 28.

128. Grisez and Ryan, "Hell and Hope for Salvation," 607.

if there are those who want to believe so evil a thing, they are anathema."[129] This point is reiterated in the *CCC* where the Church teaches that "God predestines no one to go to hell."[130] In other words, God did not create some human beings in order to be lost, for the purpose of damnation.[131] This statement must be understood against the background of the Church's rejection of the heresy of *predestinarianism*, namely, the doctrine of double predestination in the strict sense, as I described it above. For eternal damnation, as the *Catechism* adds, "a willful turning away from God (a mortal sin) is necessary, and persistence in it until the end."[132]

Thus, the importance, in the Church's teaching, of viewing God's judgment concerning the reprobate in light of the fall and man's actual sins in order to avoid the awful implication that would make God the cause of sin and unbelief.[133] That being the case, it is fundamental to a proper understanding of a Catholic doctrine of predestination to affirm the "essential asymmetry" between election and reprobation rather than placing them parallel to each other as a twofoldness of the one divine causality: God may be called the author and cause of our salvation but there is *no* parallel here with reprobation because he is not the author and cause of unbelief and sin.[134] Of course, mindful of that essential asymmetry, the question still remains regarding an explanation, not only of how supernatural grace is bestowed and how it effects our salvation, but also of those acts of the sinner that resist God's grace and hence fail to elicit a supernaturally salvific act that God intends.

Fifth, in accord with historic Catholic doctrine, in particular, the Council of Trent, which arguably with legitimacy may trace its teaching back to St. Augustine, the Catholic Church holds that the freedom of the will has not been destroyed, totally lost, or taken away by original sin. Canon 5 of the Decree of Justification states: "If any one says that, after Adam's sin the free will of man is lost and extinct or that it is an empty concept, a

129. Council of Orange II, 529, confirmed by Boniface II, against the semi-Pelagians, §370–397, and on predestination, §396–397.

130. CCC, §1037.

131. Wainwright, "Eschatology," 124.

132. CCC, §1037.

133. Berkouwer rightly calls this the *Biblical a priori*: "that God is not the Source, or the Cause, or the Author of man's sin. *Deus non est causa, auctor peccati*" (*De Zonde*, I, 20 [27]).

134. I borrow the phrase "essential asymmetry" from Berkouwer, *De Verkiezing Gods*, 213, 234 [182, 198]. Council of Trent, Sixth Session, On Justification, Canon XVII expressly affirms the "essential asymmetry": "If any one saith, that the grace of Justification is only attained to by those who are predestined unto life; but that all others who are called, are called indeed, but do not receive grace as being, by the divine power, predestined unto evil: let him be anathema" (Denzinger, §1567).

term without real foundation, indeed, a fiction, introduced by Satan into the Church, let him be anathema."[135] Yes, the natural powers of will has been corrupted by the fall, which results in our misuse of freedom that is rooted in a new inclination to evil; and, additionally, the supernatural gifts of God's grace have been taken away from the fallen will. Regarding the relationship between freedom and sin, according to CCC §1739, "Man's freedom is limited and fallible. In fact, man failed. He freely sinned. By refusing God's plan of love, he deceived himself and became a slave to sin. This first alienation engendered a multitude of others. From its outset, human history attests the wretchedness and oppression born of the human heart in consequence of the abuse of freedom." Still, the fall does not eliminate all inclination to goodness in the will and a capacity for contrary moral choice between good and evil—that is, its power to choose good over evil, or vice-versa.

In this light, we can understand that the *CCC* affirms that "Faith is a personal act—the *free* response of the human person to the initiative of God who reveals himself."[136] In other words, faith is an authentically human act that is not contrary to human freedom. To be human, "man's response to God by faith must be free, and . . . therefore nobody is to be forced to embrace the faith against his will. The act of faith is of its very nature a free act." It continues: "God calls men to serve him in spirit and in truth. Consequently they are bound to him in conscience, but not coerced . . . This fact received its fullest manifestation in Christ Jesus." Indeed, Christ invited people to faith and conversion, but never coerced them. "For he bore witness to the truth but refused to use force to impose it on those who spoke against it. His kingdom . . . grows by the love with which Christ, lifted up on the cross, draws men to himself."[137] Precisely what is the nature of this freedom will be considered in this book. This question is particularly important not only with respect to divine election and the judgment of reprobation, but also universalism that suggests "God will see to it that every person he creates will enter into the heavenly kingdom" given his universal salvific will. On this view, "God's infinite mercy and power preclude the loss of even the worst sinners."[138]

For now, in conclusion of this chapter and in preparation for the remaining chapters, let me say that the focus of this book is the dispute, not only revolving around the question of how best to reconcile the doctrine of human freedom with the doctrines of grace, providence, foreknowledge,

135. Denzinger, §1555; see also §1554.
136. CCC, §166; emphasis added.
137. CCC, §160. See also, CCC, §2002, and §1742.
138. Grisez and Ryan, "Hell and Hope for Salvation," 607.

and predestination, but also the relation between the universal salvific will of God and divine election, predestination and reprobation. In the second chapter, I examine the magisterial reformer John Calvin (1509–1564) on the human will in light of the relationship of nature and grace, the nature of freedom in view of his rejecting of libertarian free will, and the relationship between God's predestinating grace and freedom. In the third and sixth chapters, I will consider the Catholic theology of the nineteenth-century German theologian and priest, Matthias Joseph Scheeben (1835–1888), and the twentieth-century Catholic theologian Hans Urs von Balthasar (1905–1988), respectively. The Reformed tradition is further examined in the fourth and fifth chapters. In the former, we consider Karl Barth's reorientation of the classical Reformed doctrine of election, as well as the universalist implications of his reorientation; and we also consider the criticisms of Berkouwer and Balthasar of Barth. In the latter chapter, we examine the neo-Calvinist reception of "double predestination" in the writings of two Dutch masters of dogmatics and ecumenical theology, namely, Herman Bavinck (1854–1921) and G. C. Berkouwer (1903–1996).

Throughout the book at the end of each chapter, I provide some points of Catholic orientation. In a final chapter, I provide a Catholic synthesis of the doctrine of divine election in dogmatic and ecumenical perspective. I will do so in light of the boundaries just delineated.

CHAPTER 2

Calvin on the Will

How does Calvin reconcile genuine human freedom—as he sees it—with the doctrines of grace, providence, foreknowledge, and predestination? The first part of this chapter will examine Calvin's view on the relationship of nature and grace. His view on this matter is necessary in order to gain some perspective for answering the questions about the nature of freedom, given Calvin's rejection of libertarian free will, then freedom and grace, and afterwards on divine election.

Nature and Grace

Three quarters of a century past, Jacques Maritain significantly remarked regarding the question of the relation of nature and grace that it is errone-ous to ignore both the distinction between nature and grace as well as their union.[1] Nature has to do with the fundamental structures of reality, in particular, of human reality, in short, the deepest foundations of what God created. How has sin affected those foundational structures of creation? Has the *nature* of creation been corrupted or completely destroyed by sin? What has been called the Augustinian Principle[2] affirms that the *nature* of humanity persists in the regime of man's fallen state. Augustine writes: "The natures in which evil exists, in so far as they are natures, are good. And evil is removed, not by removing any nature, or part of a nature but by healing and correcting that which had been vitiated and depraved."[3] We find this principle expressed, for example, in the *Catechism of the Catholic Church*: "According to faith the disorder [in marriage] we notice so pain-fully does not stem from the *nature* of man and woman, nor from the nature

1. Maritain states, "There is one error that consists in ignoring [the] distinction between nature and grace. There is another that consists in ignoring their union," (cited in De Lubac, "Apologetics and Theology," 91–104, and at 103n28).

2. Hoitenga, *John Calvin and the Will*, 70–71.

3. Augustine, *City of God*, book 14, chapter 11.

of their relations, but from *sin*. As a break with God, the first sin had for its first consequence the rupture of the original communion between man and woman."[4] So, the essential feature of human nature remains the same, being substantial, or primary, and hence sin is a secondary element such that it is accidental to human nature.

By contrast, there is a view of the relationship between nature and grace that departs from the Augustinian Principle. It understands them to be opposed to each other in view of sin's destructive impact on nature. Nature has been rendered a corrupt vessel by the fall into sin, and needs to be replaced altogether with something new by grace. Human nature is capable of nothing but sin, with the accompanying loss or destruction of the natural power of the will to goodness or contrary moral choice between good and evil. On this view, the deepest foundations of what God created do not persist in the fallen state.

Calvin represents this view that the fallen state of nature is unquali-fiedly evil in Book 2 of the *Institutes of the Christian Religion*. Hence, he departs from the Augustinian Principle—inconsistently, as we shall show. This fallen state expresses "the unvarying corruption *of our nature*," "the ruin and destruction *of our nature*," such that our *nature* [is] utterly lost," such that "it is futile to seek anything good in our *nature*," meaning thereby that "it is not only burdened with vices, but is *utterly devoid* of all good."[5] In his own time, Calvin was criticized by Catholic theologian Albert Pighius (1490–1542) for identifying evil with human nature as originally created. Calvin summarizes Pighius' argument: "We damn the whole of nature, because we say that everything man has from his nature is corrupt."[6] Of course Calvin makes clear in his response to Pighius that he is referring to man's fallen state in speaking of nature as corrupt and not to human nature as initially constituted.[7] God created human nature good, with the ability to distinguish good from evil, right from wrong,[8] and although man ex-ists now in a fallen state, this state of evil is accidental to humanity being as such, then, "an adventitious quality which comes upon man rather than a substantial property which has been implanted from the beginning."[9] In other words, Calvin utterly rejects the view in which "man is evil not through the fall and his own fault, but through creation itself." He adds,

4. *CCC*, §1607.

5. Calvin, *Institutes of the Christian Religion*, 2.3.2; emphasis added.

6. Calvin, *Bondage and Liberation of the Will*, 2.259.

7. Ibid., 2.259, 263–264.

8. Calvin, *Institutes of the Christian Religion*, 1.15.8

9. Ibid., 2.1.11.

he rejects the view in which "the corruption did not become accidentally attached to our nature but is part of its substance, and so the substance itself is evil and corrupt."[10] In contrast, says Calvin, "Man is to be considered from two points of view, first in that condition of innocence in which he was created, and second in that wretchedness into which he has fallen through his own fault."[11]

Calvin then asks a crucial question regarding the relationship between the two different states of human nature, namely, the "*status naturae integrae*" and the "*status naturae lapsae*." He puts the question this way, "What similarity, I ask, is there between substance and accident? Between God's creation and corruption brought on himself by man?"[12] In other words, Calvin's question here is informed by the Augustinian principle. Do the deepest foundations of what God made, of what belongs to man's original constitution, still persist in any sense whatsoever in humanity's fallen state that is savagely wounded and deeply disturbed by the fall?

For Calvin it would seem not since in addition to the passages I cited above, he also states in the heading of chapter 3, "Only damnable things come from man's corrupt nature." He explains earlier: "For *our nature* is not only destitute and empty of good, but so fertile and fruitful of every evil that it cannot be idle. Those who have said that original sin is 'concupiscence' have used an appropriate word, if only it be added—something that most [Catholics[13]] will by no means concede—that whatever is in man, from the understanding to the will, from the soul even to the flesh, has been defiled

10. Calvin, *Bondage and Liberation of the Will*, 2.263, but also n58 in which the editor, A.N.S. Lane states that Calvin appeals to "the philosophical (Aristotelian) distinction between substance and accidents" in making his point about distinguishing between the order of creation and the order of the fall. See also 2.285, 291.

11. Ibid., 2.263. See also, *Institutes of the Christian Religion*, 2.1.10: "Sin is not our nature, but its derangement. Now away with those persons who dare write God's name upon their faults, because we declare that men are vicious by nature! They perversely search out God's handiwork in their own pollution, when they ought rather to have sought it in that unimpaired and uncorrupted nature of Adam. Our destruction, therefore, comes from the guilt of our flesh, not from God, inasmuch as we have perished solely because we have degenerated our original condition."

12. Ibid., 2.264.

13. Confessional Catholicism affirms that in his fallen state man's "wounded nature [is] weakened and inclined to evil" (*CCC*, §§405, 407). Earlier in 1965 we find in Vatican II's *Gaudium et spes*, "What divine revelation makes known to us agrees with experience. Examining his heart, man finds that he has inclinations toward evil too, and is engulfed by manifold ills which cannot come from his good Creator. Often refusing to acknowledge God as his beginning, man has disrupted also his proper relationship to his own ultimate goal as well as his whole relationship toward himself and others and all created things. Therefore man is split within himself" (§13).

and crammed with this concupiscence. Or to put it more briefly, the whole man is of himself nothing but concupiscence."[14] In short, "Whatever we have from nature, therefore, is flesh."[15] In particular, given man's corrupt nature in which "no good thing remains in his power,"[16] that is, the will's inclination to goodness and its power to choose freely equally of good and evil, the fallen will is "so bound to wicked desires that it cannot strive after the right."[17] The consequence of being in this fallen state is that "man has now been deprived of freedom of choice and bound over to miserable servitude."[18] Thus, he concludes, "you will not attribute to the human will the capability of seeking after the right so long as the will remains set in its own perversity."[19] Elsewhere Calvin reiterates this point: "A bound will, finally, is one which because of its corruptness is held captive under the authority of evil desires, so that it can choose nothing but evil, even if it does so of its own accord and gladly, without being driven by any external impulse."[20] Of course Calvin's affirmation of the bondage of the will raises the question of man's freedom to sin.

Calvin rejects free choice in the sense of libertarian free will in which man has free choice equally of good and evil, the agent himself is the cause of his choice. On this view that Calvin rejects, "freedom is then the liberty to do otherwise than one does in precisely the same circumstances."[21] Nonetheless, man is not "forced to serve sin," but rather is a "willing slave" such that "his will is bound by the fetters of sin."[22] So, man is not "able of his own power to turn himself toward either good or evil," but rather he turns toward evil necessarily because his will is in bondage, and yet he does so without compulsion.[23] He acts, says Calvin, "by the most eager inclination of his heart, not by forced compulsion; by the prompting of his own lust, not by compulsion from without." He adds, "Yet so depraved is his nature that he can be moved or impelled only to evil. But if this is true, then it is clearly expressed that man is surely subject to the necessity of sinning."[24]

---

14. Calvin, *Institutes of the Christian Religion*, 2.1.9.

15. Ibid., 2.3.1; emphasis added.

16. Ibid., 2.2.1.

17. Ibid., 2.2.12.

18. Ibid., 2.2.1.

19. Ibid., 2.3.4.

20. Calvin, *Bondage and Liberation of the Will*, 2.280.

21. Helm, *John Calvin's Ideas*, 164.

22. Calvin, *Institutes of the Christian Religion*, 2.2.7.

23. Ibid., 2.2.7.

24. Ibid., 2.3.5.

Calvin, then, distinguishes freedom from compulsion/coercion from freedom of choice (in the libertarian sense). "If freedom is opposed to coercion,
I both acknowledge and consistently maintain that choice is free, and I hold
anyone who thinks otherwise to be a heretic. If I say, it were called free in
the sense of not being coerced nor forcibly moved by an external impulse,
but moving of its own accord, I have no objection."[25] So, Calvin urges us
not to confuse coercion/compulsion with necessity.[26] On the one hand, "we
say that it [the will] is self-determined when of itself it directs itself in the
direction in which it is led, when it is not taken by force or dragged unwillingly," that is, by causal conditions outside the will. He adds, "we allow that
man has choice and that it is self-determined, so that if he does anything
evil, it should be imputed to him and to his own *voluntary choosing*. We do
away with coercion and force, because this contradicts the nature of will
and cannot coexist with it. [But on the other hand] We deny that choice is
free [in the libertarian sense], because through man's innate wickedness it
is of necessity driven to what is evil and cannot seek anything but evil."[27]
So Calvin thinks that the will voluntarily but necessarily choose evil.[28] Put
differently, freedom is consistent with determinism, 'because it is necessary
and sufficient for an act being free that the person did it, and wanted to do
it, even though there exists in principle a causally sufficient explanation of
what was done."[29] Therefore, Calvin is a theological compatibilist regarding
free will. This view is called compatibilism (or soft determinism).[30] On this

---

25. Calvin, *Bondage and Liberation of the Will*, 2.279.

26. Calvin, *Institutes of the Christian Religion*, 2.3.5. In light of the distinction
drawn here by Calvin between coercion/compulsion, on the one hand, and necessity
on the other, as well as his defense of "voluntarily choosing" to sin, we cannot say that
Calvin is an enemy of freedom. On this point, I agree with Anthony N. S. Lane, "Bondage and Liberation," 16–45: "Calvin explicitly states, in the context of his careful definition of terms, that fallen human beings have a choice that is self-determined, that this
choice is free in the sense of not being coerced and that sinners do evil through their
own voluntary choosing" (33–34).

27. Calvin, *Bondage and Liberation of the Will*, 2.279.

28. Calvin, *Institutes of the Christian Religion*, 2.4.1: "Besides, we posited a distinction between compulsion and necessity from which it appears that man, while he sins
of necessity, yet sins no less voluntarily."

29. Helm, *John Calvin's Ideas*, 164.

30. Does Calvin embrace an unqualified compatibilism such that we have libertarian free will in *no* area of human life, and not just regarding choices pertaining to
human salvation, sin? Or is his view a "mixed view" in which his compatibilism only
pertains to the latter choices, but not choices regarding what should I wear this morn-
ing, have for dinner, going running or walking, or the like? Recently, Oliver Crisp (in
his book, *Deviant Calvinism*, 71–96) has argued for the possibility of a mixed position
in the Reformed tradition, particularly the Westminster Confession. I see no evidence

view, an act is free if it meets three conditions: "[1] It is not compelled or caused by anything external to the agent who performs it. [2] However, it is caused by something internal to the agent who performs it, namely, a psychological state such as a belief, a desire or, more precisely, a combination of these two. [3] The agent performing it could have acted differently, if the agent had wanted to do so."[31] Is man really free on this account of human freedom? We shall return in the next section to discuss Calvin's theological compatibilism.

For now, returning to Calvin's question regarding similarity between creation and fallenness, one may wonder why Calvin appeals to the distinction between substance and accident unless he wants to preserve the *nature* of humanity as it persists in the regime of man's fallen state.[32] Indeed, Calvin rightly underscores the point that "the nub of the controversy between us is what now remains in man since he was robbed of those spiritual riches with which he was by nature endowed."[33]

The upshot of this distinction between substance and accident is to limit the impact of the fall/sin upon nature (i.e., the structures of reality) such that the fall/sin disorders human nature but human nature itself, its deepest foundations, remain in place after the fall/sin. In other words, metaphysically speaking, what human nature lost because of the fall/sin was accidental, not substantial or essential to being a human being, for the fall/sin

---

of that mixed view in any one of the three major sources I have considered for this chapter on Calvin's view of the will. Regardless, even if Calvin isn›t a compatibilist all the way down, he certainly seems to be one regarding the human will in its fallen state regarding sinning voluntarily, but necessarily—as he repeatedly states. My chief concern is, then, to understand what Calvin means by saying repeatedly that "we sin voluntarily, although necessarily." Calvin is not a hard determinist, but a compatibilist such that he thinks that freewill (weak free will, as Crisp calls compatibilist free will, *Deviant Calvinism*, 167) is compatible with necessity.

31. Walls and Dongell, *Why I Am Not a Calvinist*, 108. The authors are following a standard definition of soft determinism, or compatibilism. See William Hasker, *Metaphysics*, 29–55, especially, 34.

32. Hoitenga, *John Calvin and the Will*, 112. Similarly, Berkouwer states: "Reformed theology has been particularly inclined to walk this road [of distinguishing substance and accident]. Calvin, for example, in his commentary on 2 Peter 3:10, distinguishes between substance and quality. The cleansing of heaven and earth 'so that they may be fit for the kingdom of Christ' is not a matter of annihilation, but a judgment in which something will remain. The things will be consumed 'only in order to receive a new quality, while their substance remains the same'. According to Bavinck, the annihilation of substance is an impossibility, but the world, her appearance laid waste by sin, will vanish. There will not be a new, second creation, but a re-creation of what exists, a renaissance. Substantially, nothing will be lost" (Berkouwer, *Wederkomst van Christus*, 1:279 [225].

33. Calvin, *Bondage and Liberation of the Will*, 3.295.

did not literally turn the human being into a different kind of creature. Paul Helm appeals to this very distinction between substance and accident: "So there are essential features of being a human being–whatever they are–and also accidental features, those lost in the fall, and those restored in Christ."[34] Surely the import of this distinction between substance/accident suggests a crucial distinction between the fact that evil corrupts every aspect of our humanity, while human nature itself, its deepest foundations, remain in place after the fall/sin, on the one hand, and man's nature in its fallen state is *nothing but* evil in its totality on the other.[35]

In all fairness to Calvin, he does take note of the distinction between "corruption" and "destruction" of our whole nature, and in this connection he embraces the Augustinian Principle.[36] For instance, with respect to man's intellect, he argues that its natural gifts have been corrupted but "not completely wiped out." "Since reason, therefore, by which man distinguishes between good and evil, and by which he understands and judges, is a natural gift, it could not be completely wiped out; but it was partly weakened and partly corrupted, so that its misshapen ruins appears." Still, "in man's perverted and degenerate nature some sparks still glean."[37]

Calvin gives several examples of this corruption of reason, such as man's natural longing for truth, particular with respect to earthly things, art and science, civic order, equity, and the like. "Whenever we come upon these matters in secular writers, let that admirable light of truth shining in them teach us that the mind of man, though fallen and perverted from its wholeness, is nevertheless clothed and ornamented with God's excellent gifts."[38] Significantly, according to Calvin, it is God's common grace, his general non-salvific grace, restrains sin and evil from having its full way with our already corrupted nature, and without which "our fall would have entailed the destruction of our whole nature."[39] Still, with respect to the knowledge

---

34. Helm, *Faith, Form, and Fashion*, 28. Tony Lane, the editor of Calvin's *Bondage and Liberation of the Will*, suggests something similar to Helm's example in the Introduction to Calvin's work, "Just as we may be happy or sad without ceasing to be human (happiness and sadness are 'accidental' to humanity), so also the human race, after having been created good, became evil without ceasing to be human" (xxv).

35. Hoitenga, *John Calvin and the Will*, 76.

36. Calvin, *Institutes of the Christian Religion*, 2.2.12–17.

37. Ibid., 2.2.12. See also, similarly, The Canons of Dort (1618–1619), in *Reformed Confessions*, vol. 4, Third and Fourth Heads of Doctrine, Article 4: "There remain, however, in man since the fall, the glimmerings of natural light, whereby he retains some knowledge of God, of natural things, and of the difference between good and evil, and shows some regard for virtue and for good outward behavior."

38. Calvin, *Institutes of the Christian Religion*, 2.2.13–15.

39. Ibid., 2.2.17.

of God, what human reason can know of God, as Calvin understands it, "man's keenness of mind is mere blindness as far as the knowledge of God is concerned."[40] He explains:

> The greatest geniuses [here] are blinder than moles. Certainly I do not deny that one can read competent and apt statements about God here and there in the philosophers, but these always show a certain giddy imagination. . . . The Lord indeed gave them a slight taste of his divinity that they might not hide their impiety under a cloak of ignorance. And sometimes he impelled them to make certain utterances by the confession of which they would themselves be corrected. But they saw things in such a way that their seeing did not direct them to the truth, much less enable them to attain it. . . . Besides, although they may chance to sprinkle their books with droplets of truth, how many monstrous lies defile them! In short, they never even sensed that assurance of God's benevolence toward us (without which man's understand can only be filled with boundless confusion). Human reason, therefore, neither approaches, nor strives toward, nor even takes a straight aim at, this truth: to understand who the true God is or what sort of God he wishes to be toward us.[41]

And yet, despite the corruption of human nature and its effects upon human reason, the latter's capacity to know truth has not been destroyed. But with respect to the knowledge of heavenly things, human reason is filled with "boundless confusion," as Calvin says in the above passage. Hence, faith's knowledge of God is a gift of God's grace, says Calvin; it is God's own work. "That he understands by 'gift' a special illumination, not a common endowment of nature, is evident from his complaint that the very words with which he commended Christ to his disciples availed him not. 'I see', he says, 'that my words have no power to imbue men's minds with divine matters, unless the Lord through his Spirit gives understanding'. . . . This doubtless means man's mind can become spiritually wise only in so far as God illumines it."[42] But with respect to the will, unlike human reason, Calvin clearly suggests that evil is the *only* power at work in fallen human nature. Here Calvin does *not* take note of the distinction between "corruption" and "destruction" of our whole nature because the inclination of the will in man's fallen state is wholly evil. The crux of the matter is well stated by Calvin: "We must now examine whether in other respects the will is so

40. Ibid., 2.2.19.

41. Ibid., 2.2.18.

42. Ibid., 2.2.20.

deeply vitiated and corrupted in its every part that it can beget nothing but evil; or whether it retains any portion unimpaired, from which good desires may be born."[43] The direct answer to this examination is that man's nature is, according to Calvin, "so depraved . . . that he can be moved or impelled only to evil."[44] I think we can say with some certainty that Calvin does not preserve the *nature* of humanity's will in the regime of man's fallen state—no moral inclination to goodness and ability to choose freely between good and evil—and, as Hoitenga rightly conclude, "consequently the only available restraint for its evil desires is from beyond its nature, in the form of the regenerating grace of the Holy Spirit."[45]

And yet, Calvin occasionally acknowledges the moral virtues of fallen men. The question is whether he attributes it to their *nature*. He seems to do so in the following passage:

> In every age there have been persons who, guided by nature, have striven toward virtue throughout life. I have nothing to say against them even if many lapses can be noted in their moral conduct. For they have by the very zeal of their honesty given proof that there was some purity in their nature. . . . These examples, accordingly, seem to warn us against adjudging man's nature wholly corrupted, because some men have by its prompting not only excelled in remarkable deeds, but conducted themselves most honorably throughout life. But here it ought to occur to us that amid this corruption of nature there is some place for God's grace; not such grace as to cleanse it, but to restrain it inwardly.[46]

But given Calvin's view that man's fallen state has eradicated and not just corrupted his moral inclination to goodness, then man does not possess in that state "an inner disposition, an inclination, to pursue virtuous deeds."[47] Therefore, Calvin's appeal to nonsaving, common grace, Hoitenga rightly notes, "sheds no light on *how* the fallen will itself *functions* as a *natural power* to *produce* the good deeds and virtues that Calvin refers to. If the Augustinian principle is correct, enough of the created will must survive in the fallen state to provide the basis for a general theory of human moral agency. . . . The question is, does anything of the will's natural inclination to moral goodness and capacity for choice persist in the fallen state, in spite of the

43. Ibid., 2.2.26.
44. Ibid., 2.3.5.
45. Hoitenga, *John Calvin and the Will*, 79.
46. Calvin, *Institutes of the Christian Religion*, 2.3.3.
47. Hoitenga, *John Calvin and the Will*, 110.

corruption it brought upon itself in the fall?"[48] It would seem not because, on Calvin's view, every desire of the fallen will is evil. Hence, Calvin not only departs from the Augustinian Principle, but also his account of human nature is flawed since he is unable to give an intelligible account of "the moral choices between good and evil that human beings continue to make in their fallen state."[49] What prevents him from giving such an account is his confusion, according to Hoitenga, of two distinguishable issues, namely, "what elements of the natural will's moral capacity survive in the fallen state," and "whether the capacity of the will that do survive can assist in or conduce towards its conversion." In sum, Hoitenga concludes, "It seems evident that Calvin turns the inability of the will to restore itself to favor with God into a theory of a will that is unable to produce any moral good at all."[50] Thus, the freedom of the will in general is lost.

Another way to get at the same question regarding the status of the fallen will's natural power to produce any moral good at all is to ask whether the conversion of the will by divine grace involves the will's destruction, being removed and replaced altogether by a good will. It would seem so. Says Calvin, "everything good in the will is the work of grace alone."[51] Again, he says: "When the Lord speaks about us, he does not leave us even a drop of goodness. And he does not merely find us guilty of weakness, but he eliminates all respect for our own capacity."[52] And again, "[I]t is of their nature that human beings have it in them to will. But as a result of the corruption of that nature it came about that we can will only in an evil way. Therefore it is God's own gift that we will well."[53] Once more, "But since the whole of Scripture proclaims that faith is a free gift of God, it follows that when we, who are by nature inclined to evil with our whole heart, begin to will good, we do so out of mere grace. . . . For it always follows that nothing good can arise out of our will until it has been reformed; and after its reformation, in so far as it is good, it is from God, not from ourselves."[54]

Does this lead us to the conclusion that grace destroys the substance or faculty of the will itself and hence grace replaces it? In other words, does "divine grace operate in a total vacuum by creating an entirely new will that has

48. Ibid., 110.

49. Ibid., 89.

50. Ibid., 115.

51. Calvin, *Institutes of the Christian Religion*, 2.3.6.

52. Calvin, *Bondage and Liberation of the Will*, 6.377.

53. Ibid., 6.375.

54. Calvin, *Institutes of the Christian Religion*, 2.3.8.

little, if any, continuity with the natural will as it was originally created [?]"[55] At first reading, it would seem so since Calvin holds that in its fallen state the will lacks the inclination to do good and hence the will is simply evil. In particular, this reading is supported by Calvin's claims that the fallen state expresses "the unvarying corruption *of our nature*," "the ruin and destruction *of our nature*," such that our *nature* [is] utterly lost," such that "it is futile to seek anything good in our *nature*," meaning thereby that "it is not only burdened with vices, but is *utterly devoid* of all good."[56] Hence, Calvin says that in conversion "whatever belongs to our will is abolished and what takes its place is entirely from God."[57] This was certainly the critique of Pighius. In response to him, Calvin says that Pighius ignores something in "between the substance of the will, or the faculty of willing, and its actions or its actual effects." This "something" is habit. Calvin explains:

> The first is the faculty of willing or, if preferred, the substance. To will well and badly are qualities or opposed habits which belong to the power itself. I had omitted its acts, because they contribute nothing relevant. Having defined these three things, I had taught that the will is perpetually resident in our nature, that the evil condition of the will results from the corruption of that nature, and that by the regeneration of the Spirit the evil condition is corrected and in that way the will is made good instead of evil. . . . To be brief: I say that the will is evil not by nature (that is, by God's creation) but by the corruption of nature, and that it cannot be otherwise until it is changed to be good by the grace of the Holy Spirit. Nor do I imagine that a new product or a new creature is made in such a way that with the destruction of the former substance a new one takes its place. For I explicitly mention that the will remains in man just as it

---

55. Hoitenga, *John Calvin and the Will*, 91.

56. Calvin, *Institutes of the Christian Religion*, 2.3.2; emphasis added. On the state of post-fall will, according to Calvin, Lane states: "To criticize Calvin for teaching that fallen will has lost all inclination to goodness is fair; to criticize him for teaching that it is in total bondage to sin is fair; to criticize him for teaching the *near destruction* of the will and its choice itself is not fair" (Lane, "Bondage and Liberation," 34; emphasis added). It is particularly this last point regarding the "near destruction of the will" that is overstated by Lane. He rightly acknowledges elsewhere that "If Calvin was understood to teach that grace destroys the will he must bear some of the blame. But in fact he qualified this teaching. . . . Augustine rightly taught that grace does not destroy the will but rather repairs it" (Lane, "Calvin's Anthropology," 275–288, and at 283). Still, what remains of the will in the fallen states as originally created is minimalistic: the will *qua* will.

57. Calvin, *Bondage and Liberation of the Will*, 6.375.

was originally implanted in him, and so the change takes place
in the habit, not in the substance.[58]

So when Calvin says that the will "is created anew," it is at least clear that he
does not mean that "the will now begins to exist, but [only] that it is changed
from an evil to a good will. I affirm that this is wholly God's doing. . . . God
not only assists the weak will or corrects the depraved will, but also works
in us to will [Phil. 2:13]. From this, one may easily infer, as I have said, that
everything good in the will is the work of grace alone."[59]

But Calvin's response seems less than clear because so little of the
will originally implanted in man remains in the fallen state. Introducing
the notion of habit would be helpful to Calvin if he didn't hold that human
nature in its fallen state was ruined and destroyed and hence utterly lost.
This means that the will as originally created has been deprived as such of
any aspiration to the good and is therefore inclined exclusively to evil, or, as
he also puts it, "by nature in captivity and so useless for everything good."[60]
Elsewhere he says, "[M]an conceives, covets, and undertakes nothing
that is not evil, perverse, iniquitous, and soiled. Because the heart, totally
imbued with the poison of sin, can emit nothing but the fruits of sin."[61]
Still, Calvin holds that the will *qua* will remains in man's fallen state. For
instance, in the *Institutes* Calvin says, "I say that the will is effaced; not in so
far as it is will, for in man's conversion what belongs to his primal [pre-fall]
nature remains entire."[62]

It is difficult to understand Calvin's claim here because on his own
account of the will in its fallen state it has lost both its "created inclination
for goodness and for its created power of choice."[63] Calvin says, "Unless I
am mistaken, we sufficiently proved that man is so held captive by the yoke
of sin that he can of his own nature neither aspire to good through resolve
nor struggle after it through effort."[64] This fallen state is inconsistent with
Calvin's description of the created will in its pre-fallen condition. It is difficult to see how Calvin can consistently claim that in "man's conversion
what belongs to his primal [pre-fall] nature remains entire."[65] And again, in

58. Ibid., 6.378–379.

59. Calvin, *Institutes of the Christian Religion*, 2.3.6.

60. Calvin, *Bondage and Liberation of the Will*, 4.338.

61. John Calvin, "Calvin's Catechism (1537)," section 5, "Free Will," in Dennison,
Reformed Confessions, 1:353–92, and at 397.

62. Calvin, *Institutes of the Christian Religion*, 2.3.6.

63. Hoitenga, *John Calvin and the Will*, 74.

64. Calvin, *Institutes of the Christian Religion*, 2.4.1.

65. Ibid., 2.3.6.

rejecting libertarian free will, Calvin says, "We have free will, not in that we are equally capable of doing or thinking good and evil, but merely that we are freed from compulsion. . . . Man will then be spoken of as having this sort of free decision, not because he has free choice equally of good and evil, but because he acts wickedly by will, not by compulsion."[66] This state, too, is inconsistent with Calvin's description of man's will as created. So what remains of the will as originally implanted? Minimally, it is man's very nature to will that remains—the will *qua* will—in the fallen state if not the ability to exercise freedom properly in the sense of having "the free power of choosing between good and evil—which is called free will."[67] In his *Commentary on Ezekiel* Calvin restates this position:

> The will is naturally implanted in man, whence this faculty belongs equally to the elect and the reprobate. All therefore will, but through Adam's fall it happens that our will is depraved and rebellious against God: will, I say, remains in us, but it is enslaved and bound by sin. Whence then comes an upright will? Even from regeneration by the Spirit. Hence the Spirit does not confer on us the faculty of willing: for it is inherent to us from our birth, that is, it is hereditary, and a part of the creation which could not be blotted out by Adam's fall; but when the will is in us, God gives us to will rightly, and this is his work.[68]

By itself, of course, the will can only do evil things.[69] But it is still we who will that we will—voluntarily sinning albeit necessarily.[70] Similarly, in conversion, says Calvin, "'It is certain that it is we who will when we will, but it is he [God] who causes us to will the good. It is certain that it is we who act when we act, but it is he [God] who, by giving the will fully effective powers, causes us to act.'"[71] And again, he explains, "It is not that we ourselves do nothing or that we without any movement of our will are driven to act by pressure from him, but that we act while being acted upon by him."[72]

---

66. Ibid., 2.2.6–7.

67. Calvin, "Calvin's Catechism (1537)," in Dennison, *Reformed Confessions*, 1:397.

68. Cited by Lane, "Did Calvin Believe in Freewill?," 83.

69. Calvin, *Bondage and Liberation of the Will*, 4.329.

70. As Anthony N. S. Lane puts it: "Fallen man sins freely and his sin is the expression of his true character, and in that sense he is fully free. But he is not free in the sense of being poised between good and evil in some sort of moral neutrality" (*The Calvin Handbook*, 282).

71. The quote within the quote is from Augustine, *Grace and Free Choice*, 16.32, as cited in Calvin, *Bondage and Liberation of the Will*, 4.330.

72. Calvin, *Bondage and Liberation of the Will*, 4.337. See also, *Institutes of the Christian Religion*, 2.5.14–15.

Thus, Calvin clearly resists here the claim that only God acts and that man is completely and totally moved by the divine will such that genuine human action—as Calvin understands it—is excluded. Thus, the relationship between God and man is not mutually exclusive. What then is that relationship? Calvin's minimalist position on the will then raises the question of grace and freedom. In the next section, I address that question in Calvin's theology.

Grace and Freedom

Berkouwer argues about Calvin's opposition to libertarian freedom that it is not based on a metaphysical interpretation, namely, a philosophical theory of causality. In one sense, of course, Berkouwer is correct. "If Calvin's opposition to free will had been based on a deterministic causality, it would have been impossible for him to distinguish the situations before and after the fall: freedom would never have existed. But this is precisely not the case. Calvin views free will as something which has been lost; man has been deprived of it. The fall marks a basic change, for man lost what he once possessed."[73] As Calvin puts it, "We admit that man's condition while he still remained upright was such that he could incline to either side."[74] In other words, man lost in his fallen condition the created freedom, meaning thereby "the power to choose either good or evil."[75]

Yet, in another sense, Berkouwer's point brings to light a metaphysical question regarding the compatibility of freedom and necessity. Magisterial Reformers,[76] such as Calvin, did not "posit compulsion as over against freedom." Compulsion here refers to a state of affairs that is external to the agent causing him to do something. In this connection, recall Calvin's repeated efforts to distinguish necessity from compulsion in explaining the bondage of the will. "Man . . . sins of necessity, yet sins no less voluntarily."[77] Calvin

---

73. Berkouwer, *De Mens het Beeld Gods*, 355; in English, *Man: The Image of God*, 318. See also, Berkouwer, *De Voorzienigheid Gods*, 178–179; in English, *The Providence of God*, 162–65. Both the English and Dutch of these writings will be cited throughout this work, first the original followed by the pagination of the English translation in square brackets [ ]. Quotations are from the English translation unless otherwise indicated.

74. Calvin, *Institutes of the Christian Religion*, 2.3.10.

75. Berkouwer, *De Mens het Beeld Gods*, 376 [337].

76. For a collection of post-Reformation texts by Zanchi, Junius, Voetius, Turretin, and de Moor on the problem of free choice and determinism, see Asselt et al., *Reformed Thought on Freedom*.

77. Calvin, *Institutes of the Christian Religion*, 2.4.1.

rejects a "strong" free will, meaning thereby libertarian freewill. Instead, he seems to embrace a "weak" free will, in other words, a compatibilist free will.[78] Men voluntarily follow their evil inclinations and desires, and hence these are the immediate causes of their actions, causes that are internal to the agent. Therefore, he sins voluntarily but no less necessarily. In other words, he is unable to do otherwise than he does do because "no good thing remains in his power, and . . . he is hedged about on all sides by most miserable necessity."[79] His choices then are determined by his nature. Berkouwer recognizes this point: "When Calvin distinguishes between necessity and compulsion (*necessitas* and *coactio*), necessity refers to a *necessitas* arising from the corruption of human nature."[80] That the agent sins of necessity, even if voluntarily, may mislead us to think that he could have done differently if he had wanted to do so. But Calvin makes abundantly clear, as I have shown in the previous section, that given man's bondage of the will in his fallen state he could not want to do otherwise than he does.[81] But how, then, are freedom and necessity—it isn't possible to do the opposite—compatible?[82]

Berkouwer's judgment seems questionable, namely, that "the Reformation . . . implies the breaking through of *every* form of determinism."[83] In particular, Berkouwer claims that Calvin is "innocent of determinism" because he "approaches the whole question of the freedom of the will from the conflict between sin and grace." True enough. Yet, Berkouwer then adds that Calvin "speaks of the impotence [of the will] to which sin 'necessarily' leads."[84] In other words, he could not have done otherwise given the will's bondage into sin. Still, Calvin insists that man sins voluntarily. In other words, man sins with his will voluntarily, but necessarily. So, Berkouwer is right that Calvin rejects *hard* determinism, wherein there is a logical incompatibility between freedom and necessity and hence the denial of strong free will. He is wrong, however, in claiming that Calvin is free of determinism, in particular, *soft* determinism, namely, compatibilism.

Scott Burson and Jerry Walls (hereafter *BW*) provide us with a possible answer to this question regarding the compatibility of freedom—in

---

78. Crisp, *Deviant Calvinism*, 167.

79. Calvin, *Institutes of the Christian Religion*, 2.2.1.

80. Berkouwer, *De Mens het Beeld Gods*, 356n30 [319n13]; emphasis added.

81. Walls and Dongell, *Why I Am Not a Calvinist*, 109.

82. Georgius the Sicilian monk raises this question. Calvin says, "Georgius thinks we are involved in absurdity, because we make man free to sin, while the reprobate sin of necessity. But the freedom of which we speak, because it is too familiar to him is not really known to him" (Calvin, *Concerning the Eternal Predestination of God*, 156).

83. Berkouwer, *De Mens het Beeld Gods*, 356–357 [319]

84. Berkouwer, *De Voorzienigheid Gods*, 179 [165].

the sense of voluntary—and necessity—in the sense that a choice could not have been otherwise.[85] They consider C.S. Lewis' claim "that the most deeply compelled action is also the freest action."[86] *BW* could have added here Michael Polanyi's similar point: "The freedom of the subjective person to do as he pleases is overruled by the freedom of the responsible person to act as he must."[87] They rightly note that Lewis is not arguing here for the compatibility of freedom and determinism. Indeed, I think we might say that Lewis and Polanyi's statement suggest a standpoint that transcends determinism and indeterminism because "man is neither unfree in the sense of determinism nor free in the sense of indeterminism."[88] It is clear what being unfree means, but what is an indeterministic sense of freedom? Perhaps indeterministic freedom means unpredictability, randomness, or arbitrariness.[89] De Boer gives an illuminating example of the latter:

> Suppose that after a year of struggling in vain with philosophical and administrative problems I decide to go on vacation to the sunny island of Atlantis. I make all my preparations, buy the plane tickets, and so forth. But what happens on the scheduled day of departure? Instead of taking a taxi to the airport so that I can head south "on the wings of song," I find myself—to my amazement—riding my bicycle. I head to the Institute for the Science of Andragogy, where I spend the entire day taking part in a general meeting. This is completely unexpected, unpredictable conduct! According to the indeterminist definition, I have reached a high point of freedom.[90]

Neither Lewis nor Polanyi would see this as a high point of freedom. Indeed, random, arbitrary, or unpredictable action would be unfree.[91] As *BW*

85. Burson and Walls, *C. S. Lewis*, 100–101.

86. C. S. Lewis, *God in the Dock*, 261, as cited in Burson and Walls, *C. S. Lewis*, 100.

87. Polanyi, *Personal Knowledge*, 311.

88. De Boer, *Grondslagen van een kritische psychologie*, 65 [63].

89. Plantinga, "The Free Will Defense," 27.

90. De Boer, *Grondslagen van een kritische psychologie*, 67 [65].

91. McCabe, *God Matters*, "Freedom," 13: "There are always reasons and motives for free actions. You can say *why* Fred did this. We can even in English say, 'What made him do it?' meaning what reason did he have for doing it. When we speak of what made him do it in that sense we are certainly not denying that he did it freely. To assign a reason or motive to an action is not, however, to talk about the cause of the actions; it is to analyse *the action itself*. An action that was caused from outside could not be done for a reason, or at least not for the agent's reason. If by devious chemical or hypnotic means I cause Fred to eat his left sock, then *he* does not have a reason for doing it (though he may think he has), it is I who have a reason for his doing it, for the action is really mine, not his."

remark: "A true free choice is a holistic act, one that involves the entire person—mind, will and emotions. The freest act is the one in which there is no internal tension, each faculty is on board, harmoniously pulling in the same direction. . . . Such a scenario could easily be viewed as the freest possible act because there is no resistance or internal struggle." Put differently, the freest possible act is not uncaused, but the manner of causality is agent-causality where the act is determined by reasons and motives.[92] Even if I am free with respect to an action such that I am free to do it or not, says Plantinga, "If I know you well, I may be able to predict what action you will take in response to a certain set of conditions; it does not follow that you are not free with respect to that action."[93] This seems to be the point made by BW. Still, they rightly ask, "But in what sense is such an action compelled?" Regarding Polanyi, we might similarly ask in what sense must the responsible person act as he does? BW reply:

> After all, one certainly can be fully committed to a decision without a sense of compulsion. What was Lewis suggesting? It could be that Lewis was saying that a holistic action, one that receives the full endorsement of the entire person, is compelled in the sense that one would not do otherwise. Why would you? If your mind, will and emotions are the faculties involved in arriving at a decision and these faculties are in complete agreement, then surely you would make that choice. But it does not follow from the assertion that one would not do otherwise that one could not have done otherwise. For you ultimately had the power to choose which thoughts, emotions and impulses to attend to in the process of coming to internal consensus on the issue at hand. This might be the point of confusion for Lewis. If one could not have done otherwise, then we have a determined act. But if one possesses the power to do otherwise but simply would not, given the internal consensus on the matter, then this is not paradoxical or deterministic at all. If this is the point Lewis intended when he said, "The most deeply compelled action is also the freest action," then it would appear that he has confused the concept of a compelled choice, one that could not

---

92. On this point see De Boer, *Grondslagen van een kritische psychologie*, 66 [63]. *Pace* Benjamin B. Warfield who argued that the Pelagian conception of human freedom—by which he means libertarian freedom—"scarcely allows for the existence of a 'man'—only a willing machine is left. . . . In such a conception, there was no place for character. . . . Here lies the essential error of their doctrine of free will: they looked upon freedom in its form only, and not in its matter" ("Augustine and the Pelagian Controversy," xiii-lxxi).

93. Plantinga, "The Free Will Defense," 27.

have been otherwise, with a decisive choice, one that simply would not have been otherwise given the settled state of your decision-making faculties.[94]

Let's zero in on the different meanings of "one *would not* do otherwise" and "one *could not* have done otherwise." The former implies that the agent performing the action would not do otherwise given his fallen nature, antecedents and motives. But would not do otherwise is not the same as could not have acted differently, if he had wanted to do so, choosing *x* rather than *y*. Bavinck misses this difference when he claims that "God infallibly knows in advance what a person will do in a given case" is possible only if "the person's motives determine his or her will in one specific direction, and this will therefore does not consist in indifference."[95] In other words, Bavinck rejects libertarian freedom—i.e., the freedom of indifference—as inconsistent with divine foreknowledge, and hence embraces compatibilism. But one of the conditions of a free action according to theological compatibilism is that the person performing an action could have done otherwise, if he had wanted to do so. If then the person could not have done otherwise, it is difficult to see how he is free in any sense. Bavinck suffers from the confusion between a compelled choice and a decisive action.

Returning now to Calvin's claim about the compatibility of freedom and determinism, I think he, too, suffers from the same confusion that *BW* attributes to Lewis, namely, the difference between the a compelled choice and a decisive action. Calvin's concept of freedom understands an agent to be acting voluntarily because he does what he wants to do or chooses to do given his sinful nature. But could he have wanted to do something other than what he did want? Calvin denies that he could have.

Critics of Calvin's compatibilism argue that freedom is a matter of being able to do otherwise rather than just a matter of doing what you want to. Calvin resists this argument. He says: "If sin, they say, is a matter of necessity, it now ceases to be sin; if it is voluntary, then it can be avoided. . . . I therefore deny that sin ought less to be reckoned as sin merely because it is necessary. I deny conversely the inference they draw, that because sin is voluntary it is avoidable." He adds, "The second part of their syllogism is defective because it erroneously leaps from 'voluntary' to 'free'. For we proved above that something not subject to free choice is nevertheless voluntarily done."[96] But all Calvin showed after distinguishing necessity from

94. Burson and Walls, *C.S. Lewis*, 101. I cannot argue the point here, but I think Polanyi does not suffer from the same confusion that *BW* attribute to Lewis.

95. Bavinck, *Gereformeerde Dogmatiek*, 2:169 [202].

96. Calvin, *Institutes of the Christian Religion*, 2.5.1.

compulsion, because he rejects hard determinism, was that men voluntarily follow their evil inclinations and desires, and hence these are the immediate causes of their actions, causes that are internal to the agent. Therefore, he sins voluntarily but no less necessarily. He did what he most wanted to do given a state of affairs internal to the agent, and hence he made a compelled choice—one that could not have been otherwise. But then the person is not truly free—at least not in the libertarian sense of freedom.

Perhaps we can gain some perspective from Berkouwer about why magisterial Reformers, such as Calvin, rejected libertarian freedom. Earlier I noted Berkouwer's point that Calvin's rejection of libertarian freedom was not driven by a metaphysical interpretation. I think that Berkouwer is right that Calvin was rather driven by a redemptive historical interpretation of human freedom. Berkouwer says, "There was no suggestion that its critique of the freedom of the will meant to hold, in deterministic fashion, that only God acted, and that man was powerless, deprived of will, and driven. Such an approach to the problem was definitely not the background of the real controversy."[97] The real controversy concerned the "central religious question" regarding grace and freedom and to raise a deeper question beyond "the controversy between determinism and indeterminism," according to Berkouwer.[98] Accordingly, then, says Berkouwer:

> The absence of human freedom was expounded not in terms of a general determinism, but rather in terms of sin: the unfree nature of fallen and lost man, who because of the fall was in bondage to the dark powers of apostasy, which overpowered and ruled him in all his ways. This view of man's unfree nature comes to the fore in the history of theology in connection with the question of whether or not man had "freedom" to accept divine grace. Was it actually so that on the one hand there was a divine offer of grace, and on the other a free man, who could respond to this grace negatively as well as well as positively, so that the decision as to salvation lay in man's own hands only?[99]

He continues:

> The problem was then the condition, the state of "being" of sinful and lost mankind, the being with which he willed and acted

97. Berkouwer, *De Mens het Beeld Gods*, 352 [315].

98. Ibid., 350 [312].

99. Ibid., 351 [314]. Berkouwer speaks of the "unfree" (onvrijheid in Dutch) fallen man, which the English translator rendered as "slave," clearly in connection with the bondage of the will. I have retained the literal sense of the word and hence I speak of man's unfree nature.

and chose in all his activities. Thus it was primarily the central
religious question which was raised. Is the "being" of fallen man
of such a sort that he is "free" in each new situation of his life,
in each new decisive turning point of his existence, free in the
sense that the possibility of doing good, of obeying God's commands, of being "open" to divine grace, is always there? Or is he
enslaved to his sinful past and to the corruption of his heart, to
his alienation from God? The Reformation did not hesitate as to
the answer to these questions. And its answer did not arise from
a deterministic view of the acts of God or from an annihilation
of man's will, but rather from its belief in man's lostness, his
fallen state. The criticism of free will was not based on the assumption of a universal necessitarianism, but on the confession
of man's guileful, stony heart, which—mightily active—pushed
man forward on a way of sin and corruption which he is no
longer able to abandon by means of the "freedom" presumed to
be essentially and anthropologically his.[100]

Calvin's and Berkouwer's rejection of libertarian free will is driven by the
conviction that the will of man—given its sin, guilt, alienation, and rebellion with reference to God—is unable to restore itself to favor with God.
"Man's sin is not a manifestation of his freedom, but its perversion."[101] But
this inability is masked in the libertarian idea that man can equally choose
either good or evil. "How can we place true freedom next to a 'freedom' in
which man can say yes or no to evil?"[102] We can't, according to Calvin and
Berkouwer, not if we want to understand true freedom, namely, that it is in
Christ that the true freedom of man's humanity is found, but also the role of
grace in moving man to respond to the gospel. Let's consider the concepts
of "operating" and "cooperating" grace, and the corresponding distinction
between "prevenient" and "subsequent" grace as these concepts bear upon
the question of grace and freedom.

I quote here from Aquinas's use of Augustine's distinctions on the nature of grace in his account of grace and justification, and regarding the
latter the place of freedom. Augustine says (*De Gratia et Libero Arbitrio* xvii)
regarding the distinction between operating and cooperating grace: "'God
by cooperating with us, perfects what He began by operating in us, since
He who perfects by cooperation with such as are willing, begins by operating that they may will'. But the operations of God whereby He moves us to
good pertain to grace. Therefore grace is fittingly divided into operating

100. Ibid., 352–53 [316].
101. Ibid., 358 [321].
102. Ibid., 379 [339].

and cooperating."[103] Furthermore, the second set of distinctions is between prevenient and subsequent grace: "And hence grace, inasmuch as it causes the first effect in us, is called prevenient with respect to the second, and inasmuch as it causes the second, it is called subsequent with respect to the first effect. And as one effect is posterior to this effect, and prior to that, so may grace be called prevenient and subsequent on account of the same effect viewed relatively to divers others. And this is what Augustine says (*De Natura et Gratia* xxxi): 'It is prevenient, inasmuch as it heals, and subsequent, inasmuch as, being healed, we are strengthened; it is prevenient, inasmuch as we are called, and subsequent, inasmuch as we are glorified.'"[104] In short, prevenient grace is a grace enabling —it does more than enable because it also involves calling, convicting, and illuminating—a person to cooperate with the Holy Spirit by not resisting.[105] This grace opens a person up to the subsequent graces of justifying and sanctifying grace. I shall return in the next chapter on Matthias Joseph Scheeben to discuss the relationship between these two graces of prevenient and subsequent, which have been further distinguished, according to the efficacy of predestinating grace in time, "as *praedestinatio incompleta* or *inadequatio*, which signifies either Predestination to grace only (*praedestinatio ad gratiam tantum*) or Predestination to glory (*praedestinatio ad gloriam tantum*), or *praedestinatio completa or adaequata* which is a Predestination to both grace and glory."[106]

For now, I limit myself to Calvin's reference to Peter Lombard and Bernard of Clairvaux in his discussion of the first set of distinctions. Referring to the Master of the Sentences, Calvin says, quoting Lombard: "'We need two kinds of grace to render us capable of good works'. He calls the first kind of 'operating', which ensures that we effectively will to do good. The second he calls 'co-operating', which follows the good will as a help."[107] Calvin then expresses his suspicion regarding the idea of cooperating grace, namely, it suggests that grace is not efficacious, meaning thereby that a man can and does resist God's grace. "The thing that displeases me about this division is that, while he attributes the effective desire for good to the grace of God, yet he hints that man by his very own nature somehow seeks after the good—though ineffectively." He feared the view that "it is our right either to render it ineffectual by spurning the first [operating] grace, or to confirm it

103. Aquinas, *Summa Theologiae*, II-I, q. 111, art 2.

104. Ibid., II-I, q. 111, art 3.

105. Olson, *Arminian Theology*, 160.

106. Ott, *Fundamentals of Catholic Dogma*, 242.

107. Calvin, *Institutes of the Christian Religion*, 2.2.6.

by obediently following it."[108] In other words, the crux of Calvin's objection to co-operating grace is the suggestion that "grace does no work in us by itself but is only a co-worker with us."[109] Still, Calvin cautiously accepts the notion of co-operating grace in Augustine's sense: "God by co-operating perfects that which by operating he has begun. It is the same grace but with its name changed to fit the different mode of its effect."

Still, the question remains regarding irresistible grace, particularly when it is considered in light of libertarian free will, and hence denies the bondage of the will. Berkouwer objects as well: "The simple way in which human freedom is often defined as a double possibility, as freedom of choice, arises from an abstract and irreligious and neutral anthropological analysis of human freedom. The analysis sees this 'freedom' to choose either of two directions as belonging to the essence of man as created 'good'. Freedom is them the possibility of choice, the open choice, and the choice of sin is then the demonstration, the manifestation of human freedom."[110] But this conclusion is at odds with the biblical testimony, namely, "man's sin is not a manifestation of his freedom, but is perversion."[111]

Furthermore, regarding the second set of distinctions, prevenient and subsequent grace, here, too, Calvin's objection is similar: prevenient grace is a predisposing grace that is not itself effectual, and hence its effectiveness is dependent upon the fallen man's assent and cooperation. "As if grace did not also actuate the will itself."[112] Elsewhere in the *Institutes* Calvin says, "He does not move the will in such a manner as has been taught and believed for many ages—that it is afterward in our choice either to obey or resist the motion—but by disposing it efficaciously." He adds, "For the apostle does not teach that the grace of God's will is bestowed upon us if we accept it, but that He wills to work in us."[113] And again, Calvin says, echoing Augustine, "Not only is grace offered by the Lord, which by anyone's free choice may be accepted or rejected; but it is this very grace which forms both choice and will in the heart, so that whatever good works then follow are the fruit and effect of grace; and it has no other will obeying it except the will that it has made."[114]

---

108. Ibid., 2.2.6.
109. Ibid., 2.3.11.
110. Berkouwer, *De Mens het Beeld Gods*, 372–73 [334].
111. Ibid., 358 [321].
112. Calvin, *Institutes of the Christian Religion*, 2.3.7.
113. Ibid., 2.3.10.
114. Ibid., 2.3.14.

This raises the question of effectual grace such that it *causes* the sinner to be willing, because when grace moves us we cannot but follow, and its difference from a sufficient grace that enables the sinner to respond to the grace that is offered. This latter grace is truly sufficient, making possible a saving act, but remains inefficacious in virtue of the will's resistance.[115] Of course as the *Catechism of the Catholic Church* states regarding what is called enabling grace, or prevenient grace: "The *preparation of man* for the reception of grace is already a work of grace. The latter is needed to arouse and sustain our collaboration in justification through faith, and in sanctification through charity."[116] The crucial factor is that "God's free initiative demands *man's free response*,"[117] and God's enabling grace, or prevenient grace, makes that response possible. To be clear, it isn't the response that causes grace to elicit a saving act; rather his free response is an effect of grace. This, too, is the position of the Joint Declaration on the Doctrine of Justification: "When Catholics say that persons 'cooperate' in preparing for and accepting justification by consenting to God's justifying action, they see such personal consent *as itself an effect of grace*, not as an action arising from innate human abilities."[118] Put differently, it is not the will that is the efficient cause of salvation. "The efficient cause is the merciful God who gratuitously washes and sanctifies [cf. 1 Cor 6:11], sealing and anointing [cf. 2 Cor 1:21f.] 'with the promised Holy Spirit, who is the guarantee of our inheritance' [Eph 1:13f.]."[119] But is that so only if the grace is efficacious? Or is prevenient grace such that it can be resisted?

If the grace is resisted, then it doesn't prepare one for the reception of justifying grace. But then the grace that doesn't have this saving effect is merely sufficient grace. Does that mean that it is the will of man that makes grace efficacious? So, as Ott states, "There is a question as to whether the ground for this difference in efficacy lies in the grace itself or in human freedom."[120] But then we are back to the question whether efficacious grace *causes* the will to respond, but, if so, this seems to interfere with the freedom of the will. As Olson puts it,

> [Prevenient grace] enables the will to make the free choice to
> either cooperate with or resist grace. Cooperation does not con-
> tribute to salvation, as if God does part and humans do part;

115. Ott, *Fundamentals of Catholic Dogma*, 247.

116. *CCC*, §2001.

117. Ibid., §2002.

118. *The Joint Declaration on the Doctrine of Justification*, 4.1.20; emphasis added.

119. Denzinger, §1529.

120. Ott, *Fundamentals of Catholic Dogma*, 246.

rather cooperation with grace . . . is simply nonresistance to
grace. It is merely deciding to allow grace to do its work by lay-
ing down all attempts at self-justification and self-purification,
and admitting that only Christ can save. Nevertheless, God does
not make this decision for the individual; it is a decision individuals, under the pressure of prevenient grace, must make for
themselves . . . . None of this is based on any human merit; it is a
sheer gift, not imposed but freely received. . . . Thus salvation is
conditional, not unconditional; humans play a role and are not
passive or controlled by any force, internal or external.[121]

Perhaps then the question whether the ground of the difference between sufficient and efficacious grace lies in the grace itself or in human
freedom is a false dilemma that may only be avoided if we reject the notion
of irresistible grace. I shall return to this question in the next chapter.

For now, I shall merely note that enabling or prevenient grace is, then,
consistent with the power of contrary choice, which is the possibility of doing otherwise than cooperating with God's grace, but effectual grace is not
consistent with that power because it causes the sinner to be willing. It is
the difference between a decisive choice and a compelled one. The idea of
enabling grace, of prevenient grace that not only enable, but also convicts,
calls, and illumines,[122] is at work in Trent's teaching of human freedom. "If
anyone says that after Adam's sin the free will of man is lost and extinct
or that it is an empty concept, a term without real foundation, indeed, a
fiction introduced by Satan into the Church, let him be anathema."[123] In
other words, there is a difference between saying that "(1) because a person
is determined to do an action by God making him willing to do that thing,
the person is able to do that thing" and that "(2) a person is enabled to do
that thing by God, but it is up to the person whether he does the action in
question."[124] Enabling grace rejects irresistible grace. But it also presupposes
that "God does not move man just as we throw a stone."[125] Calvin's protest

121. Olson, *Arminian Theology*, 36–37.

122. Olson, "Election is for Everyone."

123. Denzinger, §1555. In the Bull *Exsurge Domine*, June 15, 1520, condemning the
errors of Martin Luther, the following error is rejected: "After sin, free will is a reality in
name only; and when it does what is in its power, it sins mortally" (§1486).

124. Crisp, *Deviant Calvinism*, 80. Crisp is discussing Jerry Walls work. On the difference between effectual grace and enabling grace, see Burson and Walls, *C.S. Lewis*,
102; see also, Walls and Dongell, *Why I Am Not a Calvinist*, 166.

125. Calvin, *Institutes of the Christian Religion*, 2.5.14. See also, the *Second Helvetic
Confession*, ix. Of Free Will, and so of Man's Power and Ability: "His understanding
[after the fall] indeed was not taken from him, neither was he deprived of will and altogether changed into a stone or stock. Nevertheless, these things are so altered in man

notwithstanding it is difficult to see how his view of the relation of God's grace and man's act differs from "a stone set in motion by an outside force, and borne along by no motion, sensation, or will of its own."[126] Similarly, Berkouwer protests: "Roman Catholic criticism of the Reformation often says that the Reformation teaches a monergism of grace, an exclusive activity on God's part against which all human endeavor becomes mere nothingness. . . . But this characterization is unjust and incorrect."[127] I agree with Berkouwer that this way of characterizing the Reformation is unfair, but I also think that it is not at all clear how Calvin allows for genuine human action in the relationship between God's grace and man's acts.

Nevertheless, Berkouwer is right: "In the light of the gospel it is foolish to let man's acts and decisions shrink to nothingness in a system of monergism. But it is the nature of the relationship between God's grace and man's act that is at stake."[128] Calvin agrees, but notwithstanding that agreement I don't think he shows how man is not just a stone, or as Trent puts the position that it rejects: "man himself is entirely inactive while receiving that inspiration [of the Holy Spirit]," particularly since he affirms effectual grace that is irresistible, which Trent rejects.[129] The crux is thus, according to Berkouwer: "To be sure, there is a connection between the divine and the human act. The divine act makes room, leaves open the possibility for man's act. That possibility is not absorbed or destroyed by divine superiority, but created, called forth, by it. And within that 'room', that possibility, God's work is honored according to His sovereign pleasure."[130] All of this is important because it affirms that the relationship between God's grace and man does not exclude human acts.

As the *Catechism of the Catholic Church* states: "To be human, 'man's response to God by faith must be free, and . . . therefore nobody is to be forced to embrace the faith against his will. The act of faith is of its very nature a free act."[131] This is affirmed in Trent's Canon 4 on Justification: "If anyone says that the free will of man, moved and awakened by God, in no way cooperates by an assent to God's awakening call, through which he disposes and prepares himself to obtain the grace of justification; and that

---

that they are not able to do that now which they could do before his fall" (Dennison, *Reformed Confessions*, 2:822).

126. Calvin, *Institutes of the Christian Religion*, 2.5.14.

127. Berkouwer, *De Verkiezing Gods*, 52 [50].

128. Ibid., 46, 52 [44, 50].

129. Denzinger, §1525.

130. Berkouwer, *De Verkiezing Gods*, 48 [46].

131. CCC §160. The quote within the quote is from *Dignitatis Humanae*, §10.

man cannot refuse his assent if he wishes, but that like a lifeless object he does nothing at all and is merely passive, let him be anathema."[132] And yet Berkouwer is distracted by the word "cooperation" as a way of character-izing the relationship of God's grace and man's response. Why? Berkouwer says, it isn't because the idea of cooperation denies divine election and the necessity of grace. He is right. Trent states about man's act and God's grace: "without God's grace, he cannot by his own free will move toward justice in God's sight."[133] Why then? Chiefly, Berkouwer says, because "in such a no-tion God's decision is made dependent on man's decision. . . . In no form of synergism is it possible to escape the conclusion that man owes his salvation not solely to God but also to himself."[134] More precisely, then, Berkouwer thinks that "within the synergistic idea of cooperation the sovereignty of election and grace is in danger."[135] How is it in danger?

Precisely because "man's freedom to decide" becomes "a component factor in bringing about man's salvation"[136] such that it can resist the grace of God. Berkouwer acknowledges that Catholic critics reject this way of characterizing "cooperation," as if it involves a "distribution of work" be-tween God and man. "But," adds Berkouwer, "no matter how refined syner-gism is, the force of the opposition cannot be weakened and undermined. Paradoxical as it may sound, one can truly speak of cooperation only when synergism has been completely denounced."[137] But it remains to ask: how do we reject synergism without excluding the significance of human acts? Clearly, Berkouwer emphasizes that the relationship between God and man is not mutually exclusive. He explains: "It is here, within this real realm of possibility, that man's act received its form; such a form that the nature of his act excludes cooperation. And a relation, altogether different from the one between grace and freedom, becomes visible."[138] What relation becomes visible here between God's grace and man's act such that the latter is taken seriously as mutually interpenetrating albeit the case that divine grace has priority?

In response, let us recall here the difference between effectual grace that is causally construed such that it compels man to act and enabling grace that makes it possible for the sinner to respond to the grace that is offered.

132. Denzinger, §1554.

133. Ibid., §1525.

134. Berkouwer, *De Verkiezing Gods*, 44 [42].

135. Ibid., 49 [47].

136. Ibid., 50 [48].

137. Ibid., 53 [50].

138. Ibid., 48 [46].

The latter is consistent with the power of contrary choice. One wonders what Berkouwer means when he says that the Spirit creates the "realm of possibility" for man to respond in freedom to God's grace? This way of speaking is less rigorous than Calvin's who says that when grace moves us we cannot but follow. Yes, Berkouwer underscores the superiority of grace, but it "is not that of a mechanical causality or of coercion that obstructs man's activity." Rather, he adds, "it is the personal superiority of love and grace, which in man's experience is making room for him to act by not destroying his freedom." "No man can come to me, except the Father that sent me draw him" (John 6:44). . . . It is good to observe that Christ employs the word *draw* when human resistance against His gospel seems at its strongest (John 6:41, 42). In that situation Christ knew that "everyone that hath heard from the Father, and hath learned, cometh unto me" (John 6:45). To hear, to learn, to be drawn, to be given, and *then* to come—that is the evangelical breakthrough of all synergism."[139] The crux of the question is found in the concluding clause of this citation, namely, does man come to God *freely*, and if so, how? In the last section of this chapter I turn to discuss that question and divine election in Calvin's theology.

The Will and Divine Election

Calvin treats the matter of election and reprobation in the *Institutes of the Christian Religion*, 3. 21–24. One may be excused for thinking that Calvin affirms the equal symmetry ("*eodem modo*") of election and reprobation, or what the Council of Trent called predestinarianism,[140] otherwise known as "double predestination." On the one hand, when Calvin defends himself against the charge of determinism by critics, such as Albert Pighius, he appeals to the proximate cause of sin, which is man himself, and insists that God's judgment is contingent upon man's sin.[141] On the other hand, when Calvin considers the relation between the divine counsel and man's sin, he

139. Ibid., 50–51 [47, 49]

140. Denzinger 1567: "If anyone says that the grace of justification is given only to those who are predestined to life and that all the others who are called are called indeed but do not receive grace, as they are predestined to evil by the divine power, let him be anathema." Karl Barth also rejects the understanding of predestination as an equal symmetry, that is, "when the divine election and the divine rejection came to spoken of as inter-connected divine acts similar in character and determination; when they came to be regarded and understood as though they could both be grouped under the one over-ruling concept. . . of a double divine decision from all eternity , i.e., a decision with two parallel sides" (*CD* II.2, 13–14).

141. Calvin, *Concerning the Eternal Predestination of God*, 100, 116.

rejects divine foreknowledge and permission, insists that God is not the author of sin, and affirms that God ordains whatsoever comes to pass. "Mighty therefore, are the works of God and excellent in all His acts of will, so that in a marvelous and ineffable way that cannot be done without His will which is yet done contrary to His will [not *praeter* even if contra *voluntatem Dei*]. For it would not be done if He did not permit it, and permission is given not without but by His will."[142] So, since Calvin does not seem to "operate with two equivalent metaphysical *causae*,"[143] as Berkouwer argues, therefore, in one sense, we can understand why Berkouwer insists that "there is no place in Calvin's teachings for the *eodem modo*"[144] of election and reprobation. Still, Berkouwer cautiously states: "It is not our intention to defend every one of Calvin's utterances regarding the doctrine of election. On some occasions he speaks of the relation between divine and human causes in such a manner that other expressions make us feel relieved."[145] Although Berkouwer doesn't give examples of such expressions, I think the following will provide the consternation he and others sometimes felt when reading Calvin on predestination.

Calvin says at the start of his reflections on predestination: "We shall never be clearly persuaded, as we ought to be, that our salvation flows from the wellspring of God's free mercy until we come to know his eternal election, which illumines God's grace by the contrast: that he does not indiscriminately adopt all into the hope of salvation but gives to some what he denies to others."[146] On this view, predestination is parallel, and hence double in the strict sense, when both election and reprobation are symmetrical ("*eodem modo*") with respect to the mode of divine causality. On this view, the logical implication of divine sovereignty is pressed to the point where a strict parallelism of divine operation is affirmed and the asymmetry between salvation and reprobation is denied.

This results in the heresy of *predestinarianism*,[147] which is the false teaching that God does foreordain to damnation and to the means that lead to it, namely, sins, *in the same sense* in which he foreordains to salvation and to the means that lead to it, namely faith. Calvin says, "We call predestination God's eternal decree, by which he compacted with himself what he

142. Ibid., 69.

143. Ibid., 218 [186].

144. Ibid., 223 [189].

145. Ibid., 223 [190].

146. Calvin, *Institutes of the Christian Religion*, 3.21.1.

147. For a brief review of the Church's condemnation of "Heretical Predestinarianism," see Pohle, *Grace, Actual and Habitual*, 201–2, 205–6, 212–21. See also, Ott, *Fundamentals of Catholic Dogma*, 242–49.

willed to become of each man. For all are not created in equal condition; rather, eternal life is foreordained for some, eternal damnation for others. Therefore, as any man has been created to one or the other of these ends, we speak of him as predestined to life or to death."[148] Again, Calvin states: "As Scripture, then, clearly shows, we say that God once established by his eternal and unchangeable plan those whom he long before determined once for all to receive into salvation, and those who, on the other hand, he would devote to destruction. We assert that, with respect to the elect, this plan was founded upon his freely given mercy, without regard to human worth; but by his just and irreprehensible but incomprehensible judgment he has barred the door to life to those whom he has given over to damnation."[149] And despite the assurance from Reformed theologians, such as Charles Hodge,[150] and Louis Berkhof,[151] that there is no condemnation without sin, Calvin seems to state the opposite. He says, the "foundation of divine predestination is not in works. . . . If, then, we cannot determine a reason why he vouchsafes mercy to his own, except that it so pleases him, neither shall we have any reason for rejecting others, other than his will. For when it is said that God hardens or shows mercy to whom he wills, men are warned by this to seek no cause outside his will."[152]

So, then, is Evangelical Baptist theologian Millard Erikson right: "Not only did he [Calvin] hold that God has decided to send some to hell; he did not hesitate to say that God *causes* humans to sin." And because of Calvin's supralapsarianism—"the decree to save some and damn others is logically prior to the decision to create"—Erickson claims that, according to Calvin, "God creates some persons *in order* to damn them."[153] So, too, we find a similar judgment in the work of Catholic theologian Reginald Garrigou-Lagrange: "The fundamental thesis of his [Calvin's] doctrine is that some are freely predestined, and the rest are freely and positively damned."[154] Is this true? Is there reprobation apart from sin and guilt?

Michael Horton quickly dismisses the charge against Calvinism made by theologians, such as Erikson. He says, "Reprobation (the rejection of the nonelect) was not capricious or arbitrary but took account of sin." He adds, "No one is saved by divine coercion and no one is rejected apart from

---

148. Calvin, *Institutes of the Christian Religion*, 3.21.5.

149. Ibid., 3.21.7.

150. Hodge, *Systematic Theology*, 326.

151. Berkhof, *Systematic Theology*, 119.

152. Calvin, *Institutes of the Christian Religion*, 3.22.11.

153. Erikson, *Christian Theology*, 926–27.

154. Garrigou-Lagrange, *Predestination*, 119.

his or her own will."[155] In particular, he rejects what Clark Pinnock called
Calvinism's "omnicausalism," a view of divine causality presupposed in the
equal symmetry of election and reprobation.[156] Regarding Calvin's rejection of this view he refers us to Calvin's defense of human responsibility for
sin, human guilt, and the import of secondary causality in light of God's
providence, with the implication that God is not the author of the fall or, of
course, of sin.[157] Unfortunately, Horton doesn't consider Calvin's defense of
predestination and the problem of causality with respect to sin and unbelief
that arises from what appears to be his affirmation of the equal symmetry
of election and reprobation in the passages I cited above. We may turn to
Berkouwer for help here in interpreting Calvin:

> Calvin stresses two points: eternal death through God's judg-
> ment, and man's own nature that leads him to this judgment.
> Men charge God with being the cause of their destruction, Cal-
> vin says, but disregard the cause of condemnation, which they
> are compelled to recognize in themselves.[158]

In other words, God's judgment of reprobation is not unjust because the evil
that men do is brought about by causes that lie within them. Says Calvin,
"Let them not accuse God of injustice if they are destined by his eternal
judgment to death, to which they feel—whether they will or not—that they
are led by their own nature of itself. How perverse is their disposition to
protest is apparent from the fact that they deliberately suppress the cause
of condemnation, which they are compelled to recognize in themselves, in
order to free themselves by blaming God."[159] And again, he says,

> For if predestination is nothing but the meting out of divine
> justice . . . because it is certain that they were not unworthy to
> be predestined to this condition, it is equally certain that the
> destruction they undergo by predestination is also most just.
> Besides, their perdition depends upon the predestination of

---

155. Horton, *For Calvinism*, 57.

156. Horton acknowledges that some "hyper-Calvinists" have been guilty of "omnicausalism" and the attendant equal symmetry of election and reprobation. Indeed,
Louis Berkhof also says that "it is objected that Supralapsarianism makes the decree
of reprobation as absolute as the decree of election. In other words, that it regards
reprobation as purely an act of God's sovereign good pleasure, and not as an act of
punitive justice. According to its representation sin does not come into consideration
in the decree of reprobation. But this is hardly correct, though it may be true of some
Supralapsarians" (*Systematic Theology*, 122).

157. Calvin, *Institutes of the Christian Religion*, 1.17.3, 5, 9.

158. Berkouwer, *De Verkiezing Gods*, 218 [186].

159. Calvin, *Institutes of the Christian Religion*, 3.23.3.

God in such a way that *the cause and occasion of it are found in themselves.* . . . Accordingly, man falls according as God's providence ordains, but he falls by *his own fault.* . . . Accordingly, we should contemplate the evident cause of condemnation in the corrupt nature of humanity—which is closer to us—rather than seek a hidden and utterly incomprehensible cause in God's predestination.[160]

This interpretation of Calvin is strengthened when we turn to his work, *Concerning the Eternal Predestination of God,* where Calvin draws on the distinction between proximate and remote causes. Man is the proximate cause of sin and hence the blame for his condemnation resides within him.

For if they should complain that the wound is inflicted on them from another quarter, the internal sense of their mind will hold them bound to the conclusion that evil arose from the voluntary defection of the first man. . . . But when all has been said, the internal feeling of the heart does not cease to urge on everyone the conviction that no one, even being his own judge, may be absolved. Nor truly can anyone contend against this. For as on account of the sin of the one man a lethal wound was inflicted on all, so all men acknowledge God's judgment to be just. We cannot avoid concluding that the first origin of ruin is in Adam and that we individually find the proximate cause in ourselves.[161]

The lethal wound Calvin refers to here is original sin; it has the effect of bringing the will in bondage. As I argued in the previous section, according to Calvin, men voluntarily follow their evil inclinations and desires, and hence these are the immediate causes of their actions, causes that are internal to the agent. Therefore, man sins voluntarily, with the proximate cause of his actions lying within, but he sins no less necessarily, and hence he merits divine judgment. Still, the remote or ultimate cause is traced by Calvin to the divine ordination. Significantly, Berkouwer is right that "Calvin does not put the two *causae* on the same level.[162]" He adds, "Calvin often uses a twofold *causa* concept: *causa* as decree of God's will (the actual, most profound foundation), and *causa* as *causa* in man himself, namely, the ground of guilt that is synonymous with the *materia* that is found in man."[163] Therefore, Berkouwer emphasizes, "It is clear . . . that Calvin does not operate

160. Ibid., 3.23.8; emphasis added.
161. Calvin, *Concerning the Eternal Predestination of God,* 100–101.
162. Berkouwer, *De Verkiezing Gods,* 220 [187].
163. Ibid., 219 [186].

with two equivalent metaphysical *causae*."[164] One can understand and to a certain point agree with Berkouwer that since man's sin "definitely acts as a cause of judgment" that "there is no place in Calvin's teachings for the *eodem modo*"[165] of divine causality, namely, the equal symmetry of election and reprobation. These two aspects are asymmetrical because the "cause and matter" of reprobation "in in themselves," according to Calvin.[166] And yet, understanding the struggle between God's counsel and man's sin endures, not least, as I shall argue below, because of the divine decree of preterition, meaning thereby that God wills to withhold from them his free grace. As Calvin puts it, "Those, therefore, whom God passes by he reprobates, and that for no other cause but because he is pleased to exclude them from the inheritance which he predestines his children."[167] I will return to this point below. For now, I shall return to a discussion of Berkouwer's claim that Calvin does not operate with two equivalent metaphysical *causae*.

Pighius, for one, put all his emphasis on the judgment of reprobation being contingently based on an act of sin, as the proximate cause. Calvin rejects this position of conditional reprobation. Although he affirms man's sin as the proximate cause of the divine judgment of reprobation, he resists the claim of critics like Pighius who choose to remain with the proximate cause rather than going back to the remote cause to which the former cause is subordinate. On the one hand, Calvin says, resisting Pighius' objection that he cannot maintain the significance of the human *causa*:

> But the fault of our damnation resides so entirely in ourselves that it is forbidden to assemble extraneous precepts with which to cover it. But it was permissible thus briefly to show how preposterously Pighius removes the remote cause by bringing forward the proximate. He contends that the impious will be damned because they have provoked the wrath of God on themselves by their own misdeeds. From this he concludes that their damnation does not proceed from the decree of God. But I say they have accumulated misdeeds upon misdeeds because, being depraved, they could do nothing but sin. Yet they sinned not by extrinsic impulse but by the spontaneous inclination of the heart, knowingly and voluntarily. For it cannot be denied that the fount and origin of all evils is the corruption and viciousness of nature.[168]

164. Ibid.
165. Ibid., 223 [189].
166. Calvin, *Institutes of the Christian Religion*, 3.23.8.
167. Ibid., 3.23.8.
168. Calvin, *Concerning the Eternal Predestination of God*, 116.

And again:

> For the proper and genuine cause of sin is not God's hidden counsel but the evident will of man. . . . Since a man may find the cause of his evil within himself, what is the use of looking round to seek it in heaven? Clearly the fault lies in this, that [he] willed to sin. . . . God knowingly and willingly suffers man to fall; the reason may be hidden, but it cannot be unjust. This is always to be held above controversy, that sin is always hateful to God. For truly the praise which David accords Him (Ps 5:5) is fitting: God wills not iniquity.[169]

Once again, but now in response to the monk Georgius the Sicilian:

> We do not represent the reprobate as being so deprived of the Spirit of God that they may find the fault of their crimes in God. Whatever sins men commit, let them impute them to themselves. If anyone should evade this, I say that he is too strongly bound by the chains of conscience to free himself from just condemnation. . . . Hence they will be quite inexcusable who try to elicit from the profound recesses of God the cause of their evils, which in fact operates from their own corrupt heart. . . . Let each acknowledge his own sins, condemn himself, and, confessing from the heart all his guilt, supplicate in humanity his judge. If anyone object, the answer is immediate: The destruction is thine own, O Israel [Hosea 13:9].[170]

On the other hand, "one could get the impression that God is the prime cause of the proximate causes."[171] Says Calvin, "Since the disposition of all things is in God's hand, since the decision of salvation or of death rests in his power, he so ordains by his plan and will that among men some are born destined for certain death from the womb."[172] He adds, "No other cause of this fact can be adduced but reprobation, which is hidden in God's secret plan."[173] Although the decree of reprobation takes account of man's sin without which it would not be an act of divine justice, according to Calvin, nonetheless God doesn't make a judgment of reprobation on "the basis of works but solely according to God's will."[174] This suggests that Calvin accepts "unconditioned positive Reprobation," as Ott puts it, which "leads to

169. Ibid., 122.
170. Ibid., 155–56.
171. Berkouwer, *De Verkiezing Gods*, 221 [188].
172. Calvin, *Institutes of the Christian Religion*, 3.23.6.
173. Ibid., 3.23.4.
174. Ibid., 3.22.11.

a denial of the universality of the Divine Desire for salvation, and of the Redemption, and contradicts the Justice and Holiness of God as well as the freedom of man."[175] Calvin rejects "conditional reprobation," or what Ott calls, "a conditioned positive reprobation" that "occurs with consideration of foreseen future demerits (*post et propter praevisa demerita*)."[176] He does so just as much as he rejects "conditional election" in which God's election depends on foreseen faith.[177]

By contrast, the Catholic tradition holds the "conditional nature of Positive Reprobation."[178] As *CCC* teaches: "God predestines no one to go to hell; for this, a willful turning away from God (a mortal sin) is necessary, and persistence in it until the end. In the Eucharistic liturgy and in the daily prayers of her faithful, the Church implores the mercy of God, who does not want 'any to perish, but all to come to repentance.'"[179] This teaching is demanded by, says Ott, "the generality of the Divine Resolve of salvation. [Thus] [t]his excludes God's desiring in advance the damnation of certain men (cf. 1 Tim 2: 4; Ez 33:11; 2 Peter 3:9)."[180]

Let us also recall here Berkouwer's point that the preaching of God's judgment is inherently connected, according to Lord's Day 31 of the *Heidelberg Catechism*, to "the wrath of God and eternal condemnation [that] falls upon all unbelievers and hypocrites *as long as they do not repent* [emphasis added]."[181] Indeed, these verses from the Sacred Scriptures and the *Catechism* seem to presuppose a "meaningful open situation"[182] in which we are ambassadors of God issuing the call of the gospel to all sinners—not to the elect and reprobate, with their twofold destinies—to be reconciled to

175. Ott, *Fundamentals of Catholic Dogma*, 245. Similarly, Rahner and Vorgrimler, *Theological Dictionary*, 373: "When predestination is conceived of as destroying man's freedom to work out his salvation, we have heretical Predestinationism . . . . There is no positive, active predestination to sin—a thing that would be repugnant to God's sanctity and his universal salvific will."

176. Ott, *Fundamentals of Catholic Dogma*, 245.

177. Calvin, *Institutes of the Christian Religion*, 3.22.1.

178. Ott, *Fundamentals of Catholic Dogma*, 245.

179. *CCC*, §1037. See also, Rahner and Vorgrimler, *Theological Dictionary*, "When God foresees that his creatures will freely and finally reject him (and only in this case . . .) he wills and brings about the damnation of that person (see Mt 25:41; Rom 9:15ff.) (positive, unconditional but 'consequent' reprobation [following on the person's rejection of God]). To assert a positive unconditional reprobation antecedent to human guilt and thus its cause would be heretical predestinationism" (405).

180. Ott, *Fundamentals of Catholic Dogma*, 245.

181. Lord's Day 31 is quoted by Berkouwer, *De Verkiezing Gods*, 293 [243]. *Heidelberg Catechism*, in Dennison, *Reformed Confessions*, 2:1552–56.

182. Berkouwer, *Een Halve Eeuw Theologie*, 142 [102].

God (2 Cor 5:20), persuading them to respond by faith to the gospel as the only way of salvation in view of God's liberating grace. In this connection, I should note that Calvin clearly rejects the concept of foreknowledge or of permission; election or reprobation is not based on foreknowledge, nor is it a matter of God's simply permitting sin to occur.[183] Regarding the question whether "God's eternal resolve of Predestination has been taken with or without consideration of the merits of the man (*post or ante praevisa merita*),"[184] Calvin says that it is essentially a matter of God's sovereign good pleasure. Of course ever mindful that God is not the cause of sin, he adds, "Although the will of God is the supreme and first cause of all things and God holds the devil and all impious subject to His will, God nevertheless cannot be called the cause of sin, nor the author of evil, neither is He open to any blame."[185] Calvin confesses *ignorantia nostra* regarding how we make sense of God's counsel ruling over sin, in short, God ordaining whatsoever comes to pass, and not merely "permitting" or "allowing sin." And yet since there is a cause deeper than the proximate cause of man's causality, because God's counsel also rules over sin; the latter is *contra voluntatem Dei* but not *praeter voluntatem Dei*.

> So God in ordaining the fall of man had an end most just and right which holds the name of sin in abhorrence. Though I affirm that He ordained it, I do not allow that He is properly the author of sin. Not to spend longer on the point, I am of opinion that what Augustine teaches was fulfilled: In a wonderful and ineffable way, what was done contrary to His will was not yet done without His will, because it would not have been done at all unless He had allowed it. So he permitted it not unwillingly but willingly.[186]

This claim brings us back to the enduring question of the relation of God to sin. It seems that Calvin cannot regard reprobation as an act of justice *simpliciter*, as Berkhof puts it, "contingent on the sin of man."[187] Sin cannot be the ultimate or remote cause of reprobation. As Berkouwer explains: "The first and real cause for Calvin is and remains God's predestination, also as rejection, while the [proximate] cause in man is subordinated in the sense that sinful man is condemned by God. There is causality in man but

183. Calvin, *Concerning the Eternal Predestination of God*, 69, 81.

184. Ott, *Fundamentals of Catholic Dogma*, 243.

185. Calvin, "Articles Concerning Predestination," 179. See also, Calvin, *Concerning the Eternal Predestination of God*, 169.

186. Calvin, *Concerning the Eternal Predestination of God*, 123.

187. Berkhof, *Systematic Theology*, 122.

we must look further than that. There is a deeper, a deepest *causa*. . . . The relation between sin and judgment is always present, but behind this causal connection lies another *causa*, another origin: the one of rejection!"[188] As Calvin himself puts it, "As if there were not a cause deeper than that wickedness—the corruption of their [man's] nature; as if they did not remain sunk in this corruption because, reprobate by the secret counsel of God before they were born, they were not delivered from it."[189] Berkouwer describes the limits of finding an acceptable solution to the question of the relationship between God's counsel and sin by means of the concept of cause. He argues:

> It will always be impossible to escape from the thought of a causal determination, and the divine cause and the human cause are ultimately placed beside each other as entities that are, after all is said and done, equivalent, even in the subordination of the human cause to the divine cause. And that explains why men repeatedly flee from this causality to indeterminism, in which man's freedom is placed over against the omnipotent act of God—and then, in reaction a movement is launched against this indeterminism in which causal necessity is re-emphasized. Although the notion that the divine decree is a cause of judgment, parallel to the human cause [sin], has been repeatedly denied in Christian theology, it has not always been made sufficiently clear on what basis this fatalism could be legitimately rejected.[190]

Furthermore, adds, "The Roman Catholic doctrine of election . . . opposes the so-called 'predestinationalists' who teach a double predestination in the sense that God from eternity has foreordained one group to salvation and another as decidedly to preterition, and that Christ did not die for the reprobates."[191] This "inability" that Berkouwer alludes to in the last sentence of the block citation is because the decree of reprobation includes the preterition, or an act of God's sovereign will to pass over by divine grace some men. Berkhof is right that "those who are passed by are condemned on account of their sin."[192] But they are not passed over by divine grace *because* of their sin, and hence this raises the question regarding their moral responsibility for their preterition.[193] This decree of rejection is about God passing

---

188. Berkouwer, *De Verkiezing Gods*, 220 [187].

189. Calvin, *Concerning the Eternal Predestination of God*, 94.

190. Berkouwer, *De Verkiezing Gods*, 221–22 [188].

191. Ibid., 234 [198].

192. Berkhof, *Systematic Theology*, 116–17.

193. Crisp, *Deviant Calvinism*, 198–99. The same question regarding "being passed

some by ("preterition") for good reasons known only to God himself. It is

---

over" and moral responsibility arise in section 7 of chapter 3 of the Westminster Confession of Faith: "The rest of mankind God was pleased, according to the unsearchable counsel of His own will, whereby He extendeth or withholdeth mercy, as He pleaseth, for the glory of His sovereign power over His creatures, to pass by; and to ordain them to dishonor and wrath for their sin, to the praises of His glorious justice (Matt 11:25–26; Rom 9:17–18, 21–22; 2 Tim 2:19–20; Jude 4; 1 Peter 2:8)" (Dennison, *Reformed Confessions*, 4:239). Here, too, those men who are passed over are condemned because of their sin, but they are not passed over *because* of their sin. That would make reprobation conditional, contingent upon the sins of men. The American Presbyterian philosophical theologian, Cornelius van Til defends the Westminster Confession's "equal ultimacy of election and reprobation" in his work, *The Defense of the Faith*, 398–401. Van Til states: "I must maintain [the equal ultimacy of election and reprobation] if I am to maintain that by his counsel God controls whatsoever comes to pass. Since I take my point of departure in God and his plan, I think of this plan as back of reprobation as well as back of election. God's plan is a unity. His act of election of some is itself the act of not electing others" (398). Berkouwer remarks here regarding Van Til's criticism of anyone who denies "equal ultimacy": "Van Til is reminded of Kierkegaard, who speaks of human existence 'without reference to that counsel" (397), as though in the rejection of equal ultimacy the issue at stake were a denial of God's counsel. The real issue, however, is whether one takes one's 'starting point in the counsel of God' (402).Van Til does not see a single (legitimate) question arise here" (*De Verkiezing Gods*, 207n17 [177n8]). Years later, in his short study, *The Sovereignty of Grace*, which gives an appraisal of Berkouwer's view of Dort, Van Til still doesn't see a single legitimate question arise in respect of "equal ultimacy." That there are legitimate questions here will be discussed in my chapter on Barth. In his discussion of Van Til's interpretation of Barth in the English edition of his work, *De Triomf Der Genade in De Theologie van Karl Barth*, an Appendix that isn't present in the original Dutch version, Berkouwer writes: "For Van Til says that Barth rejects the 'equal ultimacy' of election and reprobation. This is to state the problem in an absolutely inadequate way, since it suggests that whoever rejects the 'equal ultimacy' of election and reprobation by that token comes to stand in the line of Barth. Nothing could be less true. I am of the opinion that the 'equal ultimacy' of election and reprobation is rejected already by the Canons of Dort, and that one can judge soundly of the scriptural doctrine of election only when one in very fact rejects this symmetry [between election and reprobation]. I think of those beautiful words in the Conclusion of the Canons in which it is said that the signatories 'detest with their whole soul' also the view that 'in the same manner in which the election is the fountain and the cause of faith and good works, reprobation is the cause of unbelief and impiety'. This is an utterance in which the symmetry which plays so tremendous a role in theological determinism is emphatically *repudiated*. This [rejection] has nothing to do with a denial of the Counsel or Plan of God, but most certainly does have something to do with the criticism of an unbiblical distortion of the message of the Divine Election, a distortion according to which the Counsel of God is made to serve as the principle accounting for both faith and unbelief. We should be particularly grateful that the Synod of Dort warned us about that so very emphatically" (Berkouwer, *The Triumph of Grace*, 391–92). I consider Berkouwer's rejection of "equal ultimacy" in chapter 5. Both the Dutch and English of Berkouwer's work will be cited hereafter throughout this book, first the original, followed by the pagination of the English translation in square brackets [ ]. Quotations are from the English translation unless otherwise indicated.

sometimes called negative reprobation, for example, by Thomists.[194] Be that as it may, Calvin says, "God chooses some, and passes over others according to his own decision. . . . God has always been free to bestow his grace on whom he wills."[195] Says Berkhof, "Preterition is a sovereign act of God, an act of His mere good pleasure, in which the demerits of man do not come into consideration. . . . The reason for preterition is not known by man. It cannot be sin, for all men are sinners. We can only say that God passed by some for good and wise reasons sufficient unto Himself. On the other hand the reason for condemnation is known; it is sin. Preterition is purely passive, a simply passing by without any action on man, but condemnation is efficient and positive. Those who are passed by are condemned on account of their sin."[196] Again, how, then, are they morally responsible for their preterition?

Consider in this connection the question regarding the scope of the atoning work of Christ. Calvin affirms the intrinsic sufficiency of Christ's death for all, albeit efficacious only for the elect. Says Calvin, "It is incontestable that Christ came for the expiation of the sins of the whole world." Elsewhere no less emphatically, he says: "That [the Gospel] is salvific for all I do not deny. . . . All are equally called to penitence and faith; the same mediator is set forth for all to reconcile them to the Father—so much is evident."[197] And yet, those whom God passes over by grace are incapable of responding to the gospel, and so how can they be blamed for not attaining salvation? Berkouwer is right: "The demand to believe and repent goes out to everybody, but what a man who is considered to be rejected must believe becomes completely uncertain. For this man, standing in the glaring searchlight of the preaching [of the gospel], is not confronted with an invitation but with the reality of rejection. He can—in the light of this supposition—no longer be called upon to believe in Christ and salvation. There is no room left for the perspective of the Canons [of Dort], which relate the call to what is good in the sight of God, namely, that those who are called may come to Him."[198]

In this light, we can easily understand the objection raised regarding the relation between human causality and divine ordination, namely, does it "leave room for a freedom in man sufficient to sustain the burden of blame."[199] But also, how is preterition consistent with God's universal invita-

194. Ott, *Fundamentals of Catholic Dogma*, 245.

195. Calvin, *Institutes of the Christian Religion*, 3.22.1.

196. Berkhof, *Systematic Theology*, 116–17.

197. Calvin, *Concerning the Eternal Predestination of God*, 148, 103, respectively.

198. Berkouwer, *De Verkiezing Gods*, 273 [228].

199. J. K. S. Reid, "Introduction," in Calvin, *Concerning the Eternal Predestination*

tion to salvation, which is grounded in the sufficiency of Christ's atoning work for the salvation of all men, a position that Calvin seems to hold,[200] and, given his interpretative gloss of John 3:16, that "God's love holds first place as the highest cause or origin [of our salvation]?"[201]

I shall return to this crucial question in the next chapter where I discuss the theology of predestination in the writings of the nineteenth-century German theologian, Matthias Joseph Scheeben, and later in chapter 5 in my treatment of the Dutch neo-Calvinists, Bavinck and Berkouwer. For now, I conclude with the claim that preterition is a theologically problematic notion that seems to lead to the denial of the following: the sufficiency of Christ's atoning work for all men, the universality of God's salvific will (1 Tim 2:4–6), contradicting the justice of God as well as man's freedom.[202] Preterition, or negative reprobation, seems to imply the idea of an abstract, merciless, and loveless sovereign decree; it is in contradiction with the Scripture that teaches that because of his great love for us "God is rich in mercy" (Eph 2: 4), that he was reconciling the world to himself in Christ" (2 Cor 5: 19), and that it is precisely the coming of Christ, the one and only Son of the Father, sent by the Father, which is the revelation of God's love (1 John 4:9). "For the Son of God, Jesus Christ, whom we proclaimed among you . . . was not Yes and No, but in him it is always Yes. For all the promises of God find their Yes in him. That is why it is through him that we utter our Amen to God for his glory" (2 Cor 1: 19–20).

Of course, in this connection, I shall need to show how the atonement is universal scope such that it possesses the intrinsic sufficiency in atoning for all men because Christ died for all men. But also I will need to show that the divine intention, which is the purpose for which God intends the atonement, is that God wills to save all men, and hence "Christ's

---

of God, 24.

200. For an instructive discussion of the question of Calvin's view of the extent of the atonement, particular/definite or universal, see Boersma, "Calvin and the Extent of the Atonement," 333–55.

201. Calvin, *Institutes of the Christian Religion*, 2.22.2. Crisp is right that this "is a problem common to all version of Augustinianism," including, I would add, Thomism. On this problem, see Ott, *Fundamentals of Catholic Dogma*, "In the question of Reprobation, the Thomist view favor not an absolute, but only a negative Reprobation. This is conceived by most Thomists as non-election to eternal bliss (non-electio), together with the Divine resolve to permit some rational creatures to fall into sin, and thus by their own guilt to lose eternal salvation. . . . It is difficult to find an intrinsic concordance between unconditioned non-election and the universality of the Divine Resolve of salvation" (245).

202. Ott, *Fundamentals of Catholic Dogma*, 245.

work is extrinsically sufficient for the sin of all fallen humans."[203] There is another concept here that is crucial for explaining the resistance against universalism,[204] namely, the notion of efficiency or efficacy, which, as Crisp says, "has to do with the actual number of those to whom Christ's work is applied."[205] In sum, Christ's atoning work is *sufficient* for the salvation of all men, albeit not *efficient* for their salvation, but only for God's elect. We find the notion of sufficiency-efficiency at work in Trent's Decree on Justification. Iit states: "even though 'Christ died for all' [2 Cor 5:15], still not all do receive the benefit of His death, but those only to whom the merit of His passion is imparted."[206] This means that though the atoning work of Christ in God's divine intention for salvation provides a satisfaction intrinsically and extrinsically sufficient for all men, it is the efficacious means by which only those who turn to Christ are saved. Crisp sharpens our understanding of the sufficiency and end of Christ's atoning work by use of the distinction between two sorts of sufficiency, intrinsic and extrinsic, on the one hand, and efficiency, on the other. These concepts are clearly explained by Crisp:

> If some condition x is, in principle, sufficient for some end E, then x is intrinsically sufficient for E. If x is in fact sufficient for some end E, where some agent G intends that the intrinsic sufficiency of E has a particular application, then x is extrinsically sufficient for E. If x actually brings about or otherwise ensures that E obtains (where G intends that x brings about E), then x is efficient for the bringing about of E. Note that an intrinsic sufficiency does not entail an extrinsic sufficiency. A particular thing could be, in principle, sufficient to some end E but not actually or in fact [extrinsically] sufficient for E, because it is not applied to E.[207]

---

203. Crisp, *Deviant Calvinism*, 218.

204. Crisp helpfully distinguishes two sorts of universalism: "The first, an argument for contingent universalism, claims that although it is possible that some people might end up in hell, as a matter of contingent fact no one will end up there. The second, necessary universalism, states that, given the essentially benevolent nature of God, it is inconceivable that anyone will ever end up in hell forever. In fact, given divine benevolence, God will necessarily save all people" (*Deviant Calvinism*, 98). Crisp gives John Hick as an example of contingent universalism, and Thomas Talbot as an example of necessary universalism. In chapters 4 and 6 I shall address the question of universalism in the theologies of Barth and Balthasar, respectively.

205. Crisp, *Deviant Calvinism*, 219.

206. Denzinger, §1523.

207. Crisp, *Deviant Calvinism*, 217.

Another possibility, other than the one that presupposes preterition, which seems to be suggested in the concluding sentence of this citation, is that the grace of Christ's atoning work is applied for the purpose of salvation to all fallen men, but not all are saved because they resist God's grace. As CCC puts it, "To God, all moments of time are present in their immediacy. When therefore he establishes his eternal plan of 'predestination', he includes in it each person's free response to his grace."[208] In this connection, the question arises regarding the conditions under which grace efficaciously brings about the particular end of salvation for the person who receives it. This question, too, will hold our attention in my discussion of Scheeben's views in the next chapter. In particular, "does this efficacy lie in the grace itself or in the free assent of the human will foreseen by God, i.e., is the grace efficacious by its intrinsic power (*per se sive ab intrinseco*) or is it efficacious by this free assent of the will (*per accidens sive ab extrinseco*)? This gives rise to the further question: Is efficacious grace intrinsically different from sufficient grace or only extrinsically different by reason of the free assent of the will?"[209] I turn now to discuss these questions in the Catholic theology of predestination of Matthias Joseph Scheeben.

---

208. *CCC*, §599. Berkouwer is right that this position raises the question regarding what has been called *scientia media*" [middle knowledge]. "The relationship between God and man is here decisively at issue. Again and again the question arose in Roman Catholic theology, in which way it was possible to reserve a place for the creature *within* the framework of God's action without prejudicing that action itself. The problem became particularly acute in connection with the 'scientia Dei' because the free will was regarded as also being an object of God's knowing. In reflecting on the relationship between the knowledge of God and free will, theologians after Trent began to operate with the idea of 'scientia media'. This doctrine was taught especially by the Molinists as that knowledge of God whereby He saw and knew beforehand what the creature would decide and on the basis of this knowledge God then—i.e., via the scientia media—made the decision. Things future came to stand in the light of the *precognition* of God, the *praescientia* or *praevisio Dei*. The Molinists were not in the first place concerned about the doctrine of this attribute of God as such, but about the connection, the synthesis, between grace and freedom. In opposition to the Dominicans [Bañezian, Spanish Thomists], they formulated the problem in the form of the scientia media and supposed that thereby they had found the point of contact for a balanced solution" (*De Triomf Der Genade in De Theologie van Karl Barth*, 168. ET: *The Triumph of Grace in the Theology of Karl Barth*, 178). The knowledge of God that Luis de Molina (1535–1600) had in mind was the knowledge of everything not only that *could* happen but also *would* happen if an individual did something freely in any appropriately specified set of circumstances. The latter is what Molina calls middle knowledge ("scientia media"). I discuss Molinism in the next chapter on Scheeben.

209. Ott, *Fundamentals of Catholic Dogma*, 248.

Points of Catholic Orientation

Confessional Catholicism takes as it orientation point when reflecting on the will, indeed, fallen human nature, the Augustinian Principle. Nature has to do with the fundamental structures of reality, in particular, of human reality, in short, the deepest foundations of what God created. How has sin affected those foundational structures of creation? Has the *nature* of creation been corrupted or completely destroyed by sin? What has been called the Augustinian Principle[210] affirms that the *nature* of humanity persists in the regime of man's fallen state. Confessional Catholicism also definitively rejects Pelagianism and semi-Pelagianism. These are the heretical claims of forms of synergism holding that we cause our own salvation, or that we initiate our own salvation, respectively. "When Catholics say that persons 'cooperate' in preparing for and accepting justification by consenting to God's justifying action, they see such personal consent *as itself an effect of grace*, not as an action arising from innate human abilities."[211] This recent assertion of the Joint Declaration on the Doctrine of Justification reaffirms the teaching of Trent: "God touches the heart of man with the illumination of the Holy Spirit, but man himself is not entirely inactive while receiving that inspiration, since he can reject it; and yet, *without God's grace, he cannot by his own free will move toward justice in God's sight.*"[212] Confessional Catholicism also rejects the heresy of predestinarianism, as Trent called what is otherwise known as "double predestination."[213] It is essential to Catholic teaching to maintain the "essential *asymmetry*"[214] between salvation and reprobation.

---

210. Hoitenga, *John Calvin and the Will*, 70–71.

211. *The Joint Declaration on the Doctrine of Justification*, 4.1.20; emphasis added.

212. Denzinger §1525; emphasis added.

213. Denzinger §1567.

214. Berkouwer remarks that "this term comes from [Gérard]. Philips, [the Belgian Catholic ecclesiologist, and key drafter of Vatican II's *Lumen Gentium*] who sees in it a mark of Roman Catholic theology" (*De Verkiezing Gods*, 213n34 [182n16]). Berkouwer holds that this "essential asymmetry" is one of Reformed theology's "most important characteristics" (Ibid., 213 [182]).

CHAPTER 3

Scheeben on God's Universal Salvific Will, Predestination, Grace, and Freedom

Predestination, a portentous, awesome word in theology, the cross of the brooding intellect, the terror of the apprehensive conscience. At first glance it appears to be a somber mystery, and seems to be the more so, the less its true supernatural and hidden character is understood. But as soon as it is moved back to the proper distance and is inspected from the right point of view, it stands before us, for all the obscurity of its secret nature, as a luminous and splendid truth. Although its ramifications are lost in dim and, to some extent, alarming regions, its shining core emits most cheering and comforting rays.[1]

Introduction

HOW DO WE RECONCILE God's universal salvific will with the mystery of predestination, election and reprobation? Furthermore, how do we reconcile the omnipotence and sovereignty of God's grace with human freedom in the Church's understanding of God's plan of salvation? These two questions will now be addressed by considering the views of a modern Catholic theologian, namely, the nineteenth-century German theologian: Matthias Joseph Scheeben (1835–1888). The chief aim of this chapter is to show that Scheeben is right: a theology of predestination does not—as Balthasar claims it does—"blunt God's triune will for salvation, which is directed at the entire world."[2] I shall show that Scheeben provides us with a theologically satisfactory reply to critics, such as Balthasar, who charge that predestination in any sense whatsoever is irreconcilable with God's universal salvific will. This

---

1. Scheeben, *The Mysteries of Christianity* (hereafter *MC*).

2. Balthasar, *Dare We Hope* (hereafter *DWH*), 13. I return to Balthasar on predestination in chapter 6.

77

chapter is structured as follows. I begin with Scheeben's doctrine of providence, moving on then to his view of predestination, followed by analysis
of his reflections on the relationship of grace and freedom, and, last but not
least, the matter of freedom and determinism. It is helpful in answering
the questions regarding the relationship of God's universal salvific will and
predestination, on the one hand, and divine election and freedom, on the
other, to analyze Scheeben's views of these matters in light of some major
theses that occur in his Catholic version of that doctrine.

Divine Providence

> I. "*In the most general sense predestination is a decree of God,
> an inner decision of the divine wisdom and will, whereby God
> resolves and determines what He Himself will bring to pass. In
> the Apostle [Paul's] words [Eph. 1:11], it is the counsel of the di-
> vine will whereby God works all things, or, according to St. Au-
> gustine, whereby He disposes within Himself what He intends to
> accomplish.*"[3]

All Christians believe that the Sovereign God has a plan and purpose in
exercising his divine providence. Providence involves God's power, knowledge, and good purposes whereby he orders of all things in the created
universe to their ends, and he does this through secondary causes, either
directly or mediately. He is the sovereign master of this divine plan, according to his omnipotence, providentially exercising control over everything,
knowing everything which can be known, according to his omniscient foreknowledge, even of free human actions, in order to fulfill that plan for the
world in accord with his divine purpose for creation. Since God brought the
whole creation into being, his providence is as broad as that creation because he sustains the world in existence at every moment. This is that aspect
of providence called conservation or sustenance. There is another aspect of
divine providence called providence as government. "In this general sense
divine predestination has a bearing on all the works of God. Everything that
He does and effects is predestined by Him through an eternal decree before
it is carried out in time."[4] Predestination in this general sense considers the
divine works of creation in and for themselves.

There is also a third aspect of God's providence called cooperation,
or, as it is also called, concurrence—God cooperates with the activities of

---

3. Scheeben, *MC*, 698; emphasis added.
4. Ibid.

every created thing, but in particular he cooperates in the relation between Divine and human activity.[5] In general, this aspect of divine providence rejects two extremes: deism and occasionalism. The former affirms God as creator of the cosmos at its first moment, but then God takes a "hands-off" approach, having no subsequent influence on self-sufficient creatures. On this view, God just lets the causal powers of creatures in the world produce their effects. The latter denies that creatures have any true causal power of their own; whatever comes into being is produced by God as the sole and total cause of everything that exists. In contrast, however, according to the idea of concurrence, God works in and over all creaturely activity that occurs. In this light, the basic powers of created beings, such as the ability of man to make choices, cannot be exercised without God's involvement.[6] This is how the *Catechism of the Catholic Church* describes providential cooperation.

> God is the sovereign master of his plan. But to carry it out he also makes use of his creatures' cooperation. This use is not a sign of weakness, but rather a token of almighty God's greatness and goodness. For God grants his creatures not only their existence, but also the dignity of acting on their own, of being causes and principles for each other, and thus of cooperating in the accomplishment of his plan. . . . The truth that God is at work in all the actions of his creatures is inseparable from faith in God the Creator. God is the first cause who operates in and through secondary causes.[7]

But the question is how does God operate in and through secondary causes?[8] This question is particularly important with respect to the matter

5. Berkouwer critically questions the need for the idea of concurrence: "The idea of concurrence adds nothing independent or new to the confession of Providence." Bavinck willingly accepts it as an aspect of divine providence. For the former, see *De Voorzienigheid Gods*, 150–89 [137–172]; and for the latter, see *GD* II, 551–80 [591–619].

6. Davison, "Divine Providence and Human Freedom," 217–37, and on these aspects of divine providence at 218–19.

7. *CCC*, §§306, 308. See also, *CCC*, §323: "Divine providence works also through the actions of creatures. To human beings God grants the ability to cooperate freely with his plans." Similarly, see also *Catechism of the Council of Trent*, "Not only does God protect and govern all things by His Providence, but He also by an internal power impels to motion and action whatever moves and acts, and this in such a manner that, although He excludes not, He yet precedes the agency of secondary causes" (30).

8. According to Ott, "There is no decision of the Church on this. However, theologians generally hold that God co-operates immediately in every act of His creatures" (*Fundamentals of Catholic Dogma*, 88). This is accepted by some Calvinists (e.g., Herman Bavinck and Louis Berkhof) and Catholics alike. For an insightful review of Luis

of acts of free choice. Generally speaking, however, says Bavinck, "God so preserves things and so works in them that they themselves work along with him as secondary causes. This is not to say that we must stop there [in the manner of Deism]. On the contrary, we must always ascend to the cause of all being and movement, and that is the will of God alone. . . . To that extent providence is not only a positive [act of causation] but also an immediate act of God. His will, his power, his being is immediately present in every creature and every event."[9] This, too, is the view of Louis Berkhof: God's concurrence is both simultaneous and immediate.[10] Furthermore, the primary and secondary causes do not run on separate tracks. Rather, "the primary works through the secondary, [and] the effect that proceeds from the two [causes] is one and the product is one." That is, adds Bavinck, "the effect and product are *in reality* totally the effect and product of the two causes, to be sure, but *formally* they are only the effect and product of the secondary cause."[11] The effect, then, is primarily traceable to the natures and casual contributions of secondary causes rather than to God's concurrence. For example, as Freddoso explains, "when a gas flame makes a pot of water boil, the fact that the effect is the boiling of water rather than, say, the blossoming of a flower is traceable primarily not to God's causal contribution, but rather to the specific natures and causal contributions of the secondary causes (gas, water, etc.)."[12]

Thus, God not only creates and conserves contingent beings, but, according to all defenders of the doctrine of concurrence, he also acts as an immediate efficient cause of all the effects produced by secondary causes, and this includes the power of free choice that man is endowed with by nature. This means that God's providence extends to everything that happens since God does not only conserve but also immediately cooperates or concurs with the operation of every secondary cause. Yet, that does not mean that God wills positively everything that happens. For some things that happen he does not will, such as the evil choices that men make, but

---

de Molina's views on concurrence, grace and freedom, and in general providence and middle knowledge, see Freddoso, "Molina, Luis de," and "Molinism." For an in-depth analysis of Molina's view, especially with respect to middle knowledge, but one that exceeds the reach of the aims of this chapter, see Freddoso's Introduction to *On Divine Foreknowledge*, part 4 of *The Concordia*, 1–81. I am indebted to Freddoso's exposition. For a brief, but helpful, account of Luis de Molina, see Levering, *Predestination*, 110–17.

9. Bavinck, *GD* II, 570 [609–10].

10. Berkhof, *Systematic Theology*, 173–74.

11. Bavinck, *GD* II, 575 [614–15].

12. Freddoso, "Molina, Luis de." Similarly, Bavinck, *GD* II, 575 [615]: "Wood burns and it is God alone who makes it burn, yet the burning process may not be formally attributed to God but must be attributed to the wood as subject."

merely permits. Thus, just as the effect, then, is primarily traceable to the natures and casual contributions of secondary causes rather than to God's cooperation or concurrence, says Freddoso, "likewise, any defectiveness in the effect is traced back causally to a defect or impediment within the order of secondary causes rather than to God's causal contribution, which is always, within its own order, causally sufficient (in the sense of 'enough') for its intended effect, even when that effect is not produced." He adds, "When the intended effect is produced, God's concurrence is said to be *efficacious* with respect to it; when it is not produced, God's concurrence is said to be *merely sufficient* with respect to it. If a defective effect is instead produced, its defectiveness is something that God merely permits rather than intends."[13]

Berkouwer remains unpersuaded that the idea of concurrence can deepen our understanding of the relationship between divine activity and human activity, particularly man's sinful willing and doing, especially since God cannot be the author of sin.[14] I think Freddoso is helpful here in responding to Berkouwer's concern. He summarizes Molina's views on God willing positively every good thing, not willing evil choices, but merely permitting them:[15]

> This account applies straightforwardly to morally good and evil acts emanating from the power of free choice that rational creatures are endowed with by nature. No such act can occur without God's general concurrence, and in causally contributing to it God intends that the act be morally upright rather than sinful. Nonetheless, because of defects in the free agents with whom God cooperates, his general concurrence is often merely sufficient—and thus inefficacious—with respect to the morally good act he intends. So even though God must concur causally in order for even a sinful act to be elicited, nonetheless, the act's defectiveness is traced back to the free created agent rather than to God, who permits the defect without intending it. By contrast, when a morally good act is freely elicited, God's concurrence is efficacious with respect to it.[16]

This view of divine providence, which affirms God's general concurrence with regard to free human acts, has, understandably, raised the

---

13. Ibid.

14. Berkouwer, *De Voorzienigheid Gods*, 157–58 [143].

15. Molina, *Concordia* 4.53.3.17.

16. Freddoso, "Molina, Luis de." Similarly, Bavinck, *GD* II, 575 [615]:"Human persons speak, act, and believe, and it is God alone who supplies to a sinner all the vitality and strength he or she needs for the commission of a sin. Nevertheless the subject and author of the sin is not God but the human being."

question of how it leaves room for significant creaturely activity and full human responsibility, especially in the connection between God's grace and human freedom, and the resistance of some to that grace. Now, much ink has been spilt on the question regarding the nature of God's simultaneous cooperation with free human acts, particularly acts that are salvific. God effects his will through secondary causes, which include human agents, but exactly how it is that these secondary causes have an integrity of their own and hence do not causally flow ultimately from divine causation is the question; without answering that question, the significance of our own freedom of choice is doubtful, or at worst negated.

Critics of Aquinas' thought as expressed by Bañezians, Spanish Thomists, is that his thought is deterministic because "God not only supplies and conserves the power of operation in every secondary cause, but that he also acts on the secondary causes to produce their actual operations, a view that came to be known as the doctrine of promotion."[17] Molina rejects this Thomist view arguing that "God acts, not *on*, but *with* the secondary cause to produce its effects."[18] Molina explains: "God's general concurrence . . . . is *not* an influence of God *on the cause* so that the cause might act after having been previously moved and applied to its act by that influence, but is instead an influence *along with the cause directly on the effect*."[19] So, on Scheeben's view, is God's simultaneous concurrence, then, in the free decisions of human beings such that he causes a person's will to turn itself one way or the other, as the doctrine of promotion understands it? As I shall show below, this is not Scheeben's view on simultaneous concurrence. Rather, according to Scheeben, God acts, not *on* the person's will to move it to its decision, as the Bañezian (Spanish Thomists) held, but rather merely concurrently acts *with* a person's will to produce some effect, as the Molinists thought.[20] Here, too, Freddoso is particularly helpful in his explanation.

> God also cooperates with free human acts by means of the particular causal influence of supernatural grace, merited for the human race by the salvific death and resurrection of Jesus Christ. By this grace, God empowers and prompts human beings to elicit free acts of will that are supernaturally salvific, and he cooperates as a simultaneous cause in the very effecting of these acts. By eliciting such free acts of faith, hope, charity and

17. Craig, "Middle Knowledge," 154.

18. Ibid.

19. Molina, *Concordia* 4.53.3.2.

20. Ibid., 4.53.3.7. Helpful to me in understanding and formulating the difference here is Moreland and Craig, *Philosophical Foundations*, 561–62. See also, Ott, *Fundamentals of Catholic Dogma*, 89.

the other infused virtues, human agents are able to attain and foster that intimate friendship with God which in its fullness constitutes their highest fulfillment as rational beings. Still, insofar as grace operates prior to the consent of human free choice, it can be freely resisted; and when it is resisted, it is said to be inefficacious, or merely sufficient, with respect to the salvific act God intends.[21]

God's supernatural grace, which is merited for humanity by the salvific passion, death and resurrection of Jesus Christ, then, exercises a particular causal influence on free human acts, cooperating as a simultaneous cause in the very effecting of these acts. In cooperating with these acts, God's grace empowers (enables?) and spurs man to elicit free acts of will that are supernaturally salvific. This ways of expressing divine concurrence raises the question whether God's simultaneous and immediate causal cooperation with supernatural salvific free human acts is *intrinsic* or *extrinsic*. "Does this efficacy lie in the grace itself or in the free assent of the human will foreseen by God, i.e., is the grace efficacious by its intrinsic power (*per se sive ab intrinseco*) or is it efficacious by the free assent of the will (*per accidens sive ab extrinseco*)?"[22] If concurrence is intrinsic then it is efficacious concurrence because supernatural grace necessarily attains its intended effect. In contrast, if concurrence is extrinsic then it is sufficient concurrence because grace necessarily fails to attain its intended effect.

So, with respect to the question regarding the grace by which God operates to elicit supernaturally salvific acts, Freddoso describes the view of some Thomists as follows: "God grants intrinsically efficacious grace when and only when the human agent elicits the supernaturally salvific act God intends; and God grants intrinsically merely sufficient grace when and only when the human agent resists and thus fails to elicit the supernaturally salvific act that God intends."[23] Molina, according to Freddoso, rejects this Thomist view of grace and human freedom because it undermines libertarian human freedom—i.e., indeterministically free choices—by emphasizing God's omni-causality in pre-determining efficacious grace or merely sufficient grace.

> Molina argues strenuously that this Bañezian [Spanish Thomists] doctrine is incompatible with human freedom and falls into the strict determinism advocated by the Lutherans and Calvinists. For even though the Bañezians, like Molina, insist that a free

21. Freddoso, "Molina, Luis de."
22. Ott, *Fundamentals of Catholic Dogma*, 248.
23. Freddoso, "Molina, Luis de."

act of will cannot result by natural necessity from antecedently acting causes, they nonetheless assert that an act of will can be free even if God has predetermined to cooperate with it contemporaneously by a concurrence or grace that is intrinsically efficacious (or inefficacious). This Molina denies: "That agent is called free who, with all the prerequisites for acting having been posited, is able to act and able not to act, or is able to do one thing in such a way that he is also able to do some contrary thing." And numbered among these prerequisites is God's fixed intention to confer his general concurrence and grace. So if God has decided to confer only intrinsically efficacious (or intrinsically inefficacious) grace or concurrence in a given situation, the created agent's freedom is destroyed. Molina's alternative thesis is that God's grace and general concurrence are intrinsically neither efficacious nor inefficacious. Rather, they are intrinsically "neutral" and are rendered efficacious or inefficacious "extrinsically" by the human agent's free consent or lack thereof.[24]

Of course, the Calvinism that Molina has in mind affirms the equal symmetry ("*eodem modo*") of election and reprobation whereby a strict parallelism of divine causality is affirmed.[25] Similarly, according to the Bañezians—at least as Molina understands them—God has decided to confer only intrinsically efficacious, or intrinsically inefficacious, grace or concurrence in a given situation, such that this cooperation, or lack of cooperation, is predetermined, and hence the created agent's freedom is destroyed. By contrast, Molina's critics retort that his view seems to resemble Pelagianism by virtue of emphasizing the freedom of the will allowing that the efficaciousness of God's predestinating grace depends on foreseen faith. This view it was urged endangers the sovereignty of grace.[26] Furthermore, for Molina, the grace

24. Ibid.

25. I have discussed John Calvin's view on grace and freedom as well as election and reprobation in the previous chapter. I continue my discussion of predestination in the Dutch neo-Calvinist theology of Bavinck and Berkouwer in chapter 5.

26. This, too, is Berkouwer's objection: "The Molinists, too, thought of negative reprobation as conditional (strong accents on the freedom of will!), this in contrast to the Thomists who did not want to call sin the motive of negative reprobation. That is impossible, "for this negative reprobation is none other than divine permission of these demerits and thus it [unconditioned negative reprobation] logically precedes rather than follows their being foreseen. The thought of [conditional] negative reprobation is different: 'God has wanted to make manifest His goodness, not only in the form of His mercy, but also in that of His justice'. That is why there is an 'allowing'. After this allowing, *praescientia* comes into perspective, to which [conditional] positive reprobation corresponds" (*De Verkiezing Gods*, 235n128 [199n58]. We can understand why Ludwig Ott had his misgivings about the Thomist view of "unconditioned negative

whereby God cooperates with supernaturally salvific acts is not intrinsically efficacious, and hence there is only an external accidental difference between efficacious and sufficient grace. "If the free will assents to the grace and with it accomplishes the salutary act, sufficient grace is, ipso facto, efficacious grace. If the free will refuses its assent the grace remains sufficient only. God from all Eternity foresees the free assent of the will by reason of his Scientia Media [middle knowledge]."[27] Therefore, on this view, the relationship between God's omniscience and human freedom is such that the efficacy of grace itself is contingent on the free assent of the human will.

This view seems inconsistent with Christian Orthodoxy, Catholic and Protestant alike, namely, that "God is perfectly provident and has infallible and comprehensive knowledge of future contingents."[28] The response of Molina to this charge is to postulate what he called "divine middle knowledge (*scientia media*), by which God knows, before any of his free decrees regarding creatures, how any possible rational being would freely act in any possible situation."[29] But that is only part of Molina's response. The divine initiative of God's gracious gift of prevenient grace—a preparatory grace—is given to all men providing sufficient grace for the salvation of all men. As Craig puts it:

> Molina rejects as Pelagian the view . . . that predestination con-
> sist in God's creating certain persons because he knew that they
> would freely make good use of the grace God would give them
> and so be saved. Rather, Molina held that God's choosing to
> create certain persons has nothing to do with how they would
> respond to his grace; he simply chose to create the world order
> he wanted to, and no rationale for this choice is to be sought
> other than the divine will itself. In this sense, predestination is
> for Molina wholly gratuitous, the result of the divine will, and in
> no way based on the merits or demerits of creatures.[30]

Reprobation": "it is difficult to find an intrinsic concordance between unconditioned non-election and the universality of the Divine Resolve of Salvation. In practice, the unconditioned negative Reprobation of the Thomists involves the same result as the unconditioned positive Reprobation of the heretical Predestinarians" (*Fundamentals of Catholic Dogma*, 245). The Molinists shared this misgiving with Ott, but they in particular with respect to the Spanish Thomists, the Bañezians.

27. Ott, *Fundamentals of Catholic Dogma*, 249.
28. Freddoso, "Molina, Luis de."
29. Freddoso, "Molinism."
30. Craig, "Middle Knowledge," 141–64, and at 160.

What, then, is the idea of divine middle knowledge?[31] Will this idea help us to understand how Scheeben squares divine omniscience with human freedom? I think it does. Indeed, against this background, we can understand why Scheeben rejects the view that God causes a person's will to turn itself this way or that. God acts, not *on* the person's will to move it to its decision, as the Bañezian (Spanish Thomists) held, but rather merely concurrently acts *with* a person's will to produce some effect in certain circumstances, as the Molinists thought. Furthermore, Scheeben's view, arguably, then "probably comes closest to the view known as 'Congruism', associated in the later sixteenth and early seventeenth centuries with St. Robert Bellarmine and St. Francis de Sales."[32] On this developed Molinist view, the efficacy of grace, that is, its infallible success in attaining its divinely intended salvific end is due not to its own intrinsic nature, as the Bañezian held, but to the Divine middle knowledge, which foresees the congruity of the grace that is given in circumstances favorable to its reception and its infallible success. In the conclusion of this section and in preparation for the next, I turn now to give a brief account of Scheeben's view of reconciling divine foreknowledge and human freedom through divine middle knowledge of conditional future contingents.

Given divine omniscience, God knows all truths. But what sorts of truths are there for him to know? Molina distinguishes three logical moments in the truths that God knows.[33] First, he knows *necessary truths*, that is, the laws of logic and mathematics. This includes knowledge of all the possible worlds that God might create. Molina also calls this God's *natural knowledge* of metaphysically necessary truths. This "gives Him knowledge of what *could* be."[34] This set of truths is followed up by God's knowledge of "all the contingent truths about the actual world, including its past, present, and future. This was called God's *free knowledge*. It involves knowledge of what *will* be."[35] In addition to these sorts of truth known by God, he also has knowledge, sometimes said to be hypothetical knowledge, of what *would* be; in other words, of conditional future contingents or counterfactual conditionals.[36] With this knowledge, which is midway between God's natural

---

31. In addition to Freddoso's account of middle knowledge (see note 8), I have also found helpful Bavinck, GD II, 165–70 [198–203], Moreland and Craig, *Philosophical Foundations*, 521–24, 561–65; Craig, *What Does God Know?*, 41–57; and Helm, *The Providence of God*, 55–61.

32. Nichols, *Romance and System*, 421.

33. Molina, *Concordia* 4.52.9.

34. Craig, *What Does God Know?*, 43.

35. Ibid., 43.

36. Bavinck rejects divine middle knowledge but not because he denies that God

knowledge of necessary truths and his free knowledge, God has "knowledge of all true counterfactual propositions, including counterfactuals of creaturely freedom." In other words, "Whereas by his natural knowledge God knew what any free creature *could* do in any set of circumstances, now in this [knowledge] God knows what any free creature *would* do in any set of circumstances."[37]

So, distinctive about Molina's view of divine middle knowledge is that God's knowledge of all true counterfactual propositions includes conditional propositions that state what would happen if an individual performed a free action in a certain circumstance. Helm helpfully states the form of all such propositions: "In circumstances C, if Jones freely chooses between X and Y, he will choose Y."[38] Craig explains how it is that "God knows what any free creatures would do in any set of circumstances":

> This is not because the circumstances causally determine the creature's choice, but simply because this is how the creature would freely choose. God thus knows that were he to actualize certain states of affairs, then certain other contingent states of affairs would obtain. This so-called "middle" knowledge is like natural knowledge in that such knowledge does not depend on any decision of the divine will; God does not determine which counterfactuals of creaturely freedom are true or false. Thus, if it is true that "if some agent S were placed in circumstances C, then he would freely perform action *a*," then even God in his omnipotence cannot bring it about that S would freely refrain from *a* if he were placed in C. On the other hand, middle knowledge is unlike natural knowledge in that the content of his middle knowledge is not essential to God. True counterfactuals are contingently true; S could freely decide to refrain from *a* in C, so that different counterfactuals could be true and be known by God than those that are. Hence, although it is essential to God that he have middle knowledge, it is not essential to him to have middle knowledge of those particular propositions that he does in fact know.[39]

possesses hypothetical knowledge of what would be in a given set of circumstances. In fact, he cites numerous Scripture texts to support such divine knowledge: "e.g., Gen 11:6; Exod 3:19; 34:16; Deit 7:3–4; 1 Sam 23:10–13; 25:29ff.; 2 Sam 12:8; 1 Kings 11:2; 2 Kgs 2:10; 13:19; Ps 81:14–16; Jer 26:2–3; 38:17–20; Ezek 2:5–7; 3:4–6; Matt 11:21, 23; 24:22; 26:53; Luke 22:66–68; John 4:10; 6:15; Acts 2:2; 18; Rom 9:29; I Cor 2:8" (*Gereformeerde Dogmatiek* II,166 [199]).

37. Moreland and Craig, *Philosophical Foundations*, 561–62.

38. Helm, *Providence of God*, 57.

39. Moreland and Craig, *Philosophical Foundations*, 562.

The problem with this view, according to critics of Molinism, such as
Bavinck, a position he shares with Thomists, is that it makes God dependent on creatures for his middle knowledge.[40] "God does not derive his
knowledge of the free actions of human beings from his own being, his own
decrees, but from the will of creatures. God, accordingly, becomes dependent on the world, derives knowledge from the world that he did not have
and could not obtain from himself. . . . Conversely, the creature in large
part becomes independent vis-à-vis God. It did indeed at one time receive
'being' (*esse*) and 'being able' (*posse*) from God but now it has the 'volition'
(*velle*) completely in its own hand. It sovereignly makes its own decisions
and either accomplishes something or does not accomplish something apart
from any preceding divine decree. Something can therefore come into being
quite apart from God's will." Bavinck then rejects divine middle knowledge
but not because he denies that God possesses hypothetical knowledge of
what would be in a given set of circumstances. In fact, he cites numerous
Scripture texts to support such divine knowledge.[41] Says Bavinck, "There
is no doubt that Scripture acknowledges the fact that God has put things
(events, etc.) in a varied web of connections to each other, and that these
connections are frequently of a conditional nature, so that one thing cannot

---

40. Catholic theologian of the Dominican order, Thomist Garrigou-Lagrange posed
a similar objection in his study, *The One God* , 465–66: "God's knowledge cannot be
determined by anything which is extrinsic to Him, and which would not be caused
by Him. But such is the *scientia media* [middle knowledge], which depends on the
determination of the free conditioned future; for this determination does not come
from God but from the human liberty, granted that it is placed in such particular circumstances. . . . Thus God would be dependent on another, would be passive in His
knowledge, and would no longer be Pure Act. The dilemma is unsolvable: Either God
is the first determining Being, or else He is determined by another; there is no other
alternative. In other words, the *scientia media* involves an imperfection, which cannot
exist in God. Hence there is a certain tinge of anthropomorphism in this theory." This,
too, is the objection of Helm, *Providence of God*, 61: "Does this [Molinism] somehow
involve a limit upon God's omniscience? . . . So, far from middle knowledge being a
way of reconciling divine omniscience (and foreordination) and human freedom, we
must conclude that human freedom limits the scope of divine omniscience." This is
also the objection of Barth: "Yet when the Jesuit doctrine [of the divine *scientia media*]
deals with the specific form of the divine foreknowledge in which it has as its object the
free acts of the creature as such, it does so in a way which allows those acts virtually to
precede the decision of the divine will, and thus to limit and determine the divine will
itself. If there was any possibility or intention of the divine foreknowledge or its specific
object the *fides praevisa* being understood in this way, then it was indeed all up with the
basis interest of the Reformation" (*CD* II.2, 79).

41. Bavinck, *GD* II,166 [199]: "e.g., Gen 11:6; Exod 3:19; 34:16; Deit 7:3–4; 1 Sam
23:10–13; 25:29ff.; 2 Sam 12:8; 1 Kings 11:2; 2 Kings 2:10; 13:19; Ps 81"14–16; Jer
26:2–3; 38:17–20; Ezek 2:5–7; 3:4–6; Matt 11:21, 23; 24:22; 26:53; Luke 22:66–68; John
4:10; 6:15; Acts 2:2; 18; Rom 9:29; I Cor 2:8."

happen unless something else happens first."[42] Rather, he rejects the Molinist account of divine middle knowledge because it "represents contingent future events as contingent and free also in relation to God." He adds, "But none of these [Scripture] texts denies that in all cases God—though he speaks to and deals with humans in human terms—knew and determined what would surely happen."[43] So, as Craig correctly remarks: "The disputed question [between Christian theologians] was where one should place God's hypothetical knowledge of what *would be*. Is it logically prior to or posterior to the divine decree?"[44]

Briefly, then, critics of Molinism argue that since God knew and determined what would happen in a given circumstance, hypothetical knowledge of what would be is logically posterior to the divine decree because in "decreeing that a particular world exist, God also decreed which counterfactual statements are true."[45] Thus, prior to the world that God has divinely decreed to exist, there are no truths of conditional future contingents to be known, and no middle knowledge. Bavinck concludes:

> Between that which is merely possible and will never be realized—present in God only as an idea—and that which is certain and has been decreed by God, there is no longer any area left that can be controlled by the will of humans. Something always belongs either to the one or to the other. If it is only a possibility and will never be realized, it is the object of God's "necessary" knowledge; and if it will indeed one day be realized, it is the content of his "free" knowledge. There is no middle ground between the two, no "middle" knowledge.[46]

Of course the critic of Bavinck's position retorts that it leads to determinism[47] and hence the elimination of free human action since God decrees what choices a man shall make in whatever circumstances he finds himself. By contrast, the Molinists argue that God's hypothetical knowledge of the truths of conditional future contingents is logically prior to God's decree to create a particular world. This position has room "for creaturely freedom by exempting counterfactual truths from God's decree."[48] Significantly, placing the counterfactuals of creaturely freedom logically prior to God's

42. Ibid., 168–69 [201–2].

43. Ibid., 169 [202].

44. Craig, *What Does God Know?*, 43.

45. Ibid., 43.

46. Bavinck, *GD* II, 169 [202].

47. In the previous chapter on Calvin, I argued that Bavinck is a soft determinist.

48. Craig, *What Does God Know?*, 44.

divine decree doesn't diminish God's sovereignty in any sense no more that holding necessary truths of logic and arithmetic to be prior to and therefore independent of God's decrees—necessary knowledge—does. So, "*counterfactual truths* about how creatures would freely choose under various circumstances are prior to and independent of God's decrees."[49] This means that God has middle knowledge. Freddeso summarizes Molina's objection to critics like Bavinck:

> According to Molina, what God knows by His middle knowledge is, to be sure, dependent on what His creatures would do in various situations. From eternity God knew that Peter would deny Christ if placed in such-and-such circumstances. But if Peter had not been going to deny Christ in those circumstances, then God would not have believed what He in fact believed. So we may properly say that God's middle knowledge is from eternity "counterfactually dependent" on what creatures will do if placed in various circumstances. But this does not distinguish middle knowledge from any other knowledge God has about creatures. Obviously, *all* God's knowledge of created effects—of necessary effects as well as contingent effects—is counterfactually dependent on what secondary causes would do in various circumstances. In general, for any created effect S will or would obtain in circumstances H, if the relevant secondary agents were not going to cause S to obtain in H, then God would never have believed that S would obtain in H. Even Bañezians must admit this. So the mere fact that God's middle knowledge is counterfactually dependent on what creatures would do is not at all problematic, but is rather a simple consequence of God's being necessarily omniscient.[50]

Before turning to Scheeben's doctrine of predestination one other question arises here, namely, the reason of grace's efficacy in which God concurrently cooperates with supernaturally salvific acts of free choice.[51] Consider circumstances C, where in Peter is influenced by grace G, and such influence freely elicits salvific act A. There is substantial agreement among all Molinists that "God places Peter in C with G knowing full well that Peter will freely elicit A." Another matter of agreement is that G is not intrinsically efficacious and hence does not effectually predetermine A. Where there is serious disagreement, however, is whether or not grace's efficacy lies in the

49. Ibid.

50. Freddoso, "Introduction," 67.

51. Helpful here in understanding the Catholic doctrine of predestination is Scheeben, *A Manual of Catholic Theology*, 266–79. See also Pohle, *Grace*, 152–221.

free assent of the will alone such that it renders G efficacious in C with respect to A. Now, Congruism, which was worked out in detail by Robert Bellarmine and Francisco Suárez, is one possible response to this question, and it deeply influenced Scheeben—as I shall show in the next section. Freddoso helpfully explains Congruism's variation of Molinism.

> One possible scenario is that God first resolves absolutely that Peter should freely elicit A in C and then, as it were, consults his middle knowledge to see just which particular graces would, if bestowed on Peter in C, obtain his free consent and thus issue in A. It follows that, given his antecedent resolution, God would have conferred some grace other than G if he had known by his middle knowledge that G would turn out to be "merely sufficient" with respect to A, i.e., that Peter would not freely consent to G in C. So G is rendered efficacious not only by Peter's free consent but also, and indeed more principally, by God's antecedent predetermination to confer a "congruous" grace that will guarantee Peter's acting well in C.[52]

In transition to the next section, I shall draw on this helpful synopsis of the positions of Thomism, Molinism, and Congruism.[53]

Thomism	*Molinism*	*Congruism*
1. God decides absolutely and gratuitously to predestine S to glory.	1. God decides absolutely and gratuitously to give sufficient grace to every person he creates.	1. God decides absolutely and gratuitously to predestine S to glory.
2. God then decides to give S a series of intrinsically efficacious graces to cause his free assent to God's offer of salvation. Those no included in (1) are reprobate.	2. On the basis of his middle knowledge, God knows whether S would respond if given sufficient grace. If so, then in creating S, God predestines S to glory, and his grace become efficacious. If not, then S is not predestined, and God's grace remains merely sufficient.	2. On the basis of his middle knowledge, God chooses those graces to which he knows S would freely respond, if he were given them. These graces are therefore efficacious for S. Those not included in (1) are reprobate.

52. Freddoso, "Molinism."

53. Théodore Regnon, *Bannestianisme et Molinisme*, 48, as cited in Craig, "Middle Knowledge," 161.

Predestination

> II. "*At the heart of this providential purpose of God is his divine will to save, which is twofold: on the one hand it is universal, and refers to all men, even those who, as a matter of fact, fail to achieve salvation; on the other hand, it is particular, and refers to those who actually reach their foreordained end.*"[54]

Scheeben considers predestination not only in terms of the works of creation in and for themselves, but also as "*constitutive of a plan.*"[55] In this connection, Scheeben writes, "[Scripture] lays special emphasis on predestination only when it speaks of decrees that are not manifest in visible creation, but come to our knowledge through a divine communication of a very intimate sort, and in which we do not infer the decree from the work [of redemption], but know the work from God's preconceived plan. This is the case particularly with regard to those supernatural works of God that do not automatically come to our knowledge even at their realization."[56] This plan is revealed to us in God's verbal revelation, Sacred Scripture, communicating the knowledge of "the hypostatic union of the Son of God with a human nature, the inner workings of the economy of redemption, and the elevation of created nature to participation in the divine nature by grace and glory."[57] Scheeben doesn't make his doctrine of revelation explicit in his discussion of predestination.[58] Still, his view, arguably, posits the inherent connection of words (the verbal element of revelation) and acts in the Christologically concentrated structured of revelation.[59]

Be that as it may, these acts or works of redemption are essential to understanding the total mystery of predestination "that is based upon the God-man, a plan of the divine wisdom and love that will be communicated to creatures with an astounding generosity they could never have imagined."[60] He continues explaining the Christological focus of predestination. "In Christ and on account of Christ, God has extended to us the fatherly love He bore toward Christ as His Son and has made us the coheirs

---

54. Scheeben, *MC*, 702; emphasis added.

55. Nichols, *Romance and System*, 420.

56. Scheeben, *MC*, 698.

57. Ibid.

58. Scheeben presents his doctrine of revelation, the nature of theology, and the relationship of faith and reason in *MC*, 733–96.

59. On this, see Nichols, "De Lubac," 113–28, and at 124.

60. Scheeben, *MC*, 699.

of Christ. Through this love God has destined us for a supernatural end."[61] Scheeben rejects here what Berkouwer calls an abstract doctrine of election, that is, the *decretum absolutum* (absolute decree) to elect some of humanity and reject others by "a mere act of sovereignty which had nothing to do with the love and grace of God," apart from and outside of Christ.[62] Has God, then, according to Scheeben, predestined *all* men to eternal life? Does he adopt a notion of "single" predestination in which all men are predestined in Christ, and does this notion entail the universal predestination of all men, as a matter of fact, to election? In other words, does Scheeben accept universalism: the view that holds all men are or will be saved, none are reprobate? Therefore, is it no longer necessary to speak of rejection?

Alternatively, is predestination as such particular, according to Scheeben, because it refers to those individuals who actually reach their foreordained end? The brief answer to this question here is that Scheeben distinguishes two distinct phases in eternal election. First, there is an antecedent and unfulfilled decree to divine election to save all humanity on the ground of Christ's atoning work, and its scope is universal, meaning thereby that it encompasses all men. Second, there is God's consequent, unconditional and effectual decree, and its scope is limited because effectual only to those who have the gift of faith.[63]

This mystery of predestination includes the way God determines the ultimate goal of humanity, since we have been created by God and for God. But it also includes how God leads individual persons to that goal such that He actively influences that process in moving us toward our last end. In this more restrictive sense, predestination means what St. Thomas calls, says Scheeben, "the *ratio transmissionis creaturae rationalis in finem*" (the "principle of the movement of the rational creature towards its goal"[64]). Nichols rightly comments: "That this principle must include at least an element of divine agency is obvious, thinks Scheeben, the moment we acknowledge that the *finis* in question is supernatural in type."[65] Scheeben explains:

> In Christian predestination . . . man is destined by God for
> an end which lies beyond the range of natural powers, which

61. Ibid., 709.

62. Berkouwer, *De Verkiezing Gods*, 164 [143].

63. Scheeben's position is consistent with the position usually called *hypothetical universalism*. For an analysis of this position, see Crisp, "Hypothetical Universalism," in *Deviant Calvinism*, 175–211; idem, "The Election of Jesus Christ," in *God Incarnate*, 34–55. I am indebted to Crisp for his discussion of this position.

64. Aquinas, *Summa theologiae* I, q. 23, a. 1.

65. Nichols, *Romance and System*, 421.

nature of itself can neither attain nor merit, and to which of itself it stands in no vital relationship. The divine love manifested
in ordaining man to this end is truly lavish and gracious. . . .
That man may receive the power to strive after that supernatural end, he must mount above his nature. He must let himself
be elevated, raised by God. He must, as it were, let himself be
borne toward his end upon the wings of God's grace. Here the
full force of *transmissio in finem* is revealed; for man progresses
toward his goal not by any power lying in his own nature, but is
raised up and carried by a higher power that speeds him toward
it. Hence Christian predestination is essentially supernatural, as
well as in the decree of God's free, gratuitous love in which it is
anchored, as in the goal at which it aims and the activity which
it generates.[66]

Predestination in Christ is, then, the ground of election, that is, its
cause and foundation. It includes not only man's ultimate goal but also God's
effective influence by his grace in man's progress toward reaching that goal.
This latter claim raises the question: In what manner is God causally involved in our salvation, according to Scheeben's theology of predestination,
such that there is an actual efficacious grace that does not undermine human freedom? Furthermore, is this saving grace in itself efficacious, achiev-
ing the end for which God intended that grace, or is it made efficacious by
virtue of the consent of the will that God foresaw? As Garrigou-Language
asks pointedly, "In other words, how are we to conceive the divine motion
that inclines our will and causes it to perform the salutary act?"[67] I shall
return to this question below.

For now, I shall ask what the word "predestination" means for Scheeben. Predestination is composed of two separate words: "pre," meaning
beforehand, and "destiny" or "destination." Predestination then means to
determine a person's destiny beforehand. There is more, however, since God
preordains not only man's supernatural end "but also [the means]," says
Scheeben, that "leads him toward that goal, and effectively influences his
progress toward it."[68] "The mystery of predestination lies in God's sublime
decree," adds Scheeben, "unfathomable by any human wisdom, by which
He appoints men to their supernatural end and guides them toward it."[69]
What is more, adds Scheeben, "It is the decree of the divine will, whereby
God 'predestined us to be adopted as his sons through Jesus Christ' [Eph

66. Scheeben, *MC*, 701.

67. Garrigou-Lagrange, *Predestination*, 238.

68. Scheeben, *MC*, 700.

69. Ibid., 701.

1:5], 'to be conformed to the image of His Son' [Rom 8:30]."[70] Furthermore, he emphasizes the decisive significance of Christ in God's free, gratuitous love, linking Jesus Christ, the Redeemer of the world, and the content of the gospel, with predestination. Thus this decree of predestination is in Christ, and it is an ultimate expression of God's love (1 Thess 1:4; Col 3:12; Eph 2:4–5; John 13:1; Jer 31:2–3; Ps 103:17). "Christ is the center, the foundation, the ideal, and the end of the whole supernatural world order and of the decree by which it is governed and brought to realization. From Him this decree derives its sublimity, its effectiveness, and its universality. All men are predestined in the predestination of Christ; for, in assuming His own body, Christ has taken the whole race as His body."[71] Are then all men actually saved in Christ?

Admittedly, Scheeben's point here is easily misunderstood as a defense of universalism. In an effort to prevent that from happening, but also to explain the tension between God's will and its efficacy, I draw on the distinction between God's antecedent and consequent will, as I explained above; but also I draw on the distinction explained in the previous chapter between two sorts of sufficiency, intrinsic and extrinsic, on the one hand, and efficiency, on the other. The former distinction between God's antecedent and consequent will is helpful in making sense of the fact that Scheeben distinguishes between universal and particular predestination, or, as Scheeben also calls it, "virtual predestination . . . and effective predestination." He adds, "The divine will to save, according to the unanimous teaching of all Catholic theologians, is twofold: on the one hand it is universal, and refers to all men, even those who, as a matter of fact, fail to achieve salvation; on the other hand, it is particular, and refers to those actually reach their foreordained end."[72] These distinctions suggestion that the redemptive wok of Christ is sufficient for the sins of all men, and hence it is potentially universal in scope; but it is not sufficient and efficient for all men's sin; otherwise it would be actually universal in extent.

Of course, in this connection, I shall need to show how the atonement is universal in scope such that it possesses the intrinsic sufficiency in atoning for all men because Christ died for all men. But also I will need to show that the divine intention, which is the purpose for which God intends the atonement, is that God wills to save all men, and hence "Christ's work is extrinsically sufficient for the sin of all fallen humans."[73] There is another

70. Ibid.

71. Ibid., 730.

72. Ibid., 702.

73. Crisp, *Deviant Calvinism*, 218.

concept here that is crucial for explaining the resistance against universalism (all men are saved), namely, the notion of efficiency or efficacy, which,
as Crisp says, "has to do with the actual number of those to whom Christ's
work is applied."[74] In sum, Christ's atoning work is *sufficient* for the salvation of all men, albeit not *efficient* for their salvation, but only for God's
elect. I argue below that this is Scheeben's view.

In a fundamental sense, according to Scheeben, the divine intentionality expressed in God's universal salvific will is that God has created
all men for eternal bliss, and in his infinite, all-embracing love, truly and
sincerely desires the salvation of them all. This desire to provide salvation
for all men pertains to the divine intentionality. He says, "All men are predestined in the predestination of Christ; for, in assuming His own body,
Christ has taken the whole race as His body."[75] Prior to the Incarnation,
adds Scheeben, "the [human] race was a *massa damnationis*; but in Him it
has become a *massa benedictionis*, upon which God's love is lavished more
insistently, more abundantly, and more graciously than the original man."[76]
Evidently, then, Scheeben answers "yes" to the question whether all men are
predestined in Christ, but only if we understand predestination, in the first
place, as his antecedent will, that is, that will is "fundamentally identical
with God's supernatural salvific will, by which He directs the movement of
His creatures toward their supernatural end."[77] That is, predestination is
universal if seen in light of the universal salvific will of God in Christ: "God
. . . desires all men to be saved and to come to knowledge of the truth. For
there is one God, and there is one Mediator between God and men, the man
Christ Jesus, who gave himself as a ransom for all" (1 Tim. 2:4f.; cf. also 1
Tim. 4:10; Titus 2:11; 2 Pt. 3:9; Heb. 9:28). In sum, then, predestination "is
universal, and refers to all men, even those who, as a matter of fact, fail to
achieve salvation."[78]

In this last sentence, Scheeben alludes to the choice of the man who
resists the grace of God. I will return to this resistance below. For now, it is
important to explain that predestination in a universal sense involves God's
prevenient grace that he makes available to all men. "For if God's universal
will to save is in earnest, it must be efficacious, since it makes the striving after salvation abundantly possible for the creature."[79] This grace is gratuitous,

74. Ibid., 219.

75. Scheeben, *MC*, 730.

76. Ibid.

77. Ibid., 702.

78. Ibid.

79. Ibid., 704.

unmerited, "proceeding solely and entirely from God's sheer goodness and the superabundant grace He bestows on us in Christ and for the sake of Christ."[80] It is also efficacious, and hence not just merely sufficient for man's salvation, whereby that grace attains the salvific purpose for which God intended it because he foresaw man's consent to it rather than his resistance. But if God's grace is efficacious because it produces the intended effect of salvation, the salutary act, how does it attain that end? As we shall see below, efficacious grace attains its divinely intended end, not because of its own intrinsic nature, but rather by virtue of Divine *scientia media*. Of course this grace "does not exclude our co-operation, but requires and elicits it."[81] And because this grace doesn't diminish our freedom, in some cases it doesn't always attain that saving effect for which God intends it, man doesn't co-operate with God's grace, but rather he freely resists it. So, although God's prevenient grace is objectively efficacious, it is not always subjectively effective because a man may "refuse his consent and cooperation to grace."[82]

In this sense, then, predestination "is particular, and refers to those who actually reach their foreordained end." Given that predestination is also particular, according to Scheeben, as a matter of fact, then, all men are *not* actually elected in Christ. For man can "wantonly fling away [his] happiness," and "thrust aside the hand of God stretched out to saved us," and hence "frustrate the tender exertions He puts forth in our behalf out of sheer goodness and love (*pro bona voluntate*). . . . So we have it entirely in our own power to dissipate [God's prevenient grace]."[83] In short, it is possible to reject God.

Accordingly, Scheeben distinguishes universal predestination and particular predestination, that is, God's consequent, unconditional and effectual decree, that is, his particular salvific will, and identifies the latter with *election*, in conformity, he says, with "Sacred Scripture and, in the spirit of Scripture, the Fathers and theologians."[84] "All human souls are chosen, and consequently called, by God's universal salvific will to be His children and spouses. But only those who actually receive baptism, or who respond to God's choice of them up to the very end with a counterchoice of their own, effectively and absolutely constitute the elect, and are separated our from the multitude of those who are merely chosen in the sense that God

---

80. Ibid., 706.
81. Garrigou-Lagrange, *Predestination*, 236.
82. Scheeben, *MC*, 702.
83. Ibid., 725–26.
84. Ibid., 724.

has created all men for eternal bliss."[85] Put differently, essentially Scheeben adopts a notion of "single" predestination that has the different stages of universal predestination and particular predestination. That is, he qualifies the realization of universal predestination in light of man's resistance against grace,[86] which is to say in reference to man's free consent and cooperation with God's prevenient grace, or his will's withdrawal from the influence of grace.[87] Scheeben explains: "Particular, effective predestination, by which God actually assists man to procure his end, is only an offshoot, a flowering of this universal predestination, is virtually contained in it, and issues from it. . . . Universal predestination and particular predestination are at bottom only one. They are distinct only as different stages. The second is based on the first, and for its execution requires the intervention of God's foreknowledge."[88] What is it a foreknowledge of, and is Scheeben suggesting that predestination is based on the merits of man's good works? Scheeben responds:

> As the tendency and inclination to good, which precedes the deliberate advertence of the will, passes over to actual movement when the free will accedes to it, so the divine will to move really moves when the will of man accedes to it under the influence of grace, and makes God's design his own. As the carrying out of the impulse to which God inspires the creature presupposes the consent and cooperation of the creature's free will, so on the part of God the will to carry through the impulse supposes foreknowledge of this cooperation and is consequent upon it, and is therefore essentially a *praedestinatio consequens*, consequent predestination. But, as should be carefully noted, it is consequent not upon any works performed by the creature or his meritorious movement toward the supernatural [end]—with regard to these it remains antecedent, as their efficient cause—but only in reference to the creature's cooperation, which likewise precedes the work and the effective movement.[89]

Scheeben is alluding in the final sentence of this passage quoted above to the "order of salvation." [90] Some Catholic theologians, such as Scheeben, distinguish between "predestination in the full sense" and "predestination

85. Ibid., 724–725.
86. Ibid., 726.
87. Ibid., 710.
88. Ibid., 703; emphasis added.
89. Ibid., 703.
90. Ibid., 707.

in a limited sense." The former encompasses predestination to initial grace, that is, the first grace that God gives to all men,[91] "without any merit on our part,"[92] as well as every subsequent grace that leads to complete predestination to glory. By contrast, predestination in a limited sense may include the first grace, the grace of faith and justification, but may also lose that grace, and so be thwarted from receiving predestination to glory. Furthermore, Scheeben distinguishes three successive stages in the "order of salvation," as he phrases it, that is, in the manifestation of the decree of predestination of the divine will: first, the call to grace, which is the first grace of vocation and the beginning of faith (*initium fidei*), second, justification, and, third, the eventual glorification of man. In short, predestination to grace and predestination to glory are distinguishable in the order of salvation.

Significantly, the first stage of initial grace, predestinating grace, is not dependent on good works and merits. Grace is absolutely gratuitous and unmerited, preceding all good works and merits. "Strictly speaking, it is not induced or merited even by the merits springing from grace." Still, adds Scheeben,

> We do, of course, merit glory by the works of grace; and so we can, in a certain sense, say that we prevail upon God to confer glory upon on us, or that we merit the *propositum dandi gloriam*, so far as glory is a special work of God, a special stage in the order of salvation, in which one element can and does depend on another. But we merit heavenly glory only by the fact that God destines us to it as our end, and incites us to it by His grace; and predestination in the narrower sense is not exactly God's decree to give us glory, but the will by which He conducts us to it: the *consilium quo nos transmittit in finem gloriae*. Neither by natural nor by supernatural merits can we earn the actual impetus which God gives us to arrive at the goal. But the utilization of the movement itself which God gives us is dependent on the condition that we accept it, that we consent to the impulse received from God, and that we allow ourselves to be moved and carried along; in a word, that we cooperate with and through God's prevenient grace.[93]

The difference between universal and particular predestination is, then, the difference between God's universal salvific will and his particular, effective salvific will. Will the universal will to save take the form of

91. Ibid.
92. Ibid.
93. Ibid.

the particular will, passing over into the effective and definitive, or will it turn into the judgment "laid upon man by divine justice,"[94] and hence into reprobation?[95] Alternatively put, this difference is also the difference between God's antecedent will to save all men and his consequent will in which some men, failing to respond freely, refuse their consent and cooperation to grace, as Scheeben expresses it, and turn into reprobates.

Scheeben defends the claim that, in his infinite, comprehensive love, God truly and sincerely desires the salvation of all men, and hence that from eternity God, calling them to eternal life, and also, "as far as lies in Him, guides them toward it." Evidence that God truly and sincerely desires all men to be saved, and in pursuance of this desire, he provides efficacious grace to all men to turn to him and be saved. Says Scheeben, "God begins to draw man to his supernatural end, and to spur him on to the attainment of it, with the purpose of leading him to it effectively, provided man does not refuse his consent and cooperation to grace."[96] Thus, God antecedently wills to save all men, giving them all prevenient grace to respond to the gospel, but considered from the perspective of his consequent will, consequent predestination, as Scheeben phrases it, is no longer universal but particular, given the way that man actually freely responds to God's grace or not.

In this connection, Scheeben stresses that insofar as God's universal salvific will is in earnest, "it must be efficacious, since it makes the striving after salvation abundantly possible for the creature."[97] When the grace of universal predestination achieves God's intended effect, eliciting a supernaturally salvific act, it is particular predestination, implying only the effective use of God's saving power "by the will of man under the influence of grace."[98] But this raises the age-old question regarding the nature of efficacious grace. Given that grace is resistible, men sometimes freely resist its influence, and thus grace fails to elicit the response, the supernaturally salvific act that God intends. In that case, does that mean that God grants merely sufficient grace? If so, is grace only efficacious on account of our consent? Scheeben resists that conclusion for it is not apparent how grace can be sufficient if it additionally requires an individual's free consent alone to render that grace efficacious.[99] Furthermore, in that case would that not mean that it is ultimately up to the individual to be saved or not, with God

94. Ibid., 726.
95. Ibid., 728.
96. Ibid., 702.
97. Ibid., 704.
98. Ibid.
99. Ibid., 704–5n10.

choosing in response to the individual's choice? Would that not make man the primary source of supernaturally salvific acts?

I should make clear at this point that this is most definitely *not* Scheeben's view. That view is Pelagianism, in which predestination comes after the foreseeing of merits (*post praevisa merita*), and depends chiefly on man. Scheeben clearly rejects this view because of the gratuitousness, also called by him, the absolute or unconditional character of predestination. "Because it is supernatural, predestination is evidently not subject to any condition on the side of [human] nature, since God is neither moved nor can in any way be moved by [human] nature for the predestination of [human] nature." "Hence the plan or purpose by which God destines nature to the supernatural end and wills to lead it to that end," Scheeben adds, "proceeds solely and entirely from His sheer goodness and the superabundant grace He bestows on us in Christ and for the sake of Christ."[100] In sum, "predestination precedes the prevision of merits, for it is their cause."[101] Salvation is not ultimately in man's hands.

But if God's grace is sufficient why does that grace not produce its intended effect? If of itself God's universal will to save is efficacious, as Scheeben claims, does that not mean that it necessarily attains its intended effect? No, since man is able to resist and to reject the grace of God, as the Council of Trent unmistakably teaches, if the effect of grace is considered, clearly then a salvific act is not always effected.[102] But then in what sense can the grace be efficacious, if the intended effect is to elicit freely, on man's part, the supernaturally salvific act God intends? In response, Scheeben says that "all men receive sufficient grace to be saved, but retain their freedom under the influence of grace: as often as they commit sin, the proffered grace remains inefficacious, or merely sufficient."[103]

But that response leaves unanswered the question how grace may infallibly obtain the consent of free will. "Another point which Catholic theologians admit," says Scheeben, "is the power of grace to attain its object with certainty." "Whatever activity is displayed by secondary causes," he adds, "especially in the supernatural order, is directed by Divine decrees, and supported by Divine co-operation (*concursus*). No creature can frustrate the

---

100. Ibid., 706.

101. Ibid., 713.

102. Denzinger §1554, canon 4: "If any one says that the free will of man, moved and awakened by God, in no way cooperates by an assent to God's awakening call, through which he disposes and prepares himself to obtain the grace of justification, and that man cannot refuse his assent if he wishes, but that like a lifeless object he does nothing at all and is merely passive, let him be anathema."

103. This quotation is taken from Scheeben, *A Manual of Catholic Theology*, 272.

will of God. If He wills that a salutary act shall follow upon a given grace, he
so disposes the free will that the act infallibly follows."[104] Evidently, Scheeben holds that supernaturally salvific acts can be free even if God simultaneously cooperates with them by a grace that is intrinsically efficacious.
At stake here for Scheeben is the supernatural property of predestination,
namely, its infallibility, the efficaciousness of God's grace, meaning thereby
that no creature can frustrate the predestining will of God by which he
conducts the elect to their salvific goal. Again the question arises: if God's
predestinating will is infallible such that he has decided to confer only efficacious grace, and hence wills that a salvific act shall concurrently, infallibly, *and freely,* follow a given grace, what happens to that person's freedom?
How does Scheeben sustain the integrity of the freedom of the will in light
of the infallible efficacy of grace?

The brief answer to this question here must be that Scheeben's answer
has an affinity to both the Molinist and the Congruist position. On the one
hand, with all Molinists, Scheeben agrees that God places an individual in
circumstances that he knows full well will freely elicit a salvific act from this
individual. "God know what each man will do under given circumstances.
When, therefore, he wishes a grace to have an infallible effect, He offers it
to man at the right moment, *i.e.* when He knows that man will consent."[105]
Scheeben explains: "No doubt, those who are placed under a system of
providence wherein they can cooperate with grace and, as is foreseen, will
cooperate, must thank God not only for grace itself, but also for the effective
congruity of grace, and they must regard the latter as a special benefit."[106]
What, then, is the basis of efficacious grace's infallible effect? If I understand
Scheeben, his answer to this question is more in line with Congruism,[107]

---

104. Ibid.

105. Ibid., 278.

106. Scheeben, *MC*, 727.

107. According to Ott, "Congruism, which was developed by Francis Suarez (d.
1617), by St. Robert Bellarmine (d. 1621), by the Jesuit General Claddius Aquaviva
(1613) and which was prescribed as a doctrine of the [Jesuit] Order, is a further extension of Molinism" (*Fundamentals of Catholic Dogma,* 249). The Congruist model
of grace and freedom brought Molinism more into line with Banezianism, and was
worked out in detail by Robert Bellarmine and Francisco Suarez. Scheeben indicates
his alignment with this model: "In acknowledging the connection between prevenient
grace and the actual movement of the will simply as a connection founded on fact,
and in subjecting it to God's providence only so far as God foresaw it through His
scientia media, the Molinists and Congruists do not in any way impair the mystery of
Christian predestination, provided they retain what is substantially true in the doctrine
of the Thomists and Augustinians. This for the most part they have done, particularly
their leaders, Molina and Suarez" (*MC,* 720). What is substantially true in the doctrine
of the Thomists and Augustinians, according to Scheeben, is the gratuitousness and

because it is not an individual's free consent alone that "extrinsically" renders God's grace efficacious with respect to a salvific act. In other words, it is not God's mere foreknowledge of an individual's free consent alone that renders grace efficacious with respect to God's intended effect to elicit that individual's salvific act. Rather, God's grace is efficacious, not only by an individual's free consent, but also, indeed principally, by God's antecedent decree to confer a "congruous" grace that will guarantee that individual's eliciting a salvific act. Ott explains: "According to the system of congruism, the difference between efficacious and sufficient grace lies not only in the assent of the free will, but also in the congruity of the grace to the individual circumstances of the recipient. When the grace suits the individual inner and outer conditions of the man (*gratia congrua*), it becomes effective by the free assent of the will: if it does not (*gratia incongrua*), it remains by lack of the free assent of the will, ineffective. God, by *Scientia Media* [middle knowledge], foresees the congruity of the grace and its infallible success."[108] Thus, the intrinsic infallibility of God's predestining will, which is the efficaciousness of the grace whereby God in cooperating with man feely elicits supernaturally salvific acts, does not come after his foreknowledge of man's cooperation, but beforehand.

Scheeben's answer to this question is that God knows beforehand whether the man will cooperate with his grace or not in the circumstances that God has placed him. Thus the infallible success of God's universal predestination, its "intrinsic infallibility," as he phrases it, "does not consist simply in God's foreknowledge of the free activity of our will," that would be no different than Pelagianism, as Scheeben understands it, "but rather in His foreknowledge of an effect that proceeds from His unfailing, supernatural divine love and power."[109] He explains:

> Thus in virtue of His universal supernatural love, God on His part must infallibly and unfalteringly lead us toward our goal. That is, He must on his part infallibly do everything that is necessary and sufficient for the attainment of our end; the actual attainment of that end depends on our cooperation, which is inherently wavering and uncertain. Hence, so far as our hope is anchored in God, as alone it can and must be, it is unfailing. . . . The infallibility of particular predestination consists in the fact that God infallibly foresees the result of the efficacy of universal predestination, which in itself is unfailing. The infallibility that

infallibility (efficacy) of predestination.

108. Ott, *Fundamentals of Catholic Dogma*, 249.

109. Scheeben, *MC*, 710; see also 708.

corresponds to God's love and faithfulness is not necessarily rooted in a special preference of God for the effectively predestined; rather it flows *ipso facto* from His universal salvific will under the prevision [foreknowledge] of human cooperation. Hence it [the infallibility of particular predestination] is present principally and primarily in the antecedent will to save, and only as a result of this fact in particular predestination which, as consequent will . . . proceeds from the antecedent will, and objectively manifests the efficacy of the latter in man's cooperation.[110]

At issue here is not only Scheeben's account of the efficacy of efficacious grace, which is due to the fact that grace is given in circumstances favorable, and hence congruent, to its operation in which a supernatural salvific act is elicited, but also that this grace proceeds from God's universal supernatural love.

Furthermore, since God's prevenient grace depends exclusively on his unconstrained goodness that we can of ourselves in no way merit, says Scheeben, "we have grounds to fear that God will withdraw His saving hand once we have defied Him," namely, "that He will no longer help us with His prevenient grace, at least not with the same abundance of grace He had previously intended for us, that He will forsake us, since we have forsaken Him."[111] In that case, since we want to maintain the freedom of God in election, or particular predestination, there is what Scheeben calls "God's liberty in selecting graces."[112] That is, "a selection of graces, a dispensing of graces in greater or lesser measure dependent on God's free will." "We may not conceive of God's universal will to save as though it were uniform for all, or the product of equal love for all," Scheeben adds, "without any regard to the way man actually corresponds to grace."[113] One might ask why Scheeben thinks that the measure of grace is not conceived as a uniform given to each man?[114] In other words, why does that grace "differ in some respects from one individual person to another" [?][115]

Walls answers this question insightfully: "What represents measure N for Jones may completely overwhelm Smith in such a way that his freedom is destroyed. Moreover, what is effective in influencing Smith toward good may only make Jones more resistant. So the even distribution of grace does

---

110. Ibid., 709.
111. Ibid., 726.
112. Ibid., 728.
113. Ibid., 727.
114. Walls, *Hell*, 83–111, is very helpful in thinking through this question.
115. Ibid., 88–89.

not in any way entail treating all persons in just the same. It means doing what is best for each individual to elicit, if possible, a positive response from him."[116] Walls continues: "With these qualifications on what is meant by 'equal', I would say grace is distributed equally if grace of optimal measure is given to all persons and all are given full opportunity to make a decisive response to it, either positively or negatively."[117] Thus, the distribution of grace cannot destroy our freedom, and hence the man who has forsaken God wanders ever farther from his vocation and destiny, meaning that he goes the way of estrangement and judgment "laid upon man by divine justice"[118] as a result of his abusing his freedom. That judgment is not a decree by a *potentia absoluta* but the holiness of the judgment of God, which is increasingly realized in such unbelief, making the unbeliever ripe for that judgment.

Most important, to maintain the freedom of God in distributing grace selectively in response to man's abusing his freedom does not contradict God's universal will to save. Rather, Scheeben affirms a God who establishes a real salvific possibility for all men to be saved. "For if God's universal will to save is in earnest, it must be efficacious, since it makes the striving after salvation abundantly possible for the creature."[119] God does not from eternity already decide to distribute graces selectively independently of his foreseeing whether or not man cooperates with his prevenient grace. This grace is universal in scope and salvific in its intention, meaning thereby that God pursues, invites, attracts, and makes salvation possible for all men, providing to all the grace to respond appropriately to his invitation. Yet, Scheeben says, God has the freedom to distribute grace selectively in response to the man who does not avail himself of it and hence he "gives it [grace] the specific form in which it applies to particular men." He adds, "We can readily perceive that neither God's mercy nor man's free will is here jeopardized in any way."[120] God's freedom to distribute grace selectively "would contradict God's salvific will only if God, in selecting graces, were to pass over some men entirely, and were to confer on them no grace at all whereby they could attain salvation."[121]

There is more: Scheeben distinguishes God's freedom to distribute graces selectively from his effective, definitive, particular predestining will

116. Ibid., 89.
117. Ibid.
118. Scheeben, *MC*, 726.
119. Ibid., 704.
120. Ibid., 726.
121. Ibid., 728.

itself, in short, the definitive election of persons. Failure to make that distinction will result in double predestination. Failure to make that distinction suggests that there is "no difference between the antecedent and consequent will [of God] with reference to the actual attainment of salvation."[122] Scheeben elaborates further on the implications of failing to make that distinction:

> Further, as regards those who are not to attain salvation, it would be impossible to perceive how God could have a serious will effectively to admit them likewise to salvation, in the event that they would cooperate with His grace. For such a will presupposes that God has not, for His part, fixed the number of the predestined *independently of His prevision of men's cooperation*; otherwise He himself would have to see to it that none of those whom He had not predestined should find their way into that number by cooperating with grace. Although God can elect some to the effective attainment of salvation by a will that is unconditional from the very beginning, *He cannot from the outset proceed to exclude any.* There must be certain limits to the selection of grace, for God does not endeavor to bring about the salvation of all men with equal energy, with equal solicitude, with equal forebearance; nevertheless He has the serious design to assist everyone effectively *provided he cooperates*, and consequently to predestine all [who cooperate with his grace] effectively.[123]

In the above passage, Scheeben explicitly tells us that he rejects what I discussed in the previous chapter as the concept of "negative reprobation," or "preterition," as the Reformed tradition calls it, meaning thereby, as Fr. Joseph Pohle writes, "an eternal decree by which God excludes from Heaven those not absolutely predestined," in other words, those he *a priori* determined not to save by refusing to give them the grace necessary to attain salvation.[124] This is unconditional negative reprobation that is difficult to reconcile with God's universal salvific will. Indeed, negative seems indistinguishable from unconditional positive reprobation because the decree of reprobation is not contingent upon the sins of men.[125] Of course Scheeben rejects the latter because he rejects the heresy of *predestinarianism*, which is a doctrine of double predestination in which there is a *symmetrical* view of election and reprobation such that the latter is worked out in a *parallel*

---

122. Ibid., 728.
123. Ibid., 728–29; emphasis added.
124. Pohle, *Grace*, 215–16.
125. Ott, *Fundamentals of Catholic Dogma*, 245.

mode of divine causation. Furthermore, it presumes, as I noted earlier in this section, an abstract doctrine of election, that is, the *decretum absolutum* (absolute decree) to elect some of humanity and reject others by "a mere act of sovereignty which had nothing to do with the love and grace of God," apart from and outside of Christ.[126] Scheeben writes, this heresy claims that "God ha[s] from the beginning formed the absolute, unconditional resolve to admit some to glory and others not. And hence to give to some graces that would effectively lead thereto, but to refuse such graces to others."[127] I now shall argue that Scheeben refutes that objection: Scheeben's view of particular predestination does not blunt God's universal salvific will.

In doing so, his account of reprobation, given that it takes into account man's cooperation with God's prevenient grace, avoids the standard critique of negative reprobation that it is absolutely irreconcilable with God truly and sincerely desiring the salvation of all men. Indeed, it makes no difference whether God directly excludes a man from heaven," as in absolute predestination, "or refuses to give him the graces necessary to attain it." "How could God sincerely will the salvation of all men if it were true, as Suarez says, that 'it is not in man's power to work out his eternal salvation in case he falls under non-election, non-predestination, or, which amounts to the same thing, negative reprobation'?"[128] By contrast, Scheeben's account of reprobation presupposes the "truth that God in His unutterable and wonderful love has destined and chosen all men for eternal, supernatural union with Himself, and that repudiation and exclusion from this union commence only when man scorns the great love of his Creator and predestines himself to perdition."[129] In short, God gives prevenient grace, "first grace," as Scheeben phrases it, "to all men (or at least holds out the prospect of it to them), and thereby gives them the power and the impetus to consent to it, to cooperate with it, and so to draw ever close to their goal."[130] Yet, the love of God "becomes actually selective, and inextricably ties the bond between God and man, only so far as God foresees man's counterchoice and response which He evokes."[131] That is, the connecting link between God's universal, conditional salvific will and his particular, absolute salvific will is God's prevision of human cooperation. We now turn to discuss Scheeben's

---

126. Berkouwer, *De Verkiezing Gods*, 164 [143].
127. Scheeben, *MC*, 728.
128. Pohle, *Grace*, 217, 219.
129. Scheeben, *MC*, 729.
130. Ibid., 707.
131. Ibid., 725.

view of the relation between God's foreknowledge and human cooperation in the order of salvation

Grace and Freedom

III. "*Therefore it would be best to say that [particular predestination] is neither* ex praevisis meritis *nor* post praevisa merita, *nor simply* ante praevisa merita *or independent of them, but* per merita praevisa in cooperatione liberi arbitrii a gratia moti et informati, qua cum ipsa gratia praeveniente cooperator; *that is, through merits foreseen in the cooperation of the free will as moved and informed by grace, whereby the free will cooperates with the prevenient grace itself.*"[132]

Particular predestination is based on universal predestination, that is, God's predestining will to save all mankind. Accordingly, says Scheeben, "They are distinct only as different stages." "The second is based on the first," he adds, "*and for its execution requires the intervention of God's foreknowledge.*"[133] Given that predestination is particular, which is at bottom identical then with election, on what basis does God decide who to save, according to Scheeben, and what is the precise role and nature of God's foreknowledge in the order of salvation?

Scheeben defends not only the infallibility of predestination but also its gratuitousness. In a word, predestination is *unmerited* on our part. "Both properties, gratuitousness and infallibility, taken together constitute what is generally known as the absolute or unconditional character of predestination."[134] In a doctrine of predestination, God decides whom he will save, because salvation, from beginning to end, is a work of God's grace. Jesus said to his disciples, "you did not choose me, but I chose you" (John 15:16).

The controversial aspect to predestination arises when we ask on what basis God decides. Typically, the answer to this question has been posed in black and white terms. Either God chooses to save an individual apart from any condition (e.g., merits) found in that person. If so, that is unconditional election. Or God chooses to save that individual whom he foreknows will §first choose him and hence on the basis of his foreseen merits. If so, that is conditional election. Scheeben's answer to this question is more complex and nuanced than this either/or suggests. God's particular predestining will,

132. Ibid., 708; emphasis added.
133. Ibid., 703; emphasis added.
134. Ibid., 706.

his consequent predestination, as Scheeben phrases it, is willed by God neither in virtue of nor because of our foreseen merits; but neither is it willed
by him prior to or independently of our foreseen merits. But what other op-
tions are there? Suppose we distinguish the distinct phases in the whole plan
or order of salvation, first grace, which is the initiating grace of conversion,
justification, and the eventual glorification of man, and think of the whole
plan as proceeding solely and entirely from God's goodness and grace. "All
our meritorious works, including our very cooperation with grace, depend
on prevenient grace, which is given to us without any merit on our part.
. . . Strictly speaking [particular predestination] is not induced or merited
even by the [supernatural] merits springing from grace."[135] Before going on
passages such as this one and others where terms like grace and merit occur
with some frequency in Scheeben's theology, then let me define grace and
merit, according to Catholic doctrine.

The *Catechism of the Catholic Church* teaches that "Grace is *favor,* the
free and undeserved help that God gives us to respond to his call to become
children of God, adoptive sons, partakers of the divine nature and of eternal
life." Thus, "since the initiative belongs to God in the order of grace, *no one
can merit the initial grace* of forgiveness and justification, at the beginning
of conversion." Even "the preparation of man for the reception of grace is
already a work of grace," a prevenient grace, as Scheeben phrases it, which is
the grace of God that is active in human lives before the initial response, and
conversion. Prevenient grace is "needed to arouse and sustain our collaboration in justification through faith, and in sanctification through charity.
God brings to completion in us what he has begun, 'since he who completes
his work by cooperating with our will began by working so that we might
will it.'"[136] Regarding the nature and place of merit in the order of salvation,
the *Catechism* teaches that "with regard to God, there is no strict right to
any merit on the part of man. Between God and us there is an immeasurable
inequality, for we have received everything from him, our Creator."

The *Catechism* adds, making clear that the merit in question is not
natural, but rather supernatural because considered the effect of God's
grace. "The merit of man before God in the Christian life arises from the
fact that *God has freely chosen to associate man with the work of his grace.*
The fatherly action of God is first on his own initiative, and then follows
man's free acting through his collaboration, so that the merit of good works
is to be attributed in the first place to the grace of God, then to the faithful.
Man's merit, moreover, itself is due to God, for his good actions proceed in

135. Ibid., 707.
136. CCC, §§§1996, 2010, 2001, respectively.

Christ, from the predispositions and assistance given by the Holy Spirit."[137] In this sense, the order of salvation is by grace from start to finish. Of course the really interesting question regarding Scheeben's position is how grace is bestowed and how it effects our salvation.[138]

In response to this question, Scheeben answers, particular predestination is willed by God "through [supernatural] merits foreseen in the cooperation of the free will as moved and informed by grace, whereby the free will cooperates with the prevenient grace itself."[139] God's consequent predestination requires the intervention of his foreknowledge of the supernatural merits that are a fruit of man's freely cooperating with his supernatural prevenient grace. He adds: "All our meritorious works, including our very cooperation with grace, depend on prevenient grace, which is given to us without any merit on our part. But God gives this *first grace* to all men (or at least holds out the prospect of it to them), and thereby gives them the power and the impetus to consent to it, to cooperate with it, and so to draw ever closer to their goal."[140] The entire salvific process—running from the call to grace, conversion, justification, through good works in grace and perseverance to eternal life itself—falls under God's predestinating grace.

On the one hand, then, God's universal salvific will, his antecedent will, is such that "no merits, great or small . . . precede it." Of itself God's plan of salvation "precedes all meritorious works or cooperation." God unconditionally decides whom to save apart from any merits found in man. "God does not choose us because we have chosen Him; but through His choice, through the call [to grace] whereby He invites and draws us, He makes it possible for us to choose Him. The election (*election*), like predestination, issues from the unmerited, but absolutely reliable and powerful love (*dilectio*) by which God has called us to supernatural union with Himself."[141] In an earlier work, Scheeben writes, "The supernatural invitation to supernature is given to all men, for the supernatural state is meant for all."[142]

On the other hand, there is particular or consequent predestination, for the love of God's universal salvific will "becomes actually selective, and inextricably ties the bond between God and man, only so far as God foresees man's counterchoice and response which He evokes." "It is not in our

---

137. Ibid., §§, nos. 2007–2008.

138. Scheeben gives a full-length treatment of this question in a five volume popular work entitled, *Glories of Divine Grace.*

139. Scheeben, *MC*, 708.

140. Ibid., 707; emphasis added.

141. Ibid., 725.

142. Scheeben, *Natur und Gnade*; in English, *Nature and Grace*, 298. Quotations are from the English translation unless otherwise indicated.

power, of course," Scheeben adds, "to effect our choice and call; but it does depend on us to follow the call and thereby, in the words of the Apostle, to make our election and our call really effective and certain [2 Pt. 1:10]."[143] Again, in that earlier work he writes in the same vein, "Therefore every man has only himself to blame if he does not reach the supernatural state; but no man can take the credit to himself if he does possess it, because he has not merited it but has received it, and could have failed utterly to attain it if God had not drawn him to it," and the latter happens if man fails to cooperate with the prevenient grace that beckons and invites him.[144]

Now, what does God actually foresee that is the connecting link between universal and particular predestination? Since the work of salvation is a matter of grace, absolutely gratuitous and unmerited, it is "neither by natural nor by supernatural merits [that] we earn the actual impetus which God gives us to arrive at the goal."[145] Thus particular predestination is "consequent not upon any works performed by the creature or his meritorious movement toward the supernatural—with regard to these it remains antecedent, as their efficient cause." Rather, this particular predestination is consequent upon "the creature's cooperation, which likewise precedes the work and the effective movement."[146] Scheeben explains, "But the utilization of the movement itself which God gives us is dependent on the condition that we accept it, that we consent to the impulse received from God, and that we allow ourselves to be moved and carried along; in a word, that we cooperate with and through God's prevenient grace. Accordingly, particular predestination in no way takes our merit into consideration, but only our cooperation."[147]

Yet, regarding the eventual glorification of man, our cooperation with God's grace brings forth supernatural, meritorious works in us, which "leads us to our end through them." That is why Scheeben states that the eventual glorification of man is best understood "through [supernatural] merits foreseen in the cooperation of the free will as moved and informed by grace, whereby the freewill cooperates with the prevenient grace itself."[148] Hence, in regard to man's eventual glorification, then "we do . . . merit glory by the works of grace."[149] In other words, perseverance in grace until man's

143. Scheeben, *MC*, 725.

144. Scheeben, *Nature and Grace*, 298.

145. Scheeben, *MC*, 707.

146. Ibid., 703.

147. Ibid., 707.

148. Ibid., 708.

149. Ibid., 707.

eventual glorification can be supernaturally merited, because, in virtue of his covenant faithfulness, God can be trusted to fulfill his promises. Of course we cannot merit salvation for what we do; nonetheless our acts must have a significant connection with our salvation and eventual glorification, according to Scheeben. We do not merit the grace that initially moves us, but once moved and informed by grace we can supernaturally merit glory by the works of grace. "It is only fitting (congruent) that a man or woman who has done good should not be abandoned by God."[150] God's grace, which cooperates with the human will after conversion, "is the cause of our super-natural merits, and so is not subsequent but antecedent to our foreseen [su-pernatural] merits. But it is such [i.e., subsequent] only with respect to the prevision of our cooperation (*praescientia cooperationis nostrae*), and hence is not independent of our supernatural liberty and its activity as procured by universal predestination and prevenient grace."[151]

In accord with historic Catholic doctrine, in particular, the Council of Trent, which with legitimacy may trace its teaching back to St. Augustine, Scheeben holds that the freedom of the will has not been destroyed, totally lost, or taken away by original sin.[152] The *nature* of creation been corrupted but not completely destroyed by sin. Scheeben supports the Augustinian Principle, namely, the *nature* of humanity persists in the regime of man's fallen state.[153] Augustine writes: "The natures in which evil exists, in so far as they are natures, are good. And evil is removed, not by removing any nature, or part of a nature but by healing and correcting that which had been vitiated and depraved."[154] Yes, the natural powers of the will has been corrupted by the fall, which results in our misuse of freedom that is rooted in a new inclination to evil; and, additionally, the supernatural gifts of God's grace have been taken away from the fallen will.

Nevertheless, *pace* Calvin, it is not that the fallen will itself, as a consequence of the fall and the fallen state, is "capable of nothing except . . . malicious, empty self-seeking . . . possessing an insuperable bent toward evil."[155] The fall does not eliminate all inclination to goodness in the will and a capacity for contrary moral choice between good and evil—that is,

150. Nichols, *Epiphany*, 185.

151. Scheeben, *MC*, 707–8.

152. Denzinger §1555, canon 5: "If any one says that, after Adam's sin, the free will of man is lost and extinct or that it is an empty concept, a term without real foundation, indeed, a fiction introduced by Satan into the Church, let him be anathema."

153. In chapter 2, I discussed the Augustinian principle and the relationship of nature and grace in Calvin's anthropology.

154. Augustine, *City of God*, book 14, chapter 11.

155. Scheeben, *Nature and Grace*, 308.

its power to choose good over evil, or vice-versa. In short, Scheeben rejects the view that disparages the very nature of the will as God created it in order to magnify grace. His rejection of this view means that he holds man's will, even in its fallen state, to be such that he is able to give "a simple, free consent to the state of grace."[156]

Yet, Scheeben is no semi-Pelagian, that is, he does not claim that the fallen will in its fallen state has the power to turn back to God apart from grace. Thus, he adds, "even this consent is not given by nature through its own power, or through a natural movement aroused by God; it is given in response to God's supernatural excitation and attraction." Furthermore, this consent is a grace-elicited response to God's prior initiative, but it does not "merit grace," says Scheeben, "but only receives it, as it is offered by God's free goodness. God expects nothing else of nature than a willingness to take the gift held out to it."[157] It should be clear from these remarks that Scheeben rejects Pelagianism and semi-Pelagianism—the claims that we cause our own salvation, or that we initiate our own salvation—while also maintaining that the freedom of will has not been extinguished by original sin.

Yet, given the gratuitousness and the infallibility of predestination, which we noted earlier Scheeben takes to amount to its absolute or unconditional character, and, in particular, in virtue of God's universal supernatural love, he does "everything that is necessary and sufficient for the attainment of our end."[158] "In Christ and on account of Christ, God has extended to us the fatherly love He bore toward Christ as His Son and has made us the coheirs of Christ. Through this love God has destined us for a supernatural end. Therefore He owes it to His love that, as long as we are still wayfarers on this earth (*in statu viae ad finem*), He remain true to Himself, and lead us through all the intervening steps to our sublime goal. But this is so only if we do not refuse cooperation to His grace or, in the words of St. Augustine, if we do not scorn His mercy in His gifts."[159] In sum, God offers all men a grace which is efficacious with the cooperation of freedom, and hence the ultimate reason why some do not respond to God's free gift held out to them is not because he did not offer them that grace sufficient, but rather they did not cooperate with it. Given his divine foreknowledge, God knows that not only the elect will arrive at their goal but also that the reprobate will fail to attain theirs.

156. Ibid., 297.
157. Ibid.
158. Scheeben, *MC*, 709.
159. Ibid.

Most important, however, for Scheeben is that the infallibility of God's particular predestining will does not consist simply in his foreknowledge of the free activity of man's will. Rather, what God foreknows is "an effect that proceeds from His unfailing, supernatural divine love and power."[160] Of course Scheeben's view raises the question whether the infallibility—efficacy—of predestination destroys man's freedom.

I have already considered his reason for denying that the freedom of will is destroyed and lost in the fallen state. In accord with historic Catholic teaching on the freedom of the will, the will, even in its fallen state, retains both the inclination to goodness besides a new inclination to evil, and the natural capacity for contrary moral choices between good and evil, a capacity which is now corrupted but not destroyed. It was not the freedom of the will that was taken away by the fall; rather supernatural gifts of grace were taken away, and the will was only weakened and corrupted, hence its misuse in developing vices, as well as its inability to turn back to God without grace.

Significantly, on Scheeben's view, divine grace does not operate in a total vacuum as if it had to create an entirely new will that has no continuity with the natural will as originally created.[161] Rather, grace presupposes nature: "Inasmuch as effective predestination involves God's prevision of man's free cooperation, it presupposes the exercise of liberty. And inasmuch as universal predestination (as *efficax*) spurs man on to the pursuit of his end, and hence to cooperation with grace, it empowers him to exercise his liberty, or better, elevates natural liberty to the supernatural plane, and raises it so high above its natural weakness and all arresting obstacles, that failure to cooperate can in no way be ascribed to a deficiency in freedom, but only to a misuse of it."[162] Clearly, Scheeben affirms that a harmony exists between God's causal influence on man and the integrity pertaining to the exercise of his freedom. In that case, there remains to ask the following: God effects his will through secondary causes, which include human agents, but exactly how it is that these secondary causes have an integrity of their own and hence do not flow ultimately from divine causation is the question; without an answer to that question, the significance of our own freedom of choice is negated. In short, the issue here is over the relation of grace and freedom in the effectuation of supernaturally salvific acts.[163]

160. Ibid., 10.

161. Hoitenga, *John Calvin and the Will*, 91.

162. Scheeben, *MC*, 711.

163. Unfortunately, I do not have the space in this chapter to give a full account of Scheeben's theology of grace and freedom as found in his first work, *Nature and Grace*, 304–38.

Freedom and Determinism

IV. *"Where the free self-movement and self-determination of man under God's moving influence are expressly excluded, hence where predeterminism is advocated in its unmitigated crudity, we have before us an open denial of the Christian mystery of predestination. This error, no less injurious to God's power and transcendence than the opposite error of naturalism [i.e., Pelagianism], deeply degrades man in the very faculty wherein God proposes to raise him to the highest level."*[164]

The controversy over predestination is not only lively but also fundamental because at the heart of it is the question of how to define the relation between grace and freedom in such a way that the sovereignty of grace is honored and yet the freedom of the will is not ruled out as such.[165] Scheeben poses the terms of the controversy as follows: "The true mystery of predestination stands in the middle between two extremes. . . . Either the self-activity of man is too much stressed, to the exclusion of God's guidance of man's preliminary steps and continued progress, or the divine guidance is represented as driving and hurrying man along in such a way that his own movement and advance are obscured."[166] The former alternative is unacceptable to Scheeben because "it teaches that of himself man moves himself [toward his end], and thereby moves God to lend him aid and support for carrying out the purpose he has formed, and eventually to allot him an eternal award."[167] An understanding of human freedom is presupposed here to which is ascribed "an unconditional independence of God and of all divine impulse, whereby the will could of its own power determine itself to good no less than to evil."[168] Regarding the latter alternative, Scheeben expands:

> At least this is the case if God's moving influence upon the will is so conceived that the cooperation of the will or its self-determination must spring from the force of the existing impulse with an inner infallibility, if not with absolute necessity. If anyone can distinguish between this infallibility and necessity, let him approve of this view. We are unable to do so, particularly if infallibility is to be understood strictly; for from a given cause the only effect that follows with absolute infallibility is

164. Scheeben, *MC*, 717; emphasis added.

165. For a general philosophical analysis of the issues raised in connection with the relation of providence and human freedom, see Davison, "Divine Providence," 217–37.

166. Scheeben, *MC*, 712.

167. Ibid.

168. Ibid., 713.

an effect which cannot fail to result, and which therefore is so determined in its cause that it cannot be absent as long as the cause is in operation.[169]

We may best understand the point Scheeben is making here about determinism by distinguishing three different accounts of freedom: (1) libertarian freedom, or the power of contrary choice, (2) determinism, and (3) compatibilism (soft determinism), and, in this light, three theses concerning the problem of freedom and determinism. "(1) Some human actions are free. (2) All human actions are ultimately causally determined by events not under the causal control of their agents. (3) It is not possible that a free human action be ultimately causally determined by events not under the causal control of its agent."[170] If taken together, these three theses are in fact inconsistent: the conjunction of any two entails the falsity of the third.

Suppose we reject (1) and hold on to (2) and (3). If we make this move, we are claiming that human actions are determined and that free actions cannot be determined. Consequently, there are no free human actions. This view is known as hard determinism. In the above passage, Scheeben is clearly rejecting determinism. It is that view where "God's moving influence upon the will is so conceived that the cooperation of the will or its self-determination must spring from the force of the existing impulse with an inner infallibility, if not with absolute necessity." In that case "from a given cause the only effect that follows with absolute infallibility is an effect which cannot fail to result, and which therefore is so determined in its cause that it cannot be absent as long as the cause is in operation." In short, everything which happens is necessitated.

Suppose, however, we hold on to (1) and (3), rejecting (2). Consequently, there are free human actions, and such actions cannot have ultimate external determinants; otherwise they would not be free. On this view a person's acts are caused by himself, which is freedom as self-determination. This view is called libertarianism (or incompatibilism). This is Scheeben's view. He holds to a version of libertarian freedom, or incompatibilism, in as much as he describes "man's freedom *in abstracto* as a property of the will by virtue of which determination to activity rests with the man himself." That is, he adds, "this is called self-determination, because it is a determination, proceeding from the man himself, with regard to a choice that up to this point was undecided."[171] To say that up to the point of choosing a choice is undecided is to say that a free action is such that it does *not* have a suf-

---

169. Ibid., 717–18.

170. Flint, *Divine Providence*, 22–24. I am closely following Flint.

171. Scheeben, *Nature and Grace*, 318n6.

ficient condition or cause prior to its occurrence. This is "freedom from a preceding, necessary determination to activity (liberty of indifference)."[172] Denying that free actions have no antecedent, sufficient conditions or causes does not mean that *de facto* they lack causes and conditions altogether, that is, such factors as heredity and environment, intellectual development, and voluntary habits, as well as original sin and its effects; in this connection, I argued in the previous chapter, the freest possible act is not uncaused, but the manner of causality is agent-causality where the act is determined by reasons and motives. It is only to say that, absent a sufficient cause, a human action is *not* necessitated—which is denied by determinism.

Lastly, suppose we reject (3) but affirm (1) and (2). Consequently, some of our actions are free but at the same time determined in a particular way. This view is called compatibilism (or soft determinism). On this view, an act is free if it meets three conditions: "[1] It is not compelled or caused by anything external to the agent who performs it. [2] However, it is caused by something internal to the agent who performs it, namely, a psychological state such as a belief, a desire or, more precisely, a combination of these two. [3] The agent performing it could have acted differently, if the agent had wanted to do so."[173] Is man really free on this account of human freedom?

Given that soft determinism is, after all, deterministic, meaning thereby that it affirms the existence of sufficient conditions or causes of the action prior to the action itself, then even if the actions of an individual come from within—from his internal wishes, desires, beliefs, wants, and so on—and are the proximate causes thereof, the antecedents of his actions are ultimately controlled from without, namely, by God. Furthermore, adequate human freedom does not consist in merely doing what one wants to, but rather it is also a matter of being able to do otherwise, having the power of contrary choice between good and evil—which is the view of libertarian freedom. That is, "given choices *A* and *B*, one can literally choose to do either one, no circumstances exist that are sufficient to determine one's choice; a person's choice is up to him, and if he does one of them, he could have done otherwise, or at least he could have refrained from acting at all. One acts as an agent who is the ultimate originator of one's own actions and, in this sense, is in control of one's action."[174] Against this background, I turn now to answer the question, in what sense is libertarian freedom—the power of

172. Ibid.

173 Walls and Dongell, *Why I Am Not a Calvinist*, 108. As I said in the previous chapter, the authors are following a standard definition of soft determinism, or compatibilism. See Hasker, *Metaphysics*, 29–55, especially, 34.

174. Moreland and Craig, *Philosophical Foundations*, 240.

contrary choice, or the freedom of indifference—a necessary condition of possibility for man's ability to cooperate freely with grace.

Earlier in this chapter I asked whether God's concurrence in the free decisions of human beings is such that he causes a person's will to turn itself one way or the other? Alternatively, is divine concurrence such that it is simultaneous concurrence? That is, does God act, not *on* the person's will to move it to its decision, but rather merely concurrently acts *with* a person's will to produce some effect?[175] Scheeben rejects the view that God acts on the will in the sense that that causes a person's will to turn itself this way or that. He calls that action on the will a predetermination, making it utterly deterministic and incompatible with self-movement, the will's free self-determination.[176] In other words, emphasizing "God's motive influence upon the will so excessively that the latter is simply put in motion without moving itself." In short, it is destructive of free will. For "it is the very essence of a free will to be left free to choose; whosoever or whatsoever inclines it to one object or act without choice of another, destroys its freedom. Wherefore, if the will be moved according to its nature, it must be moved without . . . predetermination to one thing."[177] In addition, says Scheeben, this understanding of God's acts on the person's will is such that it deprives "God's motive influence of its noblest property, namely, that it places man in a position to determine himself, not only upon the natural plane, but also upon the supernatural plane, to which he is raised by God's grace."[178] Scheeben explains:

> In the work of salvation we attribute absolutely nothing to natural freedom, not even cooperation with grace; such cooperation does not take place either outside of or alongside of or even under grace. The power and the incentive to cooperate with grace are conferred on the natural will by grace alone. Cooperation is an act of the supernatural freedom imparted by grace; hence in the matter of salvation man is completely dependent on the grace of God. But if this dependence is to redound to man's glory, and if it is to be truly glorious also for God Himself and His grace, it must raise man so high that *he will move himself as freely, and will have as much control over himself in the supernatural order, as in the natural order.* Only thus does grace prove to be a force that ennobles natural freedom but does

175. Helpful to me in understanding and formulating the difference here is Moreland and Craig, *Philosophical Foundations*, 561–62.

176. On this, see Scheeben, *MC*, 719.

177. This quotation is taken from Scheeben, *A Manual of Catholic Theology*, 274–75.

178. Scheeben, *MC*, 717.

not destroy it. Only thus us the power of God's influence upon man revealed in its full splendor; for God does not rest content with elevating man to a supernatural life, but renders this life truly man's own, *by making the exercise of it dependent on man's own self-determination.* Is man less dependent on God simply because God in His power makes a great achievement partly dependent on man?[179]

Several important points are made here in this passage by Scheeben in his view regarding free will and grace as the two factors which co-operate in the production of every supernaturally salvific act. First, natural freedom, even when incited or drawn by grace, cannot merit saving grace, and hence in that sense man's natural freedom of itself "does not put forth a claim for grace as something due to it or earned by it"[180]—this is a point that I have already sufficiently emphasized above so we need not dwell on it again. Of particular importance, however, is Scheeben's point that the act of freely responding to the invitation of grace, receiving that gift thankfully, is *not* elicited independently of all divine influence. This brings me to Scheeben's second point.

There is a real sense in which man is able to change the direction of his will, but in order to move himself in a proper direction he needs to yield freely to the attraction and excitation of God's prevenient grace. Now, what is needed to elicit or evoke in man a self-active act of freedom to God's grace is more than a natural impulse of the will, but rather a supernatural movement of the will, a supernaturalized freedom, as Scheeben phrases it. This supernaturalized freedom is not a mere *donum superadditum*, a "plus factor," extrinsically and externally related to natural freedom and human nature. That would only be the case if human nature is capable of nothing but sin, with the accompanying loss or destruction of the natural power of the will. In this sense, nature would be the very opposite of grace, and hence cannot be united with grace but has to struggle against grace and be replaced altogether with something new by grace, meaning thereby a supernatural life and a consequent supernaturalized freedom. This is not Scheeben's view of nature and grace, the natural and the supernatural, and hence the relation between natural freedom and supernatural freedom.[181] Thus,

179. Ibid., 718–19; emphasis added.

180. Scheeben, *Nature and Grace*, 326. Says Scheeben, "On the contrary, nature avows that God is not its Debtor but its Lord to whom it belongs entirely; and the consciousness of its own baseness and lack of all claim decides it to submit to the call of His gracious love and to let itself be borne aloft to the heights to which God wishes to raise it" (326–27).

181. Scheeben, *Nature and Grace*, 319–38.

supernatural freedom is not to be construed as a "superstructure" added to natural freedom, but rather as determining and elevating our whole being, including our natural, but fallen, will.

This brings me to Scheeben's third point. Yes, of course a spiritual battle is being waged by God's grace against man's fallen nature, which as corrupted and perverted by original sin and its effects, such as, a disorientation of the will in the sense that it possesses an inclination toward evil, as well as an aversion from God. In that sense, human freedom is situated, given the state of fallen nature, namely, that of Adamic humanity. Yet, the order of creation, in particular, man's nature and natural freedom are such that they remain the Creator's handiwork, good in themselves, and involving then no direct opposition to grace, in spite of their being savagely wounded—not totally depraved or destroyed—by sin. This is a matter of God's mercy, a common grace restraining the power of evil and sin from having its full way with creation. This is why man, in fact, says Scheeben, is still capable of receiving grace and hence of choosing the good in whatever fragmentary fashion.[182] It is not that man is not free to do good in any sense unless it operates under and with the supernatural gifts of grace. No, says Scheeben, "nature is something good, a true, independent factor that is able to achieve some good for itself." And yet, nature in its fallen state is without the power, without supernaturalized freedom, to move itself to God. Thus, the will in its fallen states requires another factor, which is God's supernatural excitation and attraction "for the production of a higher good,"[183] namely, the supernatural good that is the beginning of the will's conversion to God.

In light of this third point we can easily understand why Scheeben says that grace presupposes nature. Grace does not operate in a total vacuum by creating the will anew, an entirely new will that has no continuity with the natural will. Rather, grace heals and perfects and, as Dewey Hoitenga correctly remarks, "restores several specific *exercises* of the will that it lost, like faith in God and love of him as its highest good."[184] That grace restores nature is the basic principle behind Scheeben's point in the following statement: "God does not rest content with elevating man to a supernatural life," as if the grace of regeneration creates the will anew, but rather God's supernatural gifts of grace render "this life truly man's own, by making the exercise of it dependent on man's own self-determination." Thus, the very will that God created, but is now fallen, is enabled by God's grace to exercise

---

182. Ibid., 332.

183. Scheeben, *Nature and Grace*, 320–21.

184. Hoitenga, *John Calvin and the Will*, 119.

again the supernatural gifts of grace, of faith and the love of God that it exercised before the Fall.[185]

On the one hand, then, man is a "subject that is susceptible of grace," says Scheeben, "a subject that is to reach its highest perfection in and through grace, that in the present order of the universe is to expect the satisfaction of all its wants from grace alone, and therefore advances toward grace with ardent yearning, to be enriched, enlightened, and animated by it, and to be introduced by it to the possession of the supreme good."[186] This means that original sin and its effects on human nature and natural freedom are not such that the latter is by nature capable of nothing except malicious, empty self-seeking. Otherwise, nature and freedom would be "in no way a power for good," and hence "grace, as a higher power for good, [could] find in this nature no footing, no point of contact."[187]

On the other hand, human nature and natural freedom do not possess the wherewithal, that is, the grace itself, for the generation of supernatural life and freedom in man. To produce this effect "grace comes from outside as the reflection of divine light which is to illuminate, transfigure, and inflame all rational creatures, in order to transform them into the perfect mage of the divine sun."[188] In other words, Scheeben does hold that God's moving influence upon man is accompanied by "some interior modification of the will by grace."[189] Grace must incline man's will to act by changing him internally, for example, enlightening his mind, renewing his will, giving him a new heart, thinking differently and desiring differently, so that man is impelled to respond to the gift of God's goodness and grace. This supernatural influence, however, is not merely a modification of man's natural freedom, but rather God forms, animates, and fructifies, says Scheeben, man's natural freedom so as to ennoble and transform it.

There is more, man is elevated to a higher sphere of life such that God "produces in us a new, higher nature whereby we are endowed in our interior with a capacity for and an inclination toward supernatural good."[190] This su-

185. As Sokolowski correctly puts this point: "What is good by nature remains good in the setting in which grace is required; its goodness is in fact enhanced, not distorted, by the new context. . . . What is good by nature is not set over against what is good by grace but is integrated into it. And what is good by grace is not simply a matter of convention and arbitrary decision; rather it builds on nature and shares in the reasonableness associated with nature" (God of Faith and Reason, 70, 83).

186. Scheeben, Nature and Grace, 321.

187. Ibid., 308–9.

188. Ibid., 321.

189. Scheeben, MC, 718.

190. Ibid., 721.

pernatural act springs forth from a new principle of life that has taken root within the soul, and hence is not something merely produced from outside. "There is no influence exercised by God on man which is more powerful and thoroughgoing than the movement whereby man's very nature is transformed and elevated, so there is none which more solidly established and more satisfactorily explains the independence and self-activity of the person moved. This movement gives us our supernatural freedom, which enable us to cooperate as actively in supernatural acts as we do by means of our natural freedom in natural acts."[191]

On Scheeben's view, then, grace does not do violence to man's freedom on the one hand, and freedom does not necessarily block the influence of grace. Rather, says Scheeben, grace is the basis of a supernatural freedom, and this freedom reveals the full power and significance of grace.[192] Thus, adds Scheeben, "Both factors are necessary for the generation of supernatural life in man. Both cooperate for the single purpose of uniting man with God and of glorifying God in man as in His image."[193] Given Scheeben's understanding of the natural and supernatural, nature and grace, human nature and natural freedom are not opposed to grace, as we have seen, but rather are influenced and informed by grace, raised up and endowed with supernatural power and freedom, they become an intrinsic part of the supernatural process of salvation. In conclusion, "The beginning is made by grace, which enlightens the mind and moves the will. Under its continued influence the will is endowed with supernatural freedom, and freely gives its consent to the Divine inspiration. The adequate principle of salutary acts is, therefore, neither grace alone nor the will alone, but the will supernaturalized by and freely co-operating with grace."[194]

One more thing: It seems clear that the notion of libertarian freedom, which is the power of contrary choice, variously called formal freedom, or the freedom of indifference, is never able *by itself* to bring about a solution of the real and deepest problem of human freedom, namely, that we do *not* have the wherewithal to enter into life with God. Yes, the freedom of contrary choice, of indifference, makes it possible for man to reject God, but freely rejecting God is a perversion of freedom rather than a manifestation of true freedom. As John Paul II writes, "freedom is not realized in decisions made against God. For how could it be an exercise of true freedom to refuse to be open to the very reality which enables our self-realization? Men and

191. Scheeben, *MC*, 721–22.

192. Ibid., 724.

193. Scheeben, *Nature and Grace*, 322.

194. This quotation is taken from Scheeben, *A Manual of Catholic Theology*, 271.

women can accomplish no more important act in their lives than the act of faith; it is here that freedom reaches the certainty of truth and chooses to live in that truth."[195] I take this to mean that left to itself the freedom of indifference implies that God placed man before a neutral and indifferent choice, suggesting that He gave him the freedom to choose his own way, according to the power of contrary choice, to choose between two possibilities that are placed on an equal footing. But clearly this is not the biblical notion of freedom.[196] As *CCC* rightly puts it, "As long as freedom has not bound itself definitively to its ultimate good which is God, there is the pos-

---

195. John Paul II, *Fides et Ratio*, §13. See also his *Dominum et Vivificantem*, "Man's disobedience . . . always means a *turning away from God*, and in a certain sense *the closing up* of human freedom in his regard" (§37). Guardini, *Freedom, Grace, and Destiny*, who makes the point that what freedom ultimately means really becomes actualized before God. He writes: "The real meaning of freedom . . . cannot in fact be achieved except in dependence upon God. . . . Man's freedom is a created freedom and it therefore develops essentially before God and in subordination to Him—all the more so since God is not only creator of being but also ground of truth and source of good. In consequence, obedience to God does not signify subjection to superior power but the fulfillment of what is right and good" (80–81). In the same vein, see Giussani, *At the Origin of the Christian Claim*, 97: "There may be realities which, to the free conscience, appear to possess psychologically stronger attractions than others which, in an ontological sense, are closer to the final goal [of human existence]. Thus, man feels 'tempted', more attracted to whatever is farthest from his ultimate interest. This, therefore, places him in contradiction with himself; if he does not resist the temptation, his choice is 'evil'. Normally, man alone cannot resist temptation for long. *Jesus Christ is the being who will continually give him back the power to choose well—to be free*: 'If you continue in my word, you are truly my disciples, and you will know the truth, and the truth will make you free' (John 8:31) [italics added]." Similarly, Karl Barth, "The decisive point is whether freedom in the Christian sense is identical with the freedom of Hercules: choice between two ways at a crossroad. This is a heathen notion of freedom. Is it freedom to decide for the devil? The only freedom that means something is the freedom to be myself as I am created by God. God did not create a neutral creature, but his creature. He placed him in a garden that he might build it up; his freedom is to do that. When man began to discern good and evil, this knowledge was the beginning of sin. Man should not have asked this question about good and evil, but should have remained in true created freedom. We are confused by the political idea of freedom. What is the light in the Statue of Liberty? Freedom to choose good and evil? What light that would be! Light is light and not darkness. If it shines darkness is done away with, not proposed for choice! Being a slave of Christ means being free" (*Table Talk*, 37). The *Catechism of the Catholic Church* makes the same point: "Man's freedom is limited and fallible. In fact, man failed. He freely sinned. By refusing God's plan of love, he deceived himself and became a slave to sin. This first alienation engendered a multitude of others. From its outset, human history attests the wretchedness and oppression born of the human heart in consequence of the *abuse of freedom*" (§1739; emphasis added). For an instructive analysis of the problem of man's freedom that is consistent with John Paul's as well as the *Catechism's* teaching, see Berkouwer, *De Mens het Beeld Gods*, 346–89 [310–48].

196. See Deut 30:15–20.

sibility of *choosing between good and evil*, and thus of growing in perfection or of failing and sinning. . . . The more one does what is good, the freer one becomes." Therefore, "The choice to disobey and do evil is an abuse of freedom and leads to 'the slavery of sin' [Rom 6:17]."[197] The biblical perspective makes abundantly clear that this true freedom to choose life is an exclusive fruit of God's grace. For divine grace renders man once again truly free, as God meant him to be and as he restores him. "It is for freedom that Christ has set us free. Stand firm, then, and do not let yourselves be burdened again by a yoke of slavery" (Gal 5:1; see also, Gal 5:13). This is a freedom in and through Christ, as Berkouwer puts it, in which "freedom in Christ is the true freedom of man's humanness."[198] Berkouwer elaborates on this matter.

> Freedom in the New Testament is not a formal possibility or a formal power which enables the believer to choose either of two ways. On the contrary: it is no possibility but rather an actuality, the actuality of being free (cf. Gal. 3:13, 4:4). It is materially qualified and made concrete through the relation to Christ, and is identical with coming into the service of God (Rom. 6:22), with all the wealth that is implied therein. Thus the depth and completeness of this freedom become visible. It does not compete with or limit the acts of God, as if the more powerfully God's acts affect our lives, the narrower our freedom becomes! Or, as if the accentuation of our freedom should limit the power of the grace of God! Anyone who thinks in such categories should realize that the New Testament knows no such opposition. The New Testament pictures it in precisely the opposite way: the more communion with God fills our life, the more free our life becomes.[199]

The question of the relation between libertarian freedom, or the freedom of indifference, and the freedom given by God deserves more discussion than I can give it here. Nevertheless, I think I have said enough about the relation between these two types of freedom for the purpose of this chapter. So, I conclude with a statement from Jesuit theologian, John M. McDermott, "Here, the two types of freedom, indifference and engaged, are reconciled. The finite figure preserves the distance necessary for freedom of indifference; it is possible to reject God. Yet, before the offer of prevenient

---

197. CCC, §§ 1732–33.

198. Berkouwer, *De Mens het Beeld Gods*, 367 [329].

199. Ibid., 359–60 [322].

love [grace], no neutrality is possible: all are called to respond to God. God is present in every exercise of freedom, calling men to Himself."[200]

Points of Catholic Orientation

Although confessional Catholicism affirms the priority or primacy of God's grace, it also affirms man's free response to that gracious initiative without implying that saving grace depends on human merit. "To God, all moments of time are present in their immediacy. When therefore he establishes his eternal plan of 'predestination', he includes in it each person's free response to his grace."[201] A Molinist *cum* Congruist account of the reconciliation of predestination and freedom is within the boundaries of confessional Catholicism's teaching on grace and freedom. This account overcomes the equal ultimacy of reprobation and election on the one hand, in short double predestination, and Pelagianism on the other. Confessional Catholicism rejects universalism: all men are not saved. The atoning work of Christ is sufficient for the salvation of all men, but it is efficacious only for the many. "He [Christ] became the source of eternal salvation for all who obey him" (Heb 5: 9). In its Decree on Justification Trent states: "even though 'Christ died for all' [2 Cor 5:15], still not all do receive the benefit of His death, but those only to whom the merit of His passion is imparted."[202] Confessional Catholicism holds that divine election is about the truth that it is God who takes the free and gracious initiative in salvation, calling men to himself, offering prevenient grace,[203] a preparatory grace relieving man's spiritual inability to respond to God, and enabling him to be open to the justifying and sanctifying grace of God.

---

200. McDermott, rightly remarks in "Faith, Reason, and Freedom," 307–32, and at 332.

201. CCC, §600.

202. Denzinger, §1523.

203. See Shelton, *Prevenient Grace*.

CHAPTER 4

Barth on Predestination and Its Implications

The election of grace is the sum of the Gospel—we must put it as pointedly as that. But more, the election of grace is the whole of the Gospel, the Gospel *in nuce*. It is the very essence of all good news.[1]

How can we have assurance in respect of our own election except by the Word of God? And how can even the Word of God give us assurance on this point if this Word, if Jesus Christ, is not really the electing God, not the election itself, not our election, but only an elected means whereby the electing God—electing elsewhere and in some other way—executes that which He has decreed concerning those whom He has—elsewhere and in some other way—elected?[2]

Introduction

ACCORDING TO THE MOST widespread view of the matter today in recent theology, Karl Barth's views on predestination are the most prominent and influential, not to say controversial, in the Reformed tradition. In this chapter, I propose to treat Barth's views. I make no pretense at examining the full scope of his vast writings on predestination and the voluminous secondary literature his views have spawned. This limited consideration of Barth is, accordingly, structured as follows. First, I consider Barth's critique of the "equal ultimacy" of election and reprobation, otherwise known as an equal symmetry or parallelism of divine operation between election and reprobation in the Calvinistic doctrine of the *decretum absolutum*.[3] Second,

1. Barth, *CD* II.2, 11.
2. Ibid., 117.
3. Ibid., 13–15.

I examine Barth's account of the relationship between predestination and Christology, chiefly, the understanding of Jesus Christ as the ground (i.e., cause and foundation) of divine election, and, in particular, the transformation, not rejection, of "double predestination" in terms of his Christology, namely, the atoning work of Christ. Barth holds there to be an asymmetrical relation between election and reprobation in his doctrine of election. Christ is not only the electing God; but at the same time he is the elect man whose atoning work brings about the election of all humanity. Christ is also the reprobate man because he takes on the sin of all humanity, God's wrath as well His judgments upon himself. In this way, Barth synthesizes the double predestination of classical Calvinism in the person of Christ, who is at the same time the Elect and Reprobate One.

Finally, I will examine the implications of Barth's views of predestination that is concentrated in Christ for three matters: the biblical antithesis between belief and unbelief, human freedom and grace, and, last but not least, universalism. The Bible speaks decisively of the seriousness and eternal consequences of unbelief, and hence of the call to faith as a decisive choice. Can Barth's doctrine of election in which all men are chosen in Christ and in whom the rejection of all men has been borne do justice to the role of faith's decision for partaking of salvation? Does Barth endorse a libertarian or compatibilist notion of free will? Finally, Barth's views on election and atonement have been interpreted—an interpretation that he resisted—as a version of universalism, namely, that all men will be saved. It is particularly with respect to its implications on these three matters, especially the question of Barth's universalism, that I will consider two of his earliest, most prominent and respected critics: Berkouwer and Balthasar, but also his most recent critic, Oliver Crisp.[4]

The Equal Ultimacy of Election and Reprobation

In the concluding section of chapter 3 on Calvin's view of predestination, I argued that his view—the classical Reformed doctrine of predestination—raises the question as to why God decrees to save some and not others. This

---

4. Regarding Berkouwer's *De Triomf Der Genade in De Theologie van Karl Barth*, Barth has this to say in *CD* IV.3.1: "I can only join in according it the recognition which it has won in many different circles on account of its wide range of knowledge and reading, its perspicuous and penetrating mode of exposition and the sharpness and balance of its criticism." In the preface to IV.2, Barth referred to Berkouwer's *De Triomf Der Genade* as a "great book on [Barth] and the *Church Dogmatics*." He adds, "For all its reservations and criticisms this work is written with such care and goodwill and Christian *aequitas*" (xii).

question arises particularly because the decree of reprobation includes the preterition, or an act of God's sovereign will to pass over by divine grace some men. Calvin says, "God chooses some, and passes over others according to his own decision. . . . God has always been free to bestow his grace on whom he wills."[5] What is, then, the basis for his unequal treatment of people? Berkhof is right that "those who are passed by are condemned on account of their sin."[6] But they are not passed over by divine grace *because* of their sin. For that would make reprobation conditional, contingent upon the sins of men. But men are the proximate—meaning thereby that man's own fault is the ground of reprobation—and not the ultimate cause of their reprobation. Hence, the question arises regarding their moral responsibility for their preterition. Says Berkhof, "Preterition is a sovereign act of God, an act of His mere good pleasure, in which the demerits of man do not come into consideration. . . . The reason for preterition is not known by man. It cannot be sin, for all men are sinners. We can only say that God passed by some for good and wise reasons sufficient unto Himself. On the other hand the reason for condemnation is known; it is sin. Preterition is purely passive, a simply passing by without any action on man, but condemnation is efficient and positive. Those who are passed by are condemned on account of their sin."[7] Again, condemned because of their sin, but not passed over because of it; so, then, how are they morally responsible for their preterition?

Reformed theologians Van Genderen and Velema suggest a possible answer to this question: "When it is said in the Canons of Dort, 1.15,[[8]] that

5. Calvin, *Institutes of the Christian Religion*, 3.22.1.

6. Berkhof, *Systematic Theology*, 116–17.

7. Ibid. Charles Hodge seems to take a different position: "It is a clearly revealed Scriptural principle that where there is no sin there is no condemnation." Here he agrees with Berkhof. But there seems to be a crucial difference: "Therefore, anyone who has been foreordained to death must have been regarded as already sinful." He adds, "It seems plain from the whole argument of the apostle in Romans 9:9–21 that the 'mass' out of which some are chosen and others left is the mass of fallen men . . . . Since all are equally unworthy and guilty, God has mercy on one but not on another according to His own good pleasure. . . . Moreover, in texts like Romans 1:24, 26, and 28, reprobation is declared to judicial, founded upon the sinfulness of its objects. Otherwise it could not be a manifestation of the justice of God." He explains: "It is not compatible with these divine attributes [of mercy and justice] that men should be foreordained to misery and eternal death before they apostatized from God. If they are passed by and foreordained to death *for* their sins, it must be that in predestination they are contemplated as guilty and fallen creatures" (*Systematic Theology*, 326).

8. Canons of Dort, 1.15: "What peculiarly tends to illustrate and recommend to us the eternal and unmerited grace of election is the express testimony of sacred Scripture that not all, but some only, are elected, while others are passed by in the eternal decree; when God, out of His sovereign, most just, irreprehensible, and unchangeable good pleasure, has decreed to leave in the common misery into which they have willfully

some have been bypassed by God's eternal election, then that is how it is intended," namely, "reprobation is a shadow that accentuates the light." They add, "It is grace to receive grace. This is the heart of the doctrine of double predestination. Therefore this doctrine does not give us reason to be pessimistic. 'Solely on the basis of justice and merit, we would all have been lost. But since it is a matter of grace, there is hope for the most miserable person' (Bavinck)."[9] Geerhardus Vos also attempts an answer to this vexing question.

The Apostle Paul, says Vos, held two settled and, as it turns out, irreconcilable points: "a) The free, sovereign ordination of God, which does not derive its grounds from the activity of man. B) The full responsibility of man toward his Creator." Vos adds, "The apostle has not made an attempt to reconcile these two with each other logically. Nor may we make such an attempt. . . . Both sides must remain next to each other, unreconciled for our thinking but each in its full right." Vos concludes that attempting a logical reconciliation is "rationalistic exegesis."[10] Furthermore, Vos says, "Where God from persons completely alike takes the one and leaves the other, there it is indispensable that He is the source of grace. This indication must be received by us thankfully."[11] But Vos's concluding point, as well as the answer of Van Genderen and Velema, is unpersuasive since there is no hope for those whom God has passed over "on the basis of his entirely free, most just, irreproachable, and unchangeable good pleasure." To Vos, I say, how can I receive thankfully that which I cannot understand as an act of grace? Clearly, the ones passed over will never receive the grace to respond to the Gospel. Surely, this gives men reason to be pessimistic, rendering the doctrine of predestination as something that is fallen under a shadow. And surely, *pace* Van Genderen and Velema, on this view, "reprobation [does] accompany election as shadow follows light."[12]

This is precisely where Barth's rejection of the classical doctrine of equal ultimacy of election and reprobation is pointedly heard, echoing 2 Cor 1:19–20: "For the Son of God, Jesus Christ, who was preached among

---

plunged themselves, and not to bestow upon them saving faith and the grace of conversion; but, permitting them in His just judgment to follow their own ways, at last, for the declaration of His justice, to condemn and punish them forever, not only on account of their unbelief, but also for all their other sins. And this is the decree of reprobation, which by no means makes God the Author of sin (the very thought of which is blasphemy!), but declares Him to be an awful, irreprehensible, and righteous Judge and Avenger thereof" (Dennison, *Reformed Confessions*, 4:124–25).

9. Genderen and Velema, *Concise Reformed Dogmatics*, 235.

10. Vos, *Reformed Dogmatics*, 1:116–17.

11. Ibid., 116.

12. Genderen and Velema, *Concise Reformed Dogmatics*, 235.

you by us . . . was not 'Yes' and 'No', but in him it has always been 'Yes'. For no matter how many promises God has made, they are 'Yes' in Christ. And so through him the 'Amen' is spoken by us to the glory of God." In sum, divine election in Jesus Christ is in essence the proclamation of a Yes and not a No.

> The truth of the doctrine of predestination is first and last and in all circumstances the sum of the Gospel. . . . It is itself evangel: glad tidings; news which uplifts and comforts and sustains. . . . It is not a mixed message of joy and terror, salvation and damnation. . . . It does not proclaim in the same breath both good and evil, both help and destruction, both life and death. It does, of course, throw a shadow. We cannot overlook or ignore this aspect of the matter. In itself, however, it is light and not darkness. We cannot, therefore, speak of the latter aspect in the same breath. In any case, even under this aspect, the final word is never that of warning, of judgment, of punishment, of a barrier erected, of a grave opened. We cannot speak of it without mentioning all these things. The Yes cannot be heard unless the No is also heard. But the No is said for the sake of the Yes and not for its own sake. In substance, therefore , the first and last word is Yes and not No.[13]

This passage is representative of Barth's decisive opposition to "every theological construction which makes election the *obscure* and *hidden* background of the dispensation of grace revealed in history."[14] As Barth himself puts it: "There is, then, no background, no *decretum absolutum*, no mystery of the divine good-pleasure, in which predestination might just as well be man's rejection."[15] Rather, it is the revelation of God's love and grace for sinners in Jesus Christ in whom, as Berkouwer rightly notes, "God has from eternity turned His face graciously to men in the act of election."[16] This makes it impossible to detach divine election from the revelation in Christ. Says Barth:

> As against that, we must take as our starting-point the fact that this divine choice or election is the decision of the divine will which was fulfilled in Jesus Christ, and which had as its goal the sending of the Son of God. . . . We must not seek the ground of this election anywhere but in the love of God, in His free love— otherwise it would not be His—but still in His love. If we seek it

---

13. Barth, *CD* II.2, 10.

14. Berkouwer, *De Triomf Der Genade in De Theologie van Karl Barth*, 84 [90].

15. Barth, *CD* II.2, 177.

16. Berkouwer, *De Triomf Der Genade in De Theologie van Karl Barth*, 85 [91].

elsewhere, then we are no longer talking about this election. We are no longer talking about the decision of the divine will which was fulfilled in Jesus Christ. We are looking beyond these to a supposedly greater depth in God (and that undoubtedly means nothingness, or rather the depth of Satan). What takes place in this election is always that God is for us; for us, and therefore for the world which was created by Him, which is distinct from Him, but which is yet maintained by Him.[17]

On the one hand, then, Barth rejects "equal symmetry" between election and reprobation grounded on a prior *decretum absolutum*, and this without Christ, because it presents us with an abstract doctrine of election in that there is no mention of God's love and grace.[18] Indeed, he says, "The concept which so hampered the traditional doctrine [of election] was that of an equilibrium or balance in which blessedness was ordained and declared on the right hand and perdition on the left."[19] On the other hand, Barth says "If the *decretum absolutum* is the last possible word concerning the basis of divine predestination, then it is most dangerous to think of God as the One who sees and plans and achieves His own glory in the foreordaining of certain number of individuals to heaven and of a certain number

17. Barth, *CD* II.2, 26. Elsewhere Barth says, "Of what avail is it to exhort us, ad did the Reformers, and after them orthodox Protestants of both confessions, that we must acquiesce in the hidden decision of that ultimate authority, respect it as a secret? Of what avail is it for the Calvinists to protest that as God's decision it is based on grounds which are just and adequate although beyond our comprehension, or for the Lutheran to assist us with the comforting assurance that this decision is determined by the general loving-kindness of God towards us? If it is not true that Jesus Christ Himself is for us the electing God, then all these attempts at consolation point us elsewhere that to the Word of God. We are directed to a different mystery from that of the cradle and cross of Christ, a different revelation from that of His resurrection" (116–17).

18. Balthasar, *Theology of Karl Barth*, 185. Balthasar describes Barth's view: "The flaw in most of the previous doctrines of election was a failure to contextualize election as part of God's relationship to Christ. Previous theories misconstrued the christological basis that is so clearly witnessed to in the Bible. Instead, they regarded election as a purely individual happening between an abstract (and therefore terrifying) absolute God and the isolated creature viewed atomistically" (175). See also, Berkouwer, *De Verkiezing Gods*, 163–69 [142–47].

19. Barth, *CD* II.2, 180. Richard A. Muller challenges claims like those of Barth who suggests that Christ was replaced with predestination—"as if an eternal divine decree often identified with the secret or hidden will of God could have been an epistemological foundation" (*Christ and the Decree*, x–xi. His major thesis is that "Polanus, Perkins, and their contemporaries sought to ground both the doctrine of the decrees and the doctrines concerning the economy of salvation in Christ" (176–77).

of individuals no less irresistibly to hell."[20] Barth explains why then so many
recoil in horror at this view:

> And it is most dangerous to believe that for this purpose God
> created the world, and permitted and to that extent willed the
> existence of sin and the devil and then of course, in line as it
> were with these prior acts, accomplished the work of redemp-
> tion. It is most dangerous to believe that, in virtue of His over-
> all determination, this redemptive work must itself mean both
> calling and also hardening, that it must be a means of election
> and also a means of rejection—and both with that unshakeable
> fixity, both in that indestructible equilibrium, both as the fulfill-
> ment of that secret good-pleasure of God which is wholly syn-
> onymous and completely closed in upon itself. It is quite true . . .
> [that] . . . God threatens to take on the appearance of a demon,
> and in the light of this fact we may well understand the horror
> with which Roman Catholics, Lutherans, Arminians and even
> many of the Reformed themselves recoiled from the doctrine.[21]

In light of Barth's Christological concentration of divine election in the full
and exclusive light of God's self-revelation in Christ and his Cross, there is
no going behind it to an eternal decree that is two-edged.[22] The love of God
in Christ, the Elect One, in whom all humanity is elected, is the foundation
of God's decree of election.[23]

---

20. Ibid., 150.

21. Ibid.

22. Balthasar, *Theology of Karl Barth*, 177.

23. As Crisp correctly notes, "Barth opts for a supralapsarian view of the divine
decrees. But he resists the traditional assimilation of supralapsarianism to a *decretum
absolutum* couple with a doctrine of double predestination. Instead, he weds his doctrine of Christ, the Elect and Reprobate One, to supralapsarianism. This results in God's
decreeing the salvation of humanity in and through Christ the Elect human being" (*Deviant Calvinism*, 162–63). There is also the position of infralapsarian. "Supra- and infralapsarianism are the two major views I Protestant orthodoxy concerning the logical
ordering of the divine decrees" (162n14). Adds Crisp, "Very roughly, supralapsarianism
is the view according to which the decree to elect some number of humanity logically
precedes the decree to create a world of free creatures. So, the ordering of the divine
decrees in this way of thinking typically something like this: election, creation, fall,
redemption. The infralapsarians look the view that the decree to elect some number of
humanity to salvation must be logically consequent to the decree to create a world of
free creatures. Hence, in their way of thinking, the divine decrees were thought to be
organized in the following sequence: creation, fall, election, redemption" (184). I will
return to a discuss of supra- and infralapsarianism, and to Barth's critical commentary
on these positions, in the next chapter on Bavinck and Berkouwer.

From first to least the Bible directs us to the name of Jesus Christ. It is in this name that we discern the divine decision in favor of the movement towards this people, the self-determination of God as Lord and Shepherd of this people, and the determination of this people as "his people, and the sheep of his pasture" (Ps. 100). . . . As all these things happened under this name, the will of God was done. And according to God's self-revelation attested in Scripture, it is wholly and utterly in these happenings that we are to know what really is the good-pleasure of His will, what is, therefore, His being, and the purpose and orientation of His work, as Creator of the world and Controller of history. There is no greater depth in God's being and work than that revealed in these happenings and under this name. For in these happenings and under this name He has revealed Himself.[24]

Is Barth fair to classical Reformed orthodoxy? In this connection, it is instructive to consider Berkouwer's push back against Barth's charge that the essence of the Reformed doctrine of election is the doctrine of the abstract *decretum absolutum* such that it "isolates election from the love of God in Christ." Of course Berkouwer acknowledges that "this abstraction has often threatened the solace and comfort of election, so that a serious warning is quite valid."[25] He adds, "We can and must listen to his warning not to separate God's sovereignty from His love, and His election from Jesus Christ, for in view of the many dangers and misunderstandings that have become evident in the course of history this warning remains necessary."[26] This is particularly the case since that isolation when taken as a starting-point

---

24. Barth, *CD* II.2, 53–54.

25. Berkouwer, *De Verkiezing Gods*, 179 [154]. The American Orthodox Presbyterian philosophical theologian, Cornelius van Til, rejects this claim of Berkouwer, and hence Berkouwer's apparent agreement with Barth. Van Til says, "According to classical Reformed theology this God in himself elects or reprobates individual men in themselves apart from Christ" ("Has Karl Barth Become Orthodox?," 160). Says Berkouwer, "He [Van Til] adds to this amazing statement the following: '*Even when some Reformed theologians* (emphasis mine!) connect Christ with their doctrine of election, their Christ is himself subjected to the ideas of a God in himself and a man in himself.'" Berkouwer, then, remarks critically: "Apart from Van Til's historically inaccurate statement (even when some. . .), it is impossible in *this* manner to refute Barth's claim. In any case, Van Til would have to consider Ephesian 1:4, wherein it is spoken of a connection between Christ and election (cf. 2 Tim 1:9). In Van Til's pushback against Barth there is a complete misunderstanding of the relationship of Christ and election in Reformed theology" (Berkouwer, *De Triomf Der Genade in De Theologie van Karl Barth*, 284n100; this note has been dropped from the English translation of Berkouwer's Barth book).

26. Ibid., 187 [161].

makes "it . . . impossible afterwards to connect the two."[27] Still, he adds, "classical Reformed theology has been aware that this interpretation of election depreciates Biblical testimony."[28]

Berkouwer makes three relevant points in response to Barth's charge. First, the sovereignty of God's grace in divine election was at stake in the historical context wherein Luther opposed Erasmus, Calvin opposed Pighius and Catholicism, and Dort opposed the Remonstrants. It wasn't about propounding "the concept of an abstract sovereign decree by a *potentia absoluta*."[29] Berkouwer is right about this first point, particularly with respect to Calvin since he rejects the fiction of the "absolute power" of God, meaning thereby the teaching about God that "separates God's power from His righteousness,"[30] indeed, from the fullness of God's Holy nature. Second, the sovereignty of God's gracious election in Christ when pitted against the doctrine of libertarian free will "may not be interpreted as determinism."[31] I already discussed this second point in the chapter on Calvin and so I won't say anything more about it here.

Third, understanding the historical context of these controversies regarding divine election is necessary. Say Berkouwer, "In polemics, the emphasis on sovereignty has sometimes given the impression that concern lay with sovereignty as such. However, the actual intent came repeatedly to the fore, and it is a testimony to the power of Scriptures that here the dangers of abstraction (sovereign election without the love of God) were seen and repeatedly conquered."[32] To illustrate this last point Berkouwer turns to the Canons of Dort showing that they do not omit speaking of the relation of divine election to Christ and the love of God. For example, in *CD*, I, 7, this canon states: "Election is the unchangeable purpose of God, whereby, before the foundation of the world, He has out of mere grace . . . in Christ, whom He from eternity appointed the Mediator and Head of the elect and the foundation of salvation." Berkouwer rightly notes, "Clearly there is no thought here of an abstract decree of election, for in these words our eyes are simultaneously directed to the election of God and to the Mediator, while elsewhere [in the Canons] there is mention of the 'gracious election'

27. Ibid., 179 [154].

28. Ibid., 179 [154–55].

29. Ibid., 179 [155].

30. Calvin, *Institutes of the Christian Religion*, III.23.2; idem, *Concerning the Eternal Predestination of God*, 179.

31. Berkouwer, *De Verkiezing Gods*, 179 [155].

32. Ibid.

(CD, I, 10), of the 'eternal and unmerited grace of election' (*CD*, 1, 15), and of the 'free grace of election' [*CD*, 1, 18]."[33]

Furthermore, the Canons speak of the "sovereign counsel and most gracious will and purpose of God the Father" (*CD*, 2, 8), but without detaching this counsel from the grace and love of God claiming that it "originates in the eternal love of God for the elect" (*CD*, 2, 9). In sum, concludes Berkouwer, "This shows how careful one must be if he wishes to accuse orthodoxy of overemphasizing the sovereign power of God in election. Precisely because the concept of *potentia absoluta*—against which Calvin warned . . . and which he called an invention—is so dangerous, the orthodox doctrine of election has always contained a warning against it. Therefore, it is simply irresponsible to brush aside Reformed attempts to show the harmony of election with the grace and the love of God in Jesus Christ, and to suggest that this 'arbitrary power' actually underlines the Reformed view."[34] I think Berkouwer is right about the Canons in respect of election, but much less so in respect of reprobation.

With respect to the latter reprobation is "merely and solely the good pleasure of God." In *CD*, 1, 6, we read: "That some receive the gift of faith from God, and others do not receive it proceeds from God's eternal decree." Article 15 states that "not all, but some only, are elected, while others are passed by in the eternal decree." As I have already had occasion to remark critically, those who are passed by are justly condemned by virtue of their sins, according to the Canons, but they are not passed over by divine grace *because* of their sin. For that would make reprobation conditional, contingent upon the sins of men. But men are the proximate cause—meaning thereby that man's own fault is the ground of reprobation, as *CD* 1, 5 puts it—and not the ultimate cause of their reprobation. Given this unconditioned negative reprobation that is present in the Canons, how, then, can we do justice to *CD*, 2, 5, which teaches the "kerygmatic universality" (to borrow a term from Berkouwer[35]) of the gospel to all men, calling them all to repentance and conversion: "Moreover, the promise of the gospel is that whosoever believes in Christ crucified shall not perish, but have eternal life. This promise, together with the command to repent and believe, ought to be declared and published to all nations, and to all persons

33. Ibid., 167 [145].

34. Ibid., 168 [146]. Barth concurs, "There can be no doubt that all the orthodox Reformed trends of that period [the sixteenth and seventeenth century] shared the same earnest desire to serve the main interest of Calvinistic dogma—to extol the free grace of God and the sovereignty of the freely gracious God as the beginning of all Christian truth and of all Christian apprehension of truth" (*CD* II.2, 143).

35. Berkouwer, *De Verkiezing Gods*, 289 [240].

promiscuously and without distinction, to whom God out of His good pleasure sends the gospel."

Moreover, the cause of unbelief is man rather than "any defect or insufficiency in the sacrifice offered by Christ upon the cross" (CD, 2, 6). The latter is intrinsically sufficient for the sins of all men. And it is said that "As many as are called by the gospel are unfeignedly called. For God has most earnestly and truly declared in His Word what is acceptable to Him, namely, that those who are called should come unto Him. He also seriously promises rest of soul and eternal life to all who come to Him and believe" (CD, 3/4, 8). The seriousness of preaching the calling of the gospel is underscored with the simultaneous emphasis that "It is not the fault of the gospel, nor of Christ offered therein, nor of God who calls men by the gospel and confers upon them various gifts, that those who are called by the ministry of the Word refuse to come and be converted" (CD, 3/4, 9). But given God's sovereign act of preterition, and its unconditionality, as Berkouwer himself notes, "many have wondered how it was possible to emphasize the seriousness [of preaching the gospel] and whether it was endangered because of the presupposition of the Canons."[36] The presupposition alluded to here is the differentiation between those who are elected, while others are passed by, that proceeds from God's eternal decree.

This brings us back to Barth's description of double predestination as a "double divine decision from all eternity, i.e., a decision with two parallel sides [of divine election and rejection]."[37] His decisive opposition stems from his conviction that in divine election "God has truly loved the world." He adds: "In this form and this form alone of the tiding of the divine decision made in Jesus Christ are glad tidings directed to all men, directed indeed to the whole world."[38] In sum, "In the light of this election the whole of the Gospel is light. Yes is said here, all the promises of God are Yea and Amen (2 Cor 1:20)."[39]

In other words, divine election may only be properly understood when it is election of God *in Christ*. Barth appreciates that Reformed theology posits a deep connection between election and Christ.[40] So, he

36. Ibid., 262 [220].

37. Barth, *CD* II.2, 14.

38. Ibid., 27.

39. Ibid., 11.

40. Berkouwer concurs with Barth. See Berkouwer, *De Verkiezing Gods*, 154 [135]: "Hence the question whether Christ must be regarded as the foundation or as the executor of the election of God was raised long before Barth thought of making it a critical point of Reformed doctrine. It had to be that way, for the questions concerning Christ and election stood from the very beginning in the light of clear and concrete

acknowledges that his Christological concentration is not really innova-
tive in describing the "name of Jesus Christ as the basis of the doctrine of
election."[41] The biblical center in matters of predestination is Jesus Christ.
"Indeed, Calvin . . . tried to show that Christ is the *speculum electionis* to
the extent that in the incarnation of the divine Word in the man Jesus of
Nazareth we have to do with the prototype and essence of, as it were, all
divine electing and human election."[42] But in what sense is divine election
in Christ?[43] St. Paul tells us God has elected "us in him [Christ] before the
foundation of the world, that we should be holy and without blame before
him in love, having predestined us to adoption as sons by Jesus Christ, in
accordance with his pleasure and will" or that "In him we have redemption
through his blood" and "In him we were also chosen, having been predestined according to the plan of him who works out everything in conformity
with the purpose of his will" (Eph 1: 4–5, 7, 11). St. Paul speaks elsewhere
of God's power "who saved us, and called us with a holy calling, not according to our works, but according to his own purpose and grace, which was
given us in Christ Jesus before the beginning of time" (2 Tim 1:9). Clearly,
these passages suggest that the election of God may not be detached from
the revelation in Christ. Are we then to understand Christ as the ground,
that is, the cause and foundation of election?

In response to this question, Bavinck says that "Christ is indeed the
cause or foundation of election inasmuch as election is realized in and
through him. He is also the meritorious cause of salvation, which is the purpose of election, as well as the mediator and head of the elect." So, Bavinck
thinks that a good interpretation can be made to view Christ as the cause
of election. Still, he resists asserting that Christ is the "actual, moving, and
meritorious cause" of the decree election.[44]

Several possibilities are considered inadequate understandings of
the meaning of "in Christ" and hence of viewing Christ as the cause and
foundation of election. One such possibility, which was also identified and
rejected by Bavinck, is to hold that divine election is motivated or caused by

Scriptural testimony."

41. Barth, *CD* II.2, 60.

42. Ibid., 63. Berkouwer concurs, but says about Calvin: "It certainly is not correct
to say that Calvin did not see the question [of election and Christ], although it may
be asked whether Calvin always answered that question clearly and adequately" (*De
Verkiezing Gods*, 180 [156]).

43. Helpful reflections on this question may be found in Berkouwer, *De Verkiezing
Gods*, 150–99 [132–71]. Also very instructive is Oliver Crisp, "The Election of Jesus
Christ," 34–55.

44. Bavinck, *GD* II, 365 [401].

Christ's atoning work in the sense, as Berkouwer puts it, "that He [Christ] persuaded the Father—who at first was not thus inclined—with His suffering and His death to a forgiving attitude and to an actual granting of salvation." Berkouwer rightly retorts: "This view flagrantly contradicts Scripture, which teaches that God in Christ was reconciling the world unto Himself (2 Cor 5:19), and that it is precisely the coming of Christ, sent by the Father, which is the revelation of God's love (1 John 4:9)."[45] In sum, in Bavinck's words, "Christ is a gift of the Father's love, which precedes the sending of the Son (John 3:16; Rom 5:8; 8:29; 2 Tim 1:9; 1 John 4:9). The Son did not move the Father to love; electing love arose from the Father Himself."[46]

Furthermore, Barth dismisses as inadequate the idea that Christ is simply the executor, that is, the means of realizing a decree established apart from him, making the sole cause of election God's free good-pleasure which motivates the will of God and not something outside of God himself.[47] On this view, "we have a principle which has priority over the person and work of Jesus Christ, so that Jesus Christ is to be understood only as the mighty executive organ of the divine will of grace, and [then] only a secondary place can be given to christological thinking."[48] In particular, Berkouwer asks in trying to gain clarity of Barth's objection. "Is there a *prior* decree of election which is afterward brought to realization in the work of Christ in the sense that Christ becomes the *means* for its effectuation? Is there a decree of election and reprobation which, in the final analysis, precedes the revelation

---

45. Berkouwer, *De Verkiezing Gods*, 155 [136]. See also for an in-depth treatment, Berkouwer, *Het Werk van Christus*, 277–380 [253–342].

46. Bavinck, *GD* II, 365 [401]. Reformed theologian John Murray concurs: "It would be wholly false to conceive of the work of Christ as bringing inducements to bear upon the Father so that he is thereby constrained to be loving and gracious. . . . The atonement is the provision of the Father's love and grace" (*Redemption Accomplished*, 57). Other biblical passages in the New Testament making clear that the cross of Christ is not only the supreme revelation of the love of God, but also proceeds from the merciful initiative of God's redeeming love "established in all its depth and profoundness before the foundation of the world in Christ" (Berkouwer, *De Verkiezing Gods*, 155 [136]): "In this is love, not that we loved God but that he loved us and sent his Son as an atoning sacrifice for our sins" (1 John 4:10). "For God so loved the world that he gave his own and only Son, that whoever believes in him shall not perish but have eternal life" (John 3:16). "But God demonstrates his own love for us in this: While we were still sinners, Christ died for us" (Rom 5:8). "But because of his great love for us, God, who is rich in mercy, made us alive with Christ even when we were dead in transgressions—it is by grace you have been saved" (Eph 2:4–5). And again: "In this the love of God was manifested toward us, that God has sent His only begotten Son into the world, that we might live through Him" (1 John 4:9).

47. Barth, *CD* II.2, 118.

48. Barth, *CD* IV.3.1, 175.

in Christ and is *independent* from it?"[49] If it were so, that is, if the saving work of Christ were subordinate to a pre-temporal decree of God, then the assertion that divine election is not only to be known in Jesus Christ but also that Christ's merit is the ground of election, does not "contain the first and last word on this matter, the word by which we must hold conclusively, and beyond which we must not conceive of any further word." Then there would be another basis of election that is "outside Jesus Christ," with then the sole cause of election being God's will and good pleasure.

One may begin to get a sense here that Berkouwer is right: "one must avoid the dilemma between saying that Christ is either the foundation of election or only the executor of a decree established apart from Him."[50] Why? Because—adds Berkouwer—"there is no discrepancy for [St.] Paul between 'in Christ' and 'through Christ'. The 'instrumental' and the 'comprehensive' are one in Christ."[51] In other words,

> The power and evidence of [St.] Paul's testimony have safeguarded the Church and theology at decisive moments against a devaluation of God's election to such a fixedness of decree, leading to an abstract sovereignty, which is a sovereign election that is only later realized in the work of Christ. Scripture does say "through Christ" with respect to salvation, and there is no need at all to balk at the word "instrumental"—as when Paul writes that we are reconciled with God through (*dia*) the death of His Son (Rom 5:10)—provided that the word "instrumental" is stripped of all impersonal connotations, and that we think of God's acts as being in Christ who is the author of our salvation (Heb 2:10).[52]

Returning to Barth in particular, there arises the question as to the proper sense in which Christ's atoning work is the ground, the cause and foundation of election, rather than just "being merely a consequence of the divine decree to elect."[53] In this connection, Barth asks, "must the doctrine [of election] as such be related to this basis and this basis only?"[54] That is, he continues, "Must it take account only of this basis? In this matter of election are we noetically to hold by Christ and Christ alone because ontically there is no election and no electing God outside Him?" In other words, Barth is asking

49. Berkouwer, *De Triomf Der Genade in De Theologie van Karl Barth*, 89 [95].

50. Berkouwer, *De Verkiezing Gods*, 157 [137].

51. Ibid., 172 [149].

52. Ibid., 171–72 [149].

53. Crisp, "The Election of Jesus Christ," 37.

54. Barth, *CD* II.2, 65.

here whether Christ is the ground of election not only *noetically*, namely, for saving knowledge, but also *ontically* foundational such that there is nothing *behind* Jesus Christ, the incarnate Word, as the ground of election.[55] Barth's answer is "yes."

Otherwise: "If . . . the higher authority [of election] is the general choice of the Father, and the election of Jesus Christ is only His election in execution of the decree of the Father, if the order is not to be understood as meaning that the divine election is as such the election of Jesus Christ, the passive and active election of the Son of God to be the Son of Man, and in Him the election of those who believe in Him, then it is inevitable that we should enquire concerning the decision of this higher authority, and certainly we cannot be described as elected 'in Christ', but at very best only 'for Christ'. Jesus Christ is not any sense, then, the *fundamentum electionis*."[56] But that is precisely what Jesus Christ is, according to Barth, the foundation of election. Alternatively, asks Barth, "Or is it rather the case that we are to understand this assertion merely as an impressively stated pastoral rule, a practical direction regarding the attitude which, *rebus sic stantibus*, we ought to adopt towards this matter of we are not to be plunged into doubt or despair?" Barth elaborates:

> Is it the case, in fact, that behind the pastoral (and in some measure the historico-psychological) truth that God's election meets us and is revealed to us in Jesus Christ, there stands a higher truth which, for the sake of prudence and charity, must be withdrawn from the practical usage of the Church, a truth which cannot be denied or entirely suppressed, but which is so dangerous that it must be covered over and kept out of the reach of the curious like a kind of poison? Is it the case, according to this higher and dangerous truth concealed for practical purposes in the background, while, Christ is indeed the medium and instrument of the election by which factually we must hold fast, yet the electing God Himself is not Christ but God the Father, or the triune God, in a decision which precedes the being and will

55. Berkouwer, *De Triomf Der Genade in De Theologie van Karl Barth*, 88 [94]: "What is the [ontic] *ground* of the fact that *noetically* (i.e. for the knowledge and certainty of salvation) we must look to Jesus Christ alone?" Berkouwer also remarks on Barth's view who held that "It was not seen that the epistemological ground of election (the mirror of election in its pastoral significance) was also its 'Realgrund'" (*De Triomf Der Genade in De Theologie van Karl Barth*, 98 [104]). Barth answers, "Only if Jesus Christ is the true and incontestable basis of our election can He be the basis of our knowledge of the election . . . and only then can we have any assurance of our election" (*CD* II.2, 128).

56. Barth, *CD* II.2, 119.

and word of Christ, a hidden God, who as such made, as it were, the actual resolve and decree to save such and such men and to bring them to blessedness, and then mater made, as it were, the formal or technical decree and resolve to call the elect and to bring them to that end by means of His Son, by means of His Word and Spirit? Is it the case, then, that in the divine election as such we have to do ultimately, not with a divine decision made in Jesus Christ, but with one that is independent of Jesus Christ and only executed by Him?[57]

In other words, if Christ is not the ontic ground of election because behind the revelation of God in Christ is "*the final*, deepest, and hidden will which constitutes the real decision," then, says Berkouwer about Barth's view, "it is . . . no longer possible to escape Calvin's '*decretum horribile*'. Is it really possible to comfort pastorally when 'in that hidden place the really decisive word with respect to our salvation has been spoken'?"[58] "How, then, can we attain to any sure knowledge of God or ourselves? How, then, can we have any sure knowledge of this relation? How can we be certain that it is good to be so fully in the hands of God as we are proclaimed to be when we assert that God elects?"[59] The brief answer to this question is that it is only in Jesus Christ, who is the way, the truth and the life, and hence the first and last word concerning our election, that we find both a saving knowledge and the certainty of our salvation. Berkouwer nicely summarizes: "The ontic foundation is not wanting in the noetic and consoling message; it is found in election, 'elected in Christ'."[60] Thus, concludes Barth, "If the predestination is identical with the election of Jesus Christ, there can be no question of any confusion between God's living predestinating, deciding and electing, and the vacillation of a *potentia absoluta* or a game capriciously played by the Deity with its creatures."[61]

In conclusion of this section and in transition to the next, we may sum up Barth's view of the dogma of predestination as consisting "in the assertion that the divine predestination is the election of Jesus Christ."[62] There is no divine decree behind Jesus Christ electing some men and rejecting others by a sheer act of will, a decree that Christ is an executor of in his work

57. Barth, *CD* II.2, 65.

58. Berkouwer, *De Triomf Der Genade in De Theologie van Karl Barth*, 90 [95]. The quote within the quote is from Barth, *CD* II.2, 69.

59. Barth, *CD* II.2, 66.

60. Berkouwer, *De Verkiezing Gods*, 172 [149].

61. Barth, *CD* II.2, 201.

62. Ibid., 108–9.

of redemption. And in this work of redemption Barth seeks to transform the traditional Reformed doctrine of double predestination by focusing it on the person of Christ alone. Therefore, says Barth, "in obedience and thankfulness we can only rejoice at the double predestination of God. This interpretation of double predestination stands or falls, of course, with the view that the divine predestination is to be understood only within the election of Jesus Christ."[63] It is to that interpretation that I now turn.

Double Predestination

Balthasar rightly states that, according to Barth, "It is only in Christ that we can speak of such a thing as 'double predestination.'"[64] According to Barth, the concept of election refers to Jesus Christ as the subject and object of election. It has a "double reference—to the elector and to the elected. And so, too, the name of Jesus Christ has within itself the double reference: the One called by this name is both very God and very man. Thus the simplest form of the dogma may be divided at once into the two assertions that Jesus Christ is the electing God, and that He is also elected man."[65]

With respect to Christ himself as the subject of election—Christ is the Elect One—Barth directs our attention to the Son of God in his election as the Incarnate Word in "oneness with man, and in fulfillment of God's covenant with man."[66] Of course it isn't about his election as the Eternal Son of the Father. In particular, Barth directs our attention to the Scriptural witness that refers to Christ himself as the Elect One: "I know whom I have chosen" (John 13:18); "You did not choose me, but I chose you and appointed you" (John 15:16); "But I chose you out of the world" (John 15:19). Thus, Christ himself is the subject of election, but, says, Barth, he elects together with the Father and the Holy Spirit, and hence Barth underscores the Trinitarian character of election. "He is also Himself the Elector, and in that first instance His election must be understood as active. It is true that as the Son of God given by the Father to be one with man, and to take to

63. Ibid., 183.

64. Balthasar, *Theology of Karl Barth*, 177. On the question of double predestination, Bruch McCormack has written, "[t]aken on the most superficial level, the revolution which Barth effected in the Reformed understanding of predestination was to replace Calvin's version of double predestination with a universal election. . . . Jesus Christ is the Subject of election and its Object, the electing God and the elected human. That is the fundamental thesis which shapes the whole of Barth's doctrine of election." From "Grace and Being," 92–110, and at 93.

65. Barth, *CD* II.2, 109.

66. Ibid., 109.

Himself the form of man, He is elected. It is also true that He does not elect alone, but in company with the electing of the Father and the Holy Spirit."[67] Still, of particular importance to Barth, is that "He does elect,"[68] and hence is precisely the subject of election.

But Christ is not only the Elect One, the subject of election, the electing God. He is also the Elected Man, and hence the Reprobate One in so far as God elects Jesus at "the head and in the place of all others." Why? Because: "The wrath of God, the judgment and the penalty fall, then, upon Him." In other words, "In this one man Jesus, God puts at the head and in the place of all other men the One who has the same power as Himself. . . . The rejection which all men incurred, the wrath of God under which all men lie, the death which all men must die, God in His love for men transfers from all eternity to Him in whom He loves and elects them, and whom he elects at their head and in their place. . . . Indeed, the very obedience which was exacted of Him and attained by Him was His willingness to take upon Himself the divine rejection of all others and to suffer that which they ought to have suffered. . . . He, the Elect, is appointed to check and defeat Satan on behalf of all those that are elected 'in Him', on behalf of the descendants and confederates of Adam now beloved of God."[69] This substitution is at the core of Barth's understanding the Christian doctrine of redemption.

Does Barth's view mean that all men are elect because of Christ the Elect who is at the head and place of all others? It certainly seems so. Barth says: "His election is the original and all-inclusive election; the election which is absolutely unique, but which in this very uniqueness is universally meaningful and efficacious, because it is the election of Him who Himself elects. Of none other of the elect can it be said that his election carries in it and with it the election of the rest. But that is what we must say of Jesus Christ when we think of Him in relation to the rest."[70] Of crucial importance here in understanding Barth's claim regarding the scope of Christ's atoning work is the distinction between sufficiency and efficacy or efficient.[71] It is one thing to

67. Ibid., 110. See elsewhere: "The subject of this decision is the triune God—the Son of God no less than the Father and the Holy Spirit. And the specific object of it is the Son of God in His determination as the Son of Man, the God-Man, Jesus Christ, who is as such the eternal basis of the whole divine election" (Barth, *Church Dogmatics*, II.2, 116; see also, 123).

68. Ibid.

69. Ibid., 23.

70. Ibid., 124.

71. I draw again on the distinctions Crisp employs in explaining the atonement of Christ, but this time in "On Karl Barth's Denial of Universalism," 116–30, and at 120. See also, Crisp, "Hypothetical Universalism," in *Deviant Calvinism*, 175–211.

say—and to say it is biblically justified—that Christ's death atones sufficiently for the sins of all men, but it is another thing to take that to mean that Christ's atoning death is both sufficient and efficacious for all men.

As Crisp explains that latter position: "That is, Christ's death is not simply potentially universal in scope (it could save all humanity); it is actually universal in scope (all humanity are saved by it). It might be argued that Barth's position is merely that the atonement is universal in scope, not effectiveness. However, that Barth's position does involve a universally efficient atonement can be seen from passages such as the following: 'There is no-one who does not participate in Him [Christ] in His turning to God. There is no-one who is not . . . engaged in this turning. There is no-one who is not raised and exalted with Him to true humanity. 'Jesus Christ lives, and I with Him.'"[72] So, the atoning work of Christ is universally efficacious, but then what are the implications of that for rejection?

Barth explains: "That the elected man Jesus had to suffer and die means no more and no less than that in becoming man God makes Himself responsible for man who became His enemy, and that He takes upon Himself all the consequences of man's action—his rejection and his death. This is what is involved in the self-giving of God. This is the radicalness of His grace."[73] In this connection, Barth stresses that Jesus Christ as the first of Elect is the *only* man who is rejected, given that he is at the head and in the place of all others as the Reprobate One. That is, God's wrath, judgment, and punishment fall "upon His own Son, upon Himself: upon Him, and not upon those whom He loves and elects 'in Him'; upon Him, and not upon the disobedient."[74] Barth elaborates:

> For all those, then, whom God elects in His Son, the essence of the free grace of God consists in the fact that in this same Jesus God who is the Judge takes the place of the judged, and they are fully acquitted, therefore, from sin and its guilt and penalty. Thus the wrath of God and the rejection of Satan and his kingdom no longer have any relevance for them. On the contrary, the wrath of God and the rejection of Satan, the free course of divine justice to which God Himself has subjected Himself on their behalf, has brought them to freedom. In the One in whom they are elected, that is to say, in the death which the Son of God has died for them, they themselves have died as sinners. And that means their sanctification, separation and purification for

72. Crisp, "On Karl Barth's Denial of Universalism," 120. The quote within the quote is from Barth's CD II.2, 271.

73. Barth, CD II.2, 132.

74. Ibid., 132.

> participation in a true creaturely independence, and more than
> that, for the divine sonship of the creature which is the grace for
> which from all eternity they are elected in the election of the
> man Jesus.[75]

Thus, double predestination for Barth is no longer about eternal life for some and eternal damnation for others. As Barth says, "No eternal covenant of wrath corresponds on the one side to the eternal covenant of grace on the other."[76] It is about election and reprobation in and concerning Christ alone. "To the election of Jesus Christ there belongs, then, elected man as well as the electing God. There are two sides to the will of God in the election of Jesus Christ. And since this will is identical with predestination, from the very first and in itself it is a double predestination."[77] There is, then, election and rejection. In the election in Christ "God has given to man the former: election, salvation and life; for Himself, however, He has chosen the second, rejection, damnation and death." Significantly, the Elected One has elected our rejection. "He made it his own. He bore it and suffered it with all its most bitter consequences. For the sake of this choice and for the sake of man He hazarded Himself wholly and utterly. He elected our suffering (what we as sinners must suffer towards Him and before Hum and from Him). He elected it as His own suffering. This is the extent to which His election is an election of grace, and election of love, an election to give Himself, an election to empty and abase Himself for the sake of the elect."[78] Thus, if Christ is the Reprobate One, having taken our sins and all its consequences upon himself, does that mean that no man is reprobate?

Yes it does. Barth says: "With Jesus Christ the rejected can only *have been* rejected. He cannot *be* rejected any more."[79] Elsewhere he adds: "They may indeed conduct themselves as rejected, but even if they deserved it a thousand times they have no power to bring down on themselves a second time the sword of God's wrath now that it has fallen."[80] As Crisp puts it, "We might say that Christ stands in our place as the Reprobate One so that we do not have to be cast away from God's presence."[81] Thus, because of this exchange at the cross, all those who are in Christ Jesus—which is all men—are no longer under condemnation and rejection. Indeed, this is Barth's view:

75. Ibid., 133.
76. Ibid., 450.
77. Ibid., 172.
78. Ibid., 174.
79. Ibid., 453.
80. Ibid., 349.
81. Crisp, "Barthian Universalism?," in *Deviant Calvinism*, 151–74, and at 163.

When we say that God elected as His own portion the negative side of the divine predestination, the reckoning with man's
weakness and sin and inevitable punishment, we say implicitly
that this portion is not man's portion. In so far, then, as predestination does contain a No, it is not a No spoken against
man. In so far as it does involve exclusion and rejection, it is
not the exclusion and rejection of man. In so far as it is directed
to perdition and death, it is not directed to the perdition and
death of man. . . . The justification of the sinner in Jesus Christ
is the content of predestination in so far as predestination is a
No and signifies rejection. On this side, too, it is eternal. It cannot be overthrown or reversed. Rejection cannot again become
the portion or affair of man. The exchange which took place on
Golgatha, when God chose as His throne the malefactor's cross,
when the Son of God bore what the son of man ought to have
borne, took place once and for all in fulfillment of God's eternal
will, and it can never be reversed. There is no condemnation—
literally none—for those that are in Christ Jesus. For this reason
faith in the divine predestination as such and *per se* means faith
in the non-rejection of man, or disbelief in his rejection. Man
is not rejected. In God's eternal purpose it is God himself who
is rejected in His Son. The self-rejecting of God consists, the
giving and sending of His Son is fulfilled, in the fact that He is
rejected in order that we might not be rejected.[82]

So, for Barth, rejection is no longer truly possible; indeed, Barth calls it an
"impossible possibility"[83] for a man to be reprobate.[84] In fact, says Barth,

---

82. Barth, *CD* II.2, 176–177. Similarly, elsewhere in Barth's work, *Credo*, 93–94:
"If God Himself in Jesus Christ bears the *curse* that must fall upon the transgressors of
His law, then it really *is* borne; then there can be no thought of our bearing it again and
further. Then we are acquitted according to the law, yes, declared righteous. For if God's
curse no longer falls on us, what can we be—there is no third possibility—what can we
be in His sight, and that means in reality, but righteous? If God Himself in Jesus Christ
suffers the punishment that our existence would have to incur, then that mean that He,
this Other, has sacrificed His existence for us. . . . If God will not punish us because the
punishment is over and done with, then that means that we may now live as those who
have been released by Him and who are therefore His own. Finally, if, without ceasing
to be God, God in Jesus Christ entered into the ordeal, if Jesus Christ descended into
hell and thereby actually doubted Himself as to His being God and man in one, what
else can we take that to mean that He did that also for us and so relieved us of it? It is
not necessary that we go to hell."

83. Barth, *CD* IV.3.2, 463.

84. Barth, *CD* II.2, 177–78: "There is neither cause nor authorization for the fear of
possible rejection. For in God's self-giving in Jesus Christ it is clear that rejection does
not concern us because God willed that it should concern Himself. We are not called

unbelief itself "has become an objective, real and ontological impossibility"[85] in view of the omnipotence of the divine decision fully manifested in Christ and His Cross.

Of course Barth is not suggesting by any means that there are no god-less men, rejecting God, isolating themselves over against God. Rather, what he is suggesting is that unbelief has become an impossibility because it is unable to revoke the truth of the divine act in Christ's atoning work, namely, that God's saving grace is sufficient and efficient for *all* men.[86] Barth says, "Because Jesus Christ takes his place, He takes from him the right and possibility of his own independent being and gives him His own being. With Jesus Christ the rejected can only *have been rejected*. He cannot *be* rejected any more."[87] Thus, "It is clear that the idea of the 'individual', in this decidedly negative sense of our context, involves the crisis and the limit of all 'individualism'. Let the 'individual' take warning! . . . As the 'individual' of his own intention and judgment, he now belongs, indeed, to the mass, to the *massa perditionis*. This is the mass of men isolated over against God."[88] Still, since no man is outside the scope of the divine act in which Christ atoned for the sin of all men by taking our place as the Reprobate One, man's "isolation is void in Jesus Christ."[89]

Yes, the objectivity of this divine act such that salvation is understood by Barth, as I noted above, to be both sufficient and effective for all men is such apart from and prior to any subjective reception of it. Still, it isn't that God doesn't require a human response; rather, it is that even without that subjective response a man's elected status is not void. Barth explains the meaning of the radical substitution of Christ:

> This, then, is the message with which the elect community (as the circumference of the elect man, Jesus of Nazareth) has to approach every men—the promise, that he, too, is an elect man. It is fully aware of his perverted choice. It is fully aware of his godlessness. . . . It is fully aware, too, of the eternal condemnation of the man who is isolated over against God, which is unfailingly exhibited by the godlessness of every such man. . . . It knows of

upon to bear the suffering of rejection because God has taken this suffering upon Himself. And if it is the case that in the divine self-giving in Jesus Christ we can and should believe in the divine predestination, then we can believe in our own non-rejection and the non-rejection of all men."

85. Barth, *CD* IV.1, 747, and also 746.

86. Berkouwer, *De Triomf Der Genade in De Theologie van Karl Barth*, 263 [266].

87. Barth, *CD* II.2, 452.

88. Ibid., 318.

89. Ibid.

> the wrath and judgment and punishment of God in which the
> rejection of the man isolated over against God takes its course.
> . . . It knows that God, by the decree He made in the beginning
> of all His works and ways, has taken upon Himself the rejection
> merited by the man isolated in relation to Him; that on the basis
> of this decree of His the only truly rejected man is His own Son;
> that God's rejection has taken its course and been fulfilled and
> reached its goal, with all that that involves, against this One, so
> that it can no longer fall on other men or be their concern. The
> concern of all other men is still the sin and guilt of their god-
> lessness—and it is serious and severe enough. Their concern is
> still the suffering of the existence which they have prepared for
> themselves by their godlessness (in the shadow of that which
> the One has suffered for them)—and it is bitter enough to have
> to suffer this existence. Their concern is still to be aware of the
> threat of their rejection. But it cannot now be their concern to
> suffer the execution of this threat, to suffer the eternal damna-
> tion which their godlessness deserves. Their desire and their
> undertaking are pointless in so far as their only end can be to
> make them rejected. And this is the very goal which the god-
> less cannot reach, because it has already been taken away by the
> eternally decreed offering of the Son of God to suffer in place of
> the godless, and cannot any longer be their goal.[90]

In conclusion of this section and in preparation for the next, it is important to underscore, as this passage shows, the problem of man's response
in Barth's doctrine of election, and the tension that, according to Berkouwer, "arises from the relationship between *universal election* and *human
decision*."[91] In other words, says Barth, "With the divine No and Yes spoken
in Jesus Christ the root of human unbelief, the man of sin is pulled out. . . .
For this reason unbelief has become an objective, real and ontological impossibility and faith an objective, real and ontological necessity for all men
and for every man. In the justification of the sinner which has taken place in
Jesus Christ these have both become an event which comprehends all me."[92]
Regarding, then, Barth's claim that unbelief is ontologically impossible, does
Barth draw out its implication to the point of teaching universalism?

    If unbelief cannot nullify God's decision in Christ's saving act, can
Barth do justice to the "seriousness with which the New Testament takes the

---

90. Ibid., 319.

91. Berkouwer, *De Triomf Der Genade in De Theologie van Karl Barth*, 285 [288].

92. Barth, *CD* IV.1, 747.

human response to the proclamation [?]"[93] Given Barth's view of election in which it is both sufficient and efficacious for the actual salvation of all, what can Barth mean in saying that faith is an objective, real and ontologically necessary for all men? Why is faith still necessary or even significant given that all men are actually saved? "Triumph of election—and unbelief still?" That is precisely one of the key questions I will address in the next section. Berkouwer explains:

> This can only testify to that sin of man for whom Jesus Christ died vicariously. But *this* joyful message does *not* prejudice the *open* situation of the gospel proclamation. Barth refuses to permit the concrete significance of the proclamation to disappear behind the fact of the universal divine election. On the contrary, he wishes to incorporate it *in* this fact. For unbelief is powerless and is only the recurring witness to that guilt which makes grace necessary. Therefore man is place ever anew in the *open situation* of the proclamation concerning the triumph of election, the triumph of the mercy of God.[94]

But does Barth's doctrine of election leave any room at all open for that possibility alluded to in the concluding sentence of this above passage, given the universalism that seems to be at work in that doctrine?[95] "Jesus Christ is not only *one* of the elect of God but rather is *the* Elected One, next to whom and beside whom there is none other, but only the reprobate. And even in relation to all of them, the rejected of God, even for them he alone is *the* Elected One, *the* object of God's gracious choice, so that they all need not have to be rejected of God."[96] No wonder that Barth has been found teaching universalism. Still, Barth pushes back against the charge of universalism: "It is not legitimate to make the limitless many of the elect in Jesus Christ the totality of all men."[97] Barth here seems to be suggesting, according to Balthasar, "For Barth, the Church is an *open* space, a dynamic concept from the outset . . . . And for as long as the Church is yet underway, the 'many' must be understood as referring, not to a determinate, but to a dynamic and open number."[98] There is a tension here in Barth's thought on election that I shall consider in the next section.

93. Berkouwer, *De Triomf Der Genade in De Theologie van Karl Barth*, 267 [270].

94. Ibid., 115 [122].

95. Balthasar, *Theology of Karl Barth*, 186.

96. Barth, *CD* II.2, 387.

97. Ibid., 467.

98. Balthasar, *Theology of Karl Barth*, 183.

Faith, Freedom and Universalism

Freedom

According to Barth, "Christian faith is a *free* human act."[99] What does Barth understand by human freedom?[100] On the one hand, Barth seems to reject libertarian free will. He says, "The whole idea of a possibility of faith confronted by that of unbelief, the whole conception of man as a Hercules at the crossroads able to choose between faith and sin (and therefore unbelief), is a pure illusion. Whatever may be the possibility of faith this Hercules has always already chosen unbelief."[101] It seems clear that, according to Barth, the notion of libertarian freedom, which is the power of contrary choice, the ability either to do something or not, variously called formal freedom, or the freedom of indifference, is never able *by itself* to bring about a solution of the real and deepest problem of human freedom, namely, that we do *not* have the wherewithal to enter into life with God. I emphasize "by itself" since Barth affirms that "man's God-given freedom is choice, decision, [and]

99. Barth, *CD* IV.1, 757; emphasis added; see also 769.

100. Helpful in getting at Barth's understanding of freedom is his article, "The Gift of Freedom," 75–83. Also helpful is *CD* III.2 and IV.1. Instructive discussions of Barth on this matter are Gunton, "Barth, The Trinity, and Human Freedom," 316–30; Webster, "Freedom in Limitation," 99–123; Couenhoven, "Karl Barth's Conception (s)," 239–55; and McFarlane, "Barth and Kant."

101. Barth, *CD* IV.1, 746. Barth is fond of this image of "Hercules at the crossroads." According to Couenhoven, "In speaking of Hercules at the crossroads, Barth is presumably referring to the classical theme immortalized in paintings and engravings of Hercules, accosted by females figures representing Virtue and Vice, and faced with a choice concerning which path to follows. He is, of course, literally correct that this is a pagan theme; clearly, however, he is making more than a historical observation" (in "Karl Barth's Conception (s)," 247n26). Barth also uses this image in "The Gift of Freedom," 76: "God does not put man into the situation of Hercules at the crossroads. . . . It would be a strange freedom that would leave man neutral able equally to choose, decide, and act rightly or wrongly! What kind of power would that be!" See also, Karl Barth, "The decisive point is whether freedom in the Christian sense is identical with the freedom of Hercules: choice between two ways at a crossroad. This is a heathen notion of freedom. Is it freedom to decide for the devil? The only freedom that means something is the freedom to be myself as I am created by God. God did not create a neutral creature, but his creature. He placed him in a garden that he might build it up; his freedom is to do that. When man began to discern good and evil, this knowledge was the beginning of sin. Man should not have asked this question about good and evil, but should have remained in true created freedom. We are confused by the political idea of freedom. What is the light in the Statue of Liberty? Freedom to choose good and evil? What light that would be! Light is light and not darkness. If it shines darkness is done away with, not proposed for choice! Being a slave of Christ means being free" (*Table Talk*, 37).

act."[102] That is, "Faith is the human activity . . . with a profound spontaneity and a native freedom."[103] Again, "God's election evokes and awakens faith, and meets and answers that faith as a human decision. The electing God creates for Himself as such man over against Himself. And this means that for his part man can and actually does elect God, thus attesting and activating himself as elected man."[104]

So, there is a real sense in which election is freely chosen; we are not simply passive, a stone, as it were. For Barth, "To the creature God determined, therefore, to give an individuality and autonomy, not that these gifts should be possessed outside Him, let alone against Him, but for Him, and within His kingdom; not in rivalry with His sovereignty but for its confirming and glorifying. But the sovereignty which was to be confirmed and glorified was the sovereignty of His love, which did not will to exercise mechanical force, to move the immobile from without, to rule over puppets or slaves, but willed rather to triumph in faithful servants and friends, not in their overthrow, but in their obedience, in their own free decision for Him."[105] Barth continues: "There is, then, a simple but comprehensive autonomy of the creature which is constituted originally by the act of eternal divine election and which has in this act its ultimate reality."[106] He adds, "The Word of God is not spoken merely to a psycho-physical individual in time which is simply the functioning organ of another author or element in his movement, but to a subject who is himself at all points the author, accomplishing this movement [of his own being and act in time] freely, independently and spontaneously."[107]

Still, on the other hand, this spontaneous and native freedom of man, in Barth's view, is not an end in itself, is not a "free-standing, quasi-absolute reality,"[108] but rather it is a determinate freedom, an ordered freedom, a responsible freedom. Thus, it is a self-determination that takes the form, says Barth, of "responsibility . . . decision . . . obedience . . . action."[109] "Man is, and is human, as he performs this act of responsibility, offering himself as the response to the Word of God, and conducting, shaping, and expressing

102. Barth, "The Gift of Freedom," 76.

103. Barth, CD IV.1, 744.

104. Barth, CD II.2, 186.

105. Ibid., 187.

106. Ibid., 186.

107. Barth, CD III.4, 329–30. See also, CD III.3, 87: "There can be no doubt that with an autonomous reality God does give to man and to all His creatures the freedom of individual action."

108. Webster, "Freedom in Limitation," 112.

109. Barth, CD II.2, 510.

himself as an answer to it. He is, and is man, as he does this."[110] Yes, but he "becomes free and is free by choosing, deciding, and determining himself in accordance with the freedom of God. The source of man's freedom is also its yardstick. Trying to escape from being in accord with God's own freedom is not human freedom."[111] So, the freedom of contrary choice, of indifference, in Barth's terms, of spontaneity and native freedom, makes it possible for man to reject God, but freely rejecting God is a perversion of freedom rather than a manifestation of true freedom. "It is the free but necessary work of faith." "Faith is the human activity . . . with a profound spontaneity and a native freedom, but also with an inevitability in face of His [Christ's] actuality. The reverse is equally true: with an inevitability, but with a native freedom."[112] Barth explains:

> We do not compromise its [faith's] character as a free human act if we say that as a free human act—more genuinely free than any other—it also has its origin in the very point on which it is also orientated. It is also the work of Jesus Christ who is its object. It is the will and decision and achievement of Jesus Christ the Son of God that it takes place as a free human act that man is of himself ready and willing and actually begins to believe in Him. The two things are not a contradiction but belong together. If the Son makes us free, we are free indeed (Jn 8:36). The Son makes a man free to believe in Him. Therefore faith in Him is the act of a right freedom, not although but just because it is the work of the Son.[113]

Clearly, then, Barth thinks that man's freedom—his spontaneity and native freedom, indeed, his autonomy—is compatible with divine determination. Yes, the sinner can reject God, but then he is no longer free because he does something that is contrary to "what it means to be truly human." He is, indeed, alienated, not only "from God," but also "from himself and from his true nature." That is why the gift of freedom, says Barth, "awakens the receiver to true selfhood and new life."[114] But this gift, real freedom, as it were, includes, but goes beyond the freedom of choice; it includes it because "he chooses, decides, and determines himself to be this person," and "makes man free to be not more and not less than human," but it also goes beyond it

110. Barth, *CD* III.2, 175.

111. Barth, "The Gift of Freedom," 76–77.

112. Barth, *CD* IV.1, 744.

113. Ibid., 744–45.

114. Barth, "The Gift of Freedom," 78, 76, respectively.

by including a "measure of determination by that which we choose,"[115] says Barth, "to realize in his life the divine intention of true humanity inherent in the gift." In short, "human freedom is the God-given freedom to obey."[116] Barth put it as follows:

> The Word of God, demanding hearing and obedience, presupposes a productive subject, a being capable of making for himself a new beginning with his being, conduct and action (irrespective of his co-existence and connection with other beings), of planning something new and his very own, corresponding to what he has heard from God. . . . The Word of God as it is spoken to man thus constitutes his knowledge of himself as such a free subject of his life.[117]

Since human freedom is not completely indeterminate such that it stands in a neutral position before two alternatives, then, we can't say yes or no to God. Does Barth, then, hold to a compatibilist view of human freedom, and, if so, in what sense?

Faith and Unbelief

In several instructive articles on Barth's doctrine of election, Oliver Crisp raises the question regarding what Barth understands by free will.[118] Is he a compatiblist or a libertarian regarding free will? He defines them as follows:

> C1. According to compatibilism, freedom of choice means able to actualize what one desires. More precisely, a subject S is free with respect to any action A if S desires to perform A.

> L1. According to libertarianism, freedom of choice means being able to refrain from an action. More precisely, a subject S is free with respect to an action A if S could have refrained from performing A.[119]

In this connection, Crisp distinguishes what he calls a "strong free will" (L1), from a "weak will" (C1). He elaborates:

---

115. Gunton, "Barth, The Trinity, and Human Freedom," 325.

116. Barth, "The Gift of Freedom," 79, 80.

117. Barth, *CD* III.4, 330.

118. Crisp, "Barthian Universalism?," in *Deviant Calvinism*, 151–74; "On Karl Barth's Denial of Universalism," 116–130, and "The Letter and the Spirit of Barth's Doctrine of Election," 53–67.

119. Crisp, "On Karl Barth's Denial of Universalism," 123.

According to libertarianism, a person is said to be free with respect to a particular action if that person is able to refrain from choosing that course of action and his or her free act is not caused or otherwise necessitated by an antecedent act (either temporally or logically antecedent) either of the moral agent themselves, or of some outside cause or agency. And, to the extent that the person is free to do a particular action, he or she is morally responsible for the choice made. According to compatibilism, human beings are free with respect to a particular action to the extent that they are not hindered from choosing what they want to do, or prevented from choosing what they want to do. Such actions, unlike libertarian free acts, are caused either by prior choices of the moral agent (not necessarily temporality prior choices and perhaps including several different causal factors that give rise to the choice made), or the moral agent in concert with some other causal factor or agency, such as God. And, to the extent that that person is free to do a particular action, he or she is morally responsible for acts he or she commits even if they have no alternative option open to them.[120]

Arminian or Pelagian theories of free action—and corollaries such as the conceptions of "prescientia" and the "scientia media"—are libertarian in character in respect of the question of divine election. Says Barth, "Divine election is made with due consideration of the conduct of men as foreseen by God from all eternity, i.e., of the use which, according to God's foreknowledge, they make of their freedom, whether in belief or unbelief, whether in obedience or disobedience."[121] On this view, the atoning work of Christ is sufficient for the salvation of all men but only *potentially* effective. Unlike Barth, who affirms a universal election such that this work is both sufficient and effective for the salvation of all men, the view here of the atonement is a one of possibility and realization, of objectivity and subjectivity. Therefore, on this view, faith is just a possibility, one of two, unbelief being the other, and hence Jesus is presented to us as one of two alternatives, an offer.

Barth sides with the Canons of Dort on this matter rejecting,[122] as Berkouwer puts it, "that the *possibility* of salvation was obtained for all through Him. The objection of the Canons of Dort was to the doctrine of *potential reconciliation*, according to which human decision must lead to the realization of this possibility."[123] "This election was not founded upon

120. Crisp, "The Letter and the Spirit of Barth's Doctrine of Election," 59.
121. Barth, *CD* III.2, 70.
122. Ibid., 79.
123. Berkouwer, II, *De Wederkomst van Christus*, 220 [411].

foreseen faith and the obedience of faith, holiness, or any other good quality or disposition in man, as the prerequisite, cause, or condition on which it depended; but men are chosen to faith and the obedience of faith, holiness, etc."[124] So, too, Barth argues that Arminian or Pelagian theories of free action and their corresponding views of election reject the basic interest of the Reformation, namely, the defense of the sovereign and free grace of God against every view that makes the effectiveness of Christ's atoning work dependent on man's acceptance, or as Berkouwer puts it, "on his free will, belief, and the obedience of faith."[125] The basic reason why Barth rejects Arminian or Pelagian theories of libertarian freedom is because he includes all humanity in the election of Christ.[126] Furthermore, according to Barth, man's human nature is such that "the personal reason and power of proud man [is] entangled in his pride." He adds, "How can he procure it [a new freedom in Christ and therefor his true freedom] for himself when in his proud heart and the proud being determined by it he is not the one who can have it or win it or even know about it? How can he jump over his own shadow, which is to break free from him as the one who casts this shadow?" In short, "how can sinful man—there is an obvious *contradiction in adiecto*—believe?"[127]

In a word, he cannot because, says Barth, "It is not for man to choose first whether he himself will decide (what an illusion!) for faith or for unbelief."[128] Indeed, apart from grace, and hence God's gift of freedom, man will necessarily choose sin, unbelief. In short, sinners lack freedom, but those who are in Christ are free indeed. Therefore,

> Seeing we have to do with sinful man, the mere 'possibility' of faith would obviously be confronted by the other possibility which is the only true possibility, that of the man who in his own reason and strength simply goes with the current in the opposite direction. Who is to choose between them? Who is the man who will choose aright and therefore choose the possibility of faith? The only man who enters into the picture at all is the man who not only can go in the opposite direction, but actually does go in that direction, who not only has the possibility of choosing the sin of pride, but is a proud sinner from the crown of his head to the sole of his foot. . . . In the rivalry between a possible faith

124. Canons of Dort, I, 9; II, 3, 6.

125. Berkouwer, *De Verkiezing Gods*, 276 [231].

126. Crisp, "The Letter and the Spirit of Barth's Doctrine of Election:," 60.

127. Barth, *CD* IV.1, 746.

128. Ibid., 746.

and actual sin, faith will always come off second best. The rivalry
will have ended in favor of sin even before it has begun.

Moreover, "The whole idea of a possibility of faith confronted by that of
unbelief, the whole conception of man as a Hercules at the crossroads able
to choose between faith and sin (and therefore unbelief), is a pure illusion.
Whatever may be the possibility of faith, this Hercules has always already
chosen unbelief."[129] So, for Barth, election is not conditional upon the individual concerned choosing to be saved. Again, this cannot be Barth's view
because he includes all men in the election of Christ. "His election is the
original and all-inclusive election; the election which is absolutely unique,
but which in this very uniqueness is universally meaningful and efficacious,
because it is the election of Him who Himself elects. Of none other of the
elect can it be said that his election carries in it and with it the election of
the rest. But that is what we must say of Jesus Christ when we think of Him
in relation to the rest."[130]

Barth, then, rejects libertarian freedom—Herculean freedom!—such
that we would be free to choose evil, sin, unbelief, as one of two possibilities,
the other being faith. Again, "Faith does not stand or hover somewhere in
face of the possibility of unbelief (which is not a possibility but the solid
actuality of sinful man). It [faith] is not itself a mere possibility, grand and
attractive but impotent and useless like all mere possibilities. It [faith] has
itself the character of an actuality, an actuality which is absolutely superior
to that other actuality [sin, unbelief]. It is not a mere chance, or proposition.
It is not for man to choose first whether he himself will decide (what an
illusion!) for faith or for unbelief. Faith makes the solid actuality of unbelief
an impossibility."[131] In other words, according to Barth, unbelief is an *impossible* matter in view of the omnipotence of God's grace "In the death of Jesus
Christ." He adds, "Both the destroying and the renewing have been revealed
as valid for all men in His resurrection from the dead." Therefore, "Jesus
Christ is not simply one alternative or chance which is offered to man, one
proposition which is made to him. He is not put there for man's choice, à
prendre ou à laisser [take it or leave it]. The other alternative is, in fact, swept
away in Him."[132]

In this connection, Barth speaks of the "necessity of faith" because
in Jesus Christ, who is the object of faith, that necessity is included. Why?

129. Ibid.
130. Barth, *CD* II.2, 124.
131. Barth, *CD* IV.1, 746.
132. Ibid., 747.

Because the possibility of unbelief is "rejected, destroyed, and set aside." Barth explains:

> But this necessity of faith does not lie in man. It does not lie even in the good nature of man as created for God, let alone in his being as the sinner who in denial and perversion of his good nature has turned away from God and in so doing deprived himself already of the possibility of faith. It does not even lie in faith in itself and as such. It is to be found rather in the object of faith. It is this object which forces itself necessarily on man and is in that way the basis of his faith. This object is the living Lord Jesus Christ, in whom it took place, in whom it has taken place for every man, in whom it confronts man as an absolutely superior actuality [reality], that his sin, and he himself as the actual sinner he is, and with his sin the possibility of his unbelief, is rejected, destroyed and set aside, that he is born again as a new man of obedience, who now has the freedom for faith, and only in that faith his future. In his destroying and renewing of man as it took place in Jesus Christ there consists the necessity of faith, because beyond this destroying and renewing there remains for sinful man only faith in the One in whom it has taken place. . . . For this reason unbelief has become an objective, real and ontological impossibility and faith an objective, real and ontological necessity for all men and for every man.[133]

So, when man chooses unbelief as a "possibility" as an alternative to faith, his choice is an impossible choice, an unfree choice, indeed, Barth says an illusion, given what God has accomplished, once for all, completely, and irrevocably, in Jesus Christ. But, then, as Berkouwer asks, "How can man's decision still be 'decisive' when it is preceded by God's *a priori* decision? Does faith not know that it lives only because of God's decision and that it can only accept this decision? How, then, can unbelief be *the* decision? Who can withstand *His* verdict?"[134]

Balthasar raises a similar point: "Barth basically could not explain how it was possible for a human being not to have faith. If one takes seriously Barth's presuppositions, unbelief can only be the refusal to admit the truth of the faith that is already present. Man of course has the power to say No to God, but his No can never be strong enough to annul God's Yes to man or even to call it into question. In Christ, God has triumphed for all and

---

133. Ibid.

134. Berkouwer, *De Triomf Der Genade in De Theologie van Karl Barth*, 263 [267]. I must add here that I am deeply indebted to Berkouwer for my understanding of what Barth means by saying that unbelief is an objective, real, ontological impossibility.

over all, and all human beings are what they are through Christ. . . . And
so the unbelief of sinners can only persist as a rebellion against the truth of
God that has *already* been conquered and proven to be in vain."[135] What,
then, is unbelief? Given the radical substitutionary atonement of Christ,
says Berkouwer, "This substitution can be *denied*, but it cannot be *undone*.
. . . Unbelief is a denial of the election in Christ, it is denial of the definitive
'God-for-us' and of the fact that God has taken *our* rejection upon Himself and borne it away."[136] In particular, adds Berkouwer, "unbelief does not
have its roots in not-being-elect, but it is the denial of *being-elect*."[137] Now,
given that *all* men are elected in Christ, the question may be raised whether
the implication of rejecting Christ is such that one may, ultimately, not be
saved? If so, election is conditional, but election is unconditional—all men
are elect-in-Christ—because Christ's atoning work is universally unconditional. Can, then, the atonement be opted out of by those who are already—
even if not-known—elect-in-Christ? That seems to be suggested by Barth:

> If he [the believer] believes in Him, he knows and grasps his own
> righteousness as one which is alien to him, as the righteousness
> of this other, who is justified man in his place, for him. He will
> miss his own righteousness, he will fall far from it, if he thinks
> he can and should know and grasp and realize it in his own acts
> and achievements, or in his faith and the result of it. He will be
> jeopardizing, indeed he will already have lost, the forgiveness
> of his sins, his life as a child of God, his hope of eternal life,
> if he ever thinks he can and should seek and find these things
> anywhere but at the place where as the act and work of God they
> are real as the forgiveness of his sins, as his divine sonship, as his
> hope, anywhere but in the one Jesus Christ.[138]

But this position seems to make divine election dependent upon
human decision, and that looks like a traditional Arminian and Pelagian
views of the atonement, contradicting the basis interest of the Reformation
regarding the sovereignty of God's free grace.[139] These critical comments of
Berkouwer and Balthasar pertain to the crucial matter of whether not only
the trajectory of Barth's thought leads to universalism, but also the urgency
of human repentance and the nature of the response of faith. Before I address the matter of Barthian universalism, I shall conclude this section with

---

135. Balthasar, *Theology of Karl Barth*, 245–46.

136. Berkouwer, *De Triomf Der Genade in De Theologie van Karl Barth*, 107 [113].

137. Ibid., [119].

138. Barth, *CD* IV.1, 631.

139. Barth, *CD* II.2, 69–81.

further reflections on Barth's view of human freedom and the question of faith and unbelief.

Barth asks, "How can there be any question of a possible rivalry between theonomy and autonomy?" He adds, "The perfection of God's giving of Himself to man in the person of Jesus Christ consists in the fact that far from merely playing with man, far from merely moving or using him, far from merely dealing with him as an object, this self-giving sets man up as a subject, awakens him to genuine individuality and autonomy, frees him, makes him a king, so that in his rule the kingly rule of God Himself attains form and revelation. How can there be any possible rivalry here, let alone usurpation?"[140] What, then, about compatibilist free will to make sense of how Barth overcomes a possible competition between theonomy and autonomy? Answering this question will help us to answer Berkouwer's claim above—put differently—that Barth is unable to explain how faith is a free human act given that there is no alternative option open to man. In other words, as Jesse Couenhoven puts it, "How [is] it . . . possible for God to work in us such that when we are left with only one option we are not forced to take that option" [?][141] Clearly, Barth is not a hard determinist given his affirmation, as I argued above, of a "profound spontaneity and native freedom" of the act of faith.[142] So for Barth to choose compatibilist free will does not jeopardize the opportunity that a man is free to do a particular action, or is morally responsible for that act, while he has no *legitimate* alternative option open to him to do otherwise. Crisp is right here about compatibilist freedom.[143] "If human moral freedom consists in some version of compatibilism, then, applied to Barth's views, human beings are all elect in Christ, and will all be saved. Indeed, this is *inevitable*, given the prior free act of election in Christ, the Elect One."[144] It is inevitable because in Christ "the root of human unbelief . . . is pulled out," so that unbelief has become "an objective, real and ontological impossibility and faith an objective, real and ontological necessity for all men and for every man."[145] Barth explains the inevitability, or necessity, of faith existing objectively, really, and ontologically for all men.[146]

140. Ibid., 188.

141. Couenhoven, "Karl Barth's Conception (s)," 250.

142. Barth, *CD* IV.1, 744.

143. Crisp, "The Letter and the Spirit of Barth's Doctrine of Election," 59; Crisp, "Barthian Universalism?," 167–68.

144. Crisp, "Barthian Universalism?," 168.

145. Barth, *CD* IV.1, 747.

146. Ibid., 747.

Man can certainly keep on lying (and does so); but he cannot
make truth falsehood. He can certainly rebel (he does so); but
he can accomplish nothing which abolishes the choice of God.
He can certainly flee from God (he does so); but he cannot
escape him. He can certainly hate God and be hateful to God
(he does and is so); but he cannot change into its opposite the
eternal love of God which triumphs even in His hate. . . . It is to
the man who does not yet know it—and every man continually
unlearns and forgets it!—it is to the man living in the darkness
of his own negative act, always sure of himself in his error, always hopeful in his rebellion, for ever renewing his flight from
God, for ever applying himself anew to his hatred for God,
taking himself seriously in his godlessness—it is to this man,
representing the rejected and to that extent suffering the divine
rejection, that the witness of the community to the election of
Jesus Christ is addressed. It tells him that he is erring, rebelling,
fleeing and hating, when everything points to the fact he should
not do so. *It tells him also that he does it all in vain*, because the
choice which he thus makes is eternally *denied and annulled* in
Jesus Christ, and because he for his part may deny and annul
everything else by his own choice, but cannot possibly deny or
annul the gracious choice of God. It is this very man, godless in
his negative act, wantonly representing the rejected man, who is
the predestinate.[147]

Barth is a compatibilist regarding freedom. The inevitability of faith
does not, however, "compromise its character as a free human act."[148] Indeed, Barth does say that "the action of faith . . . takes place in the free choice
beside which man has no other choice, so that it is a genuinely free choice.
The Holy Spirit is the power in which Jesus Christ the Son of God makes
a man free, makes him genuinely free for this choice and therefore for
faith."[149] Barth views human beings as free responsible subjects who exercise
a "profound spontaneity and native freedom" in the act of faith. Recall again
Barth saying, "And this means that for his part man can and actually does
elect God, thus attesting and activating himself as elected man."[150] Again,
Barth says, "the being and presence of man are not merely passive but active." He adds, "Man is, of course, purely receptive as regards the movement
from God, but he is also purely spontaneous in the movement to God. He is

147. Barth, *CD* II.2, 317; emphasis added.
148. Barth, *CD* IV.1, 744.
149. Ibid., 748.
150. Barth, *CD* II.2, 186.

not merely a partial function in a dynamic whole. He is not a mere function at all. In this matter, God is Subject, but over against God and in relation to Him man is also subject. I imply that I am subject by saying: 'I will.'"[151]

And yet, given the inevitability of faith and the ontological impossibility of unbelief, one can only wonder whether there is any "serious kerygmatic significance . . . to what Barth calls the 'fatal danger' of unbelief."[152] It seems unlikely given Barth's emphasis regarding the "*nullity* of this [rejected man's] choice and the *futility* of his desire and undertaking." Furthermore, "for all its wickedness and disastrous results this negative act as such can never be other than *impotent*. . . . He cannot reverse or change the eternal decision of God—by which He regards, considers and wills man, not in his isolation over against Him, but in His Son Jesus."[153] Moreover, even if God allows some sort of room for the dynamics of unbelief to work itself out whereby "God allows [His] creatures to respond to this election,"[154] says Barth, "their attempt [at unbelief] is powerless in the face of God's will and decree [meaning thereby] that it is only conditionally and not unconditionally that it can lack this distinction [of the elect], or, stated positively, that they can be 'rejected'. A limit is fixed by the fact that the rejected man, who alone and truly takes and bears and bears away the wrath of God, is called Jesus Christ. They can be only potentially rejected."[155] How, then, can unbelief have eternal consequences still be considered existentially serious when it is virtually already swallowed up Christ's atoning work? What does it mean to speak, as Barth does (see below), of the seriousness and severity of godlessness, of the threat of rejection in view of the actual election of all men in Christ?

Berkouwer remarks, "Barth calls unbelief 'fatally dangerous'. But this now and then repeated expression is flanked by extensive reflections on the ontologically impossibility of unbelief. This unbelief *has been* put away—the unbelief of the old man—*by* the decisive grace of God, which is *so* decisive that the *inevitability* of faith *lies involved* in it."[156] Is Barth, then, a universalist? It certainly seems so. In conclusion of this section and in preparation for the next, consider the following lengthy passage from Barth:

> This, then, is the message with which the elect community (as the circumference of the elect man, Jesus of Nazareth) has to

151. Barth, *CD* III.2, 180.

152. Berkouwer, *De Triomf Der Genade in De Theologie van Karl Barth*, 263 [267].

153. Barth, *CD* II.2, 316–17; emphasis added.

154. Crisp, *Deviant Calvinism*, 165.

155. Barth, *CD* II.2, 349.

156. Berkouwer, *De Triomf Der Genade in De Theologie van Karl Barth*, 266 [270].

approach every man—the promise, that he, too, is an elect man. It is fully aware of his perverted choice. It is fully aware of his godlessness. . . . It is fully aware, too, of the eternal condemnation of the man who is isolated over against God, which is unfailingly exhibited by the godlessness of every such man. . . . It knows of the wrath and judgment and punishment of God in which the rejection of the man isolated over and against God takes its course. . . . It knows that God, by the decree He made in the beginning of all His works and ways, has taken upon Himself the rejection merited by the man isolated in relation to Him; and on the basis of this decree of His the only truly rejected man is His own Son; that God's rejection has taken its course and been fulfilled and reached its goal, with all that that involves, against this One, so that it can no longer fall on other men or be their concern. The concern of other men is still the sin and guilt of their godlessness—and it is serious and severe enough. Their concern is still the suffering of the existence which they have prepared for themselves by their godlessness (in the shadow of that which the One has suffered for them)—and it is bitter enough to have to suffer this existence. Their concern is still be aware of the threat of their rejection. *But* it cannot now be their concern to suffer the execution of this threat, to suffer the eternal damnation which their godlessness deserves. Their desire and undertaking are pointless in so far as their only end can be to make them rejected. And this is the goal which the godless cannot reach, because it has already been taken away by the eternally decreed offering of the Son of God to suffer in place of the godless, and cannot any longer be their goal.[157]

The upshot of Barth's position above is that Christ's redemptive work, not only sufficiently accomplished the salvation of all men given its universal scope, but also effectively applied it to all men; surely, then, all *must* be saved. And given Barth's claim that the attempt to reject God is futile, null and void, impotent, in short, pointless—"this is the very goal which the godless cannot reach, because it has already been taken away by the eternally decreed offering of the Son of God to suffer in the place of the godless, and cannot any longer be their goal"[158]—therefore, all *will* be saved. And yet, Barth explicitly rejects universalism. The difficulty—perhaps, insurmountable one—in Barth's thought is that God is not "free to exclude anyone from participating in Christ's election, given the way in which God has freely

157. Barth, *CD* II.2, 318–319; emphasis added.
158. Barth, *CD* II.2, 319.

determined to be God in his self-election."[159] Can, then, God freely choose *not* to save in Christ?

Barthian Universalism?

The question posed in the title of this concluding section raises has spawned voluminous secondary literature. Briefly, what is universalism?[160] And is Barth a universalist? I shall distinguish three sorts. The first sort is contingent universalism. Crisp defines the latter as follows: "although it is possible that some people might end up in hell, as a matter of contingent fact no one will end up there." There is also a necessary universalism, namely, "given the essentially benevolent nature of God, it is inconceivable that anyone will ever end up in hell forever. In fact, given divine benevolence, God will necessarily save all people."[161] Finally, there is a version that some have called hopeful universalism: "this is the view according to which all human beings may be saved, indeed we hope *will* be saved, though we cannot say definitively *must* be saved."[162] Balthasar and Berkouwer argue that Barth's doctrine of election implies necessary universalism. Balthasar, for one, says, "Barth's doctrine of election does not leave much room open for possibility [contingency]. There is something inevitable and necessary in his views. What is definitive in Barth's thought is grace and blessing, and all reprobation and judgment are merely provisional."[163] I have supplied sufficient textual evidence above supporting Balthasar's claim.

Elsewhere he rejects Barth's claim "that Jesus, as God's chosen One, is rejected in place of all sinners, 'so that, besides him, no one may be lost'. This comment is, to be sure, surrounded by others whose tone is less absolute, and the term *apokatastasis*, or, 'universal reconciliation', is carefully avoided, even rejected. Still, one ought to stay well away from so systematic a statement and limit oneself to that Christian hope that does not mask a concealed knowing but rests essentially content with the Church's prayer, as called for in 1 Timothy 2:4, that God wills that all men be saved."[164] Berkouwer, for another, observes that:

159. McDonald, "Evangelical Questioning," 250–68, and at 253.

160. See Berkouwer's review of recent theological discussions of universalism in *De Wederkomst van Christus*, 2:202–10 [396–403].

161. Crisp, *Deviant Calvinism*, 98, 113, and 128. Crisp depends on Kvanvig, *The Problem of Hell*, 74, for these distinctions.

162. Crisp, *Deviant Calvinism*, 98, 152, respectively.

163. Balthasar, *Theology of Karl Barth*, 186.

164. Balthasar, *Dare We Hope*, 30–31. Intriguingly, Bruce McCormack claims that

Questions about universalism, especially in recent times, are
concentrated on Barth's doctrine of election, for with him there
occurs a peculiar mutation. In original universalism, the issue
is a universal offer because Christ died for all, and election
remains in the background for the moment. But with Barth,
Christ's death touches precisely upon the election of all, which
election has become manifest in Christ's death. The universality
of the message is no longer at odds with the fact of election, for
it is based on the universality of election. The message which
is carried into the world forms the transition from those who
already know (the believers) to those who do not yet know,
but who are nevertheless comprised in the election. Rejection
is now no longer an independent shadow and menace, but the
accepted and therefore withstood rejection, namely, in and
through Christ. This rejection is thus transmitted—as the rejection of Christ—into the *kerygma* and there becomes the essence
of glad tidings.[165]

Still, Bruce McCormack disputes this interpretation and holds that Barth
is a *hopeful* universalist.[166] "Universal salvation is something for which we
ought to hope and pray but it is not something we can teach."[167] There is
some textual evidence for this interpretation in Barth's work. Consider
Barth himself who drew back from drawing a universalistic conclusion
from his doctrine of election and atonement." Even though theological consistency might seem to lead out thoughts and utterances most clearly in this
direction," that is, in the direction of universalism, "we must not arrogate to

---

"Barth's position on 'universalism' is the same as von Balthasar's. Universal salvation is
something for which we ought to hope and pray but it is not something we can teach"
("So That He May Be," 227–49, and at 248). I shall return to this claim in the text.

165. Berkouwer, *De Verkiezing Gods*, 274 [229]. See also, *De Triomf Der Genade in
De Theologie van Karl Barth*, 105–6 [111–12].

166. See also, Bettis, "Is Karl Barth a Universalist?," 423–36, "Barth rejects the attempt to bridge the gap between the divine possibility and a theological statement of its
[universal salvation] actuality" (427).

167. McCormack, "So That He May Be," 248. Emil Brunner charges Barth's doctrine of election with "a fundamental perversion of the Christina message of Salvation"
(in *The Christian Doctrine of God*, 1:349). Carl F. Henry concurs with Berkouwer and
Balthasar, "Universalism is clearly implied when the election of Christ and election in
Christ merge with a doctrine of substitution that automatically embraces all human
beings. If all persons are identified in the Substitute it becomes difficult to resist the idea
that everyone is saved. . . .Instead of developing election in keeping with the biblical
teaching, his [Barth] theory aligns itself with the universalistic trend in neo-Protestant
theology" (in *God, Revelation and Authority*, 6:90–107, and at, 102–3).

ourselves that which can be given and received only as a free gift."[168] Barth suggests here that we have to be open for divine freedom despite the fact that theological consistency, he acknowledged, leads in the direction of universalism. This leaves our soteriological destiny uncertain.

> If we are to respect the freedom of divine grace, we cannot venture the statement that it must and will finally be coincident with the world of man as such (as in the doctrine of the so-called *apokatastasis*). No such right or necessity can legitimately be deduced. Just as the gracious God does not need to elect or call any single man, so He does not need to elect or call all mankind. His election and calling do not give rise to any historical metaphysics, but only to the necessity of attesting them on the ground that they have taken place in Jesus Christ and His community. But, again, in grateful recognition of the grace of the divine freedom we cannot venture the opposite statement that there cannot and will not be this final opening up and enlargement of the circle of election and calling. . . . We would be developing an opposing historical metaphysics if we were to try to attribute any limits to the lovingkindness of God.[169]

And in the following lengthy passage Barth suggests the *open* situation of the gospel proclamation such that the Church is an *open* space, underway, whereby, as Balthasar puts it, "'the many' must be understood as referring, not to a determinate, but to a dynamic and open number."[170] Barth says:

> For what many? If we cannot simply say for all, but can speak only of an unlimited many, this is not because of any weakness or limitation of the real and revealed divine will in Jesus Christ. This will of God, as is continually and rightly said in harmony with 1 Tim 2:4, is directed to the salvation of all men intention, and sufficient for the salvation of all men in power. It agrees with 1 Cor 5:19 that Jesus Christ is called the light of the world in Jn 8:12, 9:5, 11:9, 12:46; "the Lamb of God, which taketh away the sin of the world" in Jn 1:29; the Son in whose offering God "loved the world" in Jn 3:16, and who was sent "that the world through him might be saved" in Jn 3:17; "the Savior of the world" in Jn 4:42; "the bread of God which cometh down from heaven, and giveth life unto the world" in Jn 6:33 (cf. v. 51); "the propitiation for our sins: and not for ours only, but also for the sins of the whole world" in 1 Jn 2:2; and the light "which lighteth

168. Barth, *CD* IV.3, 477.
169. Barth, *CD* II.2, 417–418.
170. Balthasar, *Theology of Karl Barth*, 185.

every man" in Jn 1:9. When we remember this, we cannot follow
the classical doctrine and make the open number of those who
are elect in Jesus Christ into a closed number to which all other
men are opposed as they were rejected. Such an assumption is
shattered by the unity of the real and revealed will of God in
Jesus Christ. It is shattered by the impossibility of reckoning
with another divine rejection than the rejection whose subject
was Jesus Christ, who bore it and triumphantly bore it away. It
is shattered by the fact that Jesus Christ is the irreversible way
from the depths to the heights, from death to life; and that as
this way he is also the truth, the declaration of the heart of God,
beside which there is no other and beside which we have no
right to ask for any other. It is shattered by the fact that Jesus
Christ will not reject any who come to him, according to Jn 6:37.

At this point in the argument one must conclude that Barth's argument
for Christ's atoning work—its sufficiency and efficacy—has universalistic
implications:[171]

1. By Christ's death atonement is procured for the sin and guilt of those
    for whom he died.

2. Christ's death atones for the sin of all men.

Given the textual evidence I have provided for Barth's view of the atonement, this seems to mean that,

3. Christ's death is sufficient and efficient for all men.

    That is, Christ's death is not simply potentially universal in scope
    (it could save all humanity); it is actually universal in scope (all
    humanity are saved by it). It might be argued that Barth's position
    is merely that the atonement is universal in scope, not effective-
    ness. However, that Barth's position does involve a universally
    efficient atonement can be seen from passages such as the follow-
    ing: "There is no-one who does not participate in Him [Christ]
    in His turning to God. There is no-one who is not . . . engaged in
    this turning. There is no-one who is not raised and exalted with
    Him to true humanity. 'Jesus Christ lives, and I with Him' [CD
    II.2, 271]."[172]

4. This work is completed at the cross.

171. The following argument is an adaptation of Crisp's argument, "On Karl Barth's
Denial of Universalism," 116–30.

172. Crisp, "On Karl Barth's Denial of Universalism," 119–20.

5. This work is appropriated not via the traditional Reformation or Catholic teaching[173] describing the transition from unbelief to faith, "being-lost" to "being-saved:"[174] "In explicit terms He Himself [Jesus Christ] affirmed the necessity of faith and baptism [Mk 16:16; Jn 3.5] and thereby affirmed also the necessity of the Church, for through baptism as through a door men enter the Church."[175]

According to Barth, the contrast here is between knowing and not-knowing, and not-knowing about the saving fact of Jesus' death, says Berkouwer, "detracts nothing, however, from the fact of the objective liberation. The *subjective* knowledge of it does not yet correspond to the *objective* situation."[176] So, the difference is not between the saved and the lost, but rather "exclusively in having or not-having knowledge of the factual happening of God's decision."[177] That this is undeniably the case in Barth's thinking is evident from what he explicitly says: "If, however, the nature of faith consists in the fact . . . that man is wakened by the grace of God and is born again as a new subject, then, for that very reason, it is not possible to place him absolutely over against one who, different from himself, does not make real and visible the attitude of faith, its form, so that we regard the former, in contrast to the latter, as 'elect', and the other, conversely, as 'rejected'. If a person, as member of the Elect, is that new subject, then as such (and only in Jesus Christ is this possible) to a certain extent he is raised above himself in his best, and above the other in his worst, behavior. Thus, seen from thence, the contrast between them becomes a *relative contrast*. . . . How could the Grace of God mean His absolute favor for the one, and His absolute disfavor for the other? . . . The believer in particular cannot possibly recognize, in the unbelief of others, an *ultimate* given fact."[178] The fundamental reason for the contrast of "knowing" and "not-knowing" in

---

173. Crisp says, "This work is appropriated not via the traditional Reformation formula, 'If you repent and believe, you will be saved; if you do not repent and believe, you will not be saved', but by agents coming to realize that 'this is what God in Jesus Christ has done for your sake. Therefore repent and believe'" (ibid., 120). He adds, "The two citations are from George Hunsinger's *How to Read Karl Barth*, 130. Hunsinger points out the unconditional nature of the Barthian formula, observing. 'since, in Barth's understanding, God has already freely included us [in salvation], it falls to us henceforth freely to receive our inclusion as the gift it is proclaimed to be'" (ibid., 130–31).

174. Brunner, *Christian Doctrine of God*, 1:351.

175. Vatican II, *Lumen gentium* §14. See also, Council of Trent, Decree on Justification, Denzinger §1532.

176. Berkouwer, *De Triomf Der Genade in De Theologie van Karl Barth*, 261 [265].

177. Ibid., 271 [275].

178. Barth, *CD* II.2, 360.

Barth's doctrine of election and atonement is that Christ's death is sufficient and efficient for all men.

6. Christ is the Elect One. (That is, the set of the elect comprises one member, Christ.)

7. Christ is the Reprobate One. (That is, the set of the reprobate comprises one member, Christ.

"In this way," adds Crisp, Barth's doctrine fuses the so-called 'double decree' of Calvinism in the person of Christ, who is both the Elect and the Reprobate One. But the way in which this is applied to the set of human agents is asymmetrical.

8. All men are elect only in a derivative sense of having a saving relation to the set of the elect and its single member, Christ.

And:

9. The sin of all men is atoned for by Christ, the Reprobate One, who is the only member of the set of the reprobate.

Then, given (8), we have:

10. All men are members of the set 'elect-in-Christ'.

And yet, says Barth, countering this conclusion:

> It is not legitimate to make the limitless many of the elect in Jesus Christ the totality of all men. For in Jesus Christ we have to do with the living and personal and therefore the freewill of God in relation to the world and every man. In him we must not and may not take account of any freedom of God which is not that of his real and revealed love in Jesus Christ. But, again, we must not and may not take account of any love of God other than that which is a concern of the freedom realized and revealed in Jesus Christ, which, according to John's Gospel, finds expression in the fact that only those who are given to the Son by the Father, and drawn to the Son by the Father, come to Jesus Christ and are received by him. This means, however, that the intention and power of God in relation to the whole world and all men are always his intentions and power—an intention and power which we cannot control and the limits of which we cannot arbitrarily restrict or enlarge.[179]

179. Barth, *CD* II.2, 466–67.

Furthermore, adds Barth, "There is no good reason why we should forbid ourselves, or be forbidden, openness to the possibility that in the reality of God and man in Jesus Christ there is contained much more than we might expect and therefore the supremely unexpected withdrawal of that final threat, i.e., that in the truth of this reality there might be contained the superabundant promise of the final deliverance of all men."[180] Does divine freedom help Barth out of what seems to be a contradiction between his views of election and atonement and this possibility of universal reconciliation? Not at all.

11. Christ's atonement is universal in scope and efficacy (from (1)-(4)).

12. Christ is the Elect One and therefore the sole member of the set 'elect', in whom all men are elected (from (5)-(10)).

13. Christ is the Elect One whose atonement for the sin of men is universal in scope and efficacy, and all men are members of the set 'elect-in-Christ'.

Now, to claim, as some defenders of Barth, including Barth himself, that "Because God is free, the eschatological destiny of all human is uncertain," does not appear to be consistent with (1)-(3). Indeed, as I argued above, given Barth's claim that the attempt to reject God is futile, null and void, impotent, in short, pointless—"this is the very goal which the godless cannot reach, because it has already been taken away by the eternally decreed offering of the Son of God to suffer in the place of the godless, and cannot any longer be their goal"[181]—one cannot consistently hold that all men are elect in Christ, having been efficaciously atoned for by Christ, and yet also claim that their soteriological status is uncertain. Therefore, all *will* be saved is the only conclusion that is supported. Crisp concludes rightly: "[E]ither the question of whether all humanity is . . . elect and efficaciously atoned for by Christ is uncertain, or it is not. If humanity has been . . . elected and efficaciously atoned for by Christ (as per [(11)-(13)]), then their soteriological status simply cannot be uncertain. . . . This seems fatal to the consistency of Barth's position."[182]

---

180. Barth, *CD* IV.3, 477.

181. Barth, *CD* II.2, 319.

182. Crisp, "On Karl Barth's Denial of Universalism," 129–30.

Points of Catholic Orientation

Confessional Catholicism holds that in God's infinite, all-embracing love
in Christ, he truly and sincerely desires the salvation of all men. Therefore,
election is in Christ Jesus who is not only the ground, that is, the cause and
foundation of election (*fundamentum electionis*), but also the Mediator of
election (*fundamentum salutis electorum*). Confessional Catholicism takes
seriously the urgency of human repentance and the response of faith given
its rejection of universalism, Barthian or otherwise. *CCC* affirms that "Faith
is a personal act—the *free* response of the human person to the initiative of
God who reveals himself."[183] Confessional Catholicism stands with Barth
in rejecting the equal ultimacy of election and reprobation. On this view,
predestination is parallel, and hence double in the strict sense, because both
election and reprobation are symmetrical with respect to the mode of divine
causality. Confessional Catholicism also rejects universalism: all men are
not saved. The atoning work of Christ is sufficient for the salvation of all
men, but it is efficacious only for the many. "He [Christ] became the source
of eternal salvation for all who obey him" (Heb 5: 9). In its Decree on Justification Trent states: "even though 'Christ died for all' [2 Cor 5:15], still not
all do receive the benefit of His death, but those only to whom the merit of
His passion is imparted."[184]

---

183. *CCC*, §166; emphasis added.
184. Denzinger, §1523.

CHAPTER 5

Bavinck and Berkouwer on Double Predestination

IN THIS CHAPTER, I examine the Reformed doctrine of election in the writings of two Dutch masters of dogmatics and ecumenical theology, namely, the neo-Calvinists Herman Bavinck and G. C. Berkouwer. Both of them reject the parallelism or symmetry of election and reprobation and argue that there is an "essential asymmetry" at the heart of the Reformed doctrine of election in their theological account of double predestination. The question I will consider in my analysis of their views is about reconciling God's universal will to save all men in Christ with the mystery of predestining grace, election and reprobation.

Double Predestination?

I begin with a passage from the Synod of Dort (1618–1619) where the equal symmetry of election and reprobation is categorically rejected.

> That the same doctrine of [predestination] teaches that God, by a mere arbitrary act of his will, without the least respect or view to any sin, has predestinated the greatest part of the world to eternal damnation, and had created them for this very purpose; that in the same manner in which election is the fountain [source] and cause of faith and good works, reprobation is the cause of unbelief and impiety [ungodliness]; and many other things of the same kind which the Reformed churches not only do not acknowledge, but even detest with their whole soul.[1]

One can surely imagine that the Synod when writing this passage in the Epilogue had in mind Canon 17 of the Decree on Justification of the Council

---

1. The Canons of Dort (1618–1619), in Dennison, *Reformed Confessions* 4:120–53, and at conclusion, 152.

of Trent (1547): "If anyone says that the grace of justification is given only to those who are predestined to life and that all the others who are called are called indeed but do not receive grace, as they are predestined to evil by the divine power, let him be anathema."[2] Not to be outdone in hurling anathemas, however, the Synod of Dort "warns calumniators themselves to consider the terrible judgment of God which awaits them, for bearing false witness against the confessions of so many Churches; for distressing the consciences of the weak; and for laboring to render suspect the society of the truly faithful."[3] Herman Bavinck added emphatically and incredulously, after citing this very Canon from Trent, "as if anyone really taught what is contained in this canon!"[4] He explains, rejecting an "equal symmetry" between election and reprobation in their mode of operation: "The fall, sin, and eternal punishment are included in the divine decrees and in a sense willed by God, but then *always in a certain sense and not in the same manner as grace and blessedness*."[5]

Again, Bavinck states: "Though, on the one hand, there is every reason to consider reprobation as a part of predestination, it is *not in the same sense and manner* a component of God's decree as election, as the defenders of a double predestination have also at all times acknowledged."[6] *At all times?* Bavinck overstates his point here in rightly rejecting an equal ultimacy view of double predestination. Indeed, he emphasizes: "It is incorrect to represent the wretched state of the lost as the goal of predestination."[7] But that there have been supporters of equal ultimacy is beyond doubt. Hence the

---

2. Denzinger, §1567. See also the regional Synod of Arles (473) that condemned the idea "that the foreknowledge of God violently impels man to death, or that they who perish, perish by the will of God"(Denzinger §333); Second Synod of Orange (529): "Not only do we not believe that some are predestined to evil by the divine power, but if there are any who wish to believe such an enormity, we with great abhorrence anathematize them" (Denzinger §397); Synod of Valence (855): "Neither do we believe that anyone is condemned by a previous judgment on his [God's] part but by reason of his own iniquity. . . . In the condemnation, however, of those who are to be lost the evil they have deserved precedes the just judgment of God" (Denzinger §627–628); Council of Trent (1547): "If anyone says that it is not in man's power to make his ways evil, but that God performs the evil works just as he performs the good, not only by allowing them, but properly and directly, so that Judas' betrayal no less than Paul's vocation was God's own work, let him be anathema" (Denzinger §1556, Canon 6).

3. Canons of Dort, 152.

4. Bavinck, GD II, 315 [353].

5. Ibid., 351 [389]; emphasis added.

6. Ibid., 358 [395]; emphasis added.

7. Ibid., 351 [389].

need felt by some Calvinists, such as R.C. Sproul, to distinguish two sorts of Calvinism in the Reformed tradition:[8]

Calvinism	Hyper-Calvinism
Positive-negative decrees	Positive-positive decrees
Asymmetrical view	Symmetrical view
Unequal ultimacy	Equal ultimacy
God passes over the reprobate	God works unbelief in the hearts of the reprobate

And yet, under the type Sproul calls Calvinism, one still finds a decree of negative reprobation, or preterition, meaning thereby that some, namely, the non-elect, are passed over by divine grace. Yes, as I have said before, they are ultimately condemned because of their sin, unbelief, but they are not passed over because of their sin. Affirmed here is an unconditioned negative reprobation. So, even Calvinism, as Sproul describes this type, in distinction from hyper-Calvinism, has to deal with the question of equal ultimacy because of the decree of preterition that has a significant place in its scheme of election and reprobation, and particularly because it rejects a *conditioned* positive reprobation. According to Ott, the latter divine judgment "occurs with consideration of foreseen future demerits (*post et propter praevisa demerita*)."[9] Do they then embrace what he later calls "unconditioned positive reprobation," namely, "a positive predetermination to sin, and an unconditional Predestination to the eternal punishment of hell, that is, without consideration of future demerits [?]"[10] If so, and on this point Ott and John Wesley agree, "You believe *he hath absolutely decreed not to save them;* and what is this but decreeing to damn them? It is, in effect, neither more nor less; it comes to the same thing."[11] I shall return to this question below.

Of course, although Bavinck affirms here what Berkouwer shall later call an "essential asymmetry," which denies the parallelism or symmetry of operation between election and reprobation, the question shall need to be considered carefully about the sense in which Bavinck holds to "double predestination," and hence the sense in which the fall, sin, and eternal punishment are willed by God. Does Bavinck accept a so-called "conditioned positive reprobation, that is, when the judgment of reprobation occurs with consideration of foreseen future demerits (*post et propter praevisa demerita*)

---

8. Sproul, *Chosen by God*, 143.

9. Ott, *Fundamentals of Dogma*, 245.

10. Ibid.

11. John Wesley, "Free Grace," as cited in Olson, *Against Calvinism*, 126.

[?]" No, like Calvin before him as I showed in chapter 2, Bavinck, for one, rejects "conditional reprobation," or what Ott calls, "a conditioned positive reprobation" that "occurs with consideration of foreseen future demerits (*post et propter praevisa demerita*)."[12] He does so just as much as he rejects "conditional election" in which God's election depends on foreseen faith.[13] Election is unconditional. Furthermore, like Calvin, Bavinck affirms man's sin as the proximate cause of reprobation and unbelief, but it cannot be the ultimate cause.[14] Is this position a relapse into unconditioned positive reprobation? Let us recall here that I argued against Calvin that his acceptance of "unconditioned positive Reprobation," as Ott puts it, "leads to a denial of the universality of the Divine Desire for salvation, and of the [universal scope of] Redemption, and contradicts the Justice and Holiness of God as well as the freedom of man."[15] How does Bavinck reconcile all these aspects in his theology of predestination? I shall return to this question below as well. For now, suffice it to say that Bavinck—and, as we shall see below, Berkouwer in 1955—affirms Augustine's maxim with respect to reprobation: *contra voluntatem Dei* but not *praeter voluntatem Dei*.[16]

Berkouwer refers to the Synod's rejection of an "equal symmetry" between reprobation and election as "an emphatic denial of what many critics conceive to be an essential part of the orthodox doctrine of election." He insists that the Synod's "sharp defense [of an 'essential asymmetry'] be honored as an essential motif [of Reformed theology[17]]. For thus, very se-

12. Ott, *Fundamentals of Catholic Dogma*, 245.

13. Calvin, *Institutes of the Christian Religion*, 3.22.1.

14. Bavinck, *GD* IV, 11 [42]. See also, Bavinck, *GD* II, 349–50 [385–86].

15. Ott, *Fundamentals of Catholic Dogma*, 245.

16. This maxim is Augustine's *In Psalmos* cxi.2: "Great is the work of God, exquisite in all he wills! So that, in a manner wondrous and ineffable, *that is not done without his will, which is done contrary to it* [emphasis added], because it could not be done if he did not permit it; nor does he permit it unwillingly, but willingly; nor would he who is good permit evil to be done, were he not omnipotent to bring good out of evil" (as cited in Calvin, *Institutes of the Christian Religion*, I.18).

17. In their *Handbook of Christian Apologetics*, Kreeft and Tacelli hold that "double predestination" is "the Calvinistic doctrine" (292). They don't acknowledge the significance of "essential asymmetry" in interpreting "double predestination," even at points where Calvin doesn't operate with two equivalent metaphysical *causae* when speaking of proximate cause and remote cause, and hence they interpret double predestination in the very way that Dort vehemently rejects: equal symmetry regarding mode of operation between election and reprobation. They do acknowledge that this is not "even held by all Calvinists." But that they have in mind the very view that Bavinck and Berkouwer reject, namely, "equal symmetry," is clear: "According to this doctrine, God decrees and designs some souls for hell before they are born; God wills their damnation. This is contradicted both by Scripture (Mt 18:14) and by moral sanity—how could one love such a

riously, do the Canons [of Dort] mean to make clear that God is not the author of sin and unbelief." Throughout his magisterial study, *De Verkiezing Gods*, Berkouwer comes back to this "essential asymmetry," as central to understanding not only the Canons of Dort but also Reformed theology.[18] He concludes: "It is certainly not Reformed theology that feels called upon to protest against the 'essential asymmetry'. It is, rather, one of its most important characteristics that it emphatically affirms this asymmetry."[19] Berkouwer derives this expression of "essential asymmetry" from Gérard Philips, the Belgian Catholic ecclesiologist, and key drafter of Vatican II's *Lumen Gentium*, who, according to Berkouwer, "sees in it a mark of Roman Catholic theology."[20] There is a definite point of convergence here, he rightly insists, regarding the Reformed view as expressed by the rejection of "the *eodem modo* in the Canons," on the one hand, and "the Roman Catholic doctrine of election,"[21] on the other.[22] And yet, as we shall have occasion to note below, they differ significantly in their doctrine of predestination on "the question whether God's eternal resolve of Predestination has been taken with or without consideration of the merits of the man (*post or ante*

---

monster God?" Salza also fails to acknowledge the import of "essential asymmetry" in understanding "double predestination." He writes: "Calvinism supports the notion of a 'double predestination', whereby God leads the elect to salvation and the reprobate to damnation. Because God is directing the reprobate to their final end [damnation], Calvinism practically makes God responsible for man's sin—an idea at odds with Scripture and God's supreme goodness" (*The Mystery of Predestination*, 6). By contrast, consider Karl Barth, *CD* II.2, 171: The Doctrine of God: "The concept which so hampered the traditional doctrine [of predestination] was that of an equilibrium or balance in which blessedness was ordained and declared on the right hand and perdition on the left. This concept we must oppose with all the emphasis of which we are capable."

18. On the Canons, see *De Verkiezing Gods*, 201, 204–7, 213, 222–24, 230–31, 238, 248 [172, 175–78, 182, 189–90, 197–98, 201, 209]. The late Dutch theologian, Klaas Runia rightly remarks, "We are not saying too much, when we call the non-*eodem modo* in particular the master key which Berkouwer uses to open the door to the real teaching of the Canons, especially its teaching about reprobation" ("Recent Reformed Criticisms," 161–80).

19. Berkouwer, *De Verkiezing Gods*, 213 [182].

20. Ibid., 213n34 [182n16]; see also 20 [20].

21. Suffice it to note here the essential asymmetry in Aquinas's thought: "The causality of reprobation differs from that of predestination. Predestination is the cause both of what the predestined expect in the future life, namely glory, and of what they receive in the present, namely grace. Reprobation does not cause what there is in the present, namely moral fault, though that is why we are left without God. And it is the cause why we shall meet our deserts in the future, namely eternal punishment. The fault starts from the free decision of the one who abandons grace and is rejected, so bringing the prophecy to pass, *Your loss is from yourself, O Israel* [Hosea 13.9]" (*Summa theologiae*, I.23, a. 3, Reply to Objection 2).

22. Berkouwer, *De Verkiezing Gods*, 234 [198].

praevisa merita)."[23] For now, focusing on the Reformed view, Berkouwer explains that:

> The Canons of Dort speak of election and rejection when op-
> posing the Remonstrants [[24]] (CD, I). When in the Canons and
> other confessions [e.g., Belgic Confession of Faith, the Westmin-
> ster Confession of Faith], and also in reflection upon dogmatics,
> we repeatedly meet with these two words beside one another, we
> could get the impression that we are confronted with an obvious
> duality of two symmetrical "decrees" of the divine predestina-
> tion, decrees of the same structure as a Yes and No, side by side
> as *predestination ad vitam* and *ad mortem*. What does this con-
> junction "and" mean between these words? Is election always
> conjoined with the word "rejection," which we also encounter
> so often in Scripture? Does the confessional manner of speaking
> of rejection find its origin in the logical conclusion that elec-
> tion implies rejection? According to the "logical" paradigm, the
> doctrine of double predestination would then be described as
> a reference to God's absolute apriori sovereignty before which
> man can only bow and keep silent. Predestination would then
> be the general concept, and the two decrees of election and
> rejection would stand side by side as subordinates of the one
> denominator (predestination) of the divine *prae* in two differ-
> ent directions. Frequently the Church's doctrine of election was
> interpreted as such a transparent double predestination, and
> for that very reason people left her forever. And often fervent
> contention arose this very point. It seemed as if it was no longer
> possible to interpret the content of double predestination in
> more than one way. It ["equal symmetry"] became a traditional
> characterization which embodied everything that criticism
> wanted to bring up against the Church's doctrine of election.[25]

23. Ott, *Fundamentals of Dogma*, 245. I already addressed this difference in chapters 2 and 3 when addressing the views of Calvin and Scheeben. But I return to that
difference in this chapter because Berkouwer issues "a warning for anyone who wishes
to take the essential asymmetry seriously" that the "connection between asymmetry
and *praescientia* is nothing but a false solution" (*De Verkiezing Gods*, 236 [200]).

24. Remonstrants: "Another name by which the original Dutch Arminians [named
after Jacobus Arminius] are called. The name is derived from the *Remonstrance*, a
document they signed in 1610. While on many points their differences with the more
traditional Calvinists was subtle, they insisted on the point that Christ died for all . . .
and that grace is nor irresistible. These became two of the crucial points at which their
teachings were rejected by the Synod of Dort" (González, *Essential Theological Terms*,
152. See the essential articles of "The Remonstrance (1610)," in Dennison, *Reformed
Confessions*, 4:41–44.

25. Berkouwer, *De Verkiezing Gods*, 201–2 [172–73].

Berkouwer suggests in this passage that there is another way to interpret "double predestination" than by the "'logical' paradigm" [of equal symmetry] and its presupposition of a *decretum absolutum*, or absolute a priori sovereignty.[26] Something more about this so-called "logical paradigm" must be said.

Logical Paradigm

The "logical" reasoning here says that if God has eternally predestined some but not all to election, to save some and pass over others, it logically follows that some are eternally, not only elected, bust also predestined to rejection as well. R.C. Sproul, for one, disagrees with positions, such as Berkouwer's, that reject the "logic" that is allegedly inherent to the Reformed doctrine of predestination.[27] Here's the logic: "If there is such a thing as predestination at all, and if that predestination does not include all people, then we must not shrink from the necessary inference that there are two sides to predestination. It is not enough to talk about Jacob; we must also consider Esau [Rom 9:13]."[28] Put differently, according to Sproul, the "logic" of the Reformed position is as follows:

26. The Dutch text of *De Verkiezing Gods* does not use the term "'logical' paradigm" in describing the equal symmetry between divine election and reprobation. Berkouwer speaks of a "pure parallelism" ("zuivere parallelie"). Still, Berkouwer would agree with this characterization of the view as a logical paradigm. Examples of this logical paradigm are, for one, the famous *Collatio Hagensis*, where the Calvinists and Remonstrants met, and the former provided a response to the essential articles of latter: "The Counter Remonstrance (1611)" in Dennison, *Reformed Confessions*, 4:45–48. At this conference of The Hague, the Calvinists stated: "When we posit an eternal decree of election of certain particular persons, it clearly follows that we also posit an eternal decree of rejection or reprobation of certain particular persons, for there cannot be an election without a rejection or reprobation. When from a certain number some persons are elected, then by this very act others are rejected, for he who takes them all does not elect" (as cited in Runia, "Recent Reformed Criticisms"). The same argument is present in Reformed theologian Louis Berkhof, *Systematic Theology*, 117: "The doctrine of reprobation naturally follows from the logic of the situation. The decree of election inevitably implies the decree of reprobation. If the all-wise God, possessed of infinite knowledge, has eternally purposed to save some, then he *ipso facto* also purposed not to save others. If He has chosen or elected some, then He has by that very fact also rejected others." See also, Calvin, *Institutes* III/XXIII/1: "Indeed many, as if they wished to avert a reproach from God, accept election in such terms as to deny that anyone is condemned. But they do this very ignorantly and childishly, since election itself could not stand except as set over against reprobation."

27. In his article, "Double Predestination," Sproul is actually criticizing the view of Emil Brunner, *The Christian Doctrine of God*, 1:326.

28. Sproul, *Chosen by God*, 141.

[1] There is a divine decree of election that is eternal; [2] that divine decree is particular in scope ("There are those who are not elect"); [3] yet there is no decree of reprobation. Consider the implications. If God has predestined some but not all to election, does it not follow by what Luther called a "resistless logic" that some are not predestined to election? If . . . *all* salvation is based upon the eternal election of God and not all men are elect from eternity, does that not mean that from eternity there are non-elect who most certainly will not be saved? Has not God chosen from eternity not to elect some people? If so, then we have an eternal choice of non-election which we call reprobation. The inference is clear and necessary, yet some shrink from drawing it.[29]

Of course, Sproul is right that the notion of single predestination makes no sense, and hence that the force of logic impels us to recognize a double predestination. If predestination is the unconditional election of *some* people, then it logically follows that others have not been elected, because they have been passed over—preterition. Sproul helpfully distinguishes four possible kinds of consistent single predestination. That is: "(1) Universal predestination to election . . . ; (2) universal predestination to reprobation (which nobody holds); (3) particular predestination to election with the option of salvation by self-initiative to those not elect (a qualified Arminianism). . . ; and (4) particular predestination to reprobation with the option of salvation by self-initiative to those not reprobate (which nobody holds)." Of course some resist this argument by rejecting one or more of the premises of the argument, for example, they opt for universalism, that is, the view in which all men are saved because elected in Christ, and hence that ultimately there are no damned. This would be (1), which Berkouwer, for one, rejects because he does not hold to a necessary or contingent universalism, namely, that it is necessarily or contingently the case that all men are saved. He also rejects Arminianism, at least with respect to salvation, opting for unconditional election, and hence rejecting a conditional eelection along with its interpretation of divine election in light of the conceptions of "*praevisio*," "*praescientia*," "*permissio*," and the "*scientia media*." Berkouwer says, on this view, "Divine election was made dependent on man's decision."[30] It is, however, an intriguing question whether Berkouwer affirms something like (3), leading him to hold to a view Roger Olson calls "inconsistent single predestination view."[31] As I understand Olson's point,

29. Ibid., 139–60.

30. Berkouwer, *De Verkiezing Gods*, 249 [210].

31. Olson, *Against Calvinism*, 123.

Berkouwer's inconsistency would stem from his rejection of either unconditioned positive or negative reprobation. Be that as it may, Berkouwer would
disagree with Sproul's conclusion that "'single' predestination can be consistently maintained only within the framework of universalism or some sort
of qualified Arminianism. If particular election is to be maintained and if
the notion that all salvation is ultimately based upon that particular election
is to be maintained, then we must speak of double predestination." Berkouwer contests the claim that universalism or Arminianism are the only
alternatives, as he puts it, to "double predestination in the sense that God
from eternity has foreordained one group to salvation and another as decidedly to preterition, and that Christ did not die for the reprobate."[32] Is there
another alternative?

For now, I shall argue that Sproul wrongly understands Berkouwer's position, and hence Berkouwer's root objection to double predestination when
taken as the essential symmetry or parallelism of reprobation and election.
In short, it isn't the logic that Berkouwer rejects, it is the first principle, or
basic premise of the logic, that is the starting point of this paradigm, namely,
that from eternity there are two classes of people, those God elects and those
others that he passes over, leaving the latter without sufficient grace. Significantly, Berkouwer presses the point here that the question of opposing
this view "is not one of a mere symmetry, but [rather] that God has loved
the world (John 3:16)." Sproul, too, rejects the essential symmetry or equal
ultimacy of election and reprobation. He, like Bavinck and Berkouwer, distinguishes the equal symmetry interpretation of election and reprobation,
which he calls "hyper-Calvinism, from what he calls just plain "Calvinism,"
which subscribes to the "essential asymmetry" interpretation, and Sproul
opts for the latter as the genuine Reformed view.[33] Regarding the latter, he
distinguishes between the "*positive* and *negative* decrees of God. Positive has
to do with God's active intervention in the hearts of the elect. Negative has
to do with God's passing over the non-elect."[34] This "passing over" raises
the question of preterition that we have met before in previous chapters on
Calvin, Scheeben, and Barth. Why does God save only some, passing over
others? Does merely saying that there is a fundamental asymmetry here
between election and reprobation, positive and negative decree, really get at
the root of why symmetry or parallelism is wrong?

The issue here is not only of fairness of God's character, in which
the question is raised of the moral responsibility of non-elect given God's

32. Berkouwer, *De Verkiezing Gods*, 234 [198].
33. Sproul, *Chosen by God*, 143.
34. Ibid., 142.

preterition; it is also, indeed, chiefly, of God's love.[35] Olson rightly notes, "The main issue, which Sproul skirts, is *love*. If God could save everybody because election to salvation is unconditional and if God is by nature love, why doesn't he? The only answers Sproul can offer are (1) he doesn't love everybody, and (2) God can do whatever he wants to do because he isn't obligated to do anything for anyone. These answers demean God and impugn his goodness and do damage to his reputation, which is based on his morally perfect character."[36] Berkouwer agrees with arguments like Olson's, seeking to undercut God's seeming arbitrariness, lack of fairness, and an abstract sovereignty of divine election, namely, without divine love and grace. Views like those of Sproul "then no longer understand that God did not send the Son to condemn the world (John 3:17) but that the world should be saved through Him. *This is the profoundest reason for rejecting [essential symmetry or] parallelism.*"[37]

Rejecting a general double decree of election and reprobation, a *decretum absolutum*, as something behind the election in Christ means, according to Berkouwer, that there is no reprobation from eternity, but only judgment in history, and hence that judgment is contingent upon the sins of man. Notwithstanding Sproul's objection to "single predestination," he doesn't attend to the truth, as Bavinck puts it, "that Scripture seldom speaks of reprobation as an eternal decree." Bavinck adds, "All the more, however, does it represent reprobation as an act of God in history."[38] Does that mean the judgment of reprobation is conditional? I will return to this issue below. For now, pared down for my purpose here, Berkouwer argues as follows against essential symmetry.

First, what problems does Berkouwer have with Sproul's logic? *Pace* Sproul who claims, "Even G. C. Berkouwer seems allergic to the notion that logic should play a role in developing our understanding of election," it is the starting point of this logic and its implications, as I said above, that is the problem. So, in answering this question about Berkouwer's problems with Sproul's starting-point, let me briefly consider the phrase "good and necessary consequences" of which the Westminster Confession speaks.[39]

---

35. This, too, is the objection of Scottish Presbyterian theologian, James Orr (1844–1913), *Progress of Dogma*, "We are sure that if God is sovereign, yet not sovereignty but love must be enthroned as the central principle of His character" (394).

36. Olson, *Against Calvinism* , 117.

37. Berkouwer, *De Verkiezing Gods*, 238 [202]; italics added.

38. Bavinck, *GD* II, 355 [393].

39. Berkouwer says that he is "Wary, not of logic, but of certain logical consequences that had been drawn, consequences that are hardly recognizable as the '*good* consequences' of which the Westminster Confession speaks" (*Een Halve Eeuw Theologie,*

Regarding Sproul's point about an eternal decree of reprobation, Berkouwer asks whether that consequence is "good and necessary." Clearly, he doesn't think it is sufficient to speak of only "logically necessary consequences," but also of "good" consequences "drawn from an informed induction of the relevant biblical data," as Paul Helm puts it. Helm adds, "So there is a balance to be struck at this point between induction and deduction. Here again the prior work of good exegesis shows it importance. Biblical doctrine should . . . be formed on the basis of . . . sound exegesis of all the relevant material."[40] Put differently, let me suggest that Berkouwer sees the logical consequences that necessarily follow from the above stated premises, but he rejects, in particular, premise 2 as biblically false, namely, "reprobation from eternity." Says Berkouwer, "To me it has become increasingly clear that the *scriptural* proof of reprobation from eternity does not hold."[41]

Second, then, the "logical" paradigm of predestination results in the acceptance of an "abstract [decree of election] and isolated divine counsel . . . in which there is no mention of His [God's] love [in Jesus Christ] and grace."[42] In short, an abstract decree of election is a "sovereign election without the love of God."[43] Second, this decree of election is abstracted not only from Jesus Christ, the Word made flesh,[44] failing "to show the harmony of election with the grace and the love of God in Jesus Christ," but also election in Christ, that is, God's Yes to us in Jesus Christ: "But as God is faithful, our word to you was not Yes and No. For the Son of God, Jesus Christ, who was preached among you by us . . . was not Yes and No, but in Him was Yes. For all the promises of God in Him are Yes, and in Him Amen, to the glory of God through us" (2 Cor 1: 18–20). Here we find, says Berkouwer, that God's "yea is truly yea, and the Amen of certainty is spoken to the glory of God."[45] St. Paul's statement that God chose us in Christ "before the foundation of the world" (Eph 1:4) is about "the foundation of salvation in God's plan as immutable reality."[46] Berkouwer does not deny God's eternal counsel because "the salvation accomplished by Christ's death of reconciliation cannot be merely historical, but . . . it has its eternal foundation in the

139–40 [101]).

40. Helm, *Faith, Form, and Fashion,* 18.

41. Berkouwer, "The Authority of Scripture (A Responsible Confession)," 197–203, and at 198.

42. Berkouwer, *De Verkiezing Gods,* 161 [141].

43. Ibid., 179 [155].

44. Ibid., 198 [171].

45. Ibid., 151 [133].

46. Ibid., 174 [150].

love of God."[47] In other words, Berkouwer does not "historicize" and "actualize" God's counsel meaning thereby "the identification of God's decrees with the facts of history."[48] Berkouwer explains:

> The point at issue is the living, electing God, the *Deus decernens*, who reveals to us His sovereignty and freedom in the powerful "before" of His revelation, but who does that as the God who came to us precisely in His revelation . . . . "Before" indicates that this divine act of salvation, preached to us by the gospel, is free from what we know in the world to be arbitrary and precarious. To be sure, in this depth-aspect of God's salvation it becomes at the same time evident that this salvation did not originate in our flesh and blood, and that it is by no means of human merit or creation. But precisely this fact does not obscure the way; on the contrary, it illumines it. "Before the foundation of the world" means to direct our attention to what can be called the opposite of chance and contingence. History and the gospel are not minimized, but the riches and fullness of salvation in history are shown to be anchored in God.[49]

Third, the "logical" paradigm seems to lead us back to a symmetrical view of equal ultimacy, according to Berkouwer, in which election and reprobation are seen as a parallel mode of the divine operation of sovereign causality and the accompanying presupposition of a *decretum absolutum*. This is the case, he argues, because the corollary of this logical paradigm, according to Berkouwer, is a "metaphysical determinism," as he calls it, regarding election and reprobation, "which leaves no room for variations and difference but which subsumes everything under the one causality of God."[50] This criticism seems justified. For even when one affirms an essential asymmetry between election and reprobation, there is behind the latter the decree to election and rejection, that is, a positive and negative decree, saving some fallen humans and passing others by, such that the latter decree of negative reprobation—preterition—is not connected with a man's sin. As Berkouwer describes this view, "To be sure, in this position there is also a connection between sin and ultimate rejection (the judgment), but this happens in time, in history, and sin does not play any part in the apriori decree. Hence, rejection is, in the counsel of God, more of an act of God's sovereignty than of His justice. God's primary plan, His first apriori de-

47. Ibid., 195 [168].
48. Ibid., 242 [205].
49. Ibid., 242, 174 [204–5, 150–51].
50. Ibid., 208 [178].

cree—also as decree to rejection—is a decree of His eternal pleasure."[51] John Murray, for one, agrees with Berkouwer that "there is diversity in the mode of divine operation." Still, he seeks to defend as "inviolate," as he puts it, "the pure sovereignty of the differentiation inhering in the counsel of God," and hence, "in respect of *causality*," the "equal ultimacy . . . as it concerns both God's eternal counsel and man's everlasting destiny." Says Murray, "God differentiated between men in his eternal decree; *he* made men to differ. And, ultimately, the only explanation of the differentiation [between unbelief and belief] is the sovereign will of God." That is, "the sin of men is not the reason for the differentiation among men but simply and solely the sovereign will of God."[52] With this conclusion we come back to *decretum absolutum* and its corollary of metaphysical determinism.

Fourth, consider against the background of this determinism, for instance, Sproul's answer to what he calls "the thorny question of God predestinating the reprobate." He asks, "If God in any sense predestines or foreordains reprobation, doesn't this make the rejection of Christ by the reprobate absolutely certain and inevitable? And if the reprobate's reprobation is certain in light of predestination, doesn't this make God responsible for the sin of the reprobate? We must answer the first question in the affirmative, and the second in the negative."[53] But if absolutely certain and inevitable, how can the gospel be proclaimed to all men? How can the reprobate—those that God has passed over—be held accountable for their failure to response to the gospel? Furthermore, adds Sproul, "If God foreordains reprobation does this not obliterate the distinction between positive-negative [decrees] and involve a *necessity of force*? If God foreordains reprobation does this not mean that God forces, compels, or coerces the reprobate to sin? Again the answer must be negative." No, because preterition is a passing over of some people, a negative reprobation: "To reprobate is to be left in sin, not pushed or forced to sin. If the decree of reprobation were made without a view to the fall, then the objection to double predestination would be valid and God would be properly charged with being the author of sin." Clearly, the ones passed over will never receive the grace to respond to the Gospel. Surely, this gives men reason to be pessimistic, rendering the doctrine of predestination as something that is fallen under a shadow.

Be that as it may, these are questions of immense importance for understanding not only the Reformed but also the Catholic tradition. They have been answered throughout the history of the Reformed and Catholic

---

51. Ibid., 314 [258].

52. Murray, *Collected Writings*, 4:323–30, and at 328–30.

53. Sproul, "'Double' Predestination," 5.

theologies of election by taking us through a thorny path of subtle distinctions, not to say, labyrinth of speculative notions, such as, negative and
positive reprobation, *contra*, but not *praeter*, *voluntatem*, *praescientia* and
permissio, infra- and supra-lapsarianism, and others. Let me continue to
explore some of these issues in my further examination of the views of
Bavinck and Berkouwer.

Election and Reprobation

Pared down for my purposes here now, consider, for instance, the Thomist
who distinguishes between "negative" and "positive" reprobation. The former "consists in the decree of God to permit some of His moral creatures to
sin and thus lose salvation. It is called negative because God does not work
something, but let's something happen, on our part." Ott calls this sense
of reprobation "unconditioned non-election" because it is an act of God's
sovereignty withholding graces, occurring prior to a man's sinful acts. St.
Thomas says, "Why He chooses some for glory, and reprobates others, has
no reason, except the divine will."[54] We find the same idea in the Canons of
Dort: "What peculiarly tends to illustrate and recommend to us the eternal
and unmerited grace of election is the express testimony of sacred Scripture
that not all, but some only, are elected, while others are passed by in the eternal decree."[55] It is not that God causes man to sin because he is reprobated.
God passes them by, withholding graces on those whom he will permit to
reject him. Ott is right that "it is difficult to find an intrinsic concordance
between unconditioned non-election and the universality of the Divine resolve of salvation. In practice, the unconditioned negative reprobation of
the Thomists involves the same result as the unconditioned positive reprobation of the heretical Predestinarians [equal symmetry view]."[56] In short,
"unconditioned non-election" seems difficult to reconcile with the universal
salvific will of God, the universal scope of Christ's redemptive work, and
contradicts the justice of God, as well as man's freedom. What, then, is the
divine role in permitting final impenitence?

54. Aquinas, *Summa Theologiae* I, q. 23, art. 5, citing Augustine, *Homilies on the
Gospel of John*, 26:2. We find unconditioned non-election also in the 1646 *Westminster
Confession of Faith* (III.7; italics added): "The rest of mankind God was pleased, according to the unsearchable counsel of His own will, *whereby He extends or withholds mercy,
as He pleases*, for the glory of His sovereign power over His creatures, *to pass by*; and to
ordain them to dishonor and wrath for their sin, to the praised of His glorious justice"
(in Dennison *Reformed Confessions*, 4:239).

55. Canons of Dort, I.15, in Dennison, *Reformed Confessions*, 4:124–25.

56. Ott, *Fundamentals of Dogma*, 245.

By contrast, positive reprobation takes a man's sinful acts into account by maintaining—via the divine *praescientia*—that, given his rejection of God's sufficient grace, a man's demerits are the reason for his reprobation. So this is not absolute, or unconditional, positive reprobation; it, then, is always conditional. Still, as Salza rightly sees, there is a link between negative and positive reprobation: "God's choice to reprobate logically precedes a person's demerits, for the demerits would not exist without God's divine permission."[57] Still, on this view, the Thomist insists on God's universal salvific will, the bestowal of sufficient grace to the reprobate, and man's freedom.[58] Says Berkouwer, "Positive reprobation is apriori, but not in such a way that sin—in the *praescientia*—is discounted. A reprobation which would not indicate this connection would be contrary to God's general will to salvation, so that a positive reprobation is placed over against what is seen as essential in the Reformation: absolute apriority [unconditioned positive reprobation]. [Conditioned] Positive reprobation corresponds to sin, to the *praevisio demerita*."[59] As we shall see below, Berkouwer rejects the clarification of "essential asymmetry" with the two concepts of *praescientia* and *permissio* as a false solution with respect to both election and reprobation, because it relapses into Pelagianism—the freedom of indeterminism, human autonomy—and attempts to withdraw sin and unbelief, as well as faith and obedience, from God's eternal counsel. "Nothing can be made independent of the counsel of God."[60]

And yet, regarding reprobation, Berkouwer is very cautious about providing a theological explanation for reprobation. "One either breaks through the Augustinian *non praeter voluntatem Dei* into the making of man's life autonomous, or one weakens the grave seriousness of the *contra voluntatem Dei*. All of this results from an effort to 'explain' God's ordinances and to scrutinize His inscrutable ways."[61] Accordingly, Berkouwer is persuaded that theological reflection should stop at the Augustinian maxim: *contra*, but not *praeter voluntatem Dei*.

Regarding predestination, or election, Berkouwer's point is questionable or sufficiently inexact to miss out on the complexity of the Catholic position. Unlike Berkouwer, Bavinck does take note of the distinction between

57. Salza, *The Mystery of Predestination*, 51.

58. Ott, *Fundamentals of Dogma*, 245. Does Thomas hold that predestination is granted in accordance with the foreseen merit in the ones predestined? Thomas of course doesn't think so (*Summa theologiae*, I, 23, art. 5). Here I am just stating Berkouwer's understanding of positive reprobation.

59. Berkouwer, *De Verkiezing Gods*, 235 [199].

60. Ibid., 237 [201].

61. Ibid., 240 [203].

"predestination in the full sense," which is complete Predestination to grace and glory, on the one hand, and "predestination in a limited sense," on the other.[62] The latter, "incomplete Predestination to grace," as Ott calls it, "is independent of every merit (*ante praevisa merita*) as the first grace that cannot be merited."[63] Significantly, conjointly considered, complete Predestination "is independent of every merit, as the first grace cannot be merited and the consequent graces, as well as the merits acquired with these graces and their reward, depend like the links of a chain, on the first grace."[64] Ott continues: "If Predestination is conceived as Predestination to glory alone, then the question arises whether the Predestination to eternal bliss occurs by reason of the foreseen supernatural merits of man (*post praevisa merita*) or without consideration of them (*ante praevisa merita*). According to the former view, the Divine Resolve of Predestination is conditioned (hypothetical), [but] according to the latter, it is unconditioned (absolute)."[65] In the light of this distinction between conditional and unconditional Predestination, we may distinguish three positions in the Catholic tradition. Ott helpfully explains them:

> [1] The Thomists, the Augustinians, the majority of the Scotists, and [2] also older Molinists (Suarez, St. [Robert] Bellarmine) teach an absolute Predestination (*ad gloriam tantum*), therefore, *ante praevisa merita*. According to them, God freely resolves from all Eternity, without consideration of the merits of man's graces, to call certain men to beatification and therefore to bestow on them graces which will infallibly secure the execution of the Divine Decree (*ordo intentionis*). In time God first gives to the predestined effective graces and then eternal bliss as a reward for the merits which flow from their free co-operation with grace (*ordo executionis*).[66]

According to some Catholic critics of position [1], where predestination to glory is decreed *ante praevisa merita*, critics such as those Ott calls older Molinists (position [2]), but which strictly speaking are the Congruists, position, [1] appears to these critics to be a version of Calvinism.[67] This

62. Bavinck, *GD* II, 315 [354].

63. Ott, *Fundamentals of Dogma*, 243.

64. Ibid. Bavinck, *GD* II, 315 [354]: "Now, inasmuch as predestination to initial grace is the beginning of complete predestination, it can be said that predestination in its entirety is grace and unmerited, because it is 'gratuitous in its case', or as the Thomists say, it is 'gratuitous in itself'."

65. Ott, *Fundamentals of Dogma*, 243.

66. Ibid., 243.

67. See chapter 3 on Scheeben where Molinism and Congruism are discussed.

conclusion about reprobation was deeply unsatisfying for many as a theological explanation for reprobation, that is, for the divine role in permitting final impenitence. This is what Ott calls "unconditioned non-election" and it seems difficult to square with God's universal salvific will. Bavinck explains why he agrees with this understanding of negative reprobation.

> The negative decree of reprobation was viewed as anterior to the fall and as an act of sovereignty. It is no more based on demerits than election is based on merits. It implies the will to permit certain persons to plunge into guilt, and is the cause of abandonment. Thus many Thomists . . . taught that negative reprobation occurs prior to the fall and is purely an act of divine sovereignty and good pleasure. Only this supralapsarian reprobation was viewed as completely negative, as the decree of God not to elect certain people, to allow them to fall, and after that (positive reprobation) to destine them to eternal punishment. Essentially and materially Luther, Zwingli, Calvin, and all supralapsarian Reformed theologians taught exactly the same thing.[68]

Given this conclusion, it is no wonder that "Molina argues strenuously that this Bañezian [Spanish Thomists] doctrine is incompatible with human freedom and falls into the strict determinism advocated by the Lutherans and Calvinists."[69] In contrast, "Congruists," explains Nichols, "argued that by *scientia media*, God could foresee how souls would react to particular graces, and on this basis conferred on the elect those graces he saw would be efficacious ('congruent' with salvation), while on others he simply bestowed sufficient grace—thereby excluding them from an efficacious election to glory."[70] In response to the Congruists, Bavinck held that their position smacked of semi-Pelagianism. Yes, says Bavinck, on this view, "predestination to glory is indeed absolute." But "God first decreed to grant salvation to some before and apart from all merits, and then decreed to so shape their hearts by grace that they would be able to merit salvation by works."[71]

Furthermore, there is a third position [3] to consider, namely Molinism, which is named after the Spanish Jesuit Luis de Molina, and which we discussed in chapter 3. In sum, Ott explains: "Most of the Molinists, and also St. Francis of Sales (d. 1622), teach a conditioned Predestination (ad gloriam tantum), that is, post and propter praevisa merita. According to them, God, by His scientia media, sees beforehand how He chooses, according to

---

68. Bavinck, *GD* II, 324 [363].
69. Freddoso, "Molina, Luis de."
70. Nichols, *Epiphany*, 189.
71. Bavinck, *GD* II, 315 [354].

His free pleasure a fixed and definite order of grace. Now by His *scientia visionis*, He knows infallibly in advance what use the individual man will make of the grace bestowed on him. He elects for eternal bliss those who by virtue of their foreseen merits perseveringly cooperate with grace, while he determines for eternal punishment of hell, those who, on account of their foreseen demerits, deny cooperation."[72] According to the Molinists, justice is done to the orthodox doctrine of predestination where the omnipotence and sovereignty of divine grace is upheld; still, they came into conflict with the Thomists who held that the "will to respond to grace is itself graced," and hence charges Molinism with Pelagian or semi-Pelagian overtones.[73] Bavinck agrees. "The Molinists (Molina, Valentia, Vasquez, Tanner, Lessius, Becanus, Petavius, Lapide, and others) defended predestination to glory on a basis of foreseen merits."[74]

Accordingly, Berkouwer sees that others in the Catholic tradition, such as Molinists, have extended the influence of these two concepts of *praescientia* and *permissio* to the matter of election. This approach over-emphasizes man's responsibility, projecting it back into the divine counsel in light of these concepts. In reaction to this extension, says Berkouwer, "we can understand the inclination to prefer the symmetry [of election and reprobation] above the dangers of the doctrine of *praescientia*." He concludes: "Where all hesitation with respect to the symmetry has been overcome, we see the advancement of a doctrine of election which proceeds from one central concept, namely, causality, and this irrevocably ends up in determinism."[75] I suggest that Berkouwer would see such a relapse into determinism in Sproul's position.

Relapse into Determinism

Regarding Sproul's answer to the first question above, particularly against the background of the logical paradigm and its corollary of metaphysical determinism, we can easily understand why Berkouwer resists Sproul's "logic." That is, it too easily identifies the sovereignty of God's grace with "irrevocable 'eternal' decrees in which God would once and forever have predestined the salvation or ruin of man."[76] In this light, Berkouwer raises the following pertinent question: "The question was asked whether against

72. Ott, *Fundamentals of Dogma*, §12.b.β

73. Nichols, *Epiphany*, 188.

74. Bavinck, *GD* II, 315 [354].

75. Berkouwer, *De Verkiezing Gods*, 236 [200].

76. Ridderbos, *Paul*, 345.

this background it still was possible to speak of a gospel addressed to everyone, and whether preaching did not come to stand in the light (or shadow!) of this double predestination." [77] In this "interpretation of the doctrine of election . . . it is difficult to see the significance of preaching the gospel. It is the deterministic interpretation, which usurps all room for preaching because of its causal symmetry between election and rejection. . . . There is no room for real preaching, for a serious testimony, for a calling and admonishing appeal. The superiority of causality is too strong, and ultimately invades all traditional ways in which the preaching of the gospel is still continued. Determinism has always crowded out the *kerygma* from one direction or the other." [78] In other words, the critical question raised by Berkouwer is: "Does not double predestination render pointless everything people decide and do?" Put differently, "that decree [of election and reprobation is] fixed from eternity, the decree that determines everything and every person, [is] a decree that *must* be realized in history. Is there, within this horizon, still a possibility for genuine preaching to summon people to a decision of faith?" [79]

Now, in Berkouwer's 1955 work, *De Verkiezing Gods*, he still affirms "double predestination," but in light of his stress on the essential asymmetry of election and reprobation in respect to the mode of divine operation. He rejects the logical paradigm of predestination and its implied determinism, but still holds on to double predestination. As I will show, Berkouwer eventually came to reject the truth of premises 1 and 2 in the "logic" sketched above and embraced "single" predestination of a gracious election in Christ before the foundation of the world without falling into universalism—*in nuce*, all men are saved through the work of Christ—or some version of qualified Arminianism—divine election depends on foreseen faith. The traces of Berkouwer's own position are already found in his emphasis that we cannot "separate God's sovereignty from His love, and His election from Jesus Christ." [80] He adds, "The testimony of Scripture to the message of God's decree [that He choose us in Christ] 'before the foundation of the world' does not separate man from the gospel, but brings him closer to it. To say that God's counsel is eternal is not to make it remote, but to guarantee the inviolate reality of what is near." [81] "God in Christ was reconciling the world unto Himself (2 Cor 5:19), and that it is precisely the coming of Christ,

77. Berkouwer, *De Verkiezing Gods*, 202 [174].

78. Ibid., 261–62 [220].

79. Berkouwer, *Een Halve Eeuw Theologie*, 107–8 [83].

80. Berkouwer, *De Verkiezing Gods*, 187 [161].

81. Ibid., 198 [171].

sent by the Father which is the revelation of God's love (1 John 4:9)."[82] The point of concentration of the decree of election is the love of God in Jesus Christ. Election itself is a motive for proclamation of the Gospel to all men (Rom 16:26), says Berkouwer.[83] Berkouwer develops this point in the light of Bavinck's claim: "to believe in and to confess election is to recognize even the more unworthy and degraded human beings as a creature of God and an object of eternal love. The purpose of election is not—as it is so often proclaimed—to turn off the many but to invite all to participate in the riches of God's grace in Christ."[84]

Berkouwer agreed with those theologians who sought to free election "from the shackles of logical deduction." The main motivation behind his rejection of double predestination is "not respect for the autonomy of the free man." As Berkouwer puts it, "Criticism of the parallel is not meant to imply minimization of the sovereignty and absoluteness of God's good pleasure."[85] As I said above, Berkouwer and Bavinck[86] affirm the Augustinian maxim: *contra voluntatem Dei* but not *praeter voluntatem Dei*. Indeed, adds Berkouwer, "When it is asked wherein the reason lies for the Reformed criticism of the symmetry, it can certainly not be found in an attempt to deny the counsel of God over all things, or even, to limit it." Thus, Berkouwer affirms God's all-embracing providence. The reason for this criticism is, rather, "from a conviction that the Word of God does not warrant this idea of symmetry."[87] Why? Scripture repeatedly speaks of "God's rejection [as] a divine answer in history, as a reaction to man's sin and disobedience, not as its cause."[88] Significantly, Berkouwer then asks whether there is anything to add to "the act of divine rejection as God's answer to sin."[89] As Runia puts it in describing Berkouwer's probing: "Is there a 'plus', the 'plus' of God's eternal decree? Is there a double cause, one in man's sin and guilt, and a second and deeper one in God's predestination?"[90] I will return to this critical question below.

82. Ibid., 155 [136].

83. Berkouwer, *Een Halve Eeuw Theologie,* 139 [100].

84. Bavinck, *GD* II, 365–66 [402].

85. Berkouwer, *De Verkiezing Gods,* 214 [179].

86. Bavinck, *GD* II, 323, 349–50, 359 [238, 387, 396]

87. Berkouwer, *De Verkiezing Gods,* 214 [183], and throughout 224, 228, 237, 240, 256, 258, 337 [190, 193, 201, 203, 215, 217, 276–77].

88. Ibid., 214 [183]. In this connection, Berkouwer refers to such biblical texts as 1 Sam 15:23; 2 Kgs 17:20; Deut 28:15ff.; Lam 5:22; Pss 51:13; 78:67; Isa 50:1ff.

89. Ibid., 216 [184–85].

90. Runia, "Recent Reformed Criticisms." Runia also says, "I believe that we may say that there is no virtually no place for such a 'decree [of reprobation]' in Berkouwer's

Furthermore, the denial of parallelism or symmetry of election and reprobation is mainly about revealing "the meaning of election without creating the tension between election and preaching." This tension remains unresolved even in a theology of predestination that understands election and reprobation asymmetrically because in the background hovers a *decretum absolutum*. Even in the latter theology there remains "the aprioristic double decree with its two groups of human beings, each of which was the 'object' of one decision within the two-fold decree. The two groups were the elect and reprobate, which . . . were 'two groups, shut off from each other by a static objectification." Hence, adds Berkouwer, "The universal proclamation of the gospel could be accommodated to this notion of 'two groups of human beings' only via a contrived dogma."[91] Berkouwer continues: "This is why we ought not be seduced into thinking—in view of election—of two separate groups of people. . . . The Bible does not present us with two classes of people, but only one, the sinners who are called to salvation."[92] Looking back briefly to Dort, Berkouwer affirms what he calls the "real intention of the fathers of Dort," namely, "the sovereignty of grace was opposed to all human pretensions of merit." Yes, "There is a 'pre-,' but it is the divine preference for sinners, in support of which we can quote half of the Gospels. This is the preference we find in 1 Corinthians 1. It is a 'pre-' of divine desire, not logical determinism."

According to Berkouwer, then, the logical paradigm sets the "pre" in a "construction that does not let the grace of election come to its own, in spite of all the warnings against misunderstanding that the Epilogue [to the Canons of Dort] contains. Grace takes a back seat because of the double focus of the divine decree, a dual focus that the fathers of Dort thought necessary in order to secure the 'pre' aspect of election. Is the 'pre' dimension secured only through double predestination? Or is there something in John 3:17 that suggests a holy reserve in Scripture?"[93] "For God sent the Son into the world not to condemn the world, but that the world might be saved through him." In short, according to Berkouwer, predestination is about the absolute priority of grace, with the latter being the eternal foundation of salvation. That is, divine election is "more than just a confession of God's free grace in our life." The Bible says more. Yes, according to Runia, "There are especially in the New Testament, many passages that speak of

---

theology."

91. Berkouwer, *Een Halve Eeuw Theologie*, 139 [99–100].

92. Ibid., 127 [95].

93. Ibid., 124–25 [93–94].

God's pre-determination (cf. Acts 4:28; Rom 8:29–30; Eph 1:4–11)."[94] Ridderbos agrees: "The evidence of the pre-temporal elements in the Pauline
doctrine of election and predestination may not be denied."[95] How, then,
does Berkouwer intend to do justice to the "designation of sovereign, divine
grace as the sole motive of his [God's] work of redemption in history?"[96] I
will return to this below when briefly considering the relation between the
priority of God's counsel and plan of salvation revealed in Christ, in short,
his redemptive purposes, his election, and the preaching of the gospel.

The remainder of this chapter is structured as follow. First, I will sketch
Berkouwer's and Bavinck's defense of double predestination in light of the
essential asymmetry of election and reprobation.[97] Second, I will show
how they affirm this asymmetry, but (in Berkouwer's words) "without falling into the doctrine of *praescientia*," that is, a conditional predestination
in which election is based on man's free response to the offer of salvation
as foreknown and foreseen by God. On this view of conditional predestination, "divine election was made dependent on man's decision, resulting in 'a complete re-interpretation and mutation of the decisive concepts
because all concepts [of predestination]' were changed in the direction of
the *praevisio*, the *praescientia*, and the *permissio*. The central motif here in
this reinterpretation is defending and maintaining man's free will."[98] Berkouwer rejects that reinterpretation because "election is an election of [the
unmerited sovereign] grace [of God], that is to say: it does not take place on
the ground of works."[99] Third, I will consider their critique of the limitations
of infra- and supra-lapsarianism."[100] I will do this especially with respect to
their critique of the decree of reprobation from eternity and that creation
and fall are the ways that God seeks to realize that decree. Fourth, I will
examine Berkouwer's rejection of "reprobation from eternity" and, therefore his turn to a doctrine of "single predestination." This stems, he argues,
from the aim of upholding "the real intention, the *skopus* of the Canons [of

94. Runia, "Recent Reformed Criticisms."

95. Ridderbos, *Paul*, 347n46.

96. Ibid., 350.

97. They will only receive separate treatment in the next section when they diverge
in their accounts of double predestination and hence add something new.

98. Berkouwer, *De Verkiezing Gods*, 249 [210]. Inexplicably, the ET of *De Verkiezing Gods* leaves out this last sentence. The quote within the quote is from E. Weber, *Das
Problem der Heilsgeschichte* (1911), 18.

99. Ridderbos, *Paul*, 346.

100. Berkouwer, *De Verkiezing Gods*, 309–38 [264–77]. Bavinck, *GD* II, 322–27,
351–55 [361–66, 388–92].

Dort] (the sovereignty of grace)."[101] This last point will be considered in the context of the relationship between election and the preaching of the gospel.

A Reformed Doctrine of Predestination

I explained above that, according to Berkouwer, the doctrine of God's election . . . is not a *decretum absolutum*, abstracted from Jesus Christ." We cannot separate God's decree of election from his love and grace in Jesus Christ, God's Yes to man, of affirmation. In this light, we can understand why Berkouwer then asks about God's No to man's life of sin in history and therefore his judgment as an 'act of God in history', as a reactive deed, a holy, divine answer to the sin of man."[102] The crucial question then arises: "Is it still necessary to speak of rejection after discussing the election in Christ?"[103] Indeed, Berkouwer asks "whether God's rejection belongs, and can belong, to the *kerygma* of the Church. Is it possible to see God's rejection differently than as God's holy answer to human sin?"[104] Significantly, Berkouwer presses the point that this question "is not one of a mere symmetry, but [rather] that God has loved the world (John 3:16)." He explains in a passage, part of which I quoted earlier:

> It is then no longer understood that God did not send the Son to condemn the world (John 3:17) but that the world should be saved through Him. *This is the profoundest reason for rejecting parallelism. This rejection does not imply the triumph of a simple sort of universalism.* Immediately after John speaks of the purpose of Christ's coming, he adds: "He that believeth on him is not judged: he that believeth not has been judged already, because he hath not believed on the name of the only begotten Son of God" (John 3:18). He who contemplated and approaches the gospel from the point of view of symmetry can no longer understand that Christ has come to be a crisis in the world, but he can only see in Him the execution of the symmetrical decree. . . . The gospel can be understood and preached only if balance, symmetry, and parallelism are excluded. And by that gospel, the Holy Spirit will "convict the world in respect of sin, and of

101. Berkouwer, "The Authority of Scripture (A Responsible Confession)," 198.

102. Berkouwer, *De Verkiezing Gods*, 215 [184]. The quote within the quote is from Bavinck, *GD* II, 355 [393].

103. Ibid., 200–201 [172].

104. Ibid., 239 [202].

righteousness, and of judgments: of sin, because they believe not
on me" (John 16:8).[105]

Since the profoundest reason for rejecting the parallelism or symmetry
of election and reprobation is John 3:17, then, we can understand why
Berkouwer's thought would lead him to reject the teaching that Reformed
theologians, such as John Murray, claim is inherent to the Reformed tradition, and which, according to Berkouwer, makes it difficult to avoid fatalistic
determinism. Let me be clear: Murray himself concurs with Berkouwer that
"the fullest consent must be accorded" to the Canons of Dort's affirmation
of essential asymmetry and hence its rejection of parallelism or symmetry
of election and reprobation. Yes, he says, "there is diversity in the mode of
divine operation." Still, he seeks to defend as "inviolate," as he puts it, "the
pure sovereignty of the differentiation inhering in the counsel of God," and
hence, "in respect of *causality*," the "equal ultimacy . . . as it concerns both
God's eternal counsel and man's everlasting destiny." Says Murray, "God differentiated between men in his eternal decree; *he* made men to differ. And,
ultimately, the only explanation of the differentiation [between unbelief and
belief] is the sovereign will of God." That is, "the sin of men is not the reason
for the differentiation among men but simply and solely the sovereign will
of God."[106] Murray's view represents unconditioned positive reprobation
that leads to a denial of God's universal salvific will, of the universal scope of
the atonement (i.e., Christ did not die for all men), contradicting the justice
of God, and man's freedom.

   With respect to man's freedom, Berkouwer rejects "equal ultimacy"
because it makes it "impossible to distinguish predestination from fatalistic determinism." On the one hand, "everything seems to run causally and
thus the incisive contrast between belief and unbelief is therefore causally
explained by the Divine decree; but on the other hand, that God is thus
the author of sin is rejected, and what is highlighted is the divine response
to sin: God as Judge and Avenger."[107] In sum, then, "a doctrine of election
which proceeds from one central concept, namely, causality . . . irrevocably
ends up in determinism."[108] Resisting determinism, however, does not mean
that Berkouwer embraces human autonomy, or what he throughout calls
"indeterminism." What is a human will that is indetermined, according to
Berkouwer? He never actually says, but I think we can surmise that it is a
libertarian notion of freedom. The latter "is that freedom, in the full-blood-

105. Ibid., 238 [201–2]; emphasis added.

106. Murray, *Collected Writings*, 328–30.

107. Berkouwer, "Vragen Rondom de Belijdenis," 1–41, and at 12–13.

108. Berkouwer, *De Verkiezing Gods*, 236 [200].

ed sense of the term relevant to questions of free will, requires alternate possibilities. If a particular choice is really free, in this sense, then it must be one that was not determined in advance, whether by God or by any other cause. It must be up to me how the choice goes, and something other than what I actually chose to do." According to critics of the Reformed tradition, if this is denied then "they deny human freedom in the sense relevant to the free-will debate."[109] Berkouwer rejects indeterminism regarding free will because it implies that it is up to the individual to accept or reject salvation. Thus, according to Berkouwer, "The struggle between [causal] determinism and indeterminism in the doctrine of election is a futile one."[110]

Still, Berkouwer would agree with Murray and Bavinck that "nothing can be made independent of the counsel of God."[111] With approval, therefore, Berkouwer quotes Bavinck: "this entire sinful reality, all of world history as an interconnected series of events, is ultimately caused, not by factors inherent in itself—how indeed could it?—but by something extra-mundane: the mind and will of God."[112] Berkouwer is clear, however, that this claim of Bavinck must be seen in light of Augustine's thesis: "Against, but not in spite of, the will of God" (*contra voluntatem Dei* but not *praeter voluntatem Dei*).[113] Bavinck himself makes this point: "though sin is not outside the scope of the will of God, it is definitely against it."[114] Although Bavinck and Berkouwer take exception to terms such as "foreknowledge" and "permission," properly understood these terms help us to understand that God foresees and permits evil but does not directly will it. In other words, God permits sin but he is neither the cause of their sinning or preventing their sinning. Properly understanding these terms, however, which are not inherently wrong, means they "could not or should not be viewed in a purely passive sense."[115] By passive sense I take that to mean—in Berkouwer's words—that "God is . . . in His Providence, a balcony observer of a contest whose outcome is never certain. It suffices Him to create a playground and leave the decision to man whether it will be the scene of sin or of obedience. Sin, then, lies ultimately in man's power of decision, and God's

109. Crisp, *Deviant Calvinism*, 28.

110. Berkouwer, *De Verkiezing Gods*, 257 [216].

111. Ibid., 237 [201].

112. Bavinck, *GD* II, 360 [397], as quoted by Berkouwer in *De Verkiezing Gods*, 244 [206].

113. Berkouwer, *De Verkiezing Gods*, 237 [201].

114. Bavinck, *GD* II, 359 [397].

115. Ibid., 324 [364].

action becomes mere reaction to man's decision."[116] But if God's judgment of positive reprobation isn't a mere response to man's sinful deeds, is it decided independently of man's sin? If so, how does Berkouwer avoid making God the cause of unbelief and sin? In short, how does he, too, avoid unconditioned positive reprobation and all its implications?

In order to avoid, then, the connotation of spectator connoted by the passive sense of *praescientia* and *permissio* when speaking of "allowing sin," Berkouwer doesn't turn to posit a relation of causality between sin and the counsel of God. Yes, he cautions us to assume that he and Bavinck (in the latter's words) "explain sin as autonomous human deed, which is only known by God in a *nuda praescientia* and therefore would find its explanation in the concept of 'allowance' [permission]; for Bavinck accepts that fall, sin, and punishment are 'incorporated' in the counsel of God and 'in a sense are willed by God. But then only in a certain sense, and certainly not in the same manner as grace and salvation."[117] This concluding sentence reaffirms the "essential asymmetry" that Berkouwer holds is fundamental the Reformed doctrine of election.

Therefore, Berkouwer explains that we would be mistaken to interpret Bavinck as if he wanted "to explain everything (also evil) causally in God." He adds: "But it is clear that he wants to take fully into account what he writes repeatedly when he indicates the connection between the will of God and sin. He always adds, 'in a sense',[118] and with that he eschews every causality-explanation. He does not want to reach beyond Augustine's *non praeter voluntatem Dei*. And that explains why he speaks in this connection of the 'great difference'[119] between election and reprobation."[120] In short, "There is, indeed, a relation between sin and the counsel of God, but it is not the relation of causality."[121] Berkouwer, therefore, follows Bavinck, as he understands him, in eschewing every causality explanation in respect of reprobation and election as if God is causally responsible for eternally differentiating between men. In short, adds Berkouwer, "What is revealed in history and through sin is not the glory of abstract [causal] sovereignty, but the glory of sovereign love and loving sovereignty."[122]

---

116. Berkouwer, *De Voorzienigheid Gods*, 165 [149–50].

117. Berkouwer, *De Verkiezing Gods*, 206 [177]. The quote within the quote if from Bavinck, *GD* II, 351[389].

118. Bavinck, *GD* II, 351, 354 [389, 391].

119. Ibid., 352 [389].

120. Berkouwer, *De Verkiezing Gods*, 244 [206].

121. Ibid., 337 [276].

122. Ibid., 325 [267].

Although Berkouwer emphasizes throughout his study the sovereignty of God's election in Christ and the sovereignty of grace in election, he doesn't deny rejection or reprobation. But he does treat it differently than election in order for his treatment to conform to the essential asymmetry that the Canons affirm in denying the alleged parallelism in the way of belief and unbelief, namely, that God's election and reprobation operate in the same manner (*eodem modo*). In the language of the Canons of Dort, which Berkouwer cites: "The cause or guilt of this unbelief, as well as of all other sins, is nowise in God, but in man himself: whereas faith in Jesus Christ, and salvation through him, is the free gift of God."[123] The cause of God's rejection of man is sin and hence judgment is inextricably linked to man's sin. This judgment of God is called positive reprobation. In response, then, to the question whether rejection, indeed, reprobation belongs to the gospel, the answer is yes, but only as God's reaction to sin rather than as an eternal decree that in itself has no bearing on sin.

Indeed, the preaching of God's judgment is inherently connected, according to Lord's Day 31 of the *Heidelberg Catechism*, to "the wrath of God and eternal condemnation [that] falls upon all unbelievers and hypocrites *as long as they do not repent*."[124] Berkouwer explains: "The preaching of the judgment of God is so closely linked up with the message of Christ that Lord's Day 31 closes with the words: 'according to this witness of the gospel God will judge, both in this life and in that which is to come', a statement that is a clear echo of the testimony in Scripture (Acts 17:31), and is based on the convincing work of the Holy Spirit—'of sin, because they believe not on me'(John 16:9)."[125] Thus, God has decreed eternal punishment for the sin of the final impenitent—according to Lord's Day 31—and this has generated much reflection, in particular, on the following question. "If the grace of God is sufficient for salvation, should it not also be efficacious in causing the impenitent to become penitent, even, if need be, in the moment of death?

---

123. Berkouwer, *De Verkiezing Gods*, 210 [180], citing Canons of Dort, I.5; see also, Canons III-IV.9. This, too, is the view of Aquinas: "The causality of reprobation differs from that of predestination. Predestination is the cause both of what the predestined expect in the future life, namely glory, and of what they receive in the present, namely grace. Reprobation does not cause what there is in the present, namely moral fault, though that is why we are left without God. And it is the cause why we shall meet our deserts in the future, namely eternal punishment. The fault starts from the free decision of the one who abandons grace and is rejected, so bringing the prophecy to pass, *Your loss is from yourself, O Israel.* [Hosea 13.9]."

124. Lord's Day 31 is quoted by Berkouwer, *De Verkiezing Gods*, 293 [243].

125. Berkouwer, *De Verkiezing Gods*, 293 [243].

How is it that God mercifully grants efficacious grace to some and yet justly refuses it to others?"[126]

We don't know the answer to this last question, according to both Bavinck and Berkouwer. Of course they reject not only unconditioned positive reprobation, but also conditioned reprobation. They reject the latter because it impugns God's sovereignty. Yes, God is not the cause of unbelief and sin. Man's sin is unquestionably the proximate cause of sin, but not the ultimate cause. This point raises the vexing issue of obscuring the responsibility of the sinner and suggesting that God, somehow, is the final cause of man's reprobation. "For the imagined scenario is untenable: that God decided to create [man] without any preexisting plan, then waited and watched to see what humans would do, and then—knowing beforehand what the human response would be—proceeded to the action of election and reprobation. The ideas of 'foreknowledge' and 'permission' do not yield a solution, for God, foreseeing the fall, could have prevented it. He freely permitted it to happen, since doing so seemed good to him. Accordingly, Adam's fall, sin in general, and all the evil in the world cannot just have been foreseen by God but must also *in a sense* have been willed and determined by him. Hence, there must have been a reason (unknown to us) why God willed the fall: there has to be a higher plan of God that existed prior to the fall. . . . [Thus] the ultimate cause of reprobation and election is God's will."[127] The qualification here, as always, is "in a sense," and it follows from affirming the essential asymmetry between reprobation and election. Both Bavinck and Berkouwer—at least the Berkouwer of 1955—consistently appeal to the Augustinian maxim: *contra voluntatem Dei* but not *praeter voluntatem Dei*.

But a "double decree" still hovers in the background of this maxim—even when qualified by "essential asymmetry." Hence Berkouwer's point that the "problem of the relationship between election and reprobation pursues us still"—in 1963 and, again, in 1974. "How can divine election be pastorally comforting if it is backed by a double-focused eternal decree affirmed as an a priori judgment over all men, that is, over the destinies of two separate groups settled forever from out of God's absolute freedom?"[128] Furthermore, what also hovers in the "background" is the notion of a "predestined *numerus clausus* of the elect and whether with that . . . those who do not belong to this *numerus clausus* have not been excluded in virtue of

---

126. Nichols, *Epiphany*, 188.

127. Bavinck, *GD* II, 325–326 [364–365]; emphasis added.

128. Berkouwer, *Een Halve Eeuw Theologie*, 114 [86–87]. I have altered the English translation so as to more closely fit the Dutch text.

this same purpose before the foundation of the world."[129] Berkouwer adds, "The question is whether the notion of double destiny does not turn divine freedom into divine arbitrariness. . . . How could it be made clear that divine election was not an arbitrary decree that opened the door to a fatalism and determinism in which the events of our time and history were robbed of all genuine meaning?"[130] Berkouwer's final judgment on this question was to dispense with the identification of the sovereignty and omnipotence of God's grace "with irrevocable 'eternal' decrees in which God would once and forever have predestined the salvation or ruin of man."[131] As Berkouwer writes: "The problem of the 'background' continued to cast a shadow over all the wonderful things that were said in theology about God's gracious election. The struggle was always concentrated on our thoughts of the sovereignty and freedom of God which were affirmed by the doctrine of the divine decree. At this point, we usually spoke about the *absolute* freedom and sovereignty of God, as though to silence the opposition. But adding adjectives was not a sure way of preserving authentic orthodoxy, no matter what impression they make on first hearing. Adding 'absolute' did not really make the sun rise over the mystery of divine sovereignty and human freedom."[132] This conclusion is, arguably, a repudiation of the Augustinian maxim (*contra voluntatem Dei* but not *praeter voluntatem Dei*) as a satisfactory answer to the question regarding the divine role in the eternal punishment for the sin of the final impenitent. I turn now to consider briefly why Bavinck and Berkouwer came to reject the eternity of reprobation as God's predestining will.

---

129. Ridderbos, *Paul,* 350, and 352.
130. Berkouwer, *Een Halve Eeuw Theologie,* 114, 117 [87, 89].
131. Ridderbos, *Paul,* 345.
132. Berkouwer, *Een Halve Eeuw Theologie,* 119 [89–90].

Supralapsarianism and Infralapsarianism[133]

A. Supralapsarian	B. Infralapsarian	C. Hypothetical Universalism	D. Arminianism
1. Elect some, reprobate rest	1. Create	1. Create	1. Create
2. Create	2. Permit Fall	2. Permit Fall	2. Permit Fall
3. Permit Fall	3. Elect some, pass over the rest	3. Christ's atoning death is sufficient for all, but efficient only for the elect	3. Christ's atoning death is sufficient for all
4. Provide salvation for elect	4. Christ's atoning death is sufficient for all	4. Elect those who have faith, which distinguishes them from the reprobate	4. Call all to salvation
5. Call elect to salvation	5. Call elect to salvation	5. Call elect to salvation	5. Elect those who believe

The above chart describes four different positions regarding the relation, that is, the logical ordering of the divine decrees, between creation, fall, and redemption, on the one hand, and God's predestining grace, election and reprobation on the other. Supra- and infralapsarianism differ on the question whether God ordained the salvation of some and the damnation of others "prior to" or "before"—hence the "supra"—or "after" ("infra") the fall.[134] At issue is the question of how the fall was considered part of the counsel of God. Berkouwer explains: "There was apriori an unhesitant adhering to the doctrine that God was not the author of evil and that it was impossible to

133. I adapted this chart from Henry, *God, Revelation and Authority*, vol. 6, part 2, 88. Extremely helpful to me with understanding the ordering of divine decrees and the issue of the scope of divine grace in the atonement is Berkouwer, *De Verkiezing Gods*, 308–38 [254–77], Barth, *CD*, II.2, 135–55; but also Crisp, "Hypothetical Universalism," in *Deviant Calvinism*, 175–211. See also, "Notes on Supralapsarianism and Infralapsarianism."

134. Barth, *CD*, II.2, 153–55.

think of a predestination to evil. What, then, was to be the interpretation of the fall being part of God's counsel? Was rejection as a part of the counsel of God a reaction against sin, or had rejection apriori no bearing on that sin? It was in connection with these questions that the difference between supra and infra received its aspect of a problem of succession."[135] Regarding supralapsarianism, adds Berkouwer, "sin does not play any part in the apriori decree. Hence, rejection is, in the counsel of God, more an act of God's sovereignty than of His justice. God's primary plan, His first apriori decree—also as decree to rejection [preterition]—is a decree of His eternal pleasure."[136] Of course Berkouwer is right that, on this position, man's ultimate rejection, condemnation, is contingent upon the sins of men in time, in history; but given the apriori decree of preterition, those who are passed over by divine grace are not passed over *because* of their sin. Infralapsarianism takes an opposing view. "In this position the relation between sin and judgment (on earth) are considered as being part of the counsel of God. According to this position the decree to creation and fall logically precedes the decree to rejection and election, so that in the counsel of God rejection presupposes a fallen mankind. This rejection then changes its nature, and is more an act of His justice than of His sovereignty. This does not imply that the infra position denies the sovereignty of God, but in it the idea of God's wrath and reaction (God's justice) is dominant and central just as God's mercy is in election."[137] Furthermore, Reformed confessions, such as the Heidelberg Catechism (1563), the Belgic Confession (1561), the Second Helvetic Confession, and the Canons of Dort (1618–1619), take an infra- rather than a supralapsarian position. Explains Berkouwer:

135. Berkouwer, *De Verkiezing Gods*, 313 [257]. Crisp, "Hypothetical Universalism," 184.

136. Ibid., 314 [258].

137. Berkouwer, *De Verkiezing Gods*, 314 [258–59]. Dominant is an accurate way to put it because the Canons of Dort do affirm an apriori decree of negative reprobation—preterition. Canons of Dort, 1.15: "What peculiarly tends to illustrate and recommend to us the eternal and unmerited grace of election is the express testimony of sacred Scripture that not all, but some only, are elected, while others are passed by in the eternal decree; when God, out of His sovereign, most just, irreprehensible, and unchangeable good pleasure, has decreed to leave in the common misery into which they have willfully plunged themselves, and not to bestow upon them saving faith and the grace of conversion; but, permitting them in His just judgment to follow their own ways, at last, for the declaration of His justice, to condemn and punish them forever, not only on account of their unbelief, but also for all their other sins. And this is the decree of reprobation, which by no means makes God the Author of sin (the very thought of which is blasphemy!), but declares Him to be an awful, irreprehensible, and righteous Judge and Avenger thereof" (Dennison, *Reformed Confessions*, 4:124–25).

> The inclination toward the infra concept in the Confessions is shown by the fact that always reference is made to sin and perdition whenever predestination is mentioned. In the supra concept the condemnation in time is directly related to sin because actual judgment presupposes guilt, but not to the decree of rejection itself. This connection is not present, because the decree of predestination is thought to precede all merits and demerits, hence also the decree to creation and the "decree" of the fall.[138]

Moreover, adds Berkouwer, "But that the Confessions follow the infra presentation does not imply an obvious and exclusive choice with respect to the succession of God's decrees. . . . It can therefore be said that in spite of the contrast between supra and infra the Church has been kept from making a definite confessional statement with respect to succession in the decrees of God."[139] A good thing, too, says Berkouwer, since the problem regarding the logical ordering of the decrees of creation, fall, election, and redemption in the theological positions of supra and infra "is a self-created and therefore insoluble problem which does not touch upon the essential faith of the Church."[140] In brief, Berkouwer wants to honor the emphasis of the Reformed confessions where predestination is seen related to the fallen human race, to sin and guilt. "We find the infra motif in Article 16 of the Belgic Confession when it speaks of election from perdition. Salvation is confessed in connection with sin and guilt. There is no apriori mention of the counsel of God; but the depth and stability and the eternal source, not out of us, but out of God, are confessed in the light of salvation as it is revealed in history."[141]

In sum, Berkouwer's rejection of the concept of succession "is based on the Biblical testimony regarding the election in Christ. In that light it is impossible to speak *in abstracto* of a predestination decree which is realized by another independent decree to create and to ordain the fall. Nor may that be done for the sake of emphasizing God's sovereignty . . . What is revealed in history and through sin is not the glory of abstract sovereignty, but the glory of sovereign love and loving sovereignty."[142]

Now, taking B, C, and D together, they all agree that God's decree to creation and fall logically precedes the decree to rejection and election. Differences immediately appear once we consider the relationship between the

---

138. Berkouwer, *De Verkiezing Gods*, 322 [265].

139. Ibid.

140. Ibid., 323 [265].

141. Ibid., 324 [266].

142. Ibid., 325 [267].

redemptive work of Christ, on the one hand, and God's predestining grace, election and reprobation on the other. Both the Arminian and the Hypothetical Universalist are committed to universalism—meaning thereby that scope of Christ's atonement is sufficient for all, which is a form of universal divine love and intention to save. But there is a clear difference between them. On the one hand, according to the hypothetical universalism, God elects independent of any knowledge he has concerning foreseen faith. In short, "the hypothetical universalists claimed that God effectually applies the work of Christ only to those whom God has eternally elected according to [His] good pleasure and will."[143] On this view, the death of Christ is *sufficient* for all, but *efficient* only for the elect.

Regarding Arminianism, on the other hand, says Bavinck, "Arminius defended predestination as the eternal decree of God to save—in, on account of, and by Christ—those who he foresaw would by a prevenient grace believe and by a subsequent grace persevere; and to punish others who would not believe or persevere." His objection: "The residual objection to the still as yet certain foreknowledge of God with regard to those who would or would not believe, plus the universal offer of the *sufficient* means of grace—these gradually but necessarily resulted in making human beings the final arbiters of their own destiny."[144]

There is still one other position but it is not described on the chart, but Bavinck thought it worthwhile mentioning since it is often confused with hypothetical universalism, namely, Amyraldianism.[145] Moyse Amyraut, one of its founders, "taught a double decree." That is, explains Bavinck, "God first decreed in general that all who believed in Christ would be saved; but knowing in advance that no one can believe of himself . . . , he added to the first (universal and conditional) decree a second (particular and absolute) decree to give to some the gift of faith and save them."[146] The crucial difference between Amyraldianism and Arminianism is that the Arminian holds that God calls *all* to salvation whereas the Amyraldian is emphatically a particularist in that sense that God withholds grace from the non-elect

143. Crisp, "Hypothetical Universalism," 188.

144. Bavinck, *GD* II, 329 [368].

145. Carl R. Trueman describes the Amyraldian position: "Amyraldianism was a school of thought associated with the Academy at Saumur in France and developed by such theologians as Moses Amyraut [1596–1664] and John Cameron [1576–1641] as a means of obviating Arminian criticism of classic Reformed theology with regard to its apparent restriction of God's will to save [only the elect]" (Trueman, *John Owen*, 29–31).

146. Bavinck, *GD* II, 330[369].

(negative reprobation), passing them by, and hence he only calls the elect to salvation.

Position B—typically Reformed—is particularist regarding God's predestining will, with God again granting and withholding graces (unconditioned negative reprobation), but it is preceded by the decree of creation and of allowing the fall. So, positive reprobation is inextricably linked to sin and unbelief, because God's actual judgment in history presupposes guilt. Pared down for my purpose here, I want to underscore the difference between positions A and B in respect of reprobation from eternity. Position A significantly differs from B in that the decree of predestination precedes that of creation and fall. The first problem here with A is that it suggests that creation and fall are the *means* in which the eternal destinies of individuals are manifested. But this position raises the specter of equal symmetry regarding double predestination. In other words, as Bavinck puts it, "supralapsarianism . . . makes the eternal punishment of reprobates an object of the divine will in the same manner and in the same sense as the eternal salvation of the elect; and further, that it makes sin, which leads to eternal punishment, a means in the same manner and in the same sense as redemption in Christ is a means toward eternal salvation." Another critical question that arises here is whether it is correct to "represent the wretched state of the lost as the goal of predestination." Adds Bavinck:

> Admittedly, sin cannot be traced to a bare foreknowledge and permission of God. The fall, sin, and eternal punishment are included in the divine decree and in a sense willed by God, but then always only in a certain sense and not in the same manner as grace and blessedness. . . . [But] though on the one hand, with a view to the comprehensive and immutable character of God's counsel, there is no objection to speaking of a "double predestination," on the other hand we must bear in mind that in the one case predestination is of a different nature than in the other.[147]

How so? Where lies the difference between God's predestining election and reprobation? Chiefly, the crux of Bavinck's criticism of A here is that God does not predestine man to damnation because man was created for eternal fellowship with God.[148] Bavinck explains: "'Predestination is the disposition, end, and ordering of a means to an end. Since eternal damnation is not the goal but only the termination of human life, reprobation cannot properly be classified under predestination. For these two things—to order to a goal

---

147. Bavinck, *GD* II, 351 [389].

148. Essentially, Bavinck is arguing, as *CCC* teaches, "God predestines no one to go to hell" (no. 1037).

and to damnation—are at variance with each other. For by its very nature, every goal is the optimal end and perfect of a thing. Damnation, however, is the ultimate evil and the ultimate imperfection [of man], so that it cannot properly be said that God predestined some humans to damnation'. Hence, no matter how emphatically and often Scripture says that sin and punishment have been determined by God, the words 'purpose', 'foreknowledge', and 'predestination' are used almost exclusively with reference to 'predestination to glory.'"[149] This is where position B has an advantage over position A, namely, with its concern for inextricably linking reprobation and eternal damnation with the reality of sin and unbelief as opposition to God. Moreover, position A is also fundamentally misguided by placing predestination before creation and fall by losing sight of the independent purposes of God's plan for creation. Does God unfold his plan for creation with the defining interest being only the ultimate end, or eternal destinies, of individuals, both of the elect and reprobate? Alternatively, are there multiple divine purposes in the unfolding of God's design for the total creation?[150]

The brief answer to these two questions are "no" and "yes." No, because creation and fall are not simply a means to realize God's prime decrees of election and reprobation. Yes, because the totality of creation is not only affected by the fall into sin but also it is taken up within the purview of God's redemptive work in Christ Bavinck argues—and Berkouwer agrees. This, too, is Barth's objection: "It is absurd to suppose that first of all God arranged the eternal salvation or damnation of men and only then arranged their actual existence and fall. Creation and fall [on this view] must be regarded as necessary from the standpoint of predestination not as a *medium per quod* [means by which] but as a *conditio sine qua non* [a condition without which it could not be]. Obviously the sick man cannot be cured unless he exists as a man and is sick. But obviously, too, his existence as a man and his sickness cannot be regarded as a means to cure him."[151] Thus, it would be a case of theological reductionism to hold that creation and fall are mere means to realizing God's primal and basic purpose in election and reprobation, as if to say that creation itself with its multiple divine purposes is not itself taken up within the sweeping unfolding of God's design for creation. In sum, says Berkouwer, "To be sure, the question concerning the meaning and significance of creation entered in—whether creation did not have its

149. Bavinck, *GD* II, 352 [389]. The quote within the quote is from Bartholomew Keckermann (c. 1572–1609), German philosopher and Calvinist theologian, *Systema theologiae* (Hanoviae: Antonium, 1602), 296.

150. Mouw, *He Shines in all that's Fair*, 50. See also, chapter 4, "'Infra' versus 'Supra,'" 53–74.

151. Barth, *CD* II.2, 140.

own God-given purpose and hence was not more than just a 'means' to realize God's primary decree—but the main concern was nevertheless the question concerning the relation between predestination and fall."[152] It is particularly the infralapsarian who sees the decree to elect some human beings as logically consequent to the decrees of creation and fall. Moreover, Bavinck explains:

> Creation is not just a means for the attainment of the fall, nor is the fall only a means for the attainment of grace and persever- ance, and these components in turn are not just a means for the attainment of blessedness and eternal wretchedness. We must never lose sight of the fact that the decrees are as abundantly rich in content as the entire history of the world, for the latter is the total unfolding of the former. Who could possibly sum up world history in a logical outlines of just a few terms? Creation, fall, sin, Christ, faith, unbelief, and so forth, are certainly not just related to each other as means, so that a preceding one can fall away the moment the next one has been reached. . . . Cer- tainly the creation of the world did not just occur to make room for the event of the fall, but resulted in something that will con- tinue even in the state of glory. The fall did not just take place to produce creatures existing in a state of misery, but retains its meaning as a fact with all the consequences that have arisen from it. Christ did not only become a mediator—a position that would have been sufficient for the expiation of sin—but God also ordained him to be head of the church. The history of the world is not a means that can be dispensed with once the end has come; instead, it has continuing impact and leaves its fruits in eternity. And election and reprobation themselves do not fol- low two straight parallel lines, for in unbelievers there is much that does not arise from reprobation, and in believers there is much that cannot be attributed to election. . . . So the world as a whole is a masterpiece of divine art, in which all the parts are organically interconnected. And of that world, in all its dimen- sions, the counsel of God is the eternal design.[153]

Now, having considered the Bavinck's argument against the eternity of rep- robation, in one final section, I will consider Berkouwer's account on the relation of divine election and the general offer of the Gospel.

---

152. Berkouwer, *De Verkiezing Gods*, 320 [263].

153. Bavinck, *GD* II, 354–55 [390–92]. For Berkouwer's fundamental agreement with Bavinck, see *De Verkiezing Gods*, 333–34 [272–73].

Election and the General Offer of the Gospel

Does the free and general offer of the Gospel reveal God's universal salvific will for all men? Alternatively put, given the predestining grace of God, can the universal preaching of the Gospel really be meaningful? In response to this second question, Berkouwer argues that a "deterministically infected"[154] doctrine of election, with its causal symmetry between election and reprobation, undermines the general offer and preaching of the gospel. "We can no longer speak of glad tidings that go out into the world, except where the gospel reaches the elect. We do not know who they are, but, the purpose of the gospel is twofold: salvation and hardening [the rejected]. The symmetry casts its shadow over the *kerygma*."[155] How so? This causal symmetry "limits the *kerygma* to the elect and withholds it from the reprobate." Thus, the preaching of the gospel does not confront the rejected "with an invitation [to salvation] but with the reality of rejection. He can—in the light of this supposition—no longer be called upon to believe in Christ and salvation."[156] Distancing the Canons of Dort from a deterministic doctrine of election,[157] and understanding the basic intention of the Canons' doctrine of election to be an election of grace, "of sovereign, divine grace as the sole motive of his [God's] work of redemption in history."[158]

Berkouwer underscores not only the Canons attention to the general preaching of the gospel but also the seriousness of its call to repentance and conversion, which also comes to the reprobate. So the Canons: "Moreover, the promise of the gospel is that whosoever believes in Christ crucified shall not perish, but have eternal life. This promise, together with the command to repent and believe, ought to be declared and published to all nations, and to all persons promiscuously and without distinction, to whom God out of His good pleasure sends the gospel."[159] Thus, Berkouwer affirms the general offer of salvation.

154. Berkouwer, *De Verkiezing Gods*, 262 [220].

155. Ibid., 266–67 [223].

156. Ibid., 273 [228].

157. In 1955, Berkouwer is sure "that the background of the Canons is not to be found in a deterministic doctrine of election." In 1974, however, Berkouwer has changed his mind, arguing now that the Canons' mode of expression, if not the "central thrust and intentions of the Canons" as found in its doctrine of election itself with its emphasis on "the unmerited sovereign grace of God," is burdened with "the category of the 'universal causality' of God" (*Een Halve Eeuw Theologie*, 146 [105]). Earlier evidence of this change is found in Berkouwer's 1963 article, "Vragen Rondom de Belijdenis," 10–26. See also, Berkouwer's 1971 article, "The Authority of Scripture," 198–99.

158. Ridderbos, *Paul*, 350.

159. Canons of Dort, II, 5.

In this Canon, we hear clearly of the general offer of the gospel to all men, as Berkouwer puts it years later, "not [to] two classes of people, but only one, the sinners who are called to salvation,"[160] or, as Bavinck put it earlier in the century, "not as elect or reprobate, but as sinners, all of whom need redemption."[161] As Bavinck explains elsewhere, and Berkouwer heartily agrees, "The purpose of election is not—as it is so often proclaimed—to turn off many but to invite all to participate in the riches of God's grace in Christ." He continues:

> [E]lection operates according to grace, [and hence] there is hope even for the most wretched. . . . [T]o believe in and to confess election is to recognize even the most unworthy and degraded human being as a creature of God and an object of his eternal love. . . . No one [*may*] believe that he or she is a reprobate, for everyone is sincerely and urgently called to believe in Christ with a view to salvation. No one *can* actually believe it, for one's own life and all that makes it enjoyable is proof that God takes no delight in his death. No one *really* believes it, for that would be hell on earth. But election is a source of comfort and strength, of submissiveness and humility, of confidence and resolution. The salvation of human beings is firmly established in the gracious and omnipotent pleasure of God.[162]

Bavinck's claim in this passage brings us back to the first question posed at the start of this section: if the general offer of salvation to all sinners without exception is seriously intended, is that "proof . . . of God's infinite love," as Bavinck suggests above, "demonstrating that God does not rejoice in the destruction of sinners but therein that they repent and live [?]"[163] In short, does God desire the salvation of all men, according to Berkouwer?

I think we can say that Berkouwer, arguably, is a universalist—meaning thereby to refer to the universal salvific will of God in Christ. "Jesus Christ is the Light of the world, and in Him God loved the world and was reconciling it to Him. The grace of God hath appeared, bringing salvation to all men (Titus 2:11). . . . Thus the gospel concerns all."[164] Those who say that the preaching of the gospel is "good news" only to the elect are mistaken.

160. Berkouwer, *Een Halve Eeuw Theologie*, 127 [95]. See also, Berkouwer, *De Wederkomst van Christus*, II, 218 [408–9].

161. Bavinck, *GD* IV, 5 [36].

162. Bavinck, *GD* II, 365–66 [402]. Berkouwer cites this passage of Bavinck in *De Verkiezing Gods*, 270 [226].

163. Berkouwer, *De Verkiezing Gods*, 270 [226]. Berkouwer is here quoting Bavinck, *GD* IV, 7 [38].

164. Ibid., 280 [233].

Christ did not die solely for the elect. Of course Berkouwer resists universalism in the sense that all men will be saved either contingently or necessarily. In particular, he rejects the dilemma of "either no general offer of salvation or universal election." He explains: "We do so by repudiating the schema of objectivity-subjectivity on which it rests. According to that presupposition, one must either accept an objective universal election whereby an eternal decision for all has already been made, or a subjective offer of salvation whereby man can freely decide for himself."[165] He rejects the latter horn of this dilemma because all men are *not* elect in Christ. Yes, the work of Christ is intrinsically sufficient for the salvation of all men. "Christ's death is the only and most perfect sacrifice [and satisfaction for sin] which is 'of infinite worth and value, abundantly sufficient to expiate the sins of the whole world.'"[166] In short, as James Orr puts it, "He died *sufficienter* for all men, but *efficienter* for the elect only."[167] But it is *effectual* only for the elect who are given the gift of faith; in short, there is a correlation between salvation and faith (e.g., John 3:16; 1 Tim 2:4; 2 Pet 3:9). He rejects the other horn of the dilemma, and its attendant scheme of possibility-realization, when the significance of Christ's death is approached from the view point of the possibility of salvation, or a potential reconciliation, a possibility that can only be realized subjectively by human decision.[168] But "God's work, His acts in Christ, [is not] dependent on man's decision, nor does it state that God's acts acquire validity only through and in man's decision. Such a subjectivism is rejected by the Canons [of Dort]."[169] He adds, "If that were the case, everything would come to depend on his free will, belief, and the obedience of faith. . . . This is the old error of Pelagius."[170]

But how then can Berkouwer overcome the dilemma of universality and particularity? "On the one hand, we find a reference to a universal preaching of the gospel to all without exception and, on the other, we are

---

165. Ibid., 278–79 [232].

166. Ibid., 278 [232]. The quote between the quote is from the Canons of Dort, II.3. This, too, is the teaching of the *Confession of the Heidelberg Theologians* (1906), §§17–18, "Concerning the efficacy of the death of Christ, we believe that the death of Christ . . . is a perfect and sufficient atonement, not only for ours, but also for the sins of the whole world. . . . However, we also believe that no one will be a partaker of these benefits of Christ without believing in Him" (Dennison, *Reformed Confessions*, 4:26–40).

167. Orr, *Progress of Dogma*, 298.

168. Berkouwer, *De Wederkomst van Christus*, 2:220 [411].

169. Berkouwer, *De Verkiezing Gods*, 279 [233].

170. Ibid., 277 [231].

confronted with an unmistakable particularity."[171] I think that this dilemma can be overcome by understanding the scope of Christ's atoning work in light of the distinction between sufficiency and efficiency already alluded to above. Crisp explains: "the work of Christ is sufficient for the salvation of all humanity in principle, though it is effectual only for the elect who are given faith."[172] This is consistent with hypothetical universalism. So Bavinck puts it: "For everyone without distinction, it is proof of God's infinite love and seals the saying that he has no pleasure in the death of sinners but rather that they should turn and live (Ezek 18:23, 32). It proclaims to all that Christ's sacrifice is sufficient for the expiation of all sins, that no one is lost because the call is insufficiently rich and powerful."[173] Berkouwer "with the Canons [of Dort] . . . confess[es] the freedom of God's election and the general preaching of the gospel. In this combination we do not see an antinomy or an irrational paradox." This, too, is Bavinck's position: "However much it might seem that the confession of election and limited atonement[174] might require something else, the Reformed as a rule maintained the universal offer of grace."[175] Berkouwer explains:

> Rather, we understand something of the profound interrelations in the nature of election. He who would understand election as a formal *dominium absolutum*, as the arbitrariness of God, must consider the Canons to be very illogical indeed. But he who, with Bavinck, dares to accentuate the solace of election for both believer and unbeliever, and does not do so on the basis of a universalistic denial of the freedom of God, but on the basis "not out of work but out of grace," will understand in the practice of the Church the unity between its confession of election and the [general] offer of salvation.[176]

Berkouwer's protest to the contrary,[177] it is precisely the distinction between sufficiency end efficiency that explains how he overcomes the dilemma

171. Ibid., 275 [230].

172. Crisp, "Hypothetical Universalism," 180.

173. Bavinck, *GD*, IV, 5 [38].

174. "Limited atonement" is consistent with the claim that Christ's atoning work is intrinsically sufficient for the world, if the former is taken to mean that his work is efficacious for only those who have faith in Christ, but not that Christ died only for the elect.

175. Bavinck, *GD* IV, 5 [36]. Canons of Dort, 2.5 calls for the proclamation of the gospel "to all persons promiscuously and without distinction."

176. Berkouwer, *De Verkiezing Gods*, 290 [241].

177. Berkouwer, *De Wederkomst van Christus*, 2:219 [410].

described above.[178] Christ's atoning work on the cross is intrinsically sufficient for all men. Berkouwer writes, "The universal aspect, which is directly
connected with the universal and cosmic significance of Christ, is thereby
neglected. The *Christus pro omnibus* is attacked in such a manner that it no
longer is possible to realize fully that Christ's coming has meaning for all
of the world, and that the world in Him is confronted with a new decision
of critical significance in the history of salvation."[179] In this connection, he
says regarding what he calls "kerygmatic universality," "This *kerygma*, as the
message of God's saving act, has an essentially universal quality, and only
that explains the universality of the New Testament. . . . [A]n the message of
salvation—according to the will of God made known to the nations (Rom
16:26)—the way of repentance and of the knowledge of truth is pointed out
to us. That is the appeal, the invitation, the calling voice, and the admonition
in this will of God. . . . When Paul preaches God's act of salvation to the
nations, it is announced to 'all' that they must repent. The universality of the
gospel comprises essentially this universal call (Acts 17: 30; cf. 16:31).[180] He
follows this up by referring us to "the passages which speak so universally of
'all.'" That is, "We are reminded of what Paul said: 'This is good and acceptable in the sight of God our Savior; who would have all men to be saved, and
come to the knowledge of the truth' (1 Tim 2:3–3), and of Peter's words: 'not
wishing that any should perish, but that all should come to repentance' (2
Peter 3:9), and of John's: 'He is the propitiation for our sins, and not for ours
only, but also for the whole world' (1 John 2:2), and many other passages."[181]
How does Berkouwer understand these passages? Christ's atoning work is
intrinsically sufficient to cover the sins of all men, but it is efficacious only
for the elect who are given faith by God's grace. We find the notion of sufficiency-efficiency at work in Trent's Decree on Justification. It states: "even
though 'Christ died for all' [2 Cor 5:15], still not all do receive the benefit of
His death, but those only to whom the merit of His passion is imparted."[182]

Now, although Berkouwer does not side with the Remonstrants who
were the target of the Canons of Dort, there is a point of contact with them
in that Berkouwer affirms that, properly understood, "Christ died for all."
"The *pro omnibus* of the Remonstrants is an objective reality, a new situation, in which nothing is as yet implied regarding the obtaining of salvation."

178. Adapted from Peter Lombard, *The Sentences*, vol. 3, *On the Incarnation of the
Word*, 20.5, 86.

179. Berkouwer, *De Verkiezing Gods*, 281 [234]. See also, 279 [233].

180. Berkouwer, *De Verkiezing Gods*, 288–89 [239–40].

181. Ibid., 284 [237].

182. Denzinger, §1523.

We can read Berkouwer's point here to be saying that although Christ's sacrifice on the cross is sufficient for all, efficaciously it is for the elect alone.
Thus, the distinction between sufficiency and efficacy is introduced here to
make sense of Berkouwer's point.[183] Berkouwer reminds us here that the
Canons affirm that "the sacrifice of Christ is sufficient for the forgiveness of
all sins." "And, whereas many who are called by the gospel do not repent nor
believe in Christ, but perish in unbelief, this is not owing to any defect or
insufficiency in the sacrifice offered by Christ upon the cross, but is wholly
imputed to themselves."[184] Concurring with this last point from the Canons
of Dort, Berkouwer argues that the atoning work of Christ is effectual for
the elect who are given faith, and hence that "apart from faith man cannot
discover [Christ's atoning acts] or know of the reality of reconciliation for
all, to which he must respond with a decision." In sum, "the gospel comes
to man as a true *message* of salvation. It contains a fall to faith, which call is
implied in God's act in Christ. The *kerygma* is inseparably connected with
Christ."[185] In sum, Berkouwer reminds "the Church of the universality of the
message which is no other than the mirroring of God's love for the world."[186]

Berkouwer understands how some theologians in the Catholic tradition has sought to explain the relationship between the universalist and
particularist passages of Scripture—God wills that all men be saved, on
the one hand, unrepentant sinners will be lost—by reference to the distinction between the antecedent and consequent will of God. Alternatively
put, this is a way of bringing together the universalist—Christ's death is
sufficient for all—and particularist—but not efficacious for all—strands
of the Bible. 1 Tim 2:4 states that God wants all men to be saved and to
come to knowledge of the truth; but the Catholic and Reformed traditions
reject the view that all men will be saved, and thus it seems that the will
of God is not always fulfilled. Says Berkouwer, "The explanation has often been given that this [1 Tim 2:4] concerns the will of God as *voluntas
antecedens*, the general will to salvation, which is then followed by His

183. Berkouwer, *De Verkiezing Gods*, 279 [233].

184. Canons of Dort, II, 6. See also, II, 3: "The death of the Son of God is the only
and most perfect sacrifice and satisfaction for sin, and is of infinite worth and value,
abundantly sufficient to expiate the sins of the whole world." See also Article XXXI of
the XXXIX Articles of Religion of the Church of England, a part of which states: "The
offering of Christ once made is the perfect redemption, propitiation, and satisfaction,
for all the sins of the whole world, both original and actual; and there is none other
satisfaction for sin, but that alone" (in Dennison, *Reformed Confessions*, 2:1552–66).

185. Berkouwer, *De Verkiezing Gods*, 279 [233].

186. Ibid., 290 [241].

voluntas consequens, as the result of man's free decision."[187] Traditionally, some Catholic theologians have appealed to the distinction between God's antecedent and consequent will to deal with the difficulty regarding God's will and its efficacy. For example, John of Damascus as well as St. Thomas Aquinas and St. Bonaventure invoked that distinction to defend the thesis that the will of God is always fulfilled.[188]

Berkouwer is against the distinctions of an "antecedent" and "consequent" will in God, and hence is skeptical of any attempt to reconcile the difficulty regarding God's will and its efficacy in those terms. Indeed, Berkouwer claims that "Scholasticism pondered this problem [of God's will and

187. Ibid., 284–85 [237].

188. John of Damascus seeks to explain 1 Tim 2:4 by invoking the distinction between the antecedent and consequent will of God. He says, "God will have all men and women to be saved," when as a matter of fact, not all are saved but only those who believe. Says John, the apostle is here speaking of God's antecedent will (John of Damascus, *Of the Orthodox Faith*, 2, 29). St. Thomas Aquinas follows the Damascene. He writes, "[W]e can speak of a justice that *antecedently* wishes every man to live, but *consequently* pronounces the capital sentence. So by analogy God antecedently wills all men to be saved, yet consequently wills some to be condemned as his justice requires. Now to will antecedently is not to will downrightly, but only in a certain respect. For willing goes out to things just as they really are and standing in all their particularity, so that we downrightly will a thing surrounded by all its circumstances; this is what is meant by 'consequent will'. Accordingly we may speak of a just judge then and there quite simply willing a murderer to be hanged, though in a certain respect, when the criminal is considered as a human being, he wills him to live: this last should be termed more a wishing than a sheer willing. Clearly, then, whatever God wills simply speaking comes about, though what he wills antecedently does not" (*Summa Theologiae*, 1A, 19, 6). See also, St. Bonaventure, *In 1 Sent.*, dist. 46, a. I, q. I, "Antecedent will is the name applied by theologians to God's conditional will, or the will whereby God wills inasmuch as He Himself is concerned. The other, that is, consequent will, is called absolute. The distinction between the two has nothing to do with any difference in affection or in the manner of willing in God, but has reference to the connotation of the terms and our manner of understanding. When God is said to will the salvation of all [1 Tim. 2:4] as far as lies in Him and antecedently, the ordering of all men to salvation is connoted, with regard both to the nature that has been given to them and to the grace that has been offered them. For God has given to all a nature whereby they can know Him, seek Him when they know Him, find Him when they seek Him, and cleave to Him when they find Him, and thus obtain salvation. Likewise, he offered grace when He sent and offered His Son, whose merit suffices for the salvation of all. He also gave and made known laws and commands relating to salvation. Further, He Himself is at hand to all who seek Him, and is close to all who call upon Him. Therefore to will man's salvation antecedently means to place him on the road to salvation, and to assist him in his desire to arrive at the goal. Hence antecedently to will to save does not connote salvation [as actually conferred], but rather the fact that man is fully equipped to attain salvation. But consequently or absolutely to will to save is the same as to give salvation to him whom God foresees will achieve salvation through His help and grace, and connotes the actual obtaining of salvation."

its efficacy] at length, but it never came out of the impasse."[189] He opposes this distinction because he claims that "scripture never speaks of God's will as such." Rather, he adds, "in the universal passages –[2] Peter [3:9], [John 3:16,] Ezekiel [18:32, 33:11], and perhaps also 1 Timothy [2:4]—the issue is that the will of God which is presented to us in the dynamic and living context of the calling to repentance and to the knowledge of the truth."[190] Berkouwer, therefore, wonders whether it is still useful to describe God's *voluntas* with this distinction of antecedent and consequent will. In sum, Berkouwer's formulates his objection: "One wonders whether the gospel is not overshadowed by theology, and whether such [universal] passages can really be understood only in the light of a distinction which does nothing but undermine the *power* of these passages. . . . At any rate, the comprising of 'all' by the *voluntas antecedens* (by virtue of the nature of the distinction itself) is a very dubious matter. This will may in a sense be effective and be fulfilled, namely, as 'the will of means to salvation' . . . but it is far from absolute in its effectiveness where actual salvation is concerned."[191]

In response, I would say that the matter is cleared up satisfactorily if we turn to the distinction between the intrinsic sufficiency of Christ's aton-ing work for the sins of all men, on the one hand, and the efficacy or effec-tiveness of that work for the elect who are given faith. Berkouwer loses sight of the import of that distinction. "For if those whom God wants to bring to salvation with His *voluntas consequens* are the predestinated, the question arises about the seriousness of the *voluntas antecedens* which comes to the fore in such urgent references in Scripture."[192] In other words, why is Christ's atoning work not efficacious for all given the seriousness of God's anteced-ent will that he wants all men to be saved and come to the knowledge of the truth (1 Tim 2:4)? The brief answer to this question here must be, as Crisp puts it, "God ordains and intends that the satisfaction of Christ be a means of salvation that is truly sufficient for all but conditioned upon faith. That is its sufficiency."[193] This is what Crisp calls "conditional ordained sufficiency," and it is consistent with Berkouwer's claim that "apart from faith man can-not discover [Christ's atoning acts] or know of the reality of reconciliation for all, to which he must respond with a decision."[194] Crisp explains:

189. Berkouwer, *De Verkiezing Gods*, 286 [238].

190. Ibid.

191. Ibid., 287 [239].

192. Ibid.

193. Crisp, "Hypothetical Universalism," in *Deviant Calvinism*, 193.

194. Berkouwer, *De Verkiezing Gods*, 279 [233].

It is this conditional ordained sufficiency that applies in the case of the atonement. It is not a mere intrinsic sufficiency, such as those who defend a definite atonement claim. In other words, it is not only that Christ's death is in principle and independent of any actual divine intention sufficient to atone for all human sin because it has an infinite value, being the work of the God-man. Although this is true and may even be a necessary condition of the atonement, it is not a sufficient condition. To it must be added the following: God has ordained that the infinite sufficiency of the satisfaction of Christ is truly given for all people. We might say that it has been accomplished for the salvation of all human beings. However, the benefits of Christ can be effectually applied to fallen human beings, only where the condition of faith is met. Hence, the atonement involves a conditional ordained sufficiency.[195]

Moreover, "It is important to see that this way of construing the sufficiency of Christ's work means that the application of what Christ has accomplished in his oblation for the elect is entirely due to the divine will. It cannot be that Christ's work is intended only for an elect; it is intended for the whole world. This is conditional ordained sufficiency. But if his work in and of itself is ordained to be conditionally sufficient for all, then its efficacy for the elect alone must be due to the divine will, not to the work of Christ as such."[196] Berkouwer, then, offers no irrefutable argument for removing the distinction in God's will between antecedent and consequent will. In fact, the distinction between sufficiency and efficacy, along with the concomitant distinction Of God's antecedent and consequent will, arguably makes best interpretive sense, not only of the intrinsic sufficiency of Christ's atoning work, as well as its efficacy, but also the absolute necessity of faith for salvation in St. Paul's writings.[197]

Points of Catholic Orientation

Confessional Catholicism sides with the neo-Calvinists Herman Bavinck and G. C. Berkouwer in the rejection of the parallelism or symmetry of election and reprobation and argue that there is an "essential asymmetry" at the heart of the doctrine of divine election in their theological account

195. Crisp, "Hypothetical Universalism," in *Deviant Calvinism*, 194. Crisp is describing the position of Bishop John Davenant, one of the English Delegation to the Synod of Dort, whose position came to be called "hypothetical universalism."

196. Ibid., 195.

197. This important point is made by Dulles, "The Population of Hell."

of double predestination. Confessional Catholicism goes further in holding that the point at issue about election is not one of a "mere symmetry," but rather it is, chiefly, the point that "God has loved the world (John 3:16)." In this understanding, Confessional Catholicism sides with Berkouwer. In other words, Berkouwer is right that the deepest reason for rejecting parallelism, including the parallelism of positive predestination and negative reprobation (i.e., preterition), is that God did not send the Son to condemn the world but rather that the world should be saved through him (John 3:17). Berkouwer is also right that "This rejection [of parallelism] does not imply the triumph of a simple sort of universalism."[198] Confessional Catholicism holds that to avoid universalism the distinction between the antecedent and consequent will of God, as well as the corresponding distinction between sufficiency and efficacy, must be used in explaining the difference between the universal salvific will of God and its efficacy. In this way, we can give an account of the "kerygmatic universality" of the free and general offer of the Gospel that reveals God's universal salvific will for all men without collapsing into universalism.

198. Berkouwer, *De Verkiezing Gods*, 238 [201–2].

CHAPTER 6

Balthasar's Hopeful Universalism?

Major Themes

HOW DO WE RECONCILE God's universal salvific will with the mystery of predestination, election and reprobation? Furthermore, how do we reconcile the omnipotence and sovereignty of God's grace with human freedom in the Church's understanding of salvation? My entry point into an analysis of Balthasar's response to these questions is his dismissal of predestination. He dismisses predestination as such because, Balthasar alleges, the knowledge of the final outcome of God's "twofold judgment" regarding the final destiny of the saved and the lost in the eschaton is not available to us. Those who claim to possess such knowledge, Balthasar claims, have produced a theology of "double predestination"[1] that is irreconcilable with God's universal salvific will and hence with the biblically warranted hope, albeit not certainty that comes from knowledge,[2] as he sees it, for universal salvation. In his defense of the possibility of universal salvation, Balthasar opts for a *hopeful* universalism. Says Crisp, "Recall that this is the view according to which all human beings may be saved, indeed we hope *will* be saved, though we cannot say definitively *must* be saved."[3] The biblical impetus for this hopeful universalism is from universal texts of Scripture such as: God

1. In chapter 2, I discussed "double predestination" in the writings of John Calvin (1509–1564). See also chapter 5 for my interpretation and analysis of "double predestination" in the Dutch Reformed tradition, in particular the writings of the two great Dutch masters, Bavinck and Berkouwer.

2. Balthasar, *DWH*, 9. Balthasar claims that his words have been "continually twisted with a view to claiming that . . . he who voices such a hope advocates the 'universal redemption' (*apokatastasis*) condemned by the Church—something that I have expressly rejected: we stand completely and utterly *under* judgment and have no right, nor is it possible for us, to peer in advance at the judge's cards. How can anyone equate hoping with knowing? . . . . Certainty cannot be attained, but hope can be justified" (131, 149). On Balthasar's rejection of 'universal redemption' (*apokatastasis*), see *DWH*, 30–31, 71–72, 121, 157, and 181–89.

3. Crisp, *Deviant Calvinism*, 152.

loved the *world* (John 3:16); that the Lamb of God takes away the sin of the *world* (John 1:29); that God was in Christ reconciling the *world* to Himself (2 Cor 5:19); that Christ is the propitiation for our sins, and not for ours only but also for the sins of the whole *world* (I John 2:2); that Christ is the Savior of the *world* (John 4:42), the Savior of *all men* (1 Tim 4:10; that God desires *all men* to be saved and brought to the knowledge of truth (1 Tim 2:4), not wishing that any should perish (2 Pet 3:9); that the grace of God has appeared for the salvation of *all men* (Titus 2:11).[4] It isn't that Balthasar denies the particular texts of judgment in the New Testament in which the love of God in Jesus Christ goes hand in hand with the judgment. For example, John 3:16's statement about God's love for the world is followed by these words: "that whoever believes in him should not perish but have eternal life." St. John also says that "he who does not obey the Son shall not see life, but the wrath of God rests upon him" (vs. 36). Paul's testimony of God's reconciling acts in Christ is followed by evangelical mandate "be reconciled to God" (2 Cor 5:19f). The Gospel of Mark 16: 15–16: "He said to them, 'Go into the whole world and proclaim the gospel to every creature. Whoever believes and is baptized will be saved; whoever does not believe will be condemned.'" Throughout the New Testament a prominent place is given to the human response to salvation.[5]

And yet, all of Balthasar's arguments for this hopeful universalism, and against theological attempts to explain the discrepancy between God's universal salvific will and its efficacy by employing distinctions between God's antecedent and consequent will, between an objective redemption through Christ and its subjective acceptance,[6] are such that he leaves us asking whether his thought actually *is* a version of *necessary* universalism.[7] "Necessary universalism, states that, given the essentially benevolent nature of God, it is inconceivable that anyone will ever end up in hell forever. In fact, given divine benevolence, God will necessarily save all people."[8] This question will hold my attention throughout this chapter. But there are other

---

4. Berkouwer, *De Wederkomst van Christus*, 2:202–3 [395–96].

5. Ibid., 214–15 [405–6].

6. In discussed the theological import of these concepts in chapter 5 for giving an account of the discrepancy between God's universal salvific will and its efficacy. So, I won't be repeating that discussion in this chapter.

7. Balthasar, *DWH*, 26.

8. Crisp, *Deviant Calvinism*, 98. John Finnis charges Balthasar with implicitly supporting necessary universalism: "all his argument for hoping . . . that all men are saved are in fact arguments that it is inconsistent with God's nature, and therefore impossible, for *any* human creature to be lost" (Finnis, "Hell and Hope," 374).

issues to which I shall attend that are connected with the question of the scope of Christ's atoning work. In this first section, I give a review of them.

Of course Balthasar is deeply committed to the orthodox Christian teaching that salvation is always and entirely due to God's gracious initiative in Christ. The biblical revelation considers this gracious initiative as one that stretches back to eternity. In Titus 1:2–3 St. Paul tells us that God promised eternal life before "eternal ages." In 2 Tim 1: 9–10 St. Paul tells us that God has saved us according to his own purpose and grace, which he gave us in Christ Jesus before the "eternal ages." Indeed, widespread throughout the New Testament is the theological concept that God planned the work of salvation before creation in eternity. For instance, in Romans 8, Romans 9–11, and the first chapter of Ephesians, the Apostle Paul reaches back to the intention and purpose of God underlying the divine work of redemption in history and says that it has an electing character in Christ. Suffice it to note for now that since Balthasar's theology of hope holds that God's redemptive work for the sinful world finds its concentration point in Christ, this surely means, not only that, as Balthasar says, "from a theological point of view, election . . . [is] always pure grace,"[9] but also it is one in which God chose us in Christ before the foundation of the world (Eph 1:4).

Furthermore, as Schnelle puts it, "God's initiative and decision has priority, and in every respect is prior to all human considerations,"[10] such as human works and freedom. Still, the question arises regarding the sense in which individual human freedom is constitutive for man's response to the calling of the gospel.[11] Can a man be saved without regard in any sense whatsoever to his freedom? It would seem not, according to Balthasar: "we shall not be saved against our own will. We shall be redeemed as living agents who gave lively consent to be rescued."[12] And yet, on the one hand, man's damnation is in his own hands, as Balthasar insists, a self-determining choice,[13] but man's salvation, by contrast, is accomplished by God's grace alone in Christ's atoning work, which is the sole and sufficient ground of redemption, and that we receive as a gift offered to us. What, then, is the relationship between the salvation and grace of God and man's free will?

Consider also Balthasar's outright dismissal of predestination—election *and* reprobation. I think his dismissal is based on his polemic against the idea that divine judgment is God's final word to us such that he misses

9. Balthasar, *Theo-Drama*, 3:269.

10. Schnelle, *Theology of the New Testament*, 563.

11. Ridderbos, *Paul*, 351.

12. Balthasar, *Theo-Drama*, 5:288.

13. Balthasar, *DWH*, 37–41.

out on seeing the inextricable connection between judgment and the proclamation of salvation. As Berkouwer puts it:

> The proclamation of the gospel contains a warning against unbe-
> lief, and the way of unbelief is portrayed as the way of outermost
> darkness and lostness and the severance of all relationships. In
> a variety of images and concepts, the Gospels warn against the
> possibility of a "definitive destruction." Such warnings are not
> meant to orient us to the eschaton, but continually to confront
> us with an admonition to open our eyes to the light and see the
> salvation, not to harden our hearts (cf. Heb 3).[14]

It isn't that Balthasar doesn't attend to the Scriptural point that Berkouwer
makes here about salvation and judgment, warning and call. Of course he
is especially attentive to the Scriptural testimony regarding the universalist
(1 Tim 2:4–6; 1 Tim 4:10; John 16:33; 2 Pet 3:9; Rom 11:32; Col 1:20) and
particularist (Matt 5:22, 29f.; Matt 7:23; Matt 8:12; 10:28; 22:11ff.; 23:33;
25:12, 30, 41, 46) series of texts. The tension between these two series is
best left unresolved, according to Balthasar. And yet, it is abundantly clear
that Balthasar interprets the particularist texts in light of the universalist
ones. Indeed, the "[universalist] statements give us a right to have hope
for all men."[15] He says, "Jesus comes as the light of absolute love ('to the
end' [John 13:1]) in order to save all men. But how will this be, if there are
some who consciously draw back from this love and refuse it ([John] 3:9;
9:40–41; 12:48)? The question, to which no final answer is given or can be
given, is this: Will he who refuses it now refuse it to the last?"[16] Yes, says,
Balthasar, "I do not know, but I think it permissible to hope (on the basis of
the [universal] statements from Scripture) that the light of divine love will
ultimately be able to penetrate every human darkness and refusal."[17] What
is the ground of Balthasar's hopeful universalism?

Balthasar responds, "I think that the most serious thing that exists is
not God's punitive justice but rather his love."[18] This is true in itself, but
Balthasar interprets it to mean, as Finnis rightly says, "that for any human
person to be lost in hell is inconsistent with God's saving will and power and
with the efficacy of Christ's saving sacrifice."[19] This is why Balthasar dis-
penses with theological attempts to explain the discrepancy between God's

14. Berkouwer, *De Wederkomst van Christus*, 2:223 [413].

15. Balthasar, *DWH*, 149.

16. Ibid., 142.

17. Ibid.

18. Ibid., 130.

19. Finnis, "Hell and Hope," 375.

universal salvific will and its efficacy by employing distinctions between God's antecedent and consequent will, between an objective redemption through Christ and its subjective acceptance.[20] Thus, the apriori of divine love encourages Balthasar to hope, asking questions such as the following. "Here we come to deep waters, in which every human mind begins to flounder. Can human defiance really resist to the end the representative assumption of its sins by the incarnate God?"[21] His answer: "God gives man the capacity to make a (negative) choice against God that seems *for man* to be definitive, but which need not be taken *by God* as definitive."[22] Why not? I shall need to consider whether that is because "in the *final* analysis the irresistible power of grace will force the capitulation of all rebellion against it." Berkouwer adds, "The question is all the more valid because the context of the New Testament words about judgment never suggests that the ultimate extinction of resistance is self-evident."[23] But the objection may be raised at the outset that Balthasar takes salvation *and* judgment with biblical seriousness evidenced by opening his book with the statement that "all of us . . . are *under* judgment."[24] Indeed, he adds, quoting St. Paul (1 Cor 4:4), "'It is the Lord who judges me.'"[25] Still, we need to understand in what sense judgment is part of the gospel, according to Balthasar. What does he take the modus of this judgment to be in saying that Christ judges us?

He explains the mode of judgment. God's love in Christ is the unsurpassable truth of God's self-revelation. This supreme truth of love calls for its unconditional acceptance. Says Balthasar, "'judgment' is nothing other than love (and love is 'truth')."[26] It is not clear to me what Balthasar means here. Let me suggest the following interpretation of what it might mean: "In the presence of Christ, who is Truth itself, the truth of each man's relationship with God will be laid bare [John 12:49]."[27] In this sense, Balthasar says, "Love itself is crisis: to the extent that it is truth." That is, being under judgment is that moment of crisis where there is a separating, a judgment, a selection. He continues, "[Love] contains justice within itself, which is why Jesus, in his disputations with those lacking in love, can just as well say that

---

20. Balthasar, *DWH*, 26, 146–49.

21. Ibid., 166.

22. Balthasar, *Explorations in Theology*, 4:421, as cited in Geoffrey Wainwright, "Eschatology," 125.

23. Berkouwer, *De Wederkomst van Christus*, 2:216 [407].

24. Balthasar, *DWH*, 5 (emphasis added). He repeats that point on 6–7, 33.

25. Ibid., 22.

26. Ibid., 29.

27. *CCC*, §1039.

he (as love) 'judges not' as that he (as truth) 'judges.'" Significantly, Balthasar
adds, "He [Christ] judges, however, *only* insofar as anyone who persists
in darkness does not himself want to come into the light ([Jn] 3:20) and
thereby, in view of God's proclaimed word of love, *judges himself*."[28] Fundamental to Balthasar's understanding of judgment in the statement that all
men stand under judgment is his emphasis on the immanent dynamic in
man's sin that leads to his self-condemnation. But where is *divine* judgment
in this dynamic? Says Balthasar, "Naturally, this self-judgment by the sinner
in the face of everlasting love does not . . . occur without the will and assent
of the Judge of the world."[29] What does he mean by saying that man's self-
condemnation occurs *within* divine judgment?[30]

Is God merely supervising the immanent dynamic? Does he just ratify
the self-condemning choices a man makes? Does Balthasar mean that divine judgment is the just response of God—punishing and judging evil and
sin—to these things as an expression of his holiness and wrath? My concern
here is with the nature of God's *activity*, and of God *himself*, in the context of
his final judgment of men. I think we must say that, according to Balthasar,
there is no transcendent divine judgment after the decisive judgment that
took place at the cross. This is evident because throughout his book he emphasizes that "God does not damn anyone." "[T]he man who irrevocably
refuses loves condemns himself."[31] There is no transcendent judgment,
according to Balthasar, but only a judgment that puts the accent on man's
own causality, that is, "the individual subjectively judging himself."[32] Yes, to
be sure, as Balthasar puts it, man judges himself "in the light of the divine
truth, which is, as such, the truth of what God has done for mankind in
Jesus Christ."[33] But is Balthasar correct in claiming that the last judgment is
being effected alone by the sinner himself who turns his back upon God. In
other words, is hell a self-made judgment, the inherent consequence of being a lover-of-self without fail, refusing to love God above all? Is, then, God
passive in the conditions of man's self-condemnation? Where is God *himself*,
in particular his *activity* as judge, expressing his character as just, in the last
judgment? Balthasar seems to agree with Rahner. "The just God is 'active'
in the punishment of Hell only insofar as he does not release man from the

28. Balthasar, *DWH*, 28; emphasis added.

29. Ibid., 41.

30. Ibid., 121n10: The immanent dynamic of sin "does not exclude this [self-
judgment] from occurring within divine judgment" (121n11).

31. Ibid., 131.

32. Balthasar, *Theo-Drama*, 5:295.

33. Ibid., 292.

reality of the definitive state which man himself has achieved on his own behalf, contradictory though this state be to the world of God's creation."[34] On
this view, there seems to be a tendency to oppose the natural consequence
model of judgment to the retributive punishment model. I shall return to a
discussion of these two models later in this chapter. But *God* is the one who
is not to be mocked and it is *God* to whom man must give an account of his
life. "They will have to give account to him who is ready to judge the living
and the dead" (1 Pet 4:5).

Thus, I think we must resist the tendency to depersonalize divine
judgment that seems to be suggested by the emphasis on the natural consequence view for understanding the manner in which our freedom has
the power to make choices that bring about damnation. Otherwise, judgment seems to be "wholly impersonal," in the sense that God is not actively
and personally judging men's actions, and so it seems that judgment does
not describe an act of God but rather a self-imposed condition of man.
Balthasar himself acknowledges that "this self-judgment by the sinner in
the face of everlasting love does not . . . occur without the will and assent
of the Judge of the world."[35] But even this way of describing God's role in
the final judgment is too impersonal, suggesting that God merely permits
or supervises that self-judgment, or ratifies, rather than actively "judging
everyone" and "convicting all the ungodly of all the ungodly acts they have
done in the ungodly way" (Jude 15). Where is the place of the living God
who justly responds to man's sin at the final judgment with wrath, the latter
being tied up with the guilt that comes from our rejection of salvation? Isn't
God's wrath proclaimed by the Gospel of John as remaining on him who
"rejects the Son" (Jn 3:36)?

Balthasar rejects this way of characterizing God's response to man's ultimate self-condemnation because it rends, he argues, "God's will for salvation into two parts—or if one likes, the splitting of the divine qualities into
'sheer mercy' and 'sheer justice.'"[36] In other words, Balthasar doesn't think
that "one [may] speak of pure justice without any reference to mercy. That
would imply making his [God's mercy] finite."[37] Isolating God's love and
justice in this manner is unbiblical. As Berkouwer puts it, "Apparently one
is to think of two parallel lines, divine mercy and divine justice, two divine
properties, juxtaposed and sometimes even opposed to one another, each

34. Rahner, "Hell," 8–9.

35. Balthasar, *DWH*, 41; see also, 120n11 where Balthasar urges us to consider that
"guilt already contains within itself its own punishment, [but that] does not exclude this
from occurring within divine judgment."

36. Balthasar, *DWH*, 14.

37. Ibid., 116.

in its own right."[38] Separating these two divine properties "diminishes the perspective on the simplicity and harmony of God's virtues."[39] Furthermore, this view minimizes God's mercy, but Balthasar's objection seems to suggest that it is limitless and inexhaustible (see Exod 34:6; Ps 86:13).

Most important, this view would leave us to understand God's final judgment in a *symmetrical* way such that God shows his mercy to some and his justice to others, namely, to the save and the damned. In other words, Kasper writes agreeing with Balthasar, it would leave God's final judgment poised "in an equilibrium between a mercy that saves and justice that rejects."[40] Put differently—and here both Kasper and Balthasar[41] side with Karl Rahner[42]—"The human being's 'no' of refusal cannot be an equally powerful possibility alongside the unconditional 'yes' that God has spoken to humankind [in Christ]. The prior reality of divine mercy must have the first as well as the last word. Jesus Christ as judge of the living and the dead is, indeed, the one who has died for all on the cross. We may hope that he is a gracious judge."[43] Thus, Balthasar contests this way of understanding the relationship between God's justice and mercy, and hence between the possibilities of "yes" and "no" to God, as parallel possibilities. "Yes" and "no" are unequal because "the 'no' of a created being is '*not of equal right and stature* in relation to a "yes" to God. For every "no" always derives the life which it has from a "yes" because the "no" always becomes intelligible only in light of the "yes" and not vice versa'." . . . Therefore, human freedom "of course does not limit the sovereignty of God vis-à-vis this freedom."[44]

When Balthasar underscores the sovereignty of divine freedom and the priority of God's yes, he appears to relativize the seriousness of the gospel proclamation—at least that is what some of his critics have argued.[45] Of course, Balthasar agrees with claims like the one Berkouwer makes: "It would be a mistake to underestimate this seriousness. The Word speaks of being cast away and rejected, of curse and judgment. The proclamation of the gospel contains a warning against unbelief, and the way of unbelief is portrayed as the way of outermost darkness and lostness and the severance

---

38. Berkouwer, *De Wederkomst van Christus*, 2:199 [393].

39. Ibid.

40. Kasper, *Mercy*, 108.

41. Balthasar, *DWH*, 59, 59n8, 59n9, and 199.

42. Rahner, *Foundations of Christian Faith*, 102.

43. Kasper, *Mercy*, 108.

44. Balthasar, *DWH*, 59n9.

45. Most recently, Martin, *Will Many Be Saved?*, 129–90.

of all relationships."[46] Yet, the question remains regarding the relationship between the sovereignty of God's grace vis-à-vis human freedom, and this is particularly the case because of Balthasar's understanding of the relation of mercy and justice.

On the matter, then, regarding a symmetry between a mercy that saves and justice that rejects, Balthasar says, "I had," in *Dare We Hope*, "posed some important theological questions: for example, the one about the separability (or inseparability) of God's qualities of justice and mercy. Could God's love one day lose its patience, with the result that he would be forced to proceed on the basis of sheer (punitive) justice? The answer [of my critics] was: Yes, certainly."[47] Balthasar rejects this answer: "I think that the most serious thing that exists is not God's punitive justice but rather his love."[48] Thus, Balthasar argues, not only that God's grace is limitless and inexhaustible (see Exod 34:6; Ps 86:13), but also for the priority of grace and mercy given the death and resurrection of Christ, given that God's justice is revealed dramatically in the cross, and hence for an *asymmetry* rather than symmetry between justice and mercy. So, Balthasar is not arguing for the priority of God's grace and mercy at the expense of God's justice. No, mercy and justice meet at the cross. Yet, God in Christ does not give us what we truly deserve in view of our sin, guilt, and hence spiritual death, namely, justice and judgment. Besides, God's justice is revealed in the cross and hence a duality between mercy and justice breaks down. Therefore, according to Berkouwer, "any argument . . . that requires the justice of God to be satisfied in an eternal punishment is invalid and unbiblical."[49]

Balthasar follows in this vein. He says, "In Christ's death and Resurrection the bonds of death have been burst and eternity stands before us as our 'reward': accordingly, the Old Covenant's this worldly, symmetrical doctrine of retribution collapses. Now there is a fundamental *asymmetry* insofar as God's judgment has been pronounced once and for all in the Cross and Resurrection of Jesus; whatever follows can only be an effect and consequence of this event, already inherent in it."[50] Rather than a parallelism between mercy and justice as God's final word there now exists, in view of God's definitive judgment having already been pronounced once and for all at the cross, an essential asymmetry between mercy and justice. God's last word is mercy, but not at the expense of his justice. Berkouwer rightly says,

46. Berkouwer, *De Wederkomst van Christus*, 2:223 [413].

47. Balthasar, *DWH*, 131; see also 7.

48. Ibid., 130.

49. Berkouwer, *De Wederkomst van Christus*, 2:199 [393].

50. Balthasar *Theo-Drama*, 5:277.

There is no antithesis between God's justice and mercy. Biblically speaking, there is no "mystery" in the unity and harmony
of what seems to us irreconcilable. This harmony is manifest in
the historical reality of the cross. But how then, we may ask,
could the merciful God *not* be righteous and *not* be wrathful
against man's sin when sin itself is the *departure from his good
ways* and the *breaking of communion with him?* God is merciful
exactly in his denouncing of man's sin, or his justice and condemnation of man's sin as that way in which man *must not go.*
. . . The man who ignores God's justice and glories in his mercy
must surely be instructed in the nature of the atonement and
the fundamental principle of God's "new way" with man. . . . It is
precisely in the establishment of *enmity* that God proclaims the
depths of his *mercy.*[51]

Yes, argues Balthasar, in the same line as Berkouwer, there is no mercy
without justice, that is, God does not disregard justice, "since the pardon-
ing of a sinner without restoration, from the sinner's viewpoint as well, of
the rightness of the relation between him and God would not be a mercy
that is supreme and worthy of God."[52] So mercy in no way excludes God's
justice. As Berkouwer rightly sees, "We can only speak, at one and the same
time, of the wrath and mercy of our God. . . . In the reality of 'expiation' the
seriousness of sin and the riches of God's mercy are very evident. There is
no doubt that God himself is active in man's guilt, for guilt is bared in all its
ugliness precisely where guilt is both expiated and condemned. The event
of the cross does not consist of 'two parts'; instead it is grace and judgment,
judgment and grace, in one. Wrath and grace do not come together, in a
dualistic fashion, from 'opposite sides. . . So too, in the cross of Jesus Christ
both righteousness and mercy are one. Sin is taken away in the act of God's
gracious judgment."[53] Balthasar agrees with this account of the cross, as we

51. Berkouwer, *De Zonde*, 2:194 [412–13].

52. Balthasar, *DWH*, 118.

53. Berkouwer, *De Zonde*, 2:198 [416]. Balthasar *Theo-Drama*, 4:339–51, and at
339: "God is angry with the sinner on account of his sin. . . . Contrary to the unconsid-
ered utterances of modern theologians, we must maintain that 'anger is an essential and
ineradicable feature . . . even in the New Testament picture of God. . . . The love in God's
heart is laid bare in all its radicality, showing its absolute opposition to anything that
would injure it. . . . Can we seriously say that God unloaded his wrath upon the Man
who wrestled with his destiny on the Mount of Olives and was subsequently crucified?
Indeed we must. Even in life, Jesus had been the revealer of the whole pathos of God—
of his love and his indignation at man's scorning of this love. . . . 'What was suffered on
Israel's account and ours was suffered for Israel and for us. [Namely], The wrath of God
that we had merited. . . . The reason why the No spoken on Good Friday is so terrible,
but why there is already concealed in it the Eastertide Yes of God's righteousness, is that

shall show below. But he goes one step further to argue for the priority of mercy and then conversely that there now is in Christ no judgment without mercy. Quoting Karl Lehmann, Balthasar makes the point: "'One cannot fail to notice', says Lehmann, 'that the New Testament refashions the idea of judgment on the basis of Jesus Christ's redeeming act. Unless God allows grace to take precedence over justice, no one can be saved. Righteousness before God is not something that we can manufacture.'"[54] Of course Lehmann's point is right: mercy triumphs over judgment (James 2:13). "You see, at just the right time, when we were still powerless, Christ died for the ungodly. . . . But God demonstrates how own love for us in this: While we were still sinners Christ died for us" (Rom 5:6, 8). Significantly, returning then to the matter of man's final act of self-condemnation, Balthasar doesn't see God's response to that self-condemnation to be one of "pure justice without any reference to mercy."[55] Indeed, Balthasar echoes Aquinas here:

> God acts mercifully, not indeed by going against His justice, but by doing something more than justice; thus a man who pays another two hundred pieces of money, though owing him only one hundred, does nothing against justice, buts acts liberally or mercifully. The case is the same with one who pardons an offence committed against him, for in remitting it he may be said to bestow a gift. Hence the Apostle calls remission a forgiving; *Forgive one another, as Christ has forgiven you* (Eph 4:31). Hence it is clear that mercy does not destroy justice, but in a sense is the fullness thereof. And thus it is said: Mercy exalteth itself about judgment (Jas 2: 13).[56]

Now, it isn't that Balthasar gives man the last word; no, God has the last word, but his word must be a word of mercy, given the priority of divine mercy at the root of justice, that is, the *asymmetry* between mercy and justice. Yes, in this connection, Balthasar says that a man's life "is judged objectively by the verdict of the divine judge." He explains:

---

he who on the Cross took upon himself and suffered the wrath of God was none other than God's own Son, and therefore the eternal God himself in the unity with human nature that he freely accepted in his transcendent mercy'. . . . 'The real judgment of God is alone the crucifixion of Christ. . . . In it, the real essence of all the Old Testament threats and executions of judgment, that is, the revelation of the wrath of God against all ungodliness and unrighteousness of man (Rom 1:18)—without which revelation is not divine revelation—was embodied in a unique event.'"

54. Balthasar *Theo-Drama*, 5:291.

55. Balthasar, *DWH*, 6–7.
Ibid., 116, and also 131.

56. Aquinas, *Summa theologiae*, I, q. 21, a.3, reply, 2.

This shows that man's verdict on himself in his relation to God cannot be the last act of the Judgment. Human freedom is not self-constituted: it depends on *absolute* freedom and must necessarily transcend itself. . . in that direction. Thus it will be perfected in absolute *freedom*. While infinite freedom will respect the decisions of finite freedom, it will not allow itself to be compelled, or restricted in its own freedom, by the latter.[57]

Or as Balthasar says in *Dare we Hope*:

The question is whether God, with respect to his plan of salvation, ultimately depends, and wants to depend, upon man's choice; or whether his [God's] freedom, which wills only salvation and is absolute, might not remain above things human, created and therefore, relative.[58]

Balthasar does not mean to exclude here the negative possibility that man is not saved and hence is lost forever because he sticks to his rejection of God.[59] Quoting Gustave Martelet to explain his point that man damns himself, Balthasar says, "'[I]n speaking of love refused [ultimately by the sinner], we do not mean that God refuses his love to anyone, as if beings could be lost forever because God had not loved them sufficiently. Where God is concerned, there can never be those who are in any way deprived of his love, since he is Love itself. . . . The absolute refusal of love (which is hell) exists, therefore, only in the case of him who eternally acknowledges and affirms no one but himself; and it is inconceivable that God could have anything to do with grotesque possibility.'"[60] This conclusion brings us back to Balthasar's main point that God damns no man, that is, "that we cannot say that God has 'created hell'; no one but man can be blamed for its existence."[61]

Therefore, we cannot fail to note another question that arises in Balthasar's polemic against divine judgment as God's final word to man, namely, the question regarding the *asymmetrical* relation between mercy and justice. He says, "The question facing us is this: How do justice and love (or grace) constitute a unity in Christ's judgment of man in his failure. . . . Only after we have pursued this 'dialectic' of grace and judgment into its inner depths can we tentatively approach the final question: whether and how

57. Balthasar *Theo-Drama*, 5:295.
58. Balthasar, *DWH*, 6–7.
59. Balthasar *Theo-Drama*, 5:270.
60. Ibid., 278; see also, *DWH*, 37n10.
61. Balthasar, *DWH*, 37–38.

we can envisage a harmony or at least a convergence between the two poles [of mercy and justice] that seem to be mutually exclusive."[62] I shall return to this question below.

For now, suffice it to underscore Balthasar's upholding of the omnipotence and sovereignty of God's grace in Jesus Christ. He explains that "it would be in God's power to allow the grace that flows into the world from the self-sacrifice of his Son (2 Cor 5:19) to grow powerful enough to become his 'efficacious' grace for all sinners. But precisely this is something for which we can only *hope*."[63] In other words, Balthasar states his main thesis that we can hope that all men be saved. But why only hope? Balthasar answers, "'We shall not be saved against our own will. We shall be redeemed as living agents who give lively consent to be rescued.'"[64] And yet, Balthasar counters: "Can man's finite freedom . . . so cut itself off from God as to become entirely self-contained in its own decision?"[65] "If all sins are undercut [by the judgment of the Cross] and undergirded by God's infinite love, it suggests that sin, evil, must be *finite* and must come to an end in the love that envelopes it."[66] In short, adds Balthasar, "Can human defiance really resist to the end the representative assumption of its sins by the incarnate God?"[67] Does Balthasar's emphasis on the triumphant love of God in Christ move in a universalist direction such that his love will directly affect the unrepentant individual while he remains passive? In that case, isn't the significance of our own freedom of choice negated?

Berkouwer, too, raises this question: "It is at this point that universalism makes its appeal to the irresistible love of God, which is sufficient to overcome all obstacles in the eschaton. The question is, how can this divine love—for God is love—ever run aground on human apostasy or intransigence? If the omnipotent God is Love, and if this love is revealed in grace against human resistance, are not this love and its last word *irresistible grace*?"[68] Balthasar resists drawing that conclusion. "It is a question of the sinner's own free refusal, which God, if he respects the freedom he has given to man, cannot overrule simply because his absolute freedom is more powerful than created, finite freedom."[69] He adds, "Without my consent,

---

62. Balthasar *Theo-Drama*, 5:291, 271, respectively.

63. Balthasar, *DWH*, 167.

64. Balthasar *Theo-Drama*, 5:288.

65. Ibid., 300.

66. Ibid., 283.

67. Balthasar, *DWH*, 166.

68. Berkouwer, *De Wederkomst van Christus*, II, [389].

69. Balthasar *Theo-Drama*, 5:285.

give that I am a free person, nothing can just have its way with me. But how, then, are we to understand the grace that is effected through the representative work of Christ?"[70] Still, Balthasar persists in raising the question of the serious possibility of refusal in light of God's omnipotence and sovereignty of grace in Christ. He explains:

> If one replies to this [question regarding the serious possibility of refusal] confidently and flatly: "Yes, man can do that" and thereby fills hell with naysayers, then the theologian will again have to set up a strange distinctions within God's will for grace: there is, then, a "sufficient grace" (*gratia sufficiens*), characterized as something that, from God's viewpoint, would have to be sufficient for converting the sinner yet is rejected by the sinner in such a way that it is actually not sufficient for achieving its purpose; and an "efficacious grace" (*gratia efficax*), which is capable of attaining its goal. On the other hand, we shall not be allowed to say that this latter simply takes the sinner's will by surprise, since his assent has to be freely given. Into what sort of darkness are we straying here?[71]

It is the darkness of the relationship between efficacious grace and freedom. The issue is how efficacious grace secures salvation for the person who receives this grace. "Jesus will not 'do his work without the participation of believers. . . . They are not seized by redemption against their will'. 'The decision . . . [to believe] is not only God's gift, it is also their personal act', and that has to be performed anew again and again. It is possible to 'lose [one's] prize' (Col 2:18). 'Man is always given the possibility of saying Yes or No to God's offer.'"[72] How, then, does Balthasar understand the grace that is effected in man's free response to the Gospel? Ludwig Ott poses the alternatives: "Does this efficacy lie in the grace itself or in the free assent of the human will foreseen by God, i.e., is the grace efficacious by its intrinsic power . . . or is it efficacious by the free assent of the will?"[73] Balthasar answers:

> Tentatively, we can say this: that the Holy Spirit, the Spirit of absolute freedom, allows us to see, within our free spirits, what our *own* true freedom would be, that is, by confronting us with ourselves, with our own highest possibility. We *would* not *be* able just to say "Yes" to ourselves (that is effected for us vicariously);

70. Balthasar, *DWH*, 167.

71. Ibid., 166.

72. Balthasar *Theo-Drama*, 5:287–88.

73. Ott, *Fundamentals of Dogma*, 248.

> also, the meaningfulness of such a "Yes" and the *desire for it* are
> set before us, indeed, inspired in us. Do you really want to exist
> forevermore in contradiction to yourself?

Balthasar's description of the Holy Spirit's gift of God's grace sounds more like prevenient grace, that is, a grace that convicts, calls, illumines and enables rather than irresistible grace. So, perhaps this is why Balthasar puts the accent of man being responsible for himself. Still, his freedom is not absolute, that is, a self-sufficient good, and hence it cannot be properly realized except in dependence upon God who is not only the ground of truth but also the source of good. Freely turning away from God means then the closing up of human freedom and, consequently, being in contradiction to one's own good.

Balthasar, in his view of authentic human freedom, is consistent with the Catholic tradition's teaching, as Calvin, Barth, Scheeben, and Berkouwer also argue, that is, freely rejecting God is a perversion of freedom rather than a manifestation of true freedom. Balthasar echoes this teaching: "If created freedom chooses itself as the absolute good, it involves itself in a contradiction that will devour it: the formal object that informs it—which is in fact absolute, self-positing freedom—is in constant contradiction with finite freedom's pretentious claim to be infinite. This contradiction, if persisted in, is hell."[74] When, then, is the relation between grace and freedom? In particular, to quote Ott, "is efficacious grace intrinsically different from sufficient grace, or only extrinsically different by reason of the free assent of the will?"[75]

> [A]f one wishes to keep the distinctions [between sufficient
> and efficacious grace] noted above, then one would have to say:
> grace is "efficacious" when it presents my freedom with an image of itself so evident that it cannot do other than *freely* seize
> itself, while grace would be merely "sufficient" if this image did
> not really induce my freedom to affirm itself but left it preferring
> to persist in its self-contradiction. To push on any further into
> these deep waters is not permitted us.[76]

Although it isn't clear, Balthasar doesn't seem think that there is an intrinsic substantial difference between sufficient and efficacious grace, but only an external accidental difference. If man responds positively to God's grace, as Ott puts it, "sufficient grace is, ipso facto, efficacious grace." Ott continues:

74. Balthasar *Theo-Drama*, 5:301.

75. Ott, *Fundamentals of Dogma*, 248.

76. Balthasar, *DWH*, 167.

"If free will refuses its assent the grace remains sufficient only." Moreover, Balthasar brings us back again to hope. He circles back to the question regarding a serious possibility of refusal, asking, in the quote below, whether a man is capable of rejecting God.

> The Gospel of Jesus Christ is the revelation of God's highest, unsurpassable love for us, who care not one iota for that love, have absolutely no conception of its dimensions and are, almost, happy if someone wishes to remove the burden of our guilt before God from us and carry it himself. "While we were yet sinners Christ died for us . . . while we were enemies" (Rom 5:8, 10), that is, godforsaken ones who "have turned their back" to God, "and not their face" (Jer 2:27). But then, is any man capable of looking into the countenance of eternal, absolute love, of being "equal to" that? And would not everyone who, in earnest faith, would like to direct his life toward this love first have to become existentially aware of the infinite distance from it, of his own godforsaken half-heartedness and indifference—in order not to succumb to the delusion that he could, just as he is, throw himself into God's arms and suddenly be capable of living in the "consuming fire" of his love?[77]

As we shall see below, according to Balthasar, the gospel leaves this an open question, and he urges us to consider that it may not be closed *a priori* because man finds himself ever anew in the "open situation" of the gospel proclamation concerning the mercy of God.[78] This excludes a doctrine of predestination in any sense, according to Balthasar.[79] Given the grace that saved me in my own lostness, I must always remain open to the ever greater light of divine love for all men.[80] A brief explanation of how all these themes hang together is now warranted.

77. Balthasar, *DWH*, 155.

78. Unsurprisingly, there are Barthian influences in Balthasar's emphasis on the triumph of the mercy of God and the open situation of the gospel proclamation. On this emphasis, see Berkouwer, *The Triumph of Grace in the Theology of Karl Barth*, 89–122, and at 122.

79. Berkouwer disagrees with Balthasar's position. He writes: "It is a profound misunderstanding to think that one cannot take the open situation absolutely seriously any more because of election. Rather, it is meaningful to do so precisely because of the nature of election. See Ridderbos, *Paul*, 350: the Church belongs not to a definite number, but to Christ! For the 'open situation' see further *idem, Aan de Romeinen*, particularly 230, on the continuing openness on account of the teleological character of God's unlimited power. Only in this way is it possible to understand that the proclamation is not contrary to 'divine election', but is based in it" (*De Kerk*, 1:166n31 [135n9]).

80. Berkouwer, *De Wederkomst van Christus*, 2:205 [398].

Predestination

In his 1958 work, *The God Question & Modern Man*, Balthasar says regarding the outcome of God's judgment that the act of faith "remains truly open; it determines the judgment of the Lord neither to the one side nor to the other, nowhere establishing an *a priori* 'impossibility' that none of the brethren can be lost, or that some are certainly lost."[81] Elsewhere in his 1960 lecture, "Some Points of Eschatology," Balthasar argues more fully that three implications follow from claiming to know that in fact God will condemn some men to hell. In a passage worth citing in full, Balthasar gives us a glimpse of the major themes in his theology of hope that have a direct bearing on the question of predestination, election and reprobation.

> Once theologians (doubtless *bona fide* and thinking that faith demands it) consider they have "certainty of faith" about the outcome of the [last] judgment, they decide in advance, unknowingly, a whole range of questions, and the consequences necessarily reach into what would seem the most remote parts of theology. These unavoidable conclusions, however, are clearly inconsistent with what the Bible teaches on salvation, and so reveal their questionable nature. . . . First, despite the consistently positively conceived idea of predestination in scripture, which left the matter [of the outcome of judgment] open, men were obliged to adopt a doctrine of double predestination, equally oppressive whether *ante* [before] or *post praevisa merita* [after prevision or foreseeing of any merits]. . . . Secondly, when Christ is not looked on as the *Eschaton*, but when the results of the judgment are considered as "objects" capable of being known, the character of faith undergoes a change. Instead of a loving and trusting submission of the whole person to the personal divine truth of the Father in the Son, it becomes, of necessity, an intellectual, neutral act embracing indifferently truths both of salvation and reprobation and, therefore, only when it is directed to a truth of salvation can it comprise love and hope and trust. With this is closely connected a strangely truncated idea of hope, since it now seems against faith to hope for the salvation of all men; though this clearly conflicts with the biblical idea of hope. Furthermore it means that Christ cannot have prayed for the *reprobi* [reprobate], since his power cannot fail. Thirdly, this deciding in advance entails attributing to a most important series of scriptural texts, which make the salvation

81. Balthasar, *The God Question*, 141.

of all something to be hoped for (though unknowable), a sense
which takes away part of the force they clearly possess.[82]

In this passage, first, Balthasar refers to a positive idea of predestination.
What is that? Balthasar doesn't say, but the foremost American interpreter
of his thought is helpful here in answering this question. Fr. Edward T.
Oakes writes: "Predestination, then, is really the resulting realization that
comes upon a believer when he reflects how graciously he has been received
and how the circumstances that conspired to lead him to belief were not of
his doing; it is, in other words, a doctrine that is the outcome of gratitude
for a gift that came 'in the fullness of time.'"[83] So, God's gracious initiative
and decision has priority, in such a way—reminiscent of "congruism"—that
grace is given in circumstances favorable, and hence congruent, to its operation in which a supernatural salvific act is elicited. Predestination here
simply means the omnipotence and sovereignty of God's grace, of God's
universal saving will in Jesus Christ, who is God's Yes to man, of affirmation—which Balthasar affirms. John Paul II locates this "Yes" to man, of
affirmation, at the core of God's redemptive work in history that expresses
the purpose of God and that purpose has an electing character (Rom 9:11)
from before the foundation of the world (Eph 1:4).

> This election, with the decision which translates, that is, the plan
> of creation and redemption, belongs to the intimate life of the
> Blessed Trinity, is realized eternally by the Father with the Son
> and the Holy Spirit. It is a choice that, according to St. Paul, pre-
> cedes the creation of the world ("before the foundation of the
> world": Eph 1: 4); and man in the world. Man, even before be-
> ing created, he is "chosen" by God. This election will be fulfilled
> in the eternal Son ("in him" Eph 1: 4), that is, in the Word of
> eternal Mind. Man is therefore chosen in the Son to participate
> in the same sonship by divine adoption. Herein lies the very
> essence of the mystery of predestination, which manifests the
> eternal love of the Father ("before Him in love and predested
> us to be his sons through Jesus Christ": Eph 1: 4–5). Contended
> in predestination is, therefore, the eternal vocation of man to
> participate in the very nature of God. It is a vocation to holi-
> ness, through the grace of adoption for sons and daughters ("to
> be holy and blameless before him": Eph 1: 4). . . .In this sense,
> predestination precedes "the foundation of the world," that is, to
> the creation, as it is done in the perspective of the predestination

82. Balthasar, "Some Points of Eschatology," 255–77, and for this quotation,
266–67.

83. Oakes, *Pattern of Redemption*, 212.

of man. In divine revelation, the word "predestination" means God's eternal choice, a paternal, intelligent and positive choice, a choice of love.[84]

Clearly, John Paul II is saying in this 1986 General Audience what he was to express succinctly two years later in his Apostolic Letter on the dignity of women: "The biblical teaching taken as a whole enables us to say that predestination concerns all human persons, men and women, each and every one without exception."[85] But how are we to construe this claim that predestination in Christ concerns all men? I don't think that John Paul means to say à la Barth that there is no one who is not always already predestined in Christ. Is John Paul a universalist in the sense that Christ's atoning is intrinsically sufficient for all? Is he just saying that God wills to save all men and not to condemn? "For God did not send his Son into the world to condemn the world, but in order that the world might be saved through him" (John 3:17). Suffice it to here say that John Paul II understands God's "Yes" to man, of affirmation, at the Christological concentration point of God's redemptive work in history, to be expressive of the divine initiative stretching back to eternity, indeed before the foundation of the world (Ephesians 1:4). This is God's eternal plan of salvation that "concerns all human persons, men and women, each and every one without exception." Therefore, there remains the real possibility of choosing and adhering to unbelief, meaning thereby that unbelief is still open before us just as its opposite is as well? Belief or unbelief are still open possibilities, remaining live issues.

Second, this positive biblical idea is twisted, by Balthasar's reckoning, once the believer alleges that he possesses a putative knowledge of the outcome of God's "twofold judgment" regarding the final destiny of the saved and the lost. This knowledge presupposes a *closed* situation in which one already knows the outcome of judgment rather than one that is still open because the outcome of God's judgment is still unknown[86] and is eschatologically "bound up with the person of the Redeemer and Judge."[87] Quite simply, Balthasar holds that the situation in which the gospel is proclaimed is open in that we do not know whether "the light of divine will ultimately be able to penetrate every human darkness and refusal."[88] Put differently,

84. John Paul II, "La Providencia Divina y el destino del hombre: el misterio de la predestinación en Cristo," §§2–4. I'm grateful to Ana Echeverria for her translation of this passage from the Spanish.

85. John Paul II, *Mulieris dignitatem*, §9.

86. Balthasar, *DWH*, 14.

87. Balthasar, "Some Points of Eschatology," 268.

88. Balthasar, *DWH*, 142.

we do not know whether "some persons will in fact freely and persistently resist the grace of God and be lost."[89]

Balthasar acknowledges that he stands here against a massive reception of scriptural texts throughout the Church's history: those that appear to hold out the prospect of universal redemption and those that speak of some men being lost for all eternity. "Human thought always has the urge to 'systematize'; but scripture lets the possible, indeed the actual twofold outcome of the judgment remain 'unreconciled' alongside the prospect of universal reconciliation; nor is there any possibility of subordinating one to the other."[90] The crux of Balthasar's argument is that the supposed knowledge that faith has of the outcome of God's twofold judgment is the basis for a theology of double predestination that is irreconcilable with God's universal will to save all men, and hence with a biblical idea of hope. But is Balthasar correct? Yes, God wills that all men be saved. Yes, Christ died for all men. But the New Testament also teaches that some men, nevertheless, will be lost through their own fault (Mt 7:21–23; Mt 25:41–46; Lk 13:23–24).[91] Balthasar claims that we cannot know the outcome of people's choices. He regards the words of Jesus about the damnation of unrepentant sinners found at Matt 25 as mere threats or warnings. Balthasar claims that we cannot know "whether these threats by God, who 'reconciles himself in Christ with the world', will be actually realized in the way stated."[92] In other words, adds Balthasar, "I see no need to take the step from the threats to the positing of a hell occupied by our brothers and sisters, through which our hopes [for their salvation] would come to nought."[93] I shall return to these claims below. For now, I want to examine Balthasar's rejection of double predestination. How does he define double predestination?

He defines double predestination as "God's sublime foreknowledge [that] has from the outset appointed a number of men to eternal bliss and a number to eternal damnation [whether *ante* or *post praevisa merita*]."[94] More explicitly, Balthasar explains:

> Here [in the doctrine of double predestination] an ultimate basis
> for the alternative outcomes of human existence—eternal salva-
> tion or eternal perdition—is sought in the unfathomable abyss
> of divine freedom; so much so that, in spite of all exhortations,

89. Walls, *Heaven, Hell, and Purgatory*, 209.

90. Balthasar, "Some Points of Eschatology," 267.

91. Grisez and Ryan, "Hell and Hope for Salvation," 610.

92. Balthasar, *DWH*, 146.

93. Ibid., 149.

94. Balthasar, *Truth is Symphonic*, 66.

man's efforts slacken and fail as he loses all courage in the face of this mystery. For it is not a question (as before) of how finite freedom can develop within an infinite freedom: this infinite freedom, which is necessarily the final arbiter, now threatens to swallow up finite freedom.[95]

Intriguingly, Balthasar seems to regard as equally oppressive the two major interpretations of predestination whether *ante* or *post praevisa merita*. So, he rejects not only unconditional election but also conditional election. Briefly, let me explain.

In a doctrine of predestination, then, God decides whom he will save; salvation is a work of God. Jesus said to his disciples, "you did not choose me, but I chose you" (John 15:16). But on what basis does God decide? Balthasar's description in the above quotation gives the two basic positions on this. Does he choose to save an individual apart from any condition found in that person (*ante praevisa merita*)? If so, that is unconditional election. Alternatively, does God choose to save that individual whom he foreknows will first choose him and hence on the basis of his foreseen merits (*post and propter praevisa merita*)? If so, that is conditional election. Both interpretations have a place in the history of the reception of Romans 8: 29: "For those God foreknew he also predestined to be conformed to the likeness of his Son." Some interpreters suppose that what Paul had in view here is God's foresight of faith, and hence predestination in Christ is condition upon that foresight. Ben Witherington asks, "Is Paul then talking about a pretemporal election plan of God where the outcome is predetermined because of God's sovereign hand in and on every step of the process? This of course is how Augustine and his offspring read this text, but it is not how some of the crucial Greek Fathers that came before Augustine read it, including most importantly Chrysostom. Paul is speaking about God foreknowing and destining in advance Christians to be fully conformed to the image of Christ."[96]

Some interpreters find this interpretation valuable because it avoids the conclusion that apparently follows from the doctrine of unconditional election, namely, that God arbitrarily saves some and not others, and hence has predestined from eternity the salvation or ruin of man. The objection here is to not only an abstract concept of divine freedom in which there is no reference to God's love and grace but also to the deterministic character—causal predestinarianism of the elect and damned—of God's work of

---

95. Balthasar, *Theo-Drama*, 2:250.

96. Witherington, *Paul's Letter to the Romans*, 228. On 227n24, Witherington refers to Gerald Bray's summary of the evidence of this interpretation of predestination as conditional from his explanatory notes in *Romans*.

salvation. In this light, we can understand why, as Ridderbos puts it, "the center of gravity would have to be shifted from divine predestination to human freedom,"[97] and hence to a conditional election. "Without the individual's power of decision human responsibility toward the gospel becomes a fiction."[98]

Others, however, such as John Murray, reject conditional election for two reasons. First, if we suppose that election is conditional upon God's foreknowledge of faith, asks Murray, "whence proceeds this faith which God foresees?" He replies, "The only biblical answer is that the faith which God foresees is the faith he himself creates (cf. John 3:3–8; 6:44, 45, 65; Eph 2:8; Phil 1:29; II Pet. 1:2)." In other words, faith's knowledge of God is a gift of God's grace. Put differently, the priority of divine calling concerning the predestined suggests that it must be seen as effectual because St. Paul states that "those he called, he also justified" (Rom 8:30). As Schreiner says, "The text does not say that 'some' of those called were justified. It fuses the called and justified together so that those who have experienced calling have also inevitably received the blessing of justification. Now if all those who are called are also justified, then calling must be effectual and must create faith."[99] So, we can now understand why Murray concludes that unconditional election is exegetically justified: "Hence his eternal foresight of faith is preconditioned by his decree to generate this faith in those whom he foresees as believing, and we are thrown back upon the differentiation which proceeds from God's own eternal and sovereign election to faith and its consequents."[100]

Second, Murray argues that "the expression 'whom he foreknew' contains within itself the differentiation [of believers and unbelievers] which is presupposed." How so?

> Many times in Scripture "know" has a pregnant meaning which goes beyond that of mere cognition. It is used in a sense practically synonymous with "love," to set regard upon, to know with peculiar interest, delight, affection, and action . . . . There is no reason why this import of the word "know" should not be applied to "foreknow" in this passage. . . . When this import is appreciated, then there is no reason for adding any qualifying notion and "whom he foreknew" is seen to contain within itself the differentiating element required. It means "whom he set

---

97. Ridderbos, *Paul*, 351.

98. Ibid., 353.

99. Schreiner, *Romans*, 451.

100. Murray, *The Epistle to the Romans*, 1:316.

regard upon" or "whom he knew from eternity with distinguishing affection and delight" and is virtually equivalent to "whom
he foreloved. . . . "Foreknew" focuses attention upon the distinguishing love of God whereby the sons of God were elected."[101]

There is an even more fundamental reason why conditional election is
rejected, namely, its corresponding idea of human freedom. Ridderbos
explains: "There is nothing more contradictory of the Pauline doctrine of
salvation than if man were to become God's workmanship and new creation
in virtue of a decision of his own will. 'If a person has this possibility, he
would not be a creature but would stand on his own'. We are faced with the
unmistakable fact that Paul does not found the responsibility of man with
respect to his being saved or lost in the fact that man may be said to be free
to decide concerning it, but that through the preaching of the gospel God
calls and fits him for this responsibility; and that, where freedom has been
lost and has become spiritual impotence and blindness, the responsibility of
man as the creature of God is nevertheless not taken away or abrogated."[102]
Two things stand out here. One, human freedom here is not the neutral
freedom of indifference to decide concerning being saved or lost because
the divine initiative not only precedes his response but also prepares it by
prevenient grace. Two, human responsibility maintains its foundation even
after man becomes spiritually impotent and blind in view of the fall into sin.
I will return to these two points below.

For now, I continue understanding the reasons for Balthasar's rejection of predestination. Regardless of whether God's electing grace is conditional or unconditional, says Balthasar, "this knowledge [of a twofold
outcome is taken] as a fully secure basis upon which to construct . . . further
speculations about God's twofold predeterminations *post* or *ante praevisa
merita*."[103] It seems that Balthasar does not care whether a view of predestination has God deciding unconditionally or conditionally. Is it then the very
idea of predestination with which Balthasar has trouble?

Yes it is. Indeed, what troubles Balthasar is the idea that God, by the
eternal decree of his divine will, has appointed certain men to their eternal
blessedness and guides them toward it? Yes, but ultimately it is the claim
that we know, here and now, about the outcome of divine judgment that is
at the root of his objection to predestination. But even if predestination, in
this sense, is part of the eternal divine plan of providence, is that the same
as "double" predestination? Not at all: double predestination is the absurdity

101. Murray, *The Epistle to the Romans*, 317, 318.

102. Ridderbos, *Paul*, 353–54.

103. Balthasar, *DWH*, 47.

that makes election in Christ exactly parallel to reprobation for sin doing so in way that suggests that an individual was created *for* damnation.[104]

So, Balthasar's description above of double predestination, that is, "God's twofold predeterminations *post* or *ante praevisa merita*," is too loose for us to say that it is, indeed, a doctrine of double predestination in which an "equal symmetry" between election and reprobation is affirmed. Canon 17 of the Decree on Justification of the Council of Trent (1547) rejects this notion of double predestination: "If anyone says that the grace of justification is given only to those who are predestined to life and that all the others who are called are called indeed but do not receive grace, as they are predestined to evil by the divine power, let him be anathema."[105] As I showed in chapter 5, Reformed critics, such as Bavinck and Berkouwer, insist that a doctrine of double predestination should be understood as an "essential asymmetry," which denies the parallelism or symmetry of operation between election and reprobation. On this view, which New Testament theologian Udo Schnelle claims is Pauline, "Salvation and damnation are equally grounded in the ineluctable decision of God." But, he continues, underscoring the asymmetry, "They do not, however, stand alongside each other having the same rank." In other words, Schnelle is saying that St. Paul affirms an "essential asymmetry" between salvation and damnation "for God's universal saving will has been revealed in the gospel of Jesus Christ, whereas God's no is a mystery withdrawn from human knowledge."[106]

In the strict sense, then, a doctrine of double predestination that Balthasar rejects is a *symmetrical* view of election and reprobation such that the latter is worked out in a *parallel* mode of divine causation. But not all accounts of the doctrine of election, of salvation and reprobation, adopt double predestination in this strict sense; some posit an essential asymmetry between election and reprobation. For example, Ludwig Ott correctly states, "Predestination to hell, in Catholicism, always involves man's free will, and foreseen sins, so that man is ultimately responsible for his own damnation, not God (*double predestination* is rejected)."[107] That is, a symmetrical view of double predestination is rejected. Nevertheless, Balthasar's failure to consider the crucial point of essential asymmetry results in thinking that *any*

---

104. Oakes, *Pattern of Redemption*, 314, understands this point about double predestination more clearly than Balthasar.

105. Denzinger, §1567.

106. Schnelle, *Theology of the New Testament*, 214. Elsewhere he says, "The question of whom God chooses remains closed to human knowledge" (563).

107. Ott, *Fundamentals of Catholic Dogma*, 243.

doctrine of predestination and reprobation is incompatible with the central message of revelation, namely, God's universal salvific will.[108]

I understand why Balthasar overlooks this crucial point of symmetry. Whether symmetrical or asymmetrical, unconditional or conditional, whether *ante* or *post praevisa merita*, all theories of predestination that attempt to give an account of the saved and the damned in the divine counsel presuppose a putative knowledge of the twofold outcome of divine judgment, and it is precisely that claim to knowledge that Balthasar rejects because it allegedly presupposes a situation that is "closed" rather than still "open." A "closed situation" is one in which God's saving purpose conceives of the number of those predestined to salvation in a deterministic manner. Why is, then, an "open situation" fundamentally important?

Essentially, says Balthasar, because in a "closed situation" it makes no sense to hold that: "'God our Savior . . . desires all men to be saved and to come to the knowledge of the truth'" (1 Tim 2:4).[109] Again: "For the grace of God that brings salvation has appeared to all men" (Tit 2:11). And again: "This is a trustworthy saying that deserves full acceptance . . . that we have put our hope in the living God, who is the Savior of all men, and especially of those who believe" (1 Tim 4:9–10). In the "open situation," we are ambassadors of God issuing the call of the gospel to all sinners—not to the elect and reprobate, with their twofold destinies—to be reconciled to God (2 Cor 5:20), persuading them to respond by faith to the gospel as the only way of salvation in view of God's liberating grace. In sum, given God's love for man and his universal salvific will for all men, adds Balthasar, "this is for the fact that the Church should make 'supplications, prayers, intercessions, and thanksgivings. . . for all men' (1 Tim 2;1), which could not be asked of her if she were not allowed to have at least the hope that prayers as widely directed as these are sensible and might be heard. If, that is, she knew with certainty that this hope was too widely directed, then what is asked of her would be self-contradictory." [110]The question now that we now must ask is whether the idea of a "meaningful open situation"[111] is compatible with a doctrine of predestination and, if so, in what sense?[112]

---

108. I showed earlier in chapter 3 that Scheeben's theology of predestination answers Balthasar's objection.

109. Balthasar, *DWH*, 22–23.

110. Ibid., 23–24.

111. Berkouwer, *Een Halve Eeuw Theologie*, 142 [102].

112. Helpful to me in answering this question is the work of Ridderbos, *Paul*, 341–54. See also the commentary by Ridderbos, *Aan De Romeinen*, 193–203.

According to Balthasar, a doctrine of double predestination "threatens to swallow up finite freedom."[113] I won't repeat the arguments I discussed in chapters 2 and 3 when treating the question of freedom and determinism in Calvin and Scheeben. So, Balthasar is justified in rejecting a deterministic conception of divine election in which, as Ridderbos clearly states, "all that God does in history has been foreordained from eternity and therefore, so far as his mercy as well as his hardening is concerned, has an irresistible and inevitable issue."[114] Still, notwithstanding Balthasar's justified rejection of determinism, we cannot "understand election exclusively as an action of God in time and history and therefore entirely reject the idea of an eternal election."[115] In other words, Balthasar's apparently sees divine election exclusively and essentially as an act of God in time and history. "'Election' therefore means, not God's eternal gracious choice, but the effect of this call on the freedom of the person called."[116] It isn't only that he rightly rejects seeing divine election in terms of an abstract, eternal decree, apart from God's grace and love in Christ, but also that he "historicizes" and "actualizes" election such that "election and rejection only 'happen' in an 'open situation.'"[117] *Pace* Balthasar, God's redemptive work in history expresses the purpose of God and that purpose has an electing character (Rom 9:11), stretching back to eternity, indeed, from before the foundation of the world (Eph 1:4). Ridderbos explains:

> Paul speaks of this purpose in all sorts of places and in more than one way. In addition to purpose (*prosthesis, protithemai*; Rom 8:28; 9:11; Eph 1:9, 11; 2 Tim 1:9), he makes mention of foreknowledge (*proginōskō*; Rom 8:29; 11:2), foreordination (*proorizō*; Rom 8:29, 30; 1 Cor 2:7; Eph 1:5, 11), to prepare beforehand (*proetoimazō*; Rom 9:23; Eph 2:10), but then further of God's good pleasure (*eudokia*; Eph 1:5, 9; cf. Phil 2:13), the counsel of his will (*boulē tou thelēmatos autou*; Eph 1:11), his mystery (*mystērion*; 1 Cor 2:7; Eph 1:9; 3:9). . . . The distinguishing feature of all these pronouncements is that they have reference to God's counsel with respect to his work of redemption in Christ in the fullness of the times.[118]

113. Balthasar, *Theo-Drama*, 2:250.

114. Ridderbos, *Paul*, 345.

115. Ibid., 347n46. Ridderbos adds, "With every (justified) defense against a deterministic conception . . . the evidence of the pre-temporal elements in the Pauline doctrine of election and predestination may not be denied."

116. Balthasar *Theo-Drama*, 3:266.

117. Runia, "Recent Reformed Criticisms," 5.

118. Ridderbos, *Paul*, 346.

What is, then, the "function all [of] these *pro*-concepts fulfill in the whole of the Pauline doctrine of salvation?"[119] The brief answer to this question here must be that they all fulfill the "christocentric character of this purpose." This "finds clear expression in Ephesians 1:9, which speaks of God's good pleasure that he purposed in Christ with respect to the 'economy' of the fullness of the times; and in Ephesians 3:11, where the apostle [Paul] speaks of God's eternal purpose that he formed in Christ Jesus."[120] In this connection, we cannot fail to note that, in the relation to Christ in which God's eternal purpose is accomplished, the Church, too, has a key place, being the object of God's predestination and eternal counsel in virtue of belong to Christ. "His intent was that now, through the church, the manifold wisdom of God should be made known" (Eph 3:10). Again, clearly obviating an abstract divine freedom—sovereign election without the love and grace of God—Ephesian 1:5 states, "In love, he predestined us to be adopted as his sons through Jesus Christ." In Romans 8:29 we read, similarly, "For those God foreknew he also predestined to be conformed to the likeness of his Son"; and again in Ephesians 1:11, "In him we were also chosen, having been predestined according to the plan of him who works out everything in conformity with the purpose of his will." Ridderbos correctly remarks, "All this [the church is the object of God's predestination] finds its most pregnant expression in that God even 'before the foundation of the world' chose the church to himself in Christ (Eph 1:4).[121] He elaborates:

> Here again it is a matter, as always with election, not simply of a decree of God that only later comes to realization, but of the actual appropriation of the church to himself before the foundation of the world. How this is possible and how one is to conceive of it are seen from the words "in Christ." Paul speaks here, too, of the comprehension of the church in Christ. As it, although still on earth, has in Christ received a place in heaven (Eph 2:6), and this in Christ participates in the heavenly blessings (Eph 1:3), so—Paul makes the connection here expressly—it was already united with the pre-existent Christ and thus chosen by God in

119. Ibid., 348.

120. Ibid., 346. Eph 1:9, "And he made known to us the mystery of his will according to his good pleasure, which he purposed in Christ, to be put into effect when the times will have reached their fulfillment—to bring all things in heaven and on earth together under one head, even Christ." Eph 3:11, "according to his eternal purpose which he accomplished in Christ Jesus our Lord."

121. Bruce, *The Epistle of Paul to the Romans*, "The new creation, the community of men and women conformed to the image of Christ, who is himself the image of God (2 Cor 4:4; Col 1:15), is seen to have been from the beginning the object of God's foreknowledge and foreordaining mercy" (167).

him. The inclusion of the church in Christ, its corporate existence by God in him, Paul traces back to this pre-existence. As
its life is hid in God with the Exalted One (Col 3:3), so its election is in him before the foundation of the world. Even there the
church's being in Christ can be spoken of, and thus its election
in him in whom God purposed his good pleasure, indeed, who
himself can be called God's "Foreknown" before the foundation
of the world (1 Pet 1:20).[122]

Now, in upholding the omnipotence and sovereignty of God's grace,
as Balthasar does, doesn't the biblical revelation (e.g., Rom 8: 28–30; Eph 1:
4–5, 9, 11), arguably, also impel him to acknowledge something fundamental, namely, the pre-temporal elements of God's eternal gracious choice—
election before the foundation of the world in the Pauline of doctrine of
election and predestination? God "chose us in him before the foundation of
the world . . . . He destined us in love to be his sons through Jesus Christ"
(Eph 1:4). I think so, but Balthasar inexplicably ignores it in *DWH*. There
are two reasons why St. Paul draws our attention to "Before the foundation
of the world." One, God's purpose concerning the Church is rooted in the
antecedent counsel and divine plan of salvation that is "free from what we
know in the world to be arbitrary and precarious" and hence our attention
is directed "to what can be called the opposite of chance and contingence."
In short, "History and the gospel are not minimized, but the riches and
fullness of salvation in history are shown to be anchored in God."[123] Second, the reference to "before" underscores that the purpose of God's saving
work rests on his antecedent sovereign grace and not on human works. For
example, Romans 9:11 explains the significance of the "electing purpose of
God" by the words, "not by works but by him who calls." Again, 2 Timothy
1:9 states that "God has saved us and called us to a holy life—not because
of anything we have done but because of his own purpose and grace." Significantly, St. Paul adds, "This grace was given us in Christ Jesus before the
beginning of time [before times eternal]." The contrast here, too, is between
God's purpose and human works. It has a soteriological nature. Once again,
in Titus 3:5 we find the same soteriological contrast: "not because of righteous things we had done, but because of his mercy."

In sum, Ridderbos insists: "The reference to God's purpose and grace
[or mercy] has as its object, therefore, the placing of all the emphasis on
the precedence and priority of divine grace and thus on the absolutely gratuitous character of God's saving work and of his calling to salvation." So,

122. Ridderbos, *Paul*, 347.
123. Berkouwer, *De Verkiezing Gods*, 174 [151].

the christocentric character of God's divine purpose "is not abstract pre-destinarianism [sovereign election without the love and grace of God] or reference back to God's decrees as the final cause in the chain of event, but [rather] the designation of sovereign divine grace as the sole motive of the his work of redemption in history."[124]

There remains to ask whether God's eternal purpose includes a pre-destined *numerus clausus*—a fixed number—of those who belong to Christ and will share in his work of redemption from before the foundation of the world.[125] In this connection, St. Paul refers to the Church, known and elected beforehand (Eph 1:4; Rom 8:29), to those predestined to be adopted sons (Eph 1:5, 11), those prepared beforehand as objects of his mercy (Rom 9:23), and of those he prepared in advanced to do good works (Eph 2:10). The crux of the matter, however, concerns whether St. Paul means to include here a predestined *numerus clausus* of the elect and whether with that . . . those who do not belong to this *numerus clausus* have not been excluded in virtue of this same purpose before the foundations of the world."[126] Let's be clear here. The question here is not whether will many be saved. As John Finnis rightly says, "Of that we do not have the faintest idea and should not speculate; for on this matter there are no sufficient data to warrant any conclusion."[127] Also, I don't think the question should mislead us in think-ing that there is a decree of reprobation from eternity. This point is reiter-ated in the *CCC* where the Church teaches that "God predestines no one to go to hell."[128] For eternal damnation, as the *Catechism* adds, "a willful turn-ing away from God (a mortal sin) is necessary, and persistence in it until

---

124. Ridderbos, *Paul*, 350.

125. In Luke 13: 23, Jesus is asked, "'Lord, are only a few people going to be saved?' He said to them, 'Make every effort to enter through the narrow door, because many, I tell you, will try to enter and will not be able to'" (24). Similarly, in Matthew 7:13–14, Jesus said, "'Enter through the narrow gate. For wide is the gate and broad is the road that leads to destruction, and many enter through it. But small is the gate and narrow the road that leads to life, and only a few find it.'"

126. Ridderbos, *Paul*, 350. According to Byrne, *Romans*, 272n29: Regarding Ro-mans 8:29: "he chose beforehand" and "he also preordained": "The language of 'election' and 'preordination' here does not imply a doctrine of predestination in the classical sense of a divine fixing of individual human lives in a set of direction towards salvation or damnation. Paul does not have individuals principally in mind but is applying the biblical privilege of election communally to the Christian community made up of Jews and Gentiles. The perspective is positive and inclusive, rather than exclusive, indicating God's will to bring all to the fullness of humanity. Whether or not some individuals fail to be included is not at issue."

127. Finnis, "Hell and Hope," 374.

128. *CCC*, §1037.

the end."[129] Regarding eternal punishment for man, the *Catechism* teaches: "To die in mortal sin without repenting and accepting God's merciful love means remaining separated from him for ever by our own free choice. This state of definitive self-exclusion from communion with God and the blessed is called 'hell.'"[130] Still, we may not rest satisfied with the following statement from the 1973 Leuenberg Agreement between Lutheran and Reformed Christians about predestination.

> Faith knows by experience that the message of salvation is not accepted by all; yet it respects the mystery of God's dealings with men. It bears witness to the seriousness of human decisions, and at the same time to reality of God's universal purpose of salvation. The witness of the Scriptures to Christ forbids us to suppose that God has uttered an eternal decree for the final condemnation of specific individuals or of a particular people.[131]

The vagueness of what is meant by the "seriousness of human decision" and its relation to God's universal salvific will, as well as the idea of eternal rejection," has led some to ignore the reality of hell as an eternal implication of the guilty choices of men, or even to deny hell as a real possibility as inconsistent with God's love. Contributing to this is the denial that the New Testament's eschatological statements be interpreted as "facts" that some day will be. Rather, they argue that these should be interpreted non-literally. Karl Rahner, for one, proposes this view: "What Scripture says about hell is to be interpreted in keeping with its literary character as 'threat-discourse' and hence not to be read as a preview of something which will exist some day."[132] This, too, is Balthasar's view.[133] He regards the words of Jesus about the damnation of unrepentant sinners found at Matt 25 as mere threats or warnings. Balthasar claims that we cannot know "whether these threats by God, who 'reconciles himself in Christ with the world', will be actually

129. Ibid.

130. Ibid., §1033.

131. Rusch and Martensen, *The Leuenberg Agreement*, 139–54, and at 3 (25), 150.

132. Rahner, "Hell," in *Encyclopedia of Theology*, 603. See also, Rahner and Vorgrimler, *Theological Dictionary*, 201–2.

133. Berkouwer wonders whether this approach to eschatological statements of some Catholic theologians, such as Rahner and Balthasar, "is in complete harmony with Roman Catholic tradition" (*De Wederkomst van Christus*, II, 206 [399]). Although I cannot develop my response here, I think the answer is "no." See, for example, Denzinger §443; §411; §801; §1002; *Creed of the People of God*, Paul VI, §12; *Lumen gentium*, §48; Letter of the Congregation for the Doctrine of the Faith on *Certain Questions Concerning Eschatology*, May 17, 1979, §7; *Catechism of the Catholic Church*, §1035.

realized in the way stated."[134] In other words, adds Balthasar, "I see no need to take the step from the threats to the positing of a hell occupied by our brothers and sisters, through which our hopes [for their salvation] would come to nought."[135] Balthasar claims that this, too, pertains to Mark 16:16: "He who believes and is baptized will be saved; but he who does not believe will be condemned." That is, "[It], too, is not a report but, rather, reflects one's final placement in the position of having to decide."[136]

But there is a problem with making these Scriptural passages mere threats. Suggesting that Jesus' warnings may have been empty threats, or bluffs, argues Grisez, "implies that Jesus himself may have misrepresented the Father, making him seem other than Jesus knew him to be. But the Holy Spirit cannot have lied, and Jesus cannot have misrepresented the Father."[137] In short, "Jesus would have been dishonest had he tried to motivate people by warnings that were not truthful information about their prospects if they failed to heed his warnings."[138] Of course that is right. Furthermore, sometimes Balthasar treats these passages, adds Grisez, "as warnings that tell us nothing about what will actually happen in the future [*DWH*, 32–33] but are meant only to motivate present fidelity."

But this approach to these passages is also mistaken if what is meant, as Balthasar seems to suggest, is that motivating present fidelity is their only point. "For the very notions of threat and warning imply a reference—truthful or not, accurate or not—to what *will* happen if a certain condition is fulfilled, in this case if one dies in unrepented mortal sin."[139] Now even if not a "straightforwardly literal interpretation,"[140] meaning thereby, I take it, a *literalistic* interpretation, rather than a metaphorical one, cannot be given of the "'twofold judgment' in the Matthew 25 and other New Testament statements—a variety of metaphors are employed: everlasting fire, outer darkness, tormenting thirst, and weeping and gnashing of teeth—what reason does Balthasar give for regarding these Scriptural passages as *mere* threats and warnings, as speaking about something which *might* happen, rather than speaking about the future damnation of unrepentant sinners that *will* happen? There is no intrinsic reason since such Scriptural passages speak about the damned in a form that is grammatically future: "These will

134. Balthasar, *DWH*, 146.

135. Ibid., 149.

136. Ibid., 21.

137. Grisez, "Question 6," 25.

138. Grisez and Ryan, "Hell and Hope for Salvation," 613.

139. Grisez, "Question 6," 25–26.

140. Balthasar, *DWH*, 47.

go away into eternal punishment, but the righteous into life eternal" (Matt. 25:46). The only reason Balthasar gives is that condemning any men to eternal damnation would allow "God's benevolent will . . . to be frustrated by man's wickedness."[141] But this is unacceptable to Balthasar because it "blunts God's triune will for salvation, which is directed at the entire world."[142] In sum, adds Balthasar, "I think it is permissible to hope . . . that the light of divine love will ultimately be able to penetrate every human darkness and refusal."[143]

Now, Vatican II's *Lumen gentium* (§48) states, "at the end of the world 'those who have done good will go to the resurrection of life, and those who have done evil will go to the resurrection of condemnation' (Jn. 5:29; cf. Matt. 25:46)." Does this statement exclude the view—Balthasar's view— that damnation is a mere possibility? Is that passage teaching that there are damned *de facto* because there is a hell to which men "will go" rather just being a mere possibility that may go unrealized? Regarding this statement, Fr. James T. O'Connor informs us that at Vatican II "one bishop wanted a sentence to be included in which it would be clear that there are damned *de facto*, lest damnation remain as a mere hypothesis." This was stated in the official *Relatio*. Apparently, those responsible for drafting *Lumen Gentium*, refused to enter such a sentence, but they commented that "In [*Lumen gentium*] §48 there are cited the words of the Gospel [of Matthew 24: 1–46] in which the Lord Himself speaks about the damned in a form which is grammatically future." This is significant because it means that when the Church speaks of eternal damnation in passages like this and other magisterial statements, she speaks, as Christ himself did, in the grammatical future, about something that *will* happen, rather than in a form of grammar that is *conditional*, about something that *might* happen. As Fr. O'Connor concludes, "And it was with this understanding that the bishops of Vatican II voted upon and accepted *Lumen Gentium*."[144]

Vatican II's understanding of Matt 25 is called by New Testament scholar Ben Witherington III "apocalyptic prophecy," and it is found expressed in other commentaries of Matthew's Gospel. Matt 25 describes the ultimate fate of the damned using a variety of metaphors: everlasting fire, outer darkness, tormenting thirst, and weeping and gnashing of teeth. Witherington elaborates,

141. Ibid., 146.
142. Ibid., 13.
143. Ibid., 142.
144. O'Connor, "Von Balthasar and Salvation," 10–21.

It clearly involves parabolic images of sheep and goats symbol-izing different sorts of people, which make clear that neither the author nor the audience looked for a literal fulfillment of these words. Jesus will not be returning to sort out the world's flocks of animals! *However, it also needs to be realized that however poetic some of the images are in this prophecy, it is intended to be referential.* Jesus does envision a real second coming, he does envision a final judgment, he does envision eternal life and what we call hell. But like so much apocalyptic prophecy about the more distant horizon, it is in poetic and parabolic form. It doesn't really get into specifics, and this text tells us nothing about the timing of these events. Indeed, we would not expect it to do so. In light of the saying in Matthew 24 about no one knowing the timing of the second coming, all such speculating should cease and desist on the basis of the authority of Jesus' own word on the matter. Much of the problem of the mishan-dling of biblical prophecy in our time is that we have imposed modern hopes and expectations and preconceptions on ancient texts and so distorted their meaning. We have pressed then to tell us more than God has chosen to reveal. *The truth is that God has revealed enough about the future to give us hope, but not so much that we do not have to have faith. We should be content with what can be said with some certainty, not be frustrated by the lack of particularity of Jesus' prophecies about the end of the eschatological age.*[145]

Of course knowing that hell really exists, and that some people will end up there, and that Jesus statements on hell are hence predictive, does not mean that we should ignore them as minatory, admonitory and caution-ary. We must take very seriously the sense in which the reality of hell affects the way people live, namely, as incentive for action. It seems to me, however, that such statements can only motivate us if they imply an actual reference to what will happen if one dies in unrepented mortal sin. Otherwise, Je-sus' statements about hell would be empty threats. Thus eternal separation from God is a matter of ultimate concern. Given the evidence of Scripture regarding the abuse of human freedom, as well as the pervasive reality of sin, says Finnis, "give us reason to expect that at the end of human history, some will be found to have been lost to God's friendship and the Kingdom of Jesus."[146] Furthermore, there is no reason why we cannot understand the New Testament passages affirming an eternal separation from God, and

---

145. Witherington, *Matthew*, 468; emphasis added.
146. Finnis, "Hell and Hope," 374.

as the destiny of certain people, as passages that are also admonitory and cautionary of the terrible reality of hell. The *Catechism* observes:

> The affirmations of Sacred Scripture and the teachings of the Church on the subject of hell are a *call to the responsibility* incumbent upon man to make use of his freedom in view of his eternal destiny. They are at the same time an urgent *call to conversion*: "Enter by the narrow gate; for the gate is wide and the way is easy, that leads to destruction, and those who enter by it are many. For the gate is narrow and the way is hard, that leads to life, and those who find it are few [Mt 7:13–14].[147]

Returning now to the question posed by Ridderbos whether God's eternal purpose includes a predestined *numerus clausus*—a fixed number— of those who belong to Christ and will share in his work of redemption from before the foundation of the world. Consider in this connection the so-called *catena aurea*, the "golden chain," of Romans 8:29–30. "For those God foreknew he also predestined to be conformed to the likeness of his Son, that he might be the first-born among many brothers. And those he predestined, he also called; those he called, he also justified; those he justified, he also glorified." Those interpreters of St. Paul who support unconditional election claim that the indissoluble bond expressed here not only joins God's purpose, predestination, calling, justification, and glorification, but also make an "abstract pronouncement concerning the immutability of the number of those predestined to salvation."[148] In other words, they hold to a "causal predestinarianism abstracted from [the economy of redemption revealed and qualified in Christ]," and choose "to reduce the links of this golden chain fundamentally to one thing only, that they will inherit glory who have been foreknown and predestined by God to that end."[149]

Ridderbos, for one, contests this reading by arguing that the "golden chain" concerns a "pastoral encouragement for the persecuted and embattled church (cf. v. 36), based on the fixed and unassailable character of the divine work of redemption,"[150] namely, "faith in the trustworthiness of God's promises and in the unshakeableness of his *eudokia* in Christ (cf. e.g., Tit 1:2). . , [and] that of the revelation of the gospel as a power of God for everyone who believes (Rom 1:16), and thus of the electing character of God's grace, not resting on human power or wisdom, that he who boasts

147. *CCC*, §1036.
148. Ridderbos, *Paul*, 350.
149. Ibid., 351.
150. Ibid., 350.

should boast in the Lord (1 Cor 1:16ff)."[151] So, what is fixed here is that the Church belongs to Christ from before the foundation of the world rather than that a certain fixed number of saved belong to the Church. "Fixity does not lie in a hidden *decretum* [of a *numerus clausus* explaining the separation that comes about by the preaching of the gospel], therefore, but in the corporate unity of the church with Christ, whom it has come to know in the gospel and had learned to embrace in faith."[152] Still, on the one hand, the "golden chain" that charts the course from God's purpose, predestination, calling, justification, and glorification "begins in the eternity of God with the divine election." That is, "'Know beforehand' (*proegnō*) has its biblical sense of 'choose beforehand' (cf. Jer 1:5). Paul is applying to all believers the idea of 'election' so central to the self-understanding of Israel as People of God. Behind the existence of all who are 'in Christ'—Gentiles as well as Jews—stands the eternal 'choice' of God."[153] And yet, although there exists an indissoluble bond between the links of the *catena aurea*, such that they cannot be detached from one another both actually and cognitively, there exists a reciprocal relationship between divine predestination and the redemptive-historical "in Christ," which means that the "nature and scope of this 'chosen in Christ' are known and defined only by the realization of the divine purpose in history."[154] There has to be a reciprocal relationship here—underscoring the historical realization of the divine purpose—because God's calling is an invitation to conversion and faith. Ridderbos explains:

> Those who have been chosen in Christ before the foundation of the world are also those who in the fullness of the time have died and been raised with him, who have been called through the gospel and have been incorporated into his body in the way of faith and baptism. This means, among other things, that one can speak of the number of those who have been foreknown by God and who have died and been raised with Christ (or: for whom Christ has died) only when he at the same time takes the event of preaching into consideration and respects this to the full according to its nature (that is to say, according to the nature of the divine call to faith and conversion).[155]

---

151. Ibid., 353.
152. Ibid., 350–51.
153. Byrne, *Romans*, 268.
154. Ridderbos, *Paul*, 351.
155. Ibid.

But given this reciprocity, doesn't the emphasis now fall on human freedom? Does Ridderbos's position now swing to a conditional election as a result of eliminating every trace of a deterministic election?[156] Not at all, for human freedom is, one, not a neutral freedom of indifference to decide concerning being saved or lost because the divine initiative not only precedes his response but also prepares it. "Through the preaching of the gospel God calls and fits him for this responsibility."[157] Ridderbos adds, "He describes the calling of believers accordingly . . . as a divine creative act, a *creatio ex nihilo* (cf. Rom 4:17 with Gal 4:28), or, as he writes of the preaching of the gospel in 2 Corinthians 4:6: 'the God who said: Let light shine out of darkness, has made it to shine in our hearts.'" [158] Conversely, St. Paul "speaks of those who do not follow this call as disobedient and unbelieving, whose thoughts have been stricken with blindness by the way in which this world thinks, by the god of this age, 'so that they do not perceive the shining of the gospel of the glory of Christ' (2 Cor 4:4)." So, "Nothing could be farther from the truth than that in the relationship of election and preaching Paul takes his point of departure in individual human freedom."[159]

Two, notwithstanding the priority of the divine calling, human responsibility maintains its foundation even after man becomes spiritually impotent and blind in view of the fall into sin. In other words, speaking of man's responsibility concerning faith as obedience and unbelief as disobedience only makes sense if "the responsibility of man as the creature of God is nevertheless not taken away or abrogated."[160] Furthermore, even when St. Paul "speaks of unbelief as blinding and qualifies it as a consequence of God's righteousness and hardening (cf. Rom 11:8ff), he does not do so in an abstract and timeless manner." Rather, Ridderbos adds, "he points out precisely what the function of such a hardening is in the whole of redemptive history, and he makes it understood that this therefore 'need' not bear a definitive character, but rather, as with the reject and hardening of unbelieving Israel, presupposes a situation that is still 'open.'"[161] In conclusion, Ridderbos sketches two lines of thought that cannot be reconciled with each other from a higher standpoint:

> On the one hand, God's creative word of omnipotence by which alone the light can shine in the heart, on the other hand, human

156. Ridderbos, *Aan De Romeinen*, 195.
157. Ridderbos, *Paul*, 353–54.
158. Ibid., 251–52.
159. Ibid., 352.
160. Ibid., 254.
161. Ibid., 352.

responsibility for faith and conversion; on the one hand, blindness and spiritual impotence, on the other, struggling under
commission from God to bring back to him those who have
turned away; also on the one hand, the certainty of God's faithfulness and the irrevocableness of his election and calling, on
the other, the warning against the danger of being broken off
from the olive true on account of pride and being rejected as a
participant in salvation.[162]

Suffice it now to conclude that we have refuted Balthasar's rejection of predestination by developing the idea of a "meaningful open situation" and
shown its compatibility with a doctrine of predestination. I turn now to
consider the relationship between grace and freedom in Balthasar's theology of hope.

Two Models of Judgment:
Natural Consequence and Penalty[163]

Jesus himself tells us that he came not to judge the world but to save it (Jn
3:17; 12:47). God did not send his only Son into the world both to save and
damn. On this point St. John's Gospel is unequivocal: "For God did not send
his Son into the world to condemn the world, but to save the world through
him" (John 3:17). Still, Jesus immediately produces a judgment (*krisis*) in
respect of our response to him, whose result is, he says, that "whoever believes in him is not condemned, but whoever does not believe is condemned
already, because he has not believed in the name of the only Son of God"
(John 3:18). Those who do not believe are condemned because they are
still under the wrath of God, without saving grace, and hence dead in their
transgressions and sins (Eph 2:1). "Whoever believes in the Son has eternal
life; whoever does not obey the Son shall not see life, but the wrath of God
remains on him" (John 3:36). They have not accepted the good news that
"God, being rich in mercy, because of the great love with which he loved
us, even when we were dead in our trespasses, made us alive together with
Christ—by grace you have been saved" (Eph 2:4–5). But for those who are
in Christ Jesus there is no condemnation *here and now*, because they have
died to sin (Rom 8:1; 6:2). Asks Balthasar, "Are we therefore quite untrou-
bled in the certainty of our salvation?" He answers, "Surely not, for which

162. Ibid., 353.

163. For a critical discussion of these two models, see Murray, "Heaven and Hell,"
287–317. See also, Kvanvig, *The Problem of Hell*, 155–59. I am heavily indebted especially to Murray's analysis, but I have also profited from Kvanvig's.

man knows whether, in the course of his existence, he has lived up to God's infinite love, which chose to expend itself for him? Must be not, if he is honest and no Pharisee, assume the opposite? In attempting to respond to grace, did he allow God to act through him as God pleased, or did he presume to know better than God and act according to his own pleasure?"[164] Balthasar holds that the only way to keep the situation "open" is to reject predestination as such. We have already argued against that position. I now turn to argue against another feature of Balthasar's theology of hope, namely, his understanding of judgment.

Of course, there is an important sense in which we no longer are *under* judgment, with the latter being the fruit of the redemptive work of God the Father, in Christ, through the Holy Spirit. For Jesus Christ bore the divine wrath for sin, wrath that would otherwise have remained upon the sinner in judgment. This, then, is the indicative: "The law of the Spirit of life has made you free in Christ Jesus from the law of sin and of death" (Rom 8:2, 9). But the redemptive *indicative* of already, and hence *here and now*, dying and rising with Christ is not to be separated from the *imperative* of continuing to struggle against sin: "Let not sin therefore reign in your mortal body . . . and do not present your members any longer as weapons of unrighteousness in the service of sin" (Rom 6:12-13).

Of course the imperative is grounded in the indicative. "Nevertheless," as Ridderbos rightly notes, "The new life [in Christ] is . . . not a dormant but a militant life, a life by faith. . . . The imperative is only fulfilled when faith is vigilant, militant, sober (1 Cor 16:13; 1 Thess 5:6, 8ff.; Eph 6:11ff.). To that extent every imperative is an actualizing of the indicative. Yet it [the imperative] is not lost in that: it seeks the fruit of faith and of the Holy Spirit in sanctification (Rom 6:21, 22; Gal 5:22); it is directed toward the 'more and more', toward the increasing and abounding, toward the growth and progress of the new life (Rom 5:3; 2 Cor 8:7; 9:8ff.; 1 Tim 4:15)."[165] If those who are in Christ remain faithful to his promises, they will be able to stand in the "the day of the Lord," or as St. Paul speaks of it in Romans 2:5, the "day of wrath and righteous judgment of God," which is synonymous with the return of Jesus, the divine Son of Man, in glory. The Revelation of John (6:16) describes this judgment as "the wrath of the Lamb." New Testament scholar, R.V.G. Tasker explains the meaning of this phrase: "because Christ Himself has drunk the cup of divine wrath against sinners in His atoning passion, He has been entrusted with the task of being the agent through

---

164. Balthasar, *DWH*, 5.

165. Ridderbos, *Paul*, 257.

whom the divine wrath will be finally expressed."[166] Who, then, can stand when the day of wrath comes? The brief answer to this question must be: those whose sins have been covered in the blood of the Lamb (Rev 7:14). In other words, Tasker adds,

> The Thessalonians, Paul assures them, if they remain faithful, will find on that day complete deliverance from the wrath to come (see 1 Thess.1:10). God who had called them had not appointed them unto wrath but unto the obtaining of final salvation through their Lord Jesus Christ (see 1 Thess. 5:9). Those who at the moment were persecuted but were faithful under persecution would find "rest at the revelation of the Lord Jesus Christ from heaven with the angels of his power" (2 Thess. 1:7). But, on the other hand, to those who knew not God and obeyed not the gospel of the Lord Jesus that day would be a day of wrath, in which they would suffer "the punishment of eternal destruction and exclusion from the presence of the Lord and from the glory of his might" (2 Thess. 1:9).[167]

Is hell—clearly alluded to in the concluding sentence of the last paragraph—ordained by the eternal God as his just judgment on men to a place of final, conscious banishment from his loving presence?[168] A God of wrath—wrath being altogether determined by God's righteousness and hence expresses his holy reaction to our sin—and judgment establishes hell as a place of deserved retribution for sinners. On this view, the wrath[169] and judgment of God are intensely personal and are motivated by the sins of men. The judgment of hell is God's action rather than just a self-imposed condition of man. By contrast, if hell is merely a self-imposed condition, then the judgment of hell is the product of human choice, working itself out as a natural consequence of the choices men make in misusing their freedom, with the result that hell is a self-imposed judgment?[170] It is possible to distinguish two major theological models that have been proposed

166. Tasker, *Biblical Doctrine*, 46.

167. Ibid., 46. On St. Paul's teaching regarding the wrath of God, see also, Ridderbos, *Paul*, 108–14.

168. For the Catholic Church's teaching about hell and judgment, see *CCC*, §§1033–1041. See also, Ott, *Fundamentals of Catholic Dogma*, 479–82. For a careful discussion of the biblical basis of both judgment and hell, see Helm, *Last Things*, 57–82, 108–28.

169. The wrath (*orgē*) of God is "the expected divine reaction to human sin and evil." So says Fitzmyer, *Romans*, 107.

170. For a critique of this notion of hell as a self-imposed judgment, see Stott, *The Cross of Christ*, 104–11. See also, Morris, *The Atonement*, 153–57.

for making sense of the doctrine of hell and the last judgment: first, the natural consequence model and, second, the penalty model. The first model understands eternal damnation, or hell, to be effected by the sinner himself as a natural consequence of the choices he makes in this life. This first model is distinct from the penalty, or retributive punishment, view in which God stands over the sinner as judge such that each person's sin, "if it is not redeemed by repentance and God's forgiveness," results in that person incurring the penalty or punishment of "exclusion from Christ's kingdom and the eternal death of hell"?[171] Which model does Balthasar embrace? Balthasar's reasoning about the last judgment clearly resembles the natural consequence view. But then is his thought on the doctrine of hell and the last judgment consistent with biblical revelation as well as the dogmatic teachings of the Church? Do biblical revelation and the Church teach an understanding of judgment and hell that embraces *both* the penalty model *and* the natural consequence model?

I will argue in what follows that we do not need to choose between these two conceptions of judgment and hell. Each model has some truth that must be preserved in a hybrid model: fundamental to understanding the meaning of the cross of Jesus Christ is not only the sin, responsibility and guilt of man but also the just response of God—punishing and judging evil and sin—to these things as an expression of his holiness and wrath. Space does not permit full discussion here of the view of hell upheld by orthodox Christianity that views hell as the final righteous manifestation of God's wrath. That view of hell is called by some the strong view of hell and it involves several theses:

> (H1) The Anti-Universalism Thesis: Some persons are consigned to hell;

> (H2) The Existence Thesis: Hell is a place where people exist, if they are consigned there;

> (H3) The No Escape Thesis: There is no possibility of leaving hell and nothing one can do, change, or become in order to get out of hell, once one is consigned there; and

> (H4) The Retribution Thesis: The justification for hell is retributive in nature, hell being constituted to mete out punishment to those who earthly lives and behavior warrant it.[172]

---

171. The phrases in this sentence are from the CCC, §1861.

172. Kvanvig, *The Problem of Hell*, 25.

Now, we find a strong trace of the natural consequence or the self-determination model of judgment and hell in Balthasar. He defends the possibility of hell by referring to human freedom. That emphasis on self-determination is given by some thinkers in the nineteenth and twentieth century so as to discharge God from the responsibility of the eternal punishment of hell—which is the point of the penalty or retributive punishment model. Is that Balthasar's view as well? Yes, I think it is. Says Balthasar: "We cannot say that God has 'created hell'; no one but man can be blamed for its existence."[173] "God does not damn anyone. . . . [T]he man who irrevocably refuses love condemns himself."[174] But can we not think of God as creating hell or as damning men? Why can we not think of hell as a creation of God's love as well as of his justice; a showing of his mercy as well as of his holiness? The answer to this first question is indirectly given by Balthasar in his favorable citation of French Jesuit theologian Gustave Martelet who thinks that eternal punishment in hell is incompatible with the notion of a loving and all-merciful God.

> If God is love, as the New Testament teaches us, hell must be impossible. At the least, it represents a supreme anomaly. . . . For hell is the real absurdity. It is no part of a whole in which it might have a meaningful place but is a true outrage that is not able to be affirmed. It is an act of violence that freedom can inflict upon itself but that is not willed by God and never can be willed. . . . But hell, as a refusal of divine love, always exists on one side only: on the side of him who persists in creating it for himself. It is, however, impossible that God himself could cooperate in the slightest way in this aberration, above all, not for the purpose of vindicating the magnificence of his denied love through the triumph of his righteousness, as has, unfortunately, often enough been claimed.[175]

But God's love is inseparably connected with his holiness and his justice, and hence God therefore must manifest his wrath when confronted with sin and evil. Yes, of course the gospel is an expression of the love of God, indeed, the supreme example: "This is how God showed his love among us: He sent his one and only Son into the world that we might live through him. This is love: not that we loved God, but that he loved us and sent his Son as an atoning sacrifice for our sins" (1 John 4:9–10). But God's love is never

173. Balthasar, *DWH*, 37–38.

174. Ibid., 131.

175. Balthasar, *DWH*, 37n10. C.S. Lewis gives us a more biblical perspective in *The Problem of Pain*, 119–20.

expressed at the expense of any other attribute of his character, such as his holiness and wrath, the latter being God's holy reaction to evil and sin. "It would be offensive to speak of God's wrath if we did not also know of His holiness and love. But, just as man must repent his sins to enter into God's grace, so the believer must approach the mystery of God's anger if he will rightly approach God's love. To wish to reduce the mystery of divine wrath to a mythical expression of human experience is to mistake the seriousness of sin and to forget the tragic side of God's love. There is a fundamental incompatibility between holiness and sin."[176] In sum, the wrath of God is the real and effective opposition to sin of the all-holy God.

As I showed earlier, Balthasar raises the concern that separating God's love (mercy) and his holiness, or justice, and wrath, leads, he suggests, to an irreparable cleavage into the heart and character of God. He writes,

> Assuming that men can be divided into those who are just and those who are unjust, can one likewise, then, divide the divine qualities in such a way as to leave mercy on one side and (punitive) justice on the other? And since the two cannot . . . enter into noble competition with each other, it will probably have to be as described in a Spanish work on dogmatics: 'A healing punishment issues from sheer mercy' (this probably refers to Purgatory); 'a vindicative punishment [poena vindicativa] from pure justice, and this corresponds strictly to the offense' (this refers to hell). Thus, where God's mercy (which is obviously taken as finite here) wears thin, it remains for 'pure justice' to exert itself. Now, since precisely this sort of assumption that divine qualities are finite is not acceptable, a dispute arises about whether one who is *under* judgment, as a Christian, can have hope for all men."[177]

Elsewhere Balthasar succinctly formulates his objection: "I mentioned at the beginning the unconscious attempt of a certain dogmatism to draw a line between the qualities of God in such a way that one could speak of pure justice without any reference to mercy. That would imply making his mercy finite, against which—to our astonishment—Augustine was the first to offer energetic resistance. Both verses from Psalms must, after all, be true: 'All the paths of the Lord are mercy and truth' (Ps. 25:10), and: 'The Lord is just in all his ways' (Ps. 145:17)."[178]

176. Léon-Dufour, "Wrath," 683–88, and for this quotation, 683. See also, Berkouwer, De Zonde, II, 132–204 [354–423].

177. Balthasar, DWH, 7.

178. Ibid., 116.

Of course there is an important, and rightful, emphasis on self-determination by Balthasar, which is the core element of the natural consequence model, and which the *Catechism of the Catholic Church* also recognizes: "To die in mortal sin without repenting and accepting God's merciful love means remaining separated from him forever *by our own free choice*."[179] Hell is, the *Catechism's* Glossary adds, the "state of definitive self-exclusion from communion with God and the blessed, reserved for those who refuse by their own free choice to believe and be converted from sin, even to the end of their lives." Elsewhere in the *Catechism* we find: "Mortal sin is a radical possibility of human freedom, as is love itself. It results in the loss of charity and the privation of sanctifying grace, that is, of the state of grace. If it is not redeemed by repentance and God's forgiveness, it causes exclusion from Christ's kingdom and the eternal death of hell, *for our freedom has the power to make choices for ever, with no turning back*."[180] Furthermore, the living tradition of the Church has always taught that the eternity of hell is a consequence of a "willful turning away from God (a mortal sin)" and "persistence in it until the end."[181] "We cannot be united with God unless we freely choose to love him. But we cannot love God if we sin gravely against him, against our neighbor or against ourselves."[182] These passages raise a couple of important questions. First, how does the natural consequence view explain how it is that our freedom has the power to make choices that bring about damnation? Second, are these passages suggesting that God does not damn anyone to hell, that he does not stand over as transcendent judge but rather merely allows the sinner to determine his own condemnation by virtue of the choices he makes.[183]

Let's turn now to consider the first question. One of the theses of the strong view of hell is "The No Escape Thesis: There is no possibility of leaving hell and nothing one can do, change, or become in order to get out of hell, once one is consigned there." In short, hell is inescapable. But how is it that the very freedom of self-determination has the power to make choices whose implications redound on the individual in such a way that his character is firmly entrenched for ever, with no turning back? The brief answer to this question here must be that we are *habit formers*. A corollary of this noteworthy feature of human nature is that man possesses disposition-forming capacities. Habits then are firmly entrenched or ingrained dispositions to

179. CCC, §1033; emphasis added.
180. Ibid., §1861; emphasis added.
181. Ibid., §1037.
182. Ibid., §1033.
183. Flannery, "How to Think about Hell," 477.

desire and think and act in certain ways, and hence as habit formers we become a certain sort of person. Biblical religion teaches us that the way of Christ "leads to life" and a contrary way "leads to destruction."[184] Christians are called to be the sort of persons who make choices that are worthy of the calling that they have received in Christ, and so then there are those who are the sorts of persons who are disposed to make choices that express a firmly ingrained disposition to act as lovers-of-self *without fail*. Both kinds of persons are *maximally set in their ways*. "The result is that those who are in heaven are no longer able to break the hold of the disposition which they have acquired and likewise for those in hell."[185] Does not this view of sinful man who is maximally set in his ways, lover-of-self without fail, make sense of man's own free choice of definitive self-exclusion from the Kingdom of God?[186]

Yes, I think it does. And does it not help us to make sense of St. Paul's teaching in 1 Cor 6:9–11 (see also Gal 5:19–21) that unrighteous people will not inherit God's kingdom? Again, I think it does.

> Or do you not realize that unrighteous people will not inherit God's kingdom? Stop deceiving yourselves. Neither the sexually immoral (the *pornoi*), nor idolaters, nor adulterers, nor soft men (*malakoi*, i.e., effeminate makes who play the sexual role of females), nor men who life with males (*arsenokoitai*) . . . will inherit the kingdom of God. And these things some of you used to be. But you washed yourselves off, you were made holy (or sanctified), you were made righteous (or justified) in the name of the Lord Jesus Christ and in the Spirit of our God.

As I understand St. Paul here in this passage, an unrighteous man is one who has characteristic dispositions, emotions, desires, motives, and attitudes and, being maximally set in his ways, is the source of sinful acts. "Sin creates a proclivity to sin; it engenders vice by repetition of the same acts. This results in perverse inclinations which cloud conscience and corrupt the concrete judgment of good and evil. Thus sin tends to reproduce itself and reinforce itself."[187] St. Paul calls this unrighteous man the man who gratifies the desire of his sinful nature and walks in the flesh. The good news of the Gospel is that God is rich in mercy (cf. Eph 2: 4). Yet, "anyone who deliberately refuses to accept his mercy by repenting, rejects the forgiveness of his

---

184. CCC, §696.

185. Murray, "Heaven and Hell," 298.

186. On this question, see CCC, §§1033, 1861

187. CCC, §1865.

sins and the salvation offered by the Holy Spirit. *Such hardness of heart can lead to final impenitence and eternal loss.*" [188]

By contrast, what sort of person must I be in order to become a lover-of-God without fail, a person who is maximally set in his ways to love God above all things? This sort of man walks by the Spirit, belongs to Christ Jesus and has crucified the flesh with its passions and desires, he lives by the Spirit. "It is no longer I who live, but Christ who lives in me. And the life I now live in the flesh I live by faith in the Son of God, who loved me and gave himself for me" (Gal 2:20). This new man in Christ, who lives by the Spirit, the goal of his life is to become a lover-of-God above all things *without fail.* How then does he become maximally set in his ways? "It is not easy for man, wounded by sin, to maintain moral balance. Christ's gift of salvation offers us the grace necessary to persevere in the pursuit of the virtues."[189] But this new life in Christ must be ordered to the goal of human existence, which is to seek the love of God above all else, to become a lover-of-God without fail. In that case, the moral virtues must be rooted in the theological virtues that relate man's whole life directly to God. "[The theological virtues of faith, hope and charity] dispose Christians to live in a relationship with the Holy Trinity. [They] are the foundation of Christian moral activity; they animate it and give it its special character. They inform and give life to all the moral virtues. They are infused by God into the souls of the faithful to make them capable of acting as his children and of meriting eternal life. They are the pledge of the presence and action of the Holy Spirit in the faculties of the human being."[190] Given the necessary role of grace, especially of the theological virtues of faith, hope and charity, in founding, animating, informing, giving life, and properly ordering the moral life to the goal of human existence, the question arises how this role relates to the natural consequence or self-determination view?

Natural Consequence Model, Grace, and Righteousness

The natural consequence view makes sense of the idea that the judgment of hell is effected by the sinner himself as a natural consequence of the choices he makes in this life such that the judgment of hell is a product of that choice, a self-imposed judgment. But that cannot be the case for attaining salvation. "For by grace you have been saved through faith. And this is not

188. Ibid., §864; emphasis added.
189. Ibid., §1811.
190. *CCC*, §1812.

your own doing; it is the gift of God, not a result of works, so that no one may boast" (Eph 2:8–9). If we are to avoid "works salvation," that is, the view that salvation and eternal life is for those who have, by means of their choices in life, become God-lovers and attain salvation and heaven, then we need to explain the role of grace in becoming the sort of person who is a lover-of-God without fail.

Well, someone may say that there is surely some truth in "works righteousness." Does not Jesus himself make "entering the Kingdom" dependent upon doing the righteousness required in the Sermon on the Mount (Matt 5:20; 7:21; see also, 6:14f.)? Does not St. Matthew's Gospel speak of the rewards (6:1–6, 16–18; 25:34) and punishment (7:23; 13:42, 50; 22:13; 24:51; 25:30, 41) of the Final Judgment, emphasizing that Jesus "will repay every man for what he had done" (16:27; see also, 12:36f.)? In particular, does not Jesus himself make inheritance of the kingdom contingent upon feeding the hungry, clothing the naked, visiting the sick, and welcoming the stranger because, as he says, "as you did it to one of the least of these my brothers, you did it to me" (Matt. 25:41)?

But "works salvation" mischaracterizes the role of "good works" in the life of the faithful Christian, not only in St. Paul's Letters but also in St. Matthew's gospel. St. Matthew's stress on the doing of righteousness in God's kingdom is contingent on the righteousness made possible by Jesus' life, passion, death, and resurrection. We do not have the space here to justify fully this thesis, but a few points must be made to show why this is the correct way to think biblically about the relation between positive righteousness of the law and the Christian life. First, righteousness is a central theme in St. Matthew's gospel.

> To enter the kingdom of heaven, [1] one must have a righteousness that exceeds that of the scribes and Pharisees (5:20), [2] must perform good works so that others may glorify God (5:16), [3] must be perfect as God is perfect (5:48), and [4] must seek God's kingdom and righteousness (6:33). The doing of righteousness looms so large in Matthews's Gospel that [5] without righteousness entrance into the future kingdom is denied, even if one has prophesied and perform miracles in Jesus' name (7:21–23). The kingdom of God belongs only to [6] those who produce its fruits (21:43), and for Matthew [7] the fruit of the kingdom is the doing of righteousness.[191]

191. Holwerda, *Jesus and Israel*, 113–20, and for this quotation, 114. I am indebted to Holwerda for his theological interpretation of Matthew's gospel. Essential to my understanding of Matthew's gospel is John Paul II, *Veritatis Splendor*, §§12–18.

Second, if one's righteousness must exceed the righteousness of the scribes and pharisees, and if that righteousness is not merely increased rigor in obeying the law, what is that greater righteousness?[192] The answer to this question is summarized by what Jesus tells us is needed above everything else, "But seek first the kingdom of God and his [i.e., God's] righteousness" (Matt. 6:33). This righteousness comes as a gift from God; it is the gift of salvation in Christ who describes his mission as fulfilling all righteousness (Matt. 3:15). Indeed, Matthew's gospel is filled with themes of fulfillment in the context of Jesus' person and saving mission. For example, Jesus is the son of Abraham and David (1:1), he will save his people from their sins (Matt 1:21; cf. also 11:25–30; 20:28), and he has come to fulfill the promises of the Old Testament (1:22). "Behold, the virgin shall conceive and bear a son, and they shall call his name, Immanuel (which means, God with us)" (Matt 1:23). In short, the Christology in the early chapters of Matthew's gospel is a Christology of fulfillment. "Do not think that I have come to abolish the Law or the Prophets; I have not come to abolish them but to fulfill them" (Matt 5:17).

> Jesus in his person and mission is the embodiment of the faithful of God. He is Emmanuel, 'God with us' [Matt 1:23]. This gift of God precedes and makes possible Matthew's demand for righteousness. . . . Matthew's stress on the doing of righteousness is surrounded by the righteousness made possible by Jesus' life, death, and resurrection. The themes of fulfillment point to the grace of God that precedes and makes possible the demand for righteousness.[193]

Third, righteousness is then both a gift and a demand. Righteousness is the gift of salvation, a restored covenant relationship with God, but it also makes possible our own acts of righteous obedience.[194] Put differently, Sinai cannot be isolated from Golgotha. "The loving act of God in surrendering Christ to the cross is the presupposition (Rom. 5:8; 8:32–39; Gal. 2:20) and the origin and fountain of our love for God. All human love for God is a response to the love received from God. Love is love of (or from) the Spirit (Rom. 15:30) and fruit of the Spirit (Gal. 5:22). We must love one another, because love is of God. Everyone who loves is born of God (1 Jn. 4:7)."[195] Thus, the love demanded by the divine law is boundless and that love is only possible if the heart has been converted to God. "Let your heart

---

192. Benedict XVI, *Jesus of Nazareth*, 102.

193. Holwerda, *Jesus and Israel*, 116–17.

194. Ibid., 116.

195. Douma, *Responsible Conduct*, 99.

therefore be wholly true to the Lord our God" (1 Kgs 8:61). Indeed, Jesus
says, "You shall love the Lord your God with all your heart and with all your
soul and with all your mind. This is the great and first commandment. And
a second is like it: You shall love your neighbor as yourself. On these two
commandments depend all the Law and the Prophets" (Matt 22:37–40). In
short, Christ emphasizes the root idea of love as the fulfillment of the law
and that love is the unity of the commandments. Ridderbos explains:

> This love originates and is possible only from a whole-hearted
> readiness to serve and from our self-surrender to God. And
> because *this* love both to God and to our neighbor is the great
> content of the law, Jesus' commandments expressing the divine
> will are of such a radical nature. To put it in one statement, we
> can therefore say that *the fulfillment of the law by Jesus consists
> in his setting in the light in a matchless way the character of love
> of the obedience demanded by the law.* In this statement love is
> conceived of as the totalitarian all-embracing self-surrender.[196]

Thus, the righteous obedience that Matthew's Gospel demands has a religious root and discloses the way wherein a man stands before God, where
his heart is, his fundamental commitment, and hence the choices that he
makes in a real sense make him out to be a certain sort of person. "[W]hat
we are to be is what we *become* through individual actions."[197] This insight
presupposes the unity between "person" and "actions." In other words, in
choosing to do something I am not only determining my actions, but also
myself. "In a real sense we are choosing how we will be persons."[198] That is,
as Mark Seifred puts it,

> [O]n the one hand, taken as a whole our works reveal our per-
> sons. At the end of the day we are what we do [if our choices
> not only determine our actions, but also ourselves], not what we
> suppose ourselves to be. . . . On the other hand, the unity that
> exists between 'person' and 'works' means that even those works
> which presently appear to be good cannot be judged apart from
> the person who performs them, that is, apart from the 'heart',
> the motive and intent behind the works.[199]

---

196. Ridderbos, *Coming of the Kingdom*, 317–18.

197. Grisez and Shaw, *Beyond the New Morality*, 49.

198. Ibid., 26.

199. Seifrid, "Justified by Faith," 84–97, and for this quotation, 91.

In sum, "In the final judgment the 'work' of each life shall appear as a whole, either as perseverance in seeking 'glory, honor, and immortality', or as obedience to unrighteousness (Rom. 2:7–8)."[200]

Furthermore, Scripture does not teach that a person is saved by his deeds; the very opposite is the case, indeed. Salvation is by or account of divine grace and is appropriated by faith. "[Christ] saved us, not because of things we have done, but because of his mercy. He saved us through the washing of rebirth and renewal by the Holy Spirit, whom he poured out on us generously through Jesus Christ our Savior, so that having been justified by his grace, we might become heirs having hope of eternal life" (Titus 1:9); or "It is by grace you have been saved through faith, and this not from yourselves, it is the gift of God, not as a result of works, so that no one can boast" (Eph 2:8–9; see also, Rom 4:16). St. Paul follows this ringing affirmation of the necessity of grace by adding, "For we are God's workmanship, created in Christ Jesus *to do good works*, which God prepared in advance for us to do" (Eph 2:10; italics added). Since a man has not been saved *according to works*, but *for works*, the latter must be understood as the "fruits" of grace, that is, obedience to God. And, as Paul Helm rightly notes, "in *this* sense he is justified by works; his deeds of obedience *prove* his justification, but they do not themselves justify."[201]

Thus, man needs grace because "having been wounded in his nature by original sin, [he] is subject to error and inclined to evil in exercising his freedom."[202] One of the implications of that wound is that we can become sinners, self-absorbed and self-centered lovers of self maximally set in our ways, rather than lovers of God, cultivating God-loving habits expressive of a God-loving character. So grace is necessary in order for us to be transformed into God-lovers. The need for grace brings us back to the natural consequence or self-determination view. In order to cultivate God-loving habits we need grace to take root in our life and interiorly dispose us to live in a relationship with the Holy Trinity; the gift of God's grace in Christ grants us the ability to choose repentance and seek reconciliation with

200. Ibid.

201. Helm, *The Last Things*, 80. I don't have the space here to address the question of the sense in which good works are also supernaturally meritorious of God's grace and not merely the fruits of God's grace. But see *CCC*, §§ 2006–211. See also Morris, *The Gospel according to Matthew*, 634, Matt 25:31–46 "deals with the evidence on which people will be judged, not the cause of salvation or damnation. . . . We must bear in mind that it is common to the whole scriptural picture that we are saved by grace and judged by works (for this latter point cf. 16:27; Rom. 2:6; 2 Cor. 5:10, etc.). The works we do are the evidence either of the grace of God at work in us or of our rejection of that grace."

202. *CCC*, §1714; see also, §§403–405.

God. As Murray says, "In turn, it is only by God then granting the grace of reconciliation that the person is given the ability to be free of the power of sin and so to begin the process of becoming a lover of God, a process we call sanctification." In sum, he adds, "divine grace is a *necessary condition* for being able to seek freely reconciliation with God and for being set free from the bondage to sin that prevents us from cultivating God-loving characters (i.e., from becoming sanctified)."[203]

Can God Block the Natural Consequences of my Choices?

There is one more question to question to consider here in connection with the natural consequence or self-determination model of judgment and hell. Those who are maximally set in their ways as self-lovers will therefore be separated from God for eternity, forever unable to enjoy God's presence. Now, some have raised the question as to why cannot God block the natural consequences of my choices? In other words, why cannot he reverse the natural consequences of a life of self-love and sin rather than being a lover-of-him? I raise this question in the context of Balthasar claim: "While infinite freedom will respect the decisions of finite freedom, it will not allow itself to be compelled, or restricted in its own freedom, by the latter."[204] Can God block the natural consequences of a man's choices? It would seem not, according to Balthasar:

> God never forces his love . . . . Jesus can hardly push the sinner aside to make room for his own place. He cannot appropriate for himself the sinner's freedom to do with it what the sinner did not himself want to do. Even more pointedly: he can "redeem" (the word "redemption" refers primarily to ransom paid to release someone from prison, slavery, or debt), but never without my permission: I must continually accept this deed, letting it be true for me. Free men are not pieces of luggage, after all, that can be "redeemed" from the lost and found.[205]

Still, Balthasar suggests that God might "appropriate for himself the sinner's freedom to do with it what the sinner did not himself want to do" since man's word is not the final word, but that word is mercy. Consider here Balthasar's interpretation of Rom 5:12-21: "The whole passage gradually

203. Murray, "Heaven and Hell," 299.
204. Balthasar *Theo-Drama*, 5:295.
205. Balthasar, *Epilogue*, 118-19.

intensifies into a true hymn of triumph in which, through a continual 'much more', the surpassed state of balance that distinguished the previous, two-sided judgment [that comes from being rooted in either Adam or Christ] rises to a perduring '[grace abounding] all the more', 'above and beyond everything.'"[206] "If one casts a glance over to John['s Gospel] from here," adds Balthasar, "what dominates for him is the ring of the universal words: 'And I, when I am lifted up from the earth, will draw all men to myself' (12:32).'"[207] What is Balthasar asking God to do here, given this hymn of triumph—the triumph of grace? Is Balthasar suggesting that this drawing is, in the words of Germain Grisez, "not the powerful appeal of incarnate divine love that, nevertheless, can be refused, but an irresistible attraction."[208] Berkouwer explains the theological argument here that draws a link between universalism[209] and the irresistible love of God. He writes:

> It is at this point that universalism makes its appeal to the irresistible love of God, which is sufficient to overcome all obstacles in the eschaton. The question is, how can this divine love—for God is Love—ever run aground on human apostasy or intransigence? If the omnipotent God is Love, and if this love is revealed in grace against human resistance, are not this love and its last word *irresistible grace*? Saying this is not meant to deny the reality of sin and guilt, but to base the prospect for the future on divine love and divine omnipotence. Is there not good reason to believe that in the final revelation of all things it will be different from what has been traditionally taught about hell and damnation? Why minimize God's mercy? Is it not limitless and inexhaustible (cf. Exod 34:6; Ps 86:13)?[210]

206. Balthasar, *DWH*, 26–27.

207. Ibid., *DWH*, 27.

208. Grisez, "Question 6," 25.

209. Importantly, universalism was condemned as a heresy by the Council of Constantinople (the fifth ecumenical council, 553): "Whoever says or believes, the punishment of evil spirits or godless men is temporal and will cease after a certain period of time after which a complete restoration (*apocatastasis*) of the evil spirits and of godless men will take place, let him be anathema."

210. Berkouwer, *De Wederkomst van Christus*, II, 195–196 [389]. Berkouwer sketches the argument of universalism in his book on Barth, *De Triomf Der Genade in De Theologie van Karl Barth*, 362 [363]: "The universalistic thesis *must* be posited. There is a *must* in God's love: 'its will to lordship is inexhaustible and ultimately unendurable: the sinner must yield' [J. A. T. Robinson]. It is a question of *omnipotent* love. J. A. T. Robinson says this has nothing to do with speculation for it is a matter of 'the very necessity of God's nature'. It is not accidental that the words 'must' and 'necessity' appear in the exposition of the universalistic thesis. They belong there and constitute its foundation. God *cannot* endure possibility, 'for *that* would be the final mockery of

Alyssa Lyra Pitstick argues that this too is the basic argument of Balthasar
running through *Dare we Hope*. "Not to have hope for the salvation of all
(where *all* is taken collectively, rather than partitively) is to doubt God's
omnipotence, which is to doubt His love, as well: God's love in Christ 'is
stronger than any resistance that it encounters and. . . hope for all men is
therefore permitted."[211] We face here a dilemma. Either Love is omnipotent, in which case it *must* conquer. But then this victory of love eliminates
the very thing making God's victory a victory of *love*, namely, freedom. Or
freedom is absolutely inviolable, in which case there can be no *necessity* in
God's triumphant love in Christ.[212] Thus, as J.A.T. Robinson summarizes the
conclusion of this dilemma, "the ideas of omnipotence and love are themselves mutually contradictory. God cannot be omnipotent love."[213]

Balthasar suggests something like this argument in claiming that you
cannot adhere to the effective truth of Christ's statement that he will draw
all men to himself if you make distinctions in God's will, such as the atonement's objective and objective dimensions, or the antecedent and consequent will of God. Is not the second set of statements the triumph of grace,
he says, expressing "God's redemptive work for the sinful world . . . as a
complete triumph over all things contrary to God? Here one cannot get
by without making distinctions that, while retaining the notion of God's
benevolent will, nevertheless allow it to be frustrated by man's wickedness"
(*DWH*, 183–184; cf. also 21, 26, 39–40, 113). How is it that Jesus comes to
save all men, asks Balthasar, "if there are some who consciously draw back
from this love and refuse it ([Jn.] 3:19; 9:40–41; 12:48)?" "The question,
to which no final answer is given or can be given," adds Balthasar, "is this:
Will he who refuses it now refuse it to the last?"[214] He concludes: "Here we

His nature—and He will not."

211. Pitstick, *Light in Darkness*, 435–36n161. See also, 264: "The question arises
whether the sinner's rejection of the truth about himself and God's relation to him as
Creator, Redeemer, and Sanctifier can be maintained eternally. Although man receives
a real freedom to make a choice against God that seems definitive for him, *God* need
not take this choice as definitive. Otherwise, His absolute freedom (which is identical
to His omnipotence) would be compromised."

212. "Of course, God could always bludgeon one into submission, but presence
in heaven requires something more delicate, for the goal is a person governed by a
love of God and delight in his beauty" (Kvanvig, *The Problem of Hell*, 158). Indeed, the
problem of a forced salvation is, of course, what a contingent or necessary universalism
must face.

213. Robinson, "Universalism—Is it Heretical?" 139–55, and for this quotation,
141. For a critique of this dilemma, see Berkouwer, *De Wederkomst van Christus*, II,
222–23; [412–13].

214. Balthasar, *DWH*, 178.

come to deep waters, in which every human mind begins to flounder. Can human defiance really resist to the end the representative assumption of its sins by the incarnate God?"[215] Balthasar is struggling here with the tension between God's sovereign will to save all and man's freedom to accept or reject that salvation, and all that either choice entails. Man's freedom cannot be overpowered by God. Or does Balthasar think that it can? In fact, he suggests that human freedom can be overridden. "God gives man the capacity to make a (negative) choice against God that seems *for man* to be definitive, but which need not be taken *by God* as definitive."[216]

How far, then, can grace advance when man's assent has to be freely given? Says Balthasar, "Without my consent, given that I am a free person, nothing can just have its way with me. But how, then, are we to understand the grace that is effected through the representative work of Christ?" He replies,

> Tentatively, we can say this: that the Holy Spirit, the Spirit of absolute freedom, allows us to see, within our free spirit, what our *own* true freedom would be, that is, by confronting us with ourself, without our own highest possibility. We *would* not *be able* just to say "Yes" to ourselves (that is effected for us vicariously); also, the meaningfulness of such a "Yes" and the *desire for it* are set before us, indeed, inspired in us. Do you really want to exist forevermore in contradiction with yourself? Grace can advance as far as that. And if one wishes to keep to the distinctions noted above [between "sufficient grace" and "efficacious grace"], then one would have to say: grace is "efficacious" when it presents my freedom with an image of itself so evident that it cannot do other than *freely* seize itself, while grace would be merely "*sufficient*" if this image did not really induce my freedom to affirm itself but left it preferring to persist in self-contradiction. To push on any farther into these deep waters is not permitted us. We have to stop at this observation: it would be in God's power to allow the grace that flows into the world from the self-sacrifice of his Son (2 Cor. 5:19) to grow powerful enough to become his "efficacious" grace for all sinners. But precisely this is something that we can only *hope for*.[217]

Is Balthasar suggesting in the concluding sentences of this passage a universalist interpretation of the triumphant love of God in Christ? If so,

215. Ibid., 208.

216. Balthasar, *Explorations in Theology*, 4:421, as cited in Geoffrey Wainwright, "Eschatology," 125.

217. Balthasar, *DWH*, 27.

then this would mean that the power of that love directly affects us while we remain passive. Consequently, then, the significance of our own freedom of choice is negated. Of course this conclusion is only an implication that follows from the universalist direction of Balthasar's thought rather than something he explicitly asserts.

Indeed, Balthasar refuses to say one way or the other whether God can really "lose the game of creation through the creature's free choice to be lost." "This is a profoundly mysterious possibility," he adds, "for which we can find a certain human analogy, but which in the end must be consigned with relief to the realm of faith."[218] But can it be so consigned if the formal teaching of the Church, i.e., that impenitent sinners end in hell, faithfully reflects scriptural data? That Balthasar thinks it can is reflected in his rejection of those he calls "infernalist."[219] They are those who claim to know that not all will be saved. Alternatively, he reasons from the position of the *reverent agnostic* who does not know whether all men will be saved or have knowledge that certain individuals will be damned, concluding therefore that it is "permissible to hope (on the basis of the first series of statements from Scripture) that the light of divine love will ultimately be able to penetrate every human darkness and refusal."[220] Yes, Balthasar also maintains the belief that we, as individuals, must take account of, and be confronted relentlessly with, the most serious possibility of forfeiting our salvation, of being damned. But how real can this possibility be when Balthasar thinks there are reasons for the unreality of hell?

Yes, again, Balthasar sees correctly that "man's believing response . . . is always tied into this universality of the divine will for salvation (John 3:16; 5:24; 6:40; 17:6)."[221] He says, "God even as redeemer respects the freedom which God has bestowed upon his creature and with which it is capable of resisting his love. This respecting means that God does not overrule, pressure, or coerce with the omnipotence of his absolute freedom the precarious freedom of the creature. In doing so he would contradict himself."[222] Of course here Balthasar is right about the importance of man's believing response to the Gospel. C.S. Lewis, too, grapples with the tension between God's universal salvific will and a freedom that cannot be overpowered, and hence he speaks for us all when he says, "I would pay any price to be able to

218. Balthasar and Ratzinger, *Two Say Why*, 53, as cited in Geoffrey Wainwright, "Eschatology," 125.

219. Balthasar, *DWH*, 178.

220. Ibid.

221. Ibid., 40–41.

222. Balthasar, *Von Balthasar Reader*, 422.

say truthfully: 'All will be saved.'" The crux here is *truthfully*, and Balthasar understands that point. Lewis continues: "But my reason retorts, 'Without their will, or with it?' 'Without their will', I at once perceive a contradiction; how can the supreme voluntary act of self-surrender be involuntary? If I say, 'With their will', my reason replies, 'How if they *will not* give in?'"[223]

Still, Balthasar says, it is "infinitely improbable" (citing with approval the phrase of Edith Stein) that anyone is damned, given the complete triumph of grace over all things contrary to God's love manifested in his redemptive work in Christ.[224] But this conclusion does not necessarily follow from the triumphant love of God in Christ. For wherever the New Testament speaks of the love of God in Jesus Christ, it also mentions the judgment.

Furthermore, an individual might intellectually recognize how bad off he is in his state of self-contradiction and even desire to change, but still never seek reconciliation with God. Balthasar seems to suggest that an individual in such a state of separation from God will probably repent rather than persist in his ruined condition. But if that individual is maximally disposed to be a self-lover rather than a lover of God, he may recognize that he would be better off if he loved God, but still not *desire* to change. Consider the case of an unwilling drug addict. "The addict recognizes his ruined condition, and wishes that he no longer wanted to take drugs. But nonetheless, he *does* want to take them and thus continues to do so."[225] I suggest that the only way God's grace could be efficacious for all sinners, in the way that Balthasar is suggesting, is to save them *against their will*. But that means that if Christ is to draw all men to himself, he must reverse the natural consequences of a life of self-love. One author puts the point this way:

> If I sink deeply into moral corruption, an omnipotent being may be unable, consistent with my freedom, simply to reconstitute me with a good character, but he surely can, as often as he likes, release me from my *bondage* to a bad character. . . . [A good physician would surely give a drug addict a remedy that would break the power of the addiction if he had one. To do so would be to restore the addict to freedom.] And the same would be true of a God who releases terribly corrupt persons from their bondage to unhealthy desires or from the psychological impossibility of doing what is right; whether such bondage is their own fault or not, a God who releases them from it and restores them

223. Lewis, *The Problem of Pain*, 107.

224. Balthasar, *DWH*, 183; cf. 40.

225. I am following Michael Murray closely at this point in the argument he presents in "Heaven and Hell," 300.

to freedom, but neither causes them to act rightly nor prevents
them from continuing to act wrongly, would in no way violate
their moral freedom.[226]

Let me be clear that nowhere does Balthasar actually offer such a line
of reasoning. Yet, necessary or contingent universalists—unlike Balthasar
who embraces universal salvation as a theological possibility, as a pious
hope—have made such an argument. They have argued that God is un-
loving if he does not block those consequences. But is that true? Is it not
rather the case that if God were to block them he would make our freedom
meaningless? Making our freedom meaningless does not mean that I can no
longer make a choice among alternatives. Rather, it means that my choices
no longer have real consequences in the world, for example, with respect
to myself, my habit-formed character as virtuous or vicious, as a self-lover
or God-lover, a commitment of obedience to the "way of life" or the "way
of death" (Dt. 30:19). "If I choose to become a self-lover, but God blocks
my choices from having their effect, he has prevented my freedom from
being what it was supposed to be, that is, a means by which I can engage
in meaningful soul-making. I can engage in soul-making, but God won't
let me become the person I choose to become. I can only become the sort
of person he wants me to become. But then, of course, it looks like I don't
have freedom to engage in soul-making after all."[227] But then this is to save
a person against his will, because God would not allow his choices to have
their natural consequences, i.e., being a self-lover, and thus separated from
God for eternity in hell.

Points of Catholic Orientation

How do we reconcile God's universal salvific will with the mystery of predestination, election and reprobation? I examined Balthasar's argument
against attempts to reconcile these matters, and I found that his outright
dismissal of predestination—election *and* reprobation is based on his polemic against the idea that divine judgment is God's final word to us to the
unrepentant sinner. I argued that Balthasar misses out on seeing the inextricable connection between judgment and the proclamation of salvation.
Balthasar also rejects universalism—either contingent or necessary—and
opts for a hopeful universalism. But all of Balthasar's arguments for hopeful
universalism, and against theological attempts to explain the discrepancy

226. Talbot, "Providence, Freedom, and Human Dignity," 232, as cited in Murray,
"Heaven and Hell," 309–10.

227. Murray, "Heaven and Hell," 311.

between God's universal salvific will and its efficacy by employing distinctions between God's antecedent and consequent will, between an objective redemption and its subjective acceptance, and between the sufficiency and efficacy of Christ's atoning work, are such that he leaves us asking whether his thought actually *is* a version of *necessary* universalism. My argument is that his rejection of these concepts is not within the bounds of Confessional Catholicism. Furthermore, how do we reconcile the omnipotence and sovereignty of God's grace with human freedom in the Church's understanding of salvation? Here, too, Balthasar's arguments fall short of showing how grace and freedom can be reconciled. There is one more question to question to consider here in connection with the natural consequence or self-determination model of judgment and hell. Those who are maximally set in their ways as self-lovers will therefore be separated from God for eternity, forever unable to enjoy God's presence. Now, some have raised the question as to why cannot God block the natural consequences of my choices? In other words, why cannot he reverse the natural consequences of a life of self-love and sin rather than being a lover-of-him? I raise this question in the context of Balthasar claim: "While infinite freedom will respect the decisions of finite freedom, it will not allow itself to be compelled, or restricted in its own freedom, by the latter."[228] Can God block the natural consequences of a man's choices? It would seem not, according to Balthasar: And yet, because mercy has the last word for Balthasar, he suggests that God might "appropriate for himself the sinner's freedom to do with it what the sinner did not himself want to do." This is so, according to Balthasar, since man's word is not the final word, but that word is mercy. Indeed, Balthasar says, it is "infinitely improbable" (citing with approval the phrase of Edith Stein) that anyone is damned, given the complete triumph of grace over all things contrary to God's love manifested in his redemptive work in Christ. This conclusion is not within the bounds of Confessional Catholicism.

228. Balthasar *Theo-Drama*, 5:295.

CHAPTER 7

A Catholic Synthesis

Introduction

THROUGHOUT CHAPTERS 2-6, I have engaged not only in an exposition but also a critical assessment, both immanently and from a Catholic perspective, of the views of the theologians discussed in those chapters. In this concluding chapter, I don't repeat myself but rather I sketch an outline of a Catholic synthesis regarding the issues that have held my attention throughout this book in my analysis of Calvin, Scheeben, Barth, Bavinck, Berkouwer, and Balthasar. What I have learned from these theologians will be evident in my Catholic synthesis. For the sake of conciseness, the synthesis I present in this chapter will focus on the points of Catholic orientation I described in chapter I as well as at the conclusion of chapters 2-6, and for which I have argued in this book. These points express boundaries within which my reflections on divine election must take place—certainly for a theologian belonging to the tradition of confessional Catholicism. They are:

1. In his infinite, all-embracing love in Christ, God truly and sincerely desires the salvation of all men.[1] Therefore, election is in Christ Jesus who is not only the ground, that is, the cause and foundation of election (*fundamentum electionis*), but also the Mediator of election (*fundamentum salutis electorum*).

2. Confessional Catholicism rejects universalism: all men are not saved. The atoning work of Christ is sufficient for the salvation of all men, but it is efficacious only for the many. "He [Christ] became the source of eternal salvation for all who obey him" (Heb 5: 9). In its Decree on Justification Trent states: "even though 'Christ died for all' [2 Cor

---

1. On God's universal salvific will in Catherine of Siena (1347–1380) and Francis de Sales (1567–1622), see Levering, *Predestination*, 90–95, 117–27, respectively. For his own theology of predestination in which he integrates the essential asymmetry of election and reprobation, see 176–201.

274

5:15], still not all do receive the benefit of His death, but those only to whom the merit of His passion is imparted."[2]

3. Divine election is about the truth that it is God who takes the free and gracious initiative in salvation, calling men to himself, offering prevenient grace,[3] a preparatory grace relieving man's spiritual inability to respond to God, and enabling him to be open to the justifying and sanctifying grace of God.

4. Although confessional Catholicism affirms the priority or primacy of God's grace, it also affirms man's free response to that gracious initiative without implying that saving grace depends on human merit. "To God, all moments of time are present in their immediacy. When therefore he establishes his eternal plan of 'predestination', he includes in it each person's free response to his grace."[4] A Molinist *cum* Congruist account of the reconciliation of predestination and freedom is within the boundaries of confessional Catholicism's teaching on grace and freedom. This account overcomes the equal ultimacy of reprobation and election on the one hand, in short double predestination, and Pelagianism on the other.

Election in Jesus Christ

Jesus Christ, the Second Person of the Trinity, is the ground of election, that is, its cause and foundation, as well as the Mediator of election, the Incarnate God, in and through whom man may be reconciled to Christ. Crisp is right: "For the one electing (in the person of the Son) and the one elected as Mediator [of the] covenant [of redemption] (in the person of the God-Man) is one and the same."[5] In what sense, then, is Christ the cause and foundation of election? The cause of election has its foundation in the love of God. Confessional Catholicism rejects the heresy of predestinarianism. On this view, predestination is parallel, and hence double in the strict sense, because both election and reprobation are symmetrical with respect to the mode of divine causality. Berkouwer is right that the Catholic and Reformed tradition maintain the "essential *asymmetry*"[6] between salvation

---

2. Denzinger, §1523.

3. See Shelton, *Prevenient Grace*.

4. *CCC*, §600.

5. Crisp, "The Election of Jesus Christ," 51.

6. Berkouwer remarks that "this term comes from [Gérard]. Philips, [the Belgian Catholic ecclesiologist, and key drafter of Vatican II's *Lumen Gentium*] who sees

and reprobation. Significantly, however, is also the point that the issue about election is not one of a "mere symmetry," says Berkouwer, "but [rather] that God has loved the world (John 3:16)." In other words, Berkouwer is right that the deepest reason for rejecting parallelism, including the parallelism of positive predestination and negative reprobation (i.e., preterition), is that God did not send the Son to condemn the world but rather that the world should be saved through him (John 3:17). Berkouwer is also right that "This rejection [of parallelism] does not imply the triumph of a simple sort of universalism."[7] We shall need to distinguish here, in order to avoid universalism, the antecedent and consequent will of God.

Regarding God's antecedent will, Scheeben emphasized, as we saw, the decisive significance of Christ in God's free, gratuitous love, linking Jesus Christ, the Redeemer of the world, and the content of the gospel, with predestination. Thus this decree of predestination is in Christ, and it is an ultimate expression of God's love (1 Thess 1:4; Col 3:12; Eph 2:4–5; John 13:1; Jer 31:2–3; Ps 103:17). "Christ is the center, the foundation, the ideal, and the end of the whole supernatural world order and of the decree by which it is governed and brought to realization. From Him this decree derives its sublimity, its effectiveness, and its universality. All men are predestined in the predestination of Christ; for, in assuming His own body, Christ has taken the whole race as His body."[8] Are then all men actually saved in Christ?

No, Scheeben distinguishes between universal and particular predestination, or, as he also calls it, "virtual predestination . . . and effective predestination," or, alternatively, as he also puts it, the antecedent and consequent will of God. Scheeben says, "The divine will to save, according to the unanimous teaching of all Catholic theologians, is twofold: on the one hand it is universal, and refers to all men, even those who, as a matter of fact, fail to achieve salvation; on the other hand, it is particular, and refers to those actually reach their foreordained end."[9] Crisp describes the view of those whose position is called hypothetical universalism, which I contend is consistent with Scheeben's view: the former will is a "conditional and unfulfilled decree to elect, the scope of which is universal (encompassing all humanity)"; the latter is unconditional and effectual, as he adds, "the scope of which is limited to some number of humanity less than the total

---

in it a mark of Roman Catholic theology" (*De Verkiezing Gods*, 213n34 [182n16]). Berkouwer holds that this "essential asymmetry" is one of Reformed theology's "most important characteristics" (213 [182]).

7. Berkouwer, *De Verkiezing Gods*, 238 [201–2].

8. Scheeben, *MC*, 730.

9. Ibid., 702.

number."[10] Furthermore, the meritorious work of Christ's atonement is not the cause of election if that means that Christ's work moved the Father to love and forgiveness. According to Trent, "The meritorious cause is the most beloved only begotten Son of God, our Lord Jesus Christ, who, 'while we were enemies' [Rom 5:10], 'out of the great love with which he loved us' [Eph 2:4], merited for us justification by his most holy Passion on the wood of the Cross [can. 10] and made satisfaction for us to God the Father."[11] But God does not elect *because* of this meritorious work. Rather, Scripture teaches that God in Christ was reconciling the world unto himself (2 Cor 5:19), and that it is precisely the sending of Christ by the Father, which is the revelation of God's love (1 John 4:9). Still, even if the work of Christ is not the motivating cause of election, it is part of the cause of election. Therefore, the atoning work of Christ, the Incarnate God, has an intimate connection to God's decree to elect insofar as that work is the instrumental cause of election. That is, says Berkouwer—"there is no discrepancy . . . between 'in Christ' and 'through Christ'. The 'instrumental' and the 'comprehensive' are one in Christ."[12] In other words,

> The power and evidence of [St.] Paul's testimony have safe-guarded the Church and theology at decisive moments against a devaluation of God's election to such a fixedness of decree, leading to an abstract sovereignty, which is a sovereign election that is only later realized in the work of Christ. Scripture does say "through Christ" with respect to salvation, and there is no need at all to balk at the word "instrumental"—as when Paul writes that we are reconciled with God through (*dia*) the death of His Son (Rom 5:10)—provided that the word "instrumental" is stripped of all impersonal connotations, and that we think of God's acts as being in Christ who is the author of our salvation (Heb 2:10).[13]

In sum, Christ is not merely the means of election, that is, the instrumental cause through whose saving work the election of fallen man obtains; he is also the cause and foundation of election, its efficient cause, namely the electing love and grace of God.

---

10. Crisp, "The Election of Jesus Christ," 45.

11. Denzinger, §1529.

12. Berkouwer, *De Verkiezing Gods*, 172 [149].

13. Ibid., 171–72. [149].

The Atoning Work of Jesus Christ

A corollary to the distinction between the antecedent and consequent will of God is the distinction between the sufficiency and efficacy of Christ's atoning work. These distinctions suggestion that the redemptive wok of Christ is sufficient for the sins of all men, and hence it is potentially universal in scope; but it is not sufficient and efficient for all men's sin; otherwise it would be actually universal in extent. Of course, in this connection, I showed how the atonement is universal in scope such that it possesses the intrinsic sufficiency in atoning for all men because Christ died for all men. But also I showed that the divine intention, which is the purpose for which God intends the atonement, is that God wills to save all men, and hence "Christ's work is extrinsically sufficient for the sin of all fallen humans."[14] There is another concept here that is crucial for explaining the resistance against universalism (all men are saved), namely, the notion of efficiency or efficacy, which, as Crisp says, "has to do with the actual number of those to whom Christ's work is applied."[15] In sum, Christ's atoning work is *sufficient* for the salvation of all men, albeit not *efficient* for their salvation, but only for God's elect. The atoning work of Christ is sufficient for the salvation of all men, but it is efficacious only for the many.

The *Catechism* states, "Jesus, the Son of God, freely suffered death for us in complete and true submission to the will of God, his Father. By his death he has conquered death, and so opened the possibility of salvation to all men."[16] And again, "By his glorious Cross Christ has won salvation for all men. He redeemed them from the sin that held them in bondage."[17] The question that arises here was raised by Louis Berkhof, "Did the Father in sending Christ, and did Christ in coming into the world, to make atonement for sin, *do this with the design or for the purpose of saving only the elect or all men*?"[18] The answer of confessional Catholicism is, briefly, this: The work of Christ accomplishes the actual reality of redemption for all men, but it is only potentially efficacious for those who have faith and are able to share in the saving benefits of that work. "Believing in Jesus Christ and in the One who sent him for our salvation is necessary for obtaining that salvation [cf. Mk 16: 16; Jn 3:36; 6: 40]."[19]

14. Crisp, *Deviant Calvinism*, 218.

15. Ibid., 219.

16. CCC, §1019.

17. Ibid., §1741.

18. Berkhof, *Systematic Theology*, 394.

19. CCC, §161.

This way of expressing itself is consistent with what Crisp calls "conditional ordained sufficiency," and it is consistent with Berkouwer's claim that "apart from faith man cannot discover [Christ's atoning acts] or know of the reality of reconciliation for all, to which he must respond with a decision."[20] Again, "The Church, following the apostles, teaches that Christ died for all men without exception: 'There is not, never has been, and never will be a single human being, for whom Christ did not suffer'; [even if not all are redeemed by the mystery of his Passion]." In addition, "The omnipotent God wishes 'all men' without exception 'to be saved' [1 Tim 2:4], even if not all are saved. That some, however, are saved is the gift of the one who saves; that some, however, perish is the fault of those who perish."[21] The work of Christ is a "redemptive sacrifice *for all*."[22] Christ's atoning work manifests a "mystery of universal redemption, that is, as the ransom that would free men from the slavery of sin."[23] In sum, as John Paul II says, "[T]he merit of Christ's sacrifice is universal, that is to say, it is [valid][24] for each and every one. This is because it is based on a universal representativeness, made evident by . . . Christ's substitution for all humanity in his sacrifice. . . . All this was included in God's salvific plan and in Christ's messianic vocation." He adds,

> Jesus' teaching on faith as a condition of his saving action is summed up and confirmed in his nighttime conversation with Nicodemus. . . . Therefore faith in Christ is a constitutive condition of salvation, of eternal life. It is faith in the only-begotten Son—one in being with the Father—in whom the Father's love is manifested. "For God did not send his Son into the world to condemn the world, but that the world might be saved through him" (Jn 3:17). The judgment is implicit in the choice of accepting or rejecting faith in Christ. "Whoever believes in him will not be condemned, but whoever does not believe has already

20. Berkouwer, *De Verkiezing Gods*, 279 [233].

21. *CCC*, §605. The quote within the quote is from Denzinger, §623. See also, *CCC*, §982.

22. Ibid., §616.

23. Ibid., §601.

24. The English translation of John Paul II's General Audience, October 26, 1988, "The Redemptive Value of Christ's Sacrifice," in his, *A Catechesis on the Creed, Volume II, Jesus, Son and Savior* , 444–49, mistranslates the original Spanish ("valedero") and Italian ("valevole") of the word "valid" as "efficacious." On that translation, Christ's atoning work would be not only sufficient for the sins of all men but also efficacious. But that interpretation would make John Paul II a universalist, and he isn't. For the Spanish, see http://www.fjp2.com/us/john-paul-ii/online-library/audiences/4480-general-audience-october-26-1988; for the Italian, see http://w2.vatican.va/content/john-paul-ii/es/audiences/1988/documents/hf_jp-ii_aud_19881026.html.

been condemned, because he has not believed in the name of the only Son of God" (Jn 3:18). . . . Salvation—and therefore eternal life—is linked to Jesus Christ's messianic mission from which derives the whole "logic" and "economy" of the Christian faith. John himself proclaimed it from the prologue of his Gospel: To those who did accept him, [the Word] gave the power to become children of God, to those who believe in his name" (Jn 1:12).[25]

Christ's atoning work is, then, universally sufficient for the world, to save all men, but it is effectually redemptive only for those who have faith, which is a gift of God's grace. In sum: "It is a dogmatic teaching of the Church that Christ died on the Cross for all men and women (cf. John 11:52; 2 Corinthians 5:14–15; Titus 2:11; 1 John 2:2). The expression for many, while remaining open to the inclusion of each human person, is reflective also of the fact that this salvation is not brought about in some mechanistic way, without one's own willing or participation; rather, the believer is invited to accept in faith the gift that is being offered and to receive the supernatural life that is given to those who participate in this mystery, living it out in their lives as well so as to be numbered among the many to whom the text refers."[26]

Prevenient, Justifying, and Sanctifying Grace

Confessional Catholicism definitively rejects Pelagianism and semi-Pelagianism. These are the heretical claims of forms of synergism holding that we cause our own salvation, or that we initiate our own salvation, respectively. Salvation is the work of God's grace, from beginning to end; Christ is the full and sufficient cause of our salvation. Semi-pelagianism, in particular, affirms that the *initium fidei*, the beginning of faith, is in the human will, and not in God's grace, and consequently isolates the will from the *gratia praeveniens* (prevenient grace).[27] But as the *Catechism* says, "The *preparation of man* for the reception of grace is already a work of grace. This latter is needed to arouse and sustain our collaboration in justification through faith, and in sanctification through charity."[28] Therefore, salvation is a gift of God's grace through Jesus Christ and the Holy Spirit. Man's will is not the efficient cause of salvation. "The efficient cause is the merciful God

25. John Paul II, *A Catechesis on the Creed*, 447, 242–243, respectively.

26. Six Questions on the Translation of the *Pro Multis*: http://www.usccb.org/prayer-and-worship/the-mass/roman-missal/six-questions-on-the-translation-of-pro-multis.cfm.

27. Denzinger, §§1525, 1528. *CCC*, §§1987–2003.

28. *CCC*, §2001.

who gratuitously washes and sanctifies [cf. 1 Cor 6:11], sealing and anointing [cf. 2 Cor 1:21f.] 'with the promised Holy Spirit, who is the guarantee of our inheritance' [Eph 1:13f.]."[29] But we are not Calvinists: man is not purely passive, since prevenient grace enables man freely to love and obey God and to cooperate with him and hence to participate in God's justifying and sanctifying grace of salvation. Indeed, Trent states, "The council . . . declares that . . . the beginning of justification must be attributed to God's prevenient grace through Jesus Christ [can. 3], that is, to his call addressed to them without any previous merits of theirs."[30] "Calling" is one aspect of prevenient grace. There are others, such as "convicting," "illuminating," and "enabling."[31] These aspects, too, Trent identifies:

> Thus, those who through their sins were turned away from God, awakened and assisted by his grace are disposed to turn to their own justification by freely assenting to and cooperating with that grace [cann. 4 and 5]. In this way, God touches the heart of man with the illumination of the Holy Spirit, but man himself is not entirely inactive while receiving that inspiration, since he can reject it; and yet, without God's grace, he cannot by his own free will move toward justice in God's sights [can. 3]. Hence, when it is said in Sacred Scripture: "Return to me and I will return to you" [Zech 1:3], we are reminded of our freedom; but when we reply: "Restore us to yourself, O Lord, that we may be restored [Lam 5:21], we acknowledge that God's [prevenient] grace precedes us.[32]

Now, this Catholic form of synergism in which man's free response participates in God's gift of salvation is neither pelagian nor semi-pelagian, which are its heretical forms.[33] "When Catholics say that persons 'cooperate' in preparing for and accepting justification by consenting to God's justifying action, they see such personal consent *as itself an effect of grace*, not as an action arising from innate human abilities."[34] But this cooperation does not mean that God does part of the work of salvation and man does the rest. Rather, prevenient grace enables man's will "to make the free choice to either cooperate or resist grace."[35] Olson is right in remarking that it makes no

29. Denzinger, §1529.

30. Ibid., §1525.

31. Olson, *Arminian Theology*, 160.

32. Denzinger, §1525.

33. Olson, *Arminian Theology*, 160.

34. *The Joint Declaration on the Doctrine of Justification*, 4.1.20; emphasis added.

35. Olson, *Arminian Theology*, 36.

sense to claim that a free gift is not a free gift when it may be either accepted or rejected.[36] Man can say No as well as Yes to God's free gift—according to libertarian freedom. "The act of faith is of its very nature a free act."[37] In accord with confessional Catholicism, in particular, the Council of Trent, which with legitimacy may arguably trace its teaching back to St. Augustine, the Catholic Church holds that the freedom of the will has not been destroyed, totally lost, or taken away by original sin, and hence it provides a consistent defense of the Augustinian Principle regarding human nature, in particular, free will. But this doesn't mean that human freedom is completely indeterminate such that it stands in a neutral position before two alternatives. It seems clear that this notion of libertarian freedom, which is the power of contrary choice, variously called formal freedom, or the freedom of indifference, is a necessary but not a sufficient condition *by itself* to bring about a solution of the real and deepest problem of human freedom, namely, that we do *not* have the wherewithal to enter into salvific life with God. Yes, the freedom of contrary choice, of indifference, makes it possible for man to reject God; so we can't say that "Rome only knows of freedom *after* and *through* grace."[38] Rather, "'God willed that man should be left in the hand of his own counsel (cf. Sir 15: 14), so that he might of his own accord seek his creator and freely attain his full and blessed perfection by cleaving to him.'"[39]

Still, freely rejecting God is a perversion of freedom rather than a manifestation of true freedom. As John Paul II writes, "freedom is not realized in decisions made against God. For how could it be an exercise of true freedom to refuse to be open to the very reality which enables our self-realization? Men and women can accomplish no more important act in their lives than the act of faith; it is here that freedom reaches the certainty of truth and chooses to live in that truth."[40] Indeed, he adds, "Man's disobedience . . . always means a *turning away from God*, and in a certain sense *the closing up* of human freedom in his regard."[41] Therefore, freedom as choice, the capacity to say yes or no, to turn this way or that, without any coercion either interior or exterior, cannot be the Christian view of freedom. "For freedom Christ has set us free [Gal 5:1]." "'In him we have communion with

---

36. Ibid., 38.

37. Vatican II, *Dignitatis Humanae* §10.

38. Bernhard Bartmann, *Lehrbuch der Dogmatik*, as quoted by G. C. Berkouwer, *Conflict met Rome*, 112 [82].

39. *Gaudium et spes*, 17 §1.

40. John Paul II, *Fides et Ratio*, 1998 Encyclical Letter, §13.

41. John Paul II, *Dominum et Vivificantem*, 1986 Encyclical Letter, §37.

the 'truth that makes us free' [cf. Jn 8:32]."[42] Christian freedom is a gift of God's grace, re-coordinating fallen human freedom and divine truth, the objectively good and true, the source and foundation of the latter being in God himself, so that human freedom "finds in them its own fulfillment and raison d'être."[43]

The dynamics of grace at work in a man's life then begin with prevenient grace being an enabling power that precedes conversion, repentance, and faith. "The first work of the grace of the Holy Spirit is *conversion*, effecting justification in accordance with Jesus' proclamation at the beginning of the Gospel: 'Repent, for the Kingdom of heaven is at hand' [Mt 4:17]. Moved by grace, man turns toward God and away from sin, thus accepting forgiveness and righteousness from on high. 'Justification is not only the remission of sins, but also the sanctification and renewal of the interior man.'"[44]

Nevertheless, the question remains exactly how is grace bestowed upon us and how does it bring about our salvation, and, as Crisp states, "how much the will of a fallen individual awakened or invigorated by the secret working of the Holy Spirit may be said to be active in the process of salvation." According to confessional Catholicism, the active working of the Holy Spirit referred to here is prevenient grace. Although its workings involve a synergism of grace and man, it is not a heretical form of synergism. Crisp rightly adds, "This is not the same thing as claiming that the will of a fallen individual contributes in any substantive way to salvation. It is not even clear what it would mean for 'the will' to contribute to salvation, other than as a euphemism for the agent contributing to her or his salvation. And no evangelical theologian, Arminian or Reformed, would countenance that."[45] And I would add—neither would a Catholic theologian that remains within the boundaries of confessional Catholicism. I turn now, in one final section, to address the question regarding the question of predestination

---

42. *CCC*, §1741.

43. Barron, *Exploring Catholic Theology*, 195.

44. *CCC*, §1989. The quote within the quote is from the Council of Trent, Decree on Justification, Denzinger, §1528, and also §§1551–1553. Says Berkouwer, "Reading such sentiments, which are prolific, one would be inclined to ask again whether the conflict about grace [between Rome and the Reformation] is after all based on a misconception or on some caricature. Is all that we are discussing, in connection with the freedom of the will and the relation between grace and freedom, really irrelevant, so that it is possible to speak about the priority of grace in such a way? The answer to this question can be correct only if we remember that Rome's conception of grace is closely interwoven with a particular view of the nature of man, of the structure of human nature" (*Conflict met Rome*, 123 [90–91]). I return to this question in the text.

45. Crisp, *Deviant Calvinism*, 28.

and freedom, and, in particular, how confessional Catholicism might avoid the dilemma of double predestination and Pelagianism.

Molinism *cum* Congruism, Predestination, and Freedom

Berkouwer states the dilemma clearly of predestination and freedom: "Where falls the decision of man's redemption? Does it fall exclusively in God Himself, in His electing act, or does it fall—albeit against the background of the generative grace of God—in man's free will? Does our redemption depend on God's decision or does it depend on ours?" In response to these questions, Berkouwer understands that throughout the ages some have sought to avoid this dilemma of God or man by advancing a "synthesis between the divine and human decisions." He explains, "On the one hand, God's grace cannot be denied. God cannot be made dependent in the granting of salvation on man's decision; but on the other hand, the significance of man's decision—his belief or unbelief—is to be fully honored, and should not be allowed to be obscure by the overpowering character of God's working all things by Himself."[46] Put differently, but now with respect to Luis de Molina's reconciliation of divine election and freedom, Molinism seeks to avoid the dilemma of double predestination where divine election or reprobation is wholly wrought by God independently of the good or bad choices that men freely make on the one hand; or divine election or reprobation has been taken with consideration of future merits or demerits on the other. As William Lane Craig argues, "It is this dilemma that Molina seeks to resolve by means of the theory of middle knowledge."[47]

My thesis is that a Molinist *cum* Congruist account of the reconciliation of predestination and freedom is within the boundaries of confessional Catholicism's teaching on grace and freedom. "To God, all moments of time are present in their immediacy. When therefore he establishes his eternal plan of 'predestination', he includes in it each person's free response to his grace."[48] This passage raises the question of the nature of divine grace *in* its relation to man. Trent established that there is cooperation between grace and freedom, but the "'manner of such cooperation has been left to free discussion to define.'"[49] At least one view is excluded, however, in view of the

46. Berkouwer, *De Verkiezing Gods*, 28 [28].

47. Craig, "Middle Knowledge," 155.

48. *CCC*, §600.

49. Bartmann, *Lehrbuch der Dogmatik*, as quoted by Berkouwer, *Conflict met Rome*, 116 [85].

Augustinian Principle. Bartmann explains: "'[I]n moving our will by grace to the good in an active faultlessly certain manner, [it cannot mean that] God can do so only by destroying this will in the most sublime privilege of its nature, viz., its freedom, and leading it like a dead object to his purpose.'"[50] In particular, with respect to Molinism, Bartmann says that Molinism lays stress on freedom "without giving it priority over grace in a Pelagian way."[51] Here's the dilemma we are left with: "either to accept the Roman conception of the cooperation of the free human will, or a deterministic annihilation of any human activity in the whole of Christian life."[52] I shall return to this dilemma below.

How does the appeal to God's middle knowledge reconcile divine foreknowledge, in particular, God's hypothetical knowledge of what *would* be in a given set of circumstances, in other words, of conditional future contingents or counterfactual conditionals, and human freedom in the sense of libertarian free will where men are free either to do something or not to do it? Craig replies:

> In Molina's view, predestination is merely that aspect of providence that pertains to eternal salvation. Predestination is the concept of the order and the means by which God ensures that some free creature attains eternal life. It has its basis in (1) the divine middle knowledge, through which God knows that a certain creature will freely assent, given certain circumstances, to God's gift of grace, and (2) the divine will, which chooses to actualize such an order of circumstances and gifts. In the final analysis, the act of predestination is simply God's instantiating one of the world orders known to him via his middle knowledge.[53]

There are several claims that Molina accepts in his appeal to the theory of middle knowledge. First, God desires all men to be saved and hence he has provided unmerited sufficient grace for them by virtue of his prevenient grace, enabling them, if only they will, either assenting to or dissenting from the working of this divine enabling grace, freely to love and obey God and to cooperate with him, or not, and hence to participate in God's justifying and sanctifying grace of salvation. Second, Molina holds that God chooses to create a world of free creature without consideration of how they would respond to his prevenient grace. Rather, he chose to create the circumstances

---

50. Ibid., 118 [87].
51. Inid., 112 [82].
52. Ibid., 118 [87].
53. Craig, "Middle Knowledge," 155–56.

he wanted to for no cause other than the divine will itself. Therefore, predestination is for Molina wholly gratuitous and without consideration of the
merit or demerits of men.[54] Third, it is not simply up to us to be predestined
or not. "Predestination . . . consists in the choice made by God of an order of
things in which He foreknew that this individual will arrive at salvation. Precisely there is the delicate point, 'the unfathomable depths of God's designs';
God knew an infinite of providential orders in which the non-predestined
would freely arrive at eternal life and thus would have been predestined;
He knew as well an infinity of providential orders in which the predestined
would have freely lost beatitude and would have been reprobate; and yet
He chose for the one and for the other the order of providence in which
He foresaw that the one would be saved and other not." Moreover, "He did
this by his will alone and without consideration of their acts, but without
injustice, since he has provided them all the means [prevenient grace] of
arriving at eternal life." [55] Thus, with all Molinists, Scheeben agrees that God
places an individual in circumstances that he knows full well will freely elicit
a salvific act from this individual. "God know what each man will do under
given circumstances. When, therefore, he wishes a grace to have an infallible effect, He offers it to man at the right moment, *i.e.* when He knows that
man will consent."[56] Scheeben explains: "No doubt, those who are placed
under a system of providence wherein they can cooperate with grace and, as
is foreseen, will cooperate, must thank God not only for grace itself, but also
for the effective congruity of grace, and they must regard the latter as a special benefit."[57] What, then, is the basis of efficacious grace's infallible effect?

If I understand Scheeben, his answer to this question is more in line
with Congruism, because it is not an individual's free consent alone that
"extrinsically" renders God's grace efficacious with respect to a salvific act.
In other words, it is not God's mere foreknowledge of an individual's free
consent alone that renders grace efficacious with respect to God's intended
effect to elicit that individual's salvific act. Rather, God's grace is efficacious,
not only by an individual's free consent, but also, indeed principally, by God's
antecedent decree to confer a "congruous" grace of certain circumstances
that will guarantee eliciting a salvific act from that individual. Ott explains:
"According to the system of congruism, the difference between efficacious
and sufficient grace lies not only in the assent of the free will, but also in

54. Ibid., 156.

55. E. van Steenberghe, "Molinisme," as quoted by Craig, "Middle Knowledge,"
156.

56. Scheeben, *Manual*, 2:278.

57. Scheeben, *MC*, 727.

the congruity of the grace to the individual circumstances of the recipient. When the grace suits the individual inner and outer conditions of the man (*gratia congrua*), it becomes effective by the free assent of the will: if it does not (*gratia incongrua*), it remains by lack of the free assent of the will, ineffective. God, by *Scientia Media* [middle knowledge], foresees the congruity of the grace and its infallible success."[58] In sum, Molinism *cum* Congruism preserves human freedom while affirming God's predestination.

To be sure, this is a form of Catholic synergism, but not a heretical form, such as Pelagianism or semi-Pelagianism. There is not the denial of divine election and the necessity and primacy of grace throughout the whole process—prevenient, justifying, and sanctifying grace—from start to finish, as I argued above. Berkouwer recognizes this form of synergism, but claims that "*within* the synergistic idea of cooperation," even the one where divine election and the necessity of grace is affirmed—"the sovereignty of election and grace is in danger."[59] Intriguingly, Berkouwer also recognizes the danger that a divine monergism of grace has posed, namely, "man's acts and decision shrink to nothingness."[60] Although he recognizes this danger, he resists this characterization of the Reformed tradition throughout his writings as unjust and incorrect.[61] Still, Berkouwer suggests that cooperation in itself need not be denounced as long as it is "free of synergistic motifs."[62] Examples of such motifs would be "complementarity"[63] and an "anthropological optimism with respect to human nature,"[64] according to Berkouwer.

The former implies, says Berkouwer, that man contributes partly to salvation, as if God and man, each in their own way, do their part. The latter harkens back to the Reformed tradition's anthropology of total depravity and its corresponding account of nature and grace.[65] Nature has to do with the fundamental structures of reality, in particular, of human reality, in short, the deepest foundations of what God created. How has sin affected those foundational structures of creation? Has the *nature* of creation been corrupted or completely destroyed by sin? What has been called the

58. Ott, *Fundamentals of Catholic Dogma*, 249.

59. Berkouwer, *De Verkiezing Gods*, 49 [47].

60. Ibid., 52 [50].

61. Berkouwer, *De Verkiezing Gods*, 46, 52 [44, 50]. See also, Berkouwer, *Verdienste of Genade?*, 14–17.

62. Berkouwer, *De Verkiezing Gods*, 53 [50].

63. Ibid., 46 [44].

64. Berkouwer, *Conflict met Rome*, 123–27 [92–94].

65. I considered this matter in chapter 1 on Calvin.

Augustinian Principle affirms that the *nature* of humanity persists in the regime of man's fallen state. Confessional Catholicism is a consistent out-working of this principle whereas representatives of the Reformed tradition, such as Calvin and Berkouwer, inconsistently apply it.[66] On their view, in critical response to confessional Catholicism, they emphasize that nature has been rendered a corrupt vessel by the fall into sin, and needs to be re-placed altogether with something new by grace. Human nature is capable of nothing but sin, with the accompanying loss or destruction of the natural power of the will to goodness or contrary moral choice between good and evil. On this view, the deepest foundations of what God created do not per-sist in the fallen state. So, I dare say that Berkouwer's worry about a Catholic synergism is mistaken not only because personal cooperation in preparing for and accepting God's justifying grace is itself an effect of grace, and hence not an "action arising from innate human abilities."[67] But also, in its consis-tent maintenance of the Augustinian Principle, although human nature has not been totally corrupted, it is wounded in its totality.[68] That is, "man, who was created for freedom, bears within himself the wound of original sin, which constantly draws him towards evil and puts him in need of redemp-tion. Not only is *this doctrine an integral part of Christian revelation;* it also has great hermeneutical value insofar as it helps one to understand human reality. Man tends towards good, but he is also capable of evil."[69] Therefore, I suggest that the Catholic idea of cooperation is free of the synergistic motifs that taint heretical forms of synergism. For a Catholic form of synergism, in which man's free response participates in God's gift of salvation, is neither pelagian nor semi-pelagian, which are its heretical forms.

66. They *in*consistently depart from the Augustinian Principle because their doc-trine of common grace and a corresponding doctrine of general revelation restrains the impact of original sin on the structures of human reality. On this matter, see my book, *Berkouwer and Catholicism*, chapter 2-3.

67. *The Joint Declaration on the Doctrine of Justification*, 4.1.20.

68. *CCC*, §405.

69. John Paul II, *Centesimus Annus*, 1991 Encyclical, §25; emphasis added.

Bibliography

Asselt, Willem J. van, et al., eds. *Reformed Thought on Freedom: The Concept of Free Choice in Early Modern Reformed Theology*. Grand Rapids: Baker Academic, 2010.

Aquinas, Thomas. *Commentary on St. Paul's Epistle to Timothy, Titus, and Philemon*. South Bend, IN: St. Augustine's, 2008.

———. *De veritate*. Translated by James V. McGlynn. Chicago: Henry Regnery, 1953.

———. *Summa Theologiae*. http://www.newadvent.org/summa.

Augustine. *City of God*. Edited by Philip Schaff and Kevin Knight. Translated by Marcus Dods. Nicene and Post-Nicene Fathers, First Series 2. Buffalo: Christian Literature, 1887. http://www.newadvent.org/fathers/120114.htm.

Balthasar, Hans Urs von. *Dare We Hope "That All Men Be Saved"? With "A Short Discourse on Hell."* Translated by David Kipp and Lothar Krauth. San Francisco: Ignatius, 2014.

———. *Explorations in Theology*. 4 vols. Translated by Edward T. Oakes. San Francisco: Ignatius, 1995.

———. *Epilogue*. Translated by Edward T. Oakes. San Francisco: Ignatius, 2004.

———. *The God Question and Modern Man*. Translated by by Hilda Graef. New York: Seabury, 1967.

———. "Some Points of Eschatology." In *The Word Made Flesh*, translated by A.V. Littledale and Alexander Dru, 255–85. San Francisco: Ignatius, 1989.

———. *Theo-Drama*. 5 vols. Translated by Graham Harrison. San Francisco: Ignatius, 1990–98.

———. *The Theology of Karl Barth*. Translated by Edward T. Oakes. San Francisco: Ignatius, 1992.

———. *Truth is Symphonic: Aspects of Christian Pluralism*. Translated by Graham Harrison. San Francisco: Ignatius, 1987.

———. *The Von Balthasar Reader*. Edited by Medard Kehl and Werner Löser. Translated by Robert J. Daly and Fred Lawrence. New York: Crossroad, 1982.

Balthasar, Hans Urs von, and Joseph Ratzinger. *Two Say Why: Why I Am Still a Christian by Hans Urs Von Balthasar and Why I Am Still in the Church by Joseph Ratzinger*. Translated by John Griffiths. Chicago: Franciscan Herald, 1973.

Barron, Robert. *Exploring Catholic Theology: Essays on God, Liturgy, and Evangelization*. Grand Rapids: Baker Academic, 2015.

Barth, Karl. *Church Dogmatics II/2: The Doctrine of God*. Translated by G. W. Bromiley et al. Edinburgh: T. & T. Clark, 1957.

———. *Church Dogmatics III/2: Doctrine of Creation*. Translated by G. W. Bromiley et al. Edinburgh: T. & T. Clark, 2004.

————. *Church Dogmatics* IV/1: *The Doctrine of Reconcilation*. Translated by G. W. Bromiley, et al. Edinburgh: T. & T. Clark, 2010.

————. *Credo*. New York: Scribner's, 1963.

————. "The Gift of Freedom." In *The Humanity of God*, translated by Thomas Weser et al., 69–93. Louisville: Westminster John Knox, 1960.

————. *Table Talk*. Edited by John D. Godsey. Scottish Journal of Theology Occasional Papers 10. Edinburgh: Oliver and Boyd, 1963.

Bavinck, Herman. *Gereformeerde Dogmatiek* I. Kampen: J. H. Kok, 1895. [*Reformed Dogmatics*, vol. 1: *Prolegomena*. Edited by John Bolt. Translated by John Vriend. Grand Rapids: Baker Academic, 2003.]

————. *Gereformeerde Dogmatiek* II. Kampen: J. H. Kok, 1897. [*Reformed Dogmatics*, vol. 2: *God and Creation*. Edited by John Bolt. Translated by John Vriend. Grand Rapids: Baker Academic, 2004.]

————. *Gereformeerde Dogmatiek* IV. Kampen: J. H. Kok, 1901. [*Reformed Dogmatics*, vol. 4: *Holy Spirit, Church, and New Creation*. Edited by John Bolt. Translated by John Vriend. Grand Rapids: Baker Academic, 2008.]

Benedict XVI. *Jesus of Nazareth*. Translated by Adrian J. Walker. New York: Doubleday, 2007.

Berkhof, Louis. *Systematic Theology*. 4th rev. and enlarged ed. Grand Rapids: Eerdmans, 1949.

Berkouwer, G. C. "The Authority of Scripture (A Responsible Confession)." In *Jerusalem and Athens: Critical Discussions on the Theology and Apologetics of Cornelius van Til*, edited by E. R. Geehan, 197–203. N.p.: Presbyterian and Reformed, 1971.

————. *Een Halve Eeuw Theologie, Motieven en Stromingen van 1920 to Heden*. Kampen: J. H. Kok, 1974. [*A Half Century of Theology: Movements and Motives*. Edited and translated by Lewis B. Smedes. Grand Rapids: Eerdmans, 1977.]

————. *De Mens het Beeld Gods*. Kampen: J. H. Kok, 1957. [*Man: The Image of God*. Translated by Dirk W. Jellema. Grand Rapids: Eerdmans, 1962.]

————. *Nabetrachting op het Concilie*. Kampen: J. H. Kok, 1968.

————. *De Triomf Der Genade in De Theologie van Karl Barth*. Kampen: J. H. Kok, 1954. [*The Triumph of Grace in the Theology of Karl Barth*. Translated by Harry R. Boer. Grand Rapids: Eerdmans, 1954.]

————. *De Verkiezing Gods*. Kampen: J. H. Kok, 1955. [*Divine Election*. Translated by Hugo Bekker. Grand Rapids: Eerdmans, 1960.]

————. *De Voorzienigheid Gods*. Kampen: J. H. Kok, 1950. [*The Providence of God*. Translated by Lewis Smedes. Grand Rapids: Eerdmans, 1952.]

————. "Vragen Rondom de Belijdenis." *Gereformeerd Theologisch Tijdschrift* 63 1 (1963) 1–41.

————. *De Wederkomst van Christus* I-II. Kampen: J. H. Kok, 1961–1963. [*The Return of Christ*. Edited by Marlin J. Van Elderen. Translated by James Van Oosterom. Grand Rapids: Eerdmans, 1972.]

————. *De Zonde* I-II. J. H. Kok, 1960. [*Sin*. Translated by Philip Holtrop. Grand Rapids: Eerdmans, 1971.]

Bettis, Joseph D. "Is Karl Barth a Universalist?" *Scottish Journal of Theology* 20 4 (1967) 423–36.

Boer, Theodore de. *Grondslagen van een kritische psychologie*. Baarn: Ambo, 1980. [*Foundations of a Critical Psychology*. Translated by Theodore Plantinga. Pittsburgh: Duquesne University Press, 1983.]

Boersma, Hans. "Calvin and the Extent of the Atonement." *Evangelical Quarterly* 64 4 (1992) 333–55.

Bruce, F. F. *The Epistle of Paul to the Romans*. Grand Rapids: Eerdmans, 1963.

Brunner, Emil. *The Christian Doctrine of God*. Translated by Olive Wyon. Vol. 1 of *Dogmatics*. Philadelphia: Westminster, 1950.

Burson, Scott R., and Jerry L. Walls. *C. S. Lewis and Francis Schaeffer*. Downers Grove, IL: InterVarsity, 1998.

Byrne, Brendan. *Romans*. Edited by Daniel J. Harrington. Sacra Pagina 6. Collegeville, MN: Liturgical, 1996.

Calvin, John. "Articles Concerning Predestination." In *Calvin: Theological Treatises*. Translated by J. K. S. Reid, 178–80. Library of Christian Classics 22. Philadelphia: Westminster, 1954.

———. *The Bondage and Liberation of the Will*. Edited by A. N. S. Lane. Translated by G. I. Davies. Grand Rapids: Baker, 1996.

———. *Concerning the Eternal Predestination of God*. Translated by J. K. S. Reid. Louisville: Westminster John Knox, 1997.

———. *Institutes of the Christian Religion*. Translated by Ford Lewis Battles. Philadelphia: Westminster, 1960.

Catechism of the Council of Trent. Translated by John A. McHugh and Charles J. Callan. New York: Joseph F. Wagner, 1923.

Catechism of the Catholic Church. 1994. http://www.vatican.va/archive/ENG0015/_INDEX.HTM.

Cessario, Romanus. *Christian Faith and the Theological Life*. Washington, DC: Catholic University of America Press, 1996.

Congar, M. J. Yves. *The Meaning of Tradition*. Translated by A. N. Woodrow. San Francisco: Ignatius, 2004.

Congregation for the Doctrine of the Faith. "Doctrinal Commentary on the Concluding Formula of the *Professio fidei*." May 24, 1990. http://www.ewtn.com/library/CURIA/CDFADTU.HTM.

———. *Donum Veritatis*. Instruction on the Ecclesial Vocation of the Theologian. May 24, 1990. http://www.vatican.va/roman_curia/congregations/cfaith/documents/rc_con_cfaith_doc_19900524_theologian-vocation_en.html.

———. "Letter of the Congregation for the Doctrine of the Faith on *Certain Questions Concerning Eschatology*." May 17, 1979. http://www.vatican.va/roman_curia/congregations/cfaith/documents/rc_con_cfaith_doc_19790517_escatologia_en.html.

Couenhoven, Jesse. "Karl Barth's Conception(s) of Human and Divine Freedom(s)." In *Commanding Grace: Studies in Barth's Ethics*, edited by Daniel L. Migliore, 239–55. Grand Rapids: Eerdmans, 2010.

Craig, William L. "Middle Knowledge: A Calvinist-Arminian Rapprochement." In the *Grace of God and the Will of Man*, edited by Clark H. Pinnock, 141–64. Minneapolis: Bethany, 1989.

———. *What Does God Know? Reconciling Divine Foreknowledge and Human Freedom*. Norcross, GA: Ravi Zacharias, 2002.

Crisp, Oliver. *Deviant Calvinism: Broadening Reformed Theology*. Minneapolis: Fortress, 2014.

———. *God Incarnate: Explorations in Christology*. London: T. & T. Clark, 2009.

———. "The Letter and the Spirit of Barth's Doctrine of Election: A Response to Michael O'Neil." *Evangelical Quarterly* 79 1 (2007) 53–67.

———. "On Karl Barth's Denial of Universalism." In *Retrieving Doctrine: Essays in Reformed Theology*, 116–30. Downers Grove, IL: IVP Academic, 2010.

Davison, Scott A. "Divine Providence and Human Freedom." *Reason for the Hope Within*, edited by Michael J. Murray, 217–37. Grand Rapids: Eerdmans, 1999.

D'Costa, Gavin. *Vatican II: Catholic Doctrines on Jews and Muslims*. Oxford: Oxford University Press, 2014.

Dennision, James T. Jr., ed. *Reformed Confessions of the 16th and 17th Centuries in English Translation*. Vols. 1–4. Grand Rapids: Reformation Heritage, 2014.

Denzinger, Heinrich. *Compendium of Creeds, Definitions, and Declarations on Matters of Faith and Morals*. Edited by Peter Hünermann, et al. San Francisco: Ignatius, 2012.

Douma, J. *Responsible Conduct: Principles of Christian Ethics*. Translated by Nelson D. Kloosterman. Phillipsburg, NJ: Presbyterian & Reformed, 2003.

Dulles, Avery. Cardinalng Co. NJ: Presbyterian *First Things* (May 2003). http://www.firstthings.com/article/2003/05/the-population-of-hell.

———. *Magisterium: Teacher and Guardian of the Faith*. Naples, FL: Sapientia, 2007.

———. "Vatican II on the Interpretation of Scripture/*Letter and Spirit* 2 (2006) 7–16.

Echeverria, Eduardo. *Berkouwer and Catholicism: Disputed Questions*. Leiden: Brill, 2013.

———. *Pope Francis: The Legacy of Vatican II*. Hobe Sound, FL: Lectio, 2015.

Erikson, Millard J. *Christian Theology*. Grand Rapids: Baker Academic, 2009.

Ernst, Harold E. "The Theological Notes and the Interpretation of Doctrine." *Theological Studies* 63 (2002) 813–25.

Finnis, John. "Hell and Hope." In *Religion and Public Reasons: Collected Essays*, 5:368–80. Oxford: Oxford University Press, 2011.

Fitzmyer, Joseph. *Romans: A New Translation with Introduction and Commentary*. Edited by William Foxwell Albrights and David Noel Freedman. Anchor Bible 33. New York: Doubleday, 1992.

Flannery, Kevin L. "How to Think About Hell." *New Blackfriars* 72/854 (1991) 469–81.

Flint, Thomas R. *Divine Providence*. Ithaca: Cornell University Press, 1999.

Freddoso, Alfred J. Introduction to *On Divine Foreknowledge*, by Luis De Molina. Ithaca: Cornell University Press, 1988.

———. "Molina, Luis de." In *Routledge Encyclopedia of Philosophy*, edited by Edward Craig. London: Routledge, 1998. http://www.nd.edu/~afreddos/papers/molina.htm.

———. "Molinism." In *Routledge Encyclopedia of Philosophy*, edited by Edward Crag. London: Routledge, 1998. http://www.nd.edu/~afreddos/papers/molinism.htm.

Garrigou-Lagrange, Reginald. *Predestination*. Translated by Dom Bede Rose. Charlotte, NC: Tan, 1998.

———. *The One God*. St. Louis: N.p., 1943.

Gaudium et spes. Vatican II. December 7, 1965. http://www.vatican.va/archive/hist_councils/ii_vatican_council/documents/vat-ii_cons_19651207_gaudium-et-spes_en.html.

Genderen, J. van, and W. H. Velema. *Concise Reformed Dogmatics*. Translated by Gerrit Bilkes and Ed M. van der Maas. Phillipsburg, NJ: Presbyterian & Reformed, 2008.

George, Timothy. "An Evangelical Reflection on Scripture and Tradition." In *Your Word Is Truth. A Project of Evangelicals and Catholics Together*, edited by Charles Colson and Richard John Neuhaus, 9–34. Grand Rapids: Eerdmans, 2002.

Giussani, Luigi. *At the Origin of the Christian Claim*. Translated by Viviane Hewitt. Montreal: McGill-Queen's University Press, 1999.

González, Justo L. *Essential Theological Terms*. Louisville: Westminster John Knox, 2005.

Grisez, Germain. "Question 6, 'Should one expect that nobody will go to hell?'" In *The Way of the Lord Jesus*, 3:21–28. Quincy, IL: Franciscan, 1997.

Grisez, Germain, and Peter Ryan. "Hell and Hope for Salvation." *New Blackfriars* 95 1059 (2014) 606–15.

Grisez, Germain, and Russell Shaw. *Beyond the New Morality: The Responsibilities of Freedom*. 3rd ed. Notre Dame: University of Notre Dame Press, 1988.

Guardini, Romano. *Freedom, Grace, and Destiny: Three Chapters in the Interpretation of Existence*. Translated by John Murray. New York: Pantheon, 1960.

Gunton, Colin. "Barth, The Trinity, and Human Freedom." *Theology Today* 43 (1986–87) 316–30.

Hasker, William. *Metaphysics*. Downers Grove, IL: InterVarsity, 1983.

Healy, Nicholas J., Jr. "Vatican II and the Catholicity of Salvation: A Response to Ralph Martin." *Communio* 42 (Spring 2015) 36–60.

Helm, Paul. *Faith, Form, and Fashion*. Eugene, OR: Cascade, 2014.

———. *John Calvin's Ideas*. Oxford: Oxford University Press, 2006.

———. *The Last Things: Death, Judgment, Heaven and Hell*. Edinburgh: Banner of Truth, 1989.

———. *The Providence of God*. Downers Grove, IL: InterVarsity, 1994.

———. "The Will of Calvin's God—Can God Be Trusted?" http://paulhelmsdeep. blogspot.com/2008/02/will-of-calvins-god-be-trusted.html.

Henry, Carl F. *God, Revelation and Authority*. Vol. 6, part 2. Waco, TX: Word, 1983.

Hodge, Charles. *Systematic Theology*. Abridged ed. Edited by Edward N. Gross. Phillipsburg, NJ: Presbyterian & Reformed, 1997.

Hoitenga, Dewey Jr. *John Calvin and the Will*. Foreword by Richard A. Muller. Grand Rapids: Baker, 1997.

Holwerda, David E. *Jesus and Israel: One Covenant or Two?* Grand Rapids: Eerdmans, 1995.

Horton, Michael. *For Calvinism*. Grand Rapids: Zondervan, 2011.

International Theological Commission. "In Search of a Universal Ethics: A New Look at the Natural Law." 2009. http://www.vatican.va/roman_curia/congregations/ cfaith/cti_documents/rc_con_cfaith_doc_20090520_legge-naturale_en.html.

John Paul II. *Dominum et Vivificantem*. Encyclical Letter, 1986.

———. *Fides et Ratio*. Encyclical Letter, 1998.

———. *Mulieris dignitatem*. Apostolic Letter, 1988.

———. "La Providencia Divina y el destino del hombre: el misterio de la predestinación en Cristo." General Audience. May 28, 1986. http://w2.vatican.va/content/john-paul-ii/es/audiences/1986/documents/hf_jp-ii_aud_19860528.html.

———. "The Redemptive Value of Christ's Sacrifice." General Audience, October 26, 1988. In *A Catechesis on the Creed*. 2:444–49. Boston: Pauline, 1996. Spanish, http://www.fjp2.com/us/john-paul-ii/online-library/audiences/4480-general-audience-october-26-1988; Italian, http://w2.vatican.va/content/john-paul-ii/es/ audiences/1988/documents/hf_jp-ii_aud_19881026.html.

———. *Veritatis Splendor*. Encyclical Letter, 1993.

Johnson, Phillip R. "Notes on Supralapsarianism and Infralapsarianism." http://www. spurgeon.org/~phil/articles/sup_infr.htm.

Joint Declaration on the Doctrine of Justification. By the Lutheran World Federation and the Catholic Church, July 31, 2000. http://www.vatican.va/roman_curia/pontifical_councils/chrstuni/documents/rc_pc_chrstuni_doc_31101999_cath-luth-joint-declaration_en.html.

Journet, Charles. *What is Dogma?* Translated by Marx Pontifex. New York: Hawthorn, 1964.

Kasper, Walter. *Mercy: The Essence of the Gospel and the Key to the Christian Life.* Translated by William Madges. Mahwah, NJ: Paulist, 2013.

Kimel, Alvin. "Predestination." http://pontifications.wordpress.com/predestination/.

Kreeft, Peter, and Ronald K Tacelli. *Handbook of Christian Apologetics.* Downers Grove, IL: InterVarsity, 1994.

Kvanvig, Jonathan L. *The Problem of Hell.* New York: Oxford University Press, 1993.

Lane, Anthony. "Bondage and Liberation in Calvin's Treatise against Pighius." In, *Calvin Studies*, edited by J. H. Leith and R. A. Johnson, 9:16–45. Davidson, NC: Davidson College and Davidson College Presbyterian Church, n.d.

———. "Calvin's Anthropology." In *The Calvin Handbook*, edited by Herman J. Selderhuis, 275–88. Translated by Henry Baron, et al. Grand Rapids: Eerdmans, 2009.

———. "Did Calvin Believe in Freewill?" *Vox Evangelica* 12 (1981) 72–90.

Léon-Dufour, Xavier. "Wrath." In *Dictionary of Biblical Theology*. Updated 2nd ed. Edited by Xavier Léon-Dufour. Boston: St. Paul, 1995.

Levering, Matthew. *Predestination: Biblical and Theological Paths.* Oxford: Oxford University Press, 2011.

Lewis, C. S. *God in the Dock.* Grand Rapids: 1970.

———. *The Problem of Pain.* New York: Macmillan, 1962.

Lombard, Peter. *The Sentences.* Vol. 3. *On the Incarnation of the Word.* Translated by Giulo Silano. Toronto: Pontifical Institute of Medieval Studies, 2008.

Lubac, Henri de. "Apologetics and Theology." In *Theological Fragments*, 91–104. San Francisco: Ignatius, 1989.

Mansini, Guy. "Dogma." In *Dictionary of Fundamental Theology*, edited by René Latourelle and Rino Fisichella, 239–47. New York: Crossroad, 1994.

Marcel, Gabriel. *The Mystery of Being.* Vol. 1. *Reflection and Mystery.* Gifford Lectures, 1949–1950. South Bend, IN: St. Augustine, 2001.

Maritain, Jacques. *Clairvoyance de Rome.* Paris, 1929.

———. *A Preface to Metaphysics.* London: Sheed & Ward, 1945.

Martin, Ralph. *Will Many Be Saved? What Vatican II Actually Teaches and Its Implications for the New Evangelization.* Grand Rapids: Eerdmans, 2012.

McCabe, Herbert. *God Matters.* Springfield, IL: Templegate, 1987.

McCarthy, Margaret Harper. "Recent Developments in the Theology of Predestination." STD diss., The Lateran University, 1994.

McCormack, Bruce. "Grace and Being: The Role of God's Gracious Election in Karl Barth's Theological Ontology." In *The Cambridge Companion to Karl Barth*, edited by John Webster, 92–110. New York: Cambridge University Press, 2000.

———. "So That He May be Merciful to All: Karl Barth and the Problem of Universalism." In *Karl Barth and American Evangelicalism*, edited by Bruce L. McCormack and Clifford B. Anderson, 227–49. Grand Rapids: Eerdmans, 2011.

McDermott, John M. "Faith, Reason, and Freedom." *Irish Theological Quarterly* 67 (2002) 307–32.

McDonald, Suzanne. "Evangelical Questioning of Election in Barth: A Pneumatological Perspective from the Reformed Heritage." In *Karl Barth and American*

Evangelicalism, edited by Bruce L. McCormack and Clifford B. Anderson, 250–68. Grand Rapids: Eerdmans, 2011.

McFarlane, Andrew. "Barth and Kant on Freedom as Independence." Unpublished paper for Society for the Study of Theology, 2013.

Mill, John Stuart. *An Examination of Sir William Hamilton's Philosophy.* 4th ed. London, 1872.

Molina, Luis De. *On Divine Foreknowledge.* Part 4 of *The Concordia.* Translated by Alfred J. Freddoso. Ithaca: Cornell University Press, 1988.

Moreland, J. P., and William Lane Craig. *Philosophical Foundations for a Christian Worldview.* Downers Grove, IL: InterVarsity, 2003.

Morris, Leon. *The Atonement.* Downers Grove, IL: IVP Academic, 1984.

———. *The Gospel According to Matthew.* Grand Rapids: Eerdmans, 1992.

Mouw, Richard J. *He Shines in All that's Fair: Culture and Common Grace.* Grand Rapids: Eerdmans, 2001.

Muller, Richard A. *Christ and the Decree.* Grand Rapids: Baker Academic, 2008.

Murray, John. *Collected Writings of John Murray.* Carlisle, PA: Banner of Truth, 1982.

———. *Redemption Accomplished and Applied.* Grand Rapids: Eerdmans, 1955.

———. *The Epistle to the Romans.* Vol. 1. Grand Rapids: Eerdmans, 1959.

Murray, J. Michael. "Heaven and Hell." In *Reason for the Hope Within*, edited by Michael J. Murray, 287–317. Grand Rapids: Eerdmans, 1999.

Nichols, Aidan. "De Lubac and Réginald Garrigou-Lagrange [on Divine Revelation]." In *Engaging the Theologians*, 113–28. Milwaukee: Marquette University Press, 2013.

———. *Romance and System: The Theological Synthesis of Matthias Joseph Scheeben.* Denver: Augustine Institute, 2010.

———. *The Shape of Catholic Theology.* Collegeville, MN: Liturgical, 1991.

Oakes, Edward T. *Pattern of Redemption:The Theology of Hans Urs von Balthasar.* New York: Continuum, 1994.

O'Connor, James T. "Von Balthasar and Salvation." *Homiletic and Pastoral Review* (1989) 10–21. http://www.catholicculture.or/culture/library/view.cfm?recnum=565.

Olson, Roger E. *Against Calvinism.* Grand Rapids: Zondervan, 2011.

———. *Arminian Theology: Myths and Realities.* Downers Grove, IL: IVP Academic, 2006.

———. "A Crucial but Much Ignored (or Misunderstood) Distinction for Theology: 'Mystery' versus 'Contradiction.'" February 10, 2016. http://www.patheos.com/blogs/rogereolson/2016/02/a-crucial-but-much-ignored-or-misunderstood-distinction-for-theology-mystery-versus-contradiction/.

———. "Election Is for Everyone." February 13, 2016. http://www.patheos.com/blogs/rogereolson/2016/02/election-is-for-everyone/.

Orr, James. *Progress of Dogma.* Old Tappan, NJ: Fleming H. Revell, 1901.

Ott, Ludwig. *Fundamentals of Dogma.* Edited by James Canon Bastible. Translated by Patrick Lynch. Rockford, IL: Tan, 1974.

Paul VI. "Apostolic Letter. Credo of the People of God, June 30, 1968." http://w2.vatican.va/content/paul-vi/en/motu_proprio/documents/hf_p-vi_motu-proprio_19680630_credo.html.

Pitstick, Alyssa Lyra. *Light in Darkness: Hans Urs von Balthasar and the Catholic Doctrine of Christ's Descent into Hell.* Grand Rapids: Eerdmans, 2007.

Plantinga, Alvin. "The Free Will Defense." In *The Analytic Theist: An Alvin Plantinga Reader*, edited by James F. Sennett, 23–49. Grand Rapids: Eerdmans, 1998.

Pohle, Joseph. *Grace, Actual and Habitual: A Dogmatic Treatise.* Edited and translated by Arthur Preuss. St. Louis: B. Herder, 1915.

Polanyi, Michael. *Personal Knowledge: Towards a Post-Critical Philosophy.* Chicago: University of Chicago Press, 1958.

Rahner, Karl. "Dogmatic Constitution on the Church: Chapter III, Articles 18–27." In *Commentary on the Documents of Vatican II,* edited by Herbert Vorgrimler, 208–16. Translated by Lalit Adophus et al. London: Burn & Oates, 1967–69.

———. *Foundations of Christian Faith.* Translated by William V. Dych. London: Darton Longman & Todd, 1978.

———. "Hell." In *Sacramentum Mundi* 3:7–9. New York: Herder and Herder, 1969.

———. "Hell." In *Encyclopedia of Theology: A Concise "Sacramentum Mundi,"*602–4. London: Burns Oates, 1975.

Rahner, Karl, and Herbert Vorgrimler. *Theological Dictionary.* Edited by Cornelius Ernst. Translated by Richard Strachan. New York: Herder & Herder, 1965.

Regnon, Théodore. *Bannestianisme et Molinisme.* Paris: Retaux-Bray, 1890.

Reid, J. K. S. "Introduction." In *Concerning the Eternal Predestination of God,* translated by J. K. S. Reid, 9–44. Louisville: Westminster John Knox, 1997.

Ridderbos, Herman. *Aan De Romeinen.* Kampen: J. H. Kok, 1959.

———. *The Coming of the Kingdom.* Edited by Raymond O. Zorn. Translated by H. de Jongste. Philadelphia: Presbyterian & Reformed, 1962.

———. *Paulus: Ontwerp van zijn Theologie.* Kampen: J. H. Kok, 1973. [*Paul: An Outline of His Theology.* Translated by John Richard De Witt. Grand Rapids: Eerdmans, 1975.]

Robinson, J. A. T. "Universalism—Is it Heretical?" *Scottish Journal of Theology* 2 (1949) 139–55.

Runia, Klaas. "Recent Reformed Criticisms of the Canons." In *Crisis in the Reformed Churches,* edited by Peter Y. De Jong, 161–80. Grand Rapids: Reformed Fellowship, 1968.

Rusch, William G., and Daniel F. Martensen, eds. *The Leuenberg Agreement and Lutheran-Reformed Relationships: Evaluations by North American and European Theologians.* Minneapolis: Augsburg Fortress, 1989.

Salza, John. *The Mystery of Predestination.* Charlotte, NC: Tan, 2010.

Saward, John. "Christ, The Light of the Nations." Part 1. 2003. http://christendom-awake.org/pages/jsaward/lightofnations1.htm.

———. "The Church as Mystery." Part 2. 2003. http://christendom-awake.org/pages/jsaward/lightofnations2.htm.

Schnelle, Udo. *Theology of the New Testament.* Translated by M. Eugene Boring. Grand Rapids: Baker Academic, 2009.

Schreiner, Thomas R. *Romans.* Grand Rapids: Baker, 1998.

Shelton, W. Brian. *Prevenient Grace: God's Provision for Fallen Humanity.* Anderson, IN: Warner, 2014.

Sokolowski, Robert. *The God of Faith and Reason.* Washington, DC: Catholic University of America Press, 1982.

Scheeben, Matthias Joseph. *Glories of Divine Grace.* Translated by Patrick Shaughnessy. St. Meinrad, IN: Grail, 1946.

———. *A Manual of Catholic Theology: Based on Scheeben's "Dogmatik."* Vol. 2, *The Fall, Redemption, Grace, The Church and the Sacraments, The Last Things.* Edited by Joseph Wilhelm and Thomas B. Scannell. London: Kegan Paul, 1901.

———. *Die Mysterien des Christenthums, Wesen, Bedeutung und Zusammenhang derselben nach der in ihrem übernatürlichen Charakter gegebenen Perspective dargestellt.* Freiburg im Breisgau: Herder, 1865. [*The Mysteries of Christianity.* Translated by Cyril Vollert. London: Herder, 1946.]

―――. *Natur und Gnade. Versuch einer systematischen, wissenschaftlichen Darstellung der natürlichen und übernatürlichen Lebensordnung im Menschen.* Mainz, 1861. [*Nature and Grace.* Translated by Cyril Vollert. London: Herder, 1954.]

Seifrid, Mark A. "Justified by Faith and Judged by Works: A Biblical Paradox and Its Significance." *Southern Baptist Journal of Theology* 5 4 (2001) 84–97.

Sokolowski, Robert. *The God of Faith and Reason.* Washington, DC: Catholic University of America Press, 1982.

Sproul, R. C. *Chosen by God.* Wheaton, IL: Tyndale, 1986.

―――. "Double Predestination." http://www.ligonier.org/learn/articles/double-predestination/.

Stott, John R. W. *The Cross of Christ.* Downers Grove, IL: InterVarsity, 2006.

Talbot, Thomas. "Providence, Freedom, and Human Dignity." *Religious Studies* 26 (1990) 227–45.

Tasker, R. V. G. *The Biblical Doctrine of the Wrath of God.* London: Tyndale, 1951.

Til, Cornelius van. *The Defense of the Faith.* Edited by K. Scott Oliphint. Phillipsburg, NJ: Presbyterian & Reformed, 2008.

―――. "Has Karl Barth Become Orthodox?" *Westminster Theological Journal* 16 2 (1954) 135–81.

―――. *The Sovereignty of Grace: An Appraisal of G. C. Berkouwer's View of Dordt.* Phillipsburg, NJ: Presbyterian & Reformed, 1969.

Trueman, Carl. *John Owen.* Aldershot: Ashgate, 2007.

Vatican II. *Dei Verbum.* Dogmatic Constitution on Divine Revelation, 1965.

―――. *Dignitatis Humanae.* Declaration on Religious Freedom, 1965.

―――. *Lumen Gentium.* Dogmatic Constitution on the Church, 1965.

Vos, Geerhardus. *Reformed Dogmatics.* Vol. 1. *Theology Proper.* Edited and translated by Richard B. Gaffin Jr. Bellingham, WA: Lexham, 2012.

Wainwright, Geoffrey. "Eschatology." In *The Cambridge Companion to Hans Urs von Balthasar,* edited by Edward T. Oakes and David Moss, 113–27. Cambridge: Cambridge University Press, 2004.

Walls, Jerry L. *Hell: The Logic of Damnation.* Notre Dame: University of Notre Dame Press, 1992.

Walls, Jerry L., and Joseph R. Dongell. *Why I Am Not a Calvinist.* Downers Grove, IL: InterVarsity, 2004.

Warfield, B. B. "Augustine and the Pelagian Controversy." In *Saint Augustine: Anti-Pelagian Writings,* edited by Philip Schaff and B. B. Warfield, xiii–lxxi. Select Library of Nicene and Post-Nicene Fathers 5. Grand Rapids: Eerdmans, 1971.

Webster, John. "Freedom in Limitation: Human Freedom and False Necessity in Barth." In *Barth's Moral Theology: Human Action in Barth's Thought,* 99–123. Grand Rapids: Eerdmans, 1998.

Weinandy, Thomas. *Does God Suffer?* Notre Dame: University of Notre Dame Press, 2000.

Witherington, Ben, III. *Matthew.* Smyth & Helwys Bible Commentary. Macon, GA: Smyth & Helwys, 2006.

―――. *Paul's Letter to the Romans: A Socio-Rhetorical Commentary.* Grand Rapids: Eerdmans, 2004.

Index

Antecedent/Consequent Will of God,
    95, 100, 102, 212–14, 218, 221,
    273, 276
Apocalyptic Prophecy, 248
Aquinas, Thomas, 3, 4, 29, 55n103, 93,
    175n21, 184, 197n123
Amyraldianism, 203
Arminianism, 200, 203
Augustine, 32, 35, 54–56, 112, 174, 185,
    190, 192, 196, 198, 199
Augustinian Principle, 35–37, 44, 76,
    112, 288

Balthasar, H. Urs von, 34, 77, 131n18,
    132n22, 149, 158, 163, 165
    universalist and particularist,
        217–32
    justice and mercy, 220–29, 258
    grace and freedom, 225, 229–32,
        242, 259–61
    predestination, 233–53
    models of judgment, 253–61
    grace and action, 261–66
    natural consequence view, 266–72
Barron, R., 283
Barth, K., 15n66, 26, 34, 61n140, 88n40,
    123n195, 174n17, 205
    equal ultimacy of reprobation/
        election, 127–42
    double predestination, 142–50
    faith and freedom, 150–53
    faith and unbelief, 153–63
    universalism, 163–70
Bavinck, H., 2n8, 6–8, 26n104, 34, 52,
    80, 81n16, 86n36, 88–89, 137,

138n46, 179, 195–96, 198, 203,
    205, 208
    double predestination, 171–77
    election and reprobation, 185–87,
        190
    supralapsarianism and
        infralapsarianism, 200–206
    election and the general offer of the
        Gospel, 207–15
Benedict XVI, 263n192
Berkhof, L., 13, 63, 64n156, 69n187, 70,
    72, 80, 128, 278
Berkouwer, G.C., 1n1, 8n35, 10, 13–15,
    16–19, 20n83, 27n113, 32n133,
    32n134, 34, 40n32, 48–49,
    53–54, 56, 59–60, 64, 65–66,
    67n171, 68, 68n182, 69–70,
    70n193, 72, 79n5, 81n14, 84n26,
    93n62, 124, 130, 133, 134–36,
    137n42, 138n46, 139–40, 141,
    147n86, 148n91, 149, 155,
    157–58, 161, 163, 181, 185, 205,
    225n46, 226, 232n79, 246n133,
    267n210, 277, 287
    double predestination, 171–77,
        188–91
    logic of predestination, 177–84
    election and reprobation, 184–88,
        191–93
    Reformed doctrine of
        predestination, 193–200
    supralapsarianism and
        infralapsarianism, 200–206
    election and the general offer of the
        Gospel, 307–215

Boersma, H., 73n200
Bonaventure, 213n188
Bruce, F.F., 243n121.
Brunner, E., 164n167, 167n174
Burson, S.R., 49, 50n85, 51
Bryne, B., 245n126, 251n153

Calvin, J., 10–13, 15–16, 23, 25, 34, 52,
    127, 134n30, 177n26
  nature and grace, 35–48
  grace and freedom, 48–61
  divine election, 61–76
Calvin's *Catechism*, 47n67
Canons of Dort, 17, 41n37, 72, 128,
    135, 154, 176, 184, 197n123,
    201n137, 207, 212
Catechism of the Catholic Church, 2,
    5n20, 28n116, 29, 32–33, 36,
    37n13, 57, 59, 68, 75, 79, 109,
    123n195, 125, 170, 204n148,
    245–46, 250, 255n168, 256, 259,
    260, 261n190, 265n202, 275,
    278, 279n21, 288n69
Causes, proximate and remote, 65, 67,
    68
Centesimus annus, 288n69
Cessario, R., 4
Christian freedom, 122, 124, 150–53
Compatibilism, 16, 39–40, 49, 52,
    159–60
Concurrence, 82–84, 118
Conditional Ordained Sufficiency,
    214–15
Conditioned Positive Reprobation, 68,
    173, 185
Congruism, 86, 91, 92, 102, 102n97,
    103, 125, 187, 234, 284–87
Contra Voluntatem Dei, 69, 185, 190,
    199
Controversy of Grace, 24n100, 25
Cooperating Grace, 31, 57, 107, 122
Couenhoven, J., 150n100, 159
Council of Trent, 17, 23–24, 24n100,
    26–27, 29, 30n124, 32, 58, 60,
    61, 112, 170, 211, 274–75
Congar, Y., 20
Craig, W.L., 82n17, 85, 86n34, 87,
    89n44, 91n53, 118n175

Crisp, O., 15, 27n111, 31, 39n30, 49n78,
    58n124, 70n193, 73–74, 74n204,
    95n73, 132n23, 137n43, 139n53,
    143n71, 144, 145, 153–55,
    159n143, 161n164, 163, 166–67,
    168–69, 185n109, 210, 214–15,
    217–18, 278

Davison, S.A., 115n165
D'Costa, G., 22
De Boer, T., 50, 51n92
Decretum Absolutum, 11, 13, 93, 105,
    107, 126, 130, 131, 131n18, 133,
    141, 177, 180, 182, 183, 193
Deism, 79
Dei verbum, 5, 20
Denzinger, 22n89, 23n94, 24n98,
    25n102, 27n110, 29n117,
    58n123, 101n102, 172n2,
    211n182
Dignitatis humanae, 59n131
Divine Cooperation, 78, 79, 101
Dominum et vivificantem, 123n195
Donum veritatis, 2–3
Dongell, J.R., 40, 49
Double Predestination, 26, 34, 61,
    63, 70, 76, 136, 142–50, 198,
    239–40,
Dulles, A., 21, 22n88

Echeverria, E.J., 8n35, 8n37, 288n66
Effectual grace, 57, 60–61
Enabling grace, 57, 58, 60–61
Equal Symmetry, reprobation/election,
    28, 84, 174–75, 240
Equal Ultimacy, reprobation/election,
    70n193, 126, 131, 170
Erikson, M., 63
Essential Asymmetry, 27–28, 32

Fides et ratio, 3n5, 5n22, 6n24, 10n46,
    123n195
Finnis, J., 218n8, 220, 245, 249
Fitzmyer, J., 255n169
Flannery, K., 259n183
Flint, T., 116n170
Freddoso, F., 80–81, 82–84, 90, 91

George, T., 19n82
Garrigou-Lagrange, R., 27n109, 31n124,
    63, 88n40, 94, 97
Guarino, T., 5n20
Gaudium et spes, 37n13
Genderen, van J., 128–29
Giussani, L., 123n195
Grisez, G., 31n128, 33n138, 236n91,
    248, 264, 267
Guardini, R., 123n195

Hard Determinism, 49, 53, 116–17, 194
Hasker, W., 40n31, 117n173
Heidelberg Catechism, 68, 197
Hell, 223n34, 231, 249, 255–59
Helm, P., 3n13, 8n38, 11, 13n56, 14,
    38n21, 39n29, 41, 87n38, 88n40,
    181, 265
Henry, C.F., 9n44, 164n167, 201n133
Hodge, C., 63, 128n7
Hoitenga, D., 24, 35, 40n32, 41, 43, 44,
    45n55, 46n63, 120
Hopeful Universalism, 163n164, 217,
    218, 220, 229, 248
Horton, M., 63–64
Holwerda, D., 262, 263
Hunsinger, G., 167n173
Hypothetical Universalism, 93n63, 200,
    203, 210

Infralapsarianism, 132n23, 200–206
International Theological Commission,
    12n54
Irresistible Grace, 56, 229–30

John of Damascus, 213n188
John Paul II, 3, 5–6, 10, 122–23, 234–35,
    279, 280
Joint Declaration Justification, 31, 57,
    76, 288n67
Journet, C., 4–5

Kasper, W., 224
Kerygmatic Universality, 135, 209, 211,
    216
Kimel, A., 28n114, 30
Kreeft, P., 174n17

Kvanvig, J. L., 163n161, 253n163, 256,
    268n212

Lane, A.N.S., 37n10, 39n26, 45n56,
    47n68, 47n70
Lehman, K., 227
Leuenberg Agreement, 246
Lewis, C.S., 50, 270
Libertarian Freedom, 16, 38, 83, 116,
    117–18, 155–56
Lombard, P., 211n178
Lumen gentium, 167n175, 248
Luther, M., 58n123

Mansini, G., 5
Marcel, G., 8
Maritain, J., 9, 35
Martelet, G., 257
Martin, R., 224n45
McCabe, H., 50n91
McCarthy, M., 25–26
McCormack, B., 142n64, 163n164,
    164n167
McDermott, J.M., 124–25
McDonald, S., 162n159
Middle Knowledge (*scientia media*),
    75n208, 85, 86–90, 103
Mill, J.S., 14
Models of Judgment, 253–61
Molina, Luis de, 75n208, 79n8, 82, 84
Molinism, 25, 84, 89, 92, 102, 125, 187,
    284–87
Moreland, J.P., 82n20, 87n37, 118n175
Morris, L., 255n170, 265n201
Mouw, R., 205n150
Muller, R., 131n19
Murray, J., 138n46, 183, 194, 238–39
Murray, J.M., 253n163, 260n185, 266,
    271n225, 272

Natural Consequence View, 253–61
Nature and Grace, 35–48, 112–14,
    119–25
Negative Reprobation, 73n201, 106, 184
Nichols, A., 6n26, 86, 92n55, 92n58,
    187, 188n73, 198n126

Oakes, E., 234

Occasionalism, 79

O'Connor, J.T., 248

Olson, R., 8n39, 31n125, 55n105, 57–
58, 58n122, 180

Omnicausalism, 64

Operating/cooperating grace, 54, 112

Orr, J., 180n35, 209

Ott, L., 13n59, 22n88, 28n114, 55,
57n115, 67–68, 69n184, 72n194,
73n202, 75n209, 79n8, 82n20,
83n22, 84n26, 85n27, 102n107,
103, 173–74, 184, 230, 231

Particular Predestination, 97–99, 108,
110, 111, 276

Pelagianism, 23, 30, 51n92, 101, 103,
113

Penalty View, 253–61

Philips, G., 27n113, 76n214, 175, 275n6

Pieper, J., 8

Pighius, A., 36, 61, 66

Pitstick, A.L., 268

Plantinga, A., 50n89, 51

Pohle, J., 26n106, 62n147, 82n20,
90n51, 106

Polanyi, M., 50, 51, 52n94

Post et propter praevisa demerita, 68, 69,
101, 108, 173, 174, 175–76, 186,
236, 240

Praescientia (foreknowledge), 108, 112,
113, 179, 183, 185, 188, 192,
196, 198

Praeter Voluntatem Dei, 69, 185, 190,
199

Predestinarianism, 26–27, 32, 61–62,
106, 275

Preterition, 66, 70, 72–73, 106, 128, 136,
178, 179, 201n37

Prevenient grace, 54, 56, 57–58, 85, 109,
125, 275, 280–81

Problems and Mysteries, 6–10

Pro Multis, 29n120

Przywara, E., 16

Rahner, K., 21, 23n92, 68n175, 68n179,
224, 223n34, 224n42, 246

Ratzinger, J., 22n88

Regnon, T., 91n52

Reid, J.K.S., 10n49, 72

Ridderbos, H., 238, 239, 241n112, 242–
43, 244, 250–51, 252, 254, 264

Robinson, J.A.T., 268

Runia, K., 175n18, 177n26, 190, 191–92

Ryan, P., 31n128, 33n138, 236n91

Salza, J., 174n17, 185

Saward, J., 8

Scheeben, M.J., 1n2, 34, 55, 73, 75,
90n51
Divine providence, 78–92
Predestination, 92–108
Grace and Freedom, 108–14
Freedom and Determinism, 115–25

Seifred, M., 264

Shelton, W.B., 125n203

Schnelle, U., 1, 219, 220, 240

Schreiner, T., 238

Scripture and Tradition, 19–20

Second Helvitic Confession, 58

Soft Determinism, 39, 49, 89, 116–17

Sokolowski, R., 121n185

Sproul, R.C., 8n39, 27, 173, 177–81, 183

Stakemeier, E., 19–20

Stott, J., 255n170

Strong Free Will, 49

Sufficiency/Efficacy, 72, 74, 96, 209–210,
274, 278

Sufficiency, Extrinsic/Intrinsic, 74, 95,
96

Supralapsarianism, 63, 132n23, 200–206

Substance/Accident, 40, 41, 44–45

Synergism, 30–31, 281–84, 287–88

Tacelli, R., 174n17

Tasker, R.V.G., 254–55

Theological Notes, 21–22

Thomism, 82, 83, 92

Trueman, C., 203n145

Unconditioned Positive Reprobation,
67, 68n179, 106, 184, 194

Universal Predestination, 97–99, 108,
111, 276

Universalism, 74n204, 95, 163–70, 216,
218, 266–72, 273

Universal Salvific Will, 95, 96, 110, 207, 209, 274n1

Van Til, C., 70n193, 133n25
Vatican I, 7
Vatican II, 21
Velema, W.H., 128–29
Vos, G., 129

Wainwright, G., 32n131

Walls, J., 40, 49–50, 51, 104–5, 236n89
Warfield, B.B., 51n92
Wrath, 226–29, 257–58
Weak Free Will, 49
Weber, M. 14n62
Webster, J., 150n100, 151n108
Weinandy, T., 2–3, 9
Westminster Confession of Faith, 70n193, 180–81, 184n54
Witherington, B., 237, 248–49